Smiling at the World

A Woman's Passionate Yearlong Quest for Adventure and Love

Joyce Major

Editor: Jill Kelly
Cover design: Dunn+Associates Design
Text design: Another Jones Graphics

Library of Congress Number: 2007907136

ISBN 978-0-97997400-7

Printed in the USA

To all of the sanctuaries and projects that are working to improve planet earth, I dedicate this book. I am deeply grateful for all of your love, smiles, laughter and joy that I encountered along the way. I hold you in my heart.

In gratitude to my mom and my dad, my sons, my sister, Paul, and Bob, who have all encouraged me to explore, to dream and to discover and to write this book. I could not have done this without your help and your love.

"Twenty years from now you will be more disappointed by the

things that you didn't do than by the ones you did do.

So throw off the bowlines. Sail away from the safe harbor.

Catch the trade winds in your sails. Explore. Dream. Discover."

— *Mark Twain*

Carrie O.

My houseboat neighbor wrote this book and I thought you would really enjoy it. All the best wherever your travels take you!

Many Wishes,
Amy + Mesa

Contents

The Places that I went and How to Find them on the Internet:

Italian Restoration Project
Write Tonio Creanz at sinergie.altamura@virgilio.it, $500 for 2 weeks

Lesbian Wildlife Hospital, Lesvos, Greece
http://www.wildlifeonlesvos.org free

The Monkey Sanctuary in Looe, England
http://www.ethicalworks.co.uk/monkeysanctuary/index2.htm $100/ week

Baboon Monitoring in Cape Town, South Africa
The group I went with no longer exists but contact
http://www.keag.org.za/projects/adopt-a-baboon.html and they may
be able to help you

The Lion Park in Johannesburg, South Africa
The author's group was disbanded. Contact www.i-to-i.com $1000/week

Conservation and Portuguese lessons in Rio
www.Bridgelinguatec.com $1700/mo.

Roo Gully Sanctuary in Boyup Brook, Australia
http://members.iinet.net.au/~roogully/ $100/week

Tararu Valley Sanctuary in New Zealand
www.tararuvalley.org $380/week

The Elephant Nature Park in Chiang Mai, Thailand
www.elephantnaturepark.org $275/week – you can also do a day trip here

Global Network Volunteers in Yantai, China
www.volunteer.org.nz - teaching was around $500/month

Newspaper reporting in Ireland -
This program is no longer available in Ireland

These prices are just approximations.

Readers interested in obtaining the full list of global volunteer
opportunities compiled by the author may request an email version only
at info@smilingattheworld.com

Carbon offsetting websites to balance your travel emissions:
www.Sustainabletravelinternational.org

PROLOGUE

NOTHING LEFT TO BUY. Time has run out. The red and black backpack sits crumpled in the corner of my bedroom wondering no doubt where it's headed and why it's still empty. I turn my gaze to the mountain of clothes on my bed wondering what to pack for my yearlong solo adventure. Exactly how many shirts, pants, jackets, bras, panties, and socks does one need for 365 days of travel?

Starting with the easy stuff, I pack the quick-dry underwear that is advertised to be good for 16 countries. As I'm only scheduled to go to 11 countries, the underwear will be okay even if I change my plans and add five more places. I carefully roll everything else up placing it inside until the backpack is bulging. Yet turning to my bed, I see that half a mountain of clothes remains. Dumping everything back on the bed, I crumble. How in the world can I take this trip around the world if I can't even pack for it? What was I thinking?

With only 36 hours till takeoff, I am still wrestling with myself about this year-long journey, a trip of a lifetime. My spirit, which created this trip, is desperate for freedom but still clashing with the remaining anchors that keep me here. The internal battle that has been waging since I bought the plane tickets brings large round tears rolling down my cheeks with a sob thrown in.

Harley, the cat, jumps on the bed lying on top of the giant mound of clothes. He is very pleased with my new decorating scheme. More sobs. Harley, the best damn cat in the world, has to leave our happy houseboat life to live with a good woman he doesn't know for the year while I am gone. What was I thinking? Exactly how bad is my life now anyway and why do I need a year-long trip? Can't I rejuvenate my spirit with a facial, a massage, and a two-week yoga retreat?

Still the battle rages between the adventurer and the stable, predictable 57-year-old mother and realtor even as the countdown approaches. You have made a mistake, some voice inside says, because only the young trek around the world with backpacks strapped to their backs, not mothers.

No. No. NO! I am not wrong. Adventure and change are not just for the young. I am full of spirit. I carry wisdom and confidence now. I am perfectly suited to take this adventure. Looking into the mirror, I don't see an old woman ready to live a safe, quiet life planting flowers in clay pots and playing bridge on Tuesdays. I see a woman full of energy, ready to challenge herself, and fueled by an intense curiosity about the world, by the ability to take a risk to follow the dream. I have this ability and I am leaving for a one-year solo trip around the world! Round 213 of the constant internal battle goes to the Spirited Adventurer!

Returning to my packing task, I decide that if two of everything was good enough for Noah, it is good enough for me. The pattern of two pants, two shirts, two of each continues till the backpack is full.

With my oldest son Joe graduated from college and my youngest son Dan graduating at the year's end, I had been ruminating about what I wanted to do, what I wanted to be. It seemed that my entire reason for existence was ending with his graduation. With this Termination Notice of Purpose, I was forced into hours of introspection, the kind that nags continually with no escape. A time of endless questions. Was he graduating or was I? How do I take what I have learned and continue to challenge myself? What is my heart's desire? How do I want to live my life consistent with my spirit? Is this really enough? The song lyric "scared, scared to run out of time" played in my head at the oddest times. These questions followed me everywhere begging for answers… driving in my car, rollerblading, out in my kayak, busy doing something and then bam! Is this how you want to use the gifts in your life? Is this life I am living now filled with the truth of who I am? Where is my new dream? And how do I find my heart's desire?

Low-grade emotions had been coloring my view of the world like a thick fog at the airport, like a dull knife rubbing over a tomato. My spark, my passion, my creativity was hidden under layers of getting by and doing what was expected. And yet, a small candle still flickered deep inside my heart begging me to find my life, to feel my life, to live it my way.

Am I content with this life? The voice kept asking. Is it full enough and rich enough to take me through the next 30 years? Being a realtor for the last 16 years had taught me many things and given me financial stability and freedom with my time. But now my spirit was asking for freedom, actually demanding it based on the barrage of soul-searching questions it was continually throwing at me.

Seeking a place of maximum "dreamability," I decided to take a hike. The outdoors always breaks me free. My senses love getting lost in the feelings I find in the woods. I headed up Rattlesnake Mountain a vigorous hike, east of Seattle. My feet made a steady thumping sound on the fallen leaves covering the dirt trail. Brushing by evergreens, breathing in the fresh moist smell, and listening to water gurgle over rocks, I could feel peacefulness come easily. Breaking a sweat on the steep switchbacks, appreciating the exercise, I felt shades of green fill my eyes and the sound of my own breathing gave me a steady climbing rhythm. I could live here in these woods with nature.

But steady breathing switched to huffing and puffing when my conditioning hit its limit. I started gazing up the trail hoping for light, the light at the top of the mountain. Singularly focused on getting up the trail, suddenly a small tickle of an idea began to form. The only sound the rustle of trees and the hollow sound of earth as my feet climbed the path, an idea flashed in my mind. A couple of years before, I had taken a great two-week solo trip to Israel to work on an archeological site as a volunteer. What if now I traveled around the world working at volunteer projects back to back wherever I went? Could I do that?

Yes. Yes. Yes! I shouted. I can! I can travel solo around the world volunteering at different projects in different countries on my own not waiting for anyone to join me! Excitement started bubbling up inside of me like finding the right answer to a math problem after hours of missed solutions. An epiphany, finally. Now all of my attention was focused on this dream, this idea as I reached the clearing at the top of Rattlesnake Mountain. I can do this.

Bursting with exhilaration, I flew up the mountain, sat down on a big rock as a grin from ear to ear spread across my face. I remember it was like being struck by lightning.

I needed a year, a full year, to truly remove the layers. I wanted out of the comfort of my cocoon. Bring on adventure and uncertainty! I wanted to rely on my own spirit, my own abilities to cope. I wanted new lessons and new challenges to open the door to change. The ultimate road trip with no one to please but myself. I wanted to celebrate my love of life and honor my spirit with the gift of freedom for one full year. Freedom. A release from everything. I was fired up with bundles of excitement, certain that this dream was the one, the answer to my soul's nagging questions. Finally, a solution: a quest. I leaned back on my warm rock smiling at the clouds rolling by in the deep blue Seattle sky and fell asleep with a commitment to take this trip to learn about the world and my place in it.

Down from the mountain, every spare minute away from work was spent searching the Internet for volunteer opportunities around the globe. Putting in weeks and hours researching projects, I was determined to bring my dream to life as I gathered information about projects, locations, and costs. Six months before the start date, I had the list narrowed down to 20 projects but I needed to bring it down to 12, a month in each country. With a huge piece of paper on my living room floor and a column for each month, I drew up various possibilities until I found the one that made sense and wouldn't cost a fortune.

The budgeting process was painful as I agonized over a full year's living expenses: airline tickets, ferry and train tickets, project tuitions, bed and breakfasts, hotels, health insurance, visas, and shots. Everything needed to be budgeted and paid for before I left including my bills in Seattle! Running out of money was an ever-looming fear with only $25,000 available and no more. When my friend Jennifer asked how much I was budgeting for food away from the projects during the year, I realized that I had completely forgotten to budget for that! What else was I forgetting?

Finally every detail fell in place with 11 projects in 10 countries producing an enormous grin across my face every time I thought about it. The dream was reality and it was exactly what I had hoped for! My final selections ran a wide gamut of interests across all but one continent. I would volunteer with lion cubs, monkeys, baboons, and sea turtles in Johannesburg, England, Cape Town, and Thailand. I would volunteer on conservation projects in Brazil and Australia and at a sustainability sanctuary in New Zealand. I would teach English in China, work on a restoration project in Italy, and spend two months volunteering as a reporter in Ireland! The best part about my selections was my complete lack of all skills and experience for all of these projects. I didn't have a clue how to be a reporter or feed a lion cub but I was jumping up and down inside with unstoppable glee every time I thought about my year of travel!

With the details of my trip completed and my houseboat rented, I announced my decision to travel around the world for one year to my family and friends wondering how they would react.

My sweet mom surprised me. "Great honey! Sounds wonderful! I am happy for you."

Hmm, I think, did she really hear me?

Dan, my younger son, said, "Mom, this is your soul telling you to do this."

Joe, my older, said, "Wow, Mom, is this your mid-life crisis?"

Both sons were dead-on about their mom's motivation and I smiled at their keen perceptions. Both gave me their uncompromising support. My sister, Norine, worried about my safety but promised to work on adjusting to the idea. My friends were a mix of happy, sad, angry, jealous, and just plain flabbergasted.

But as takeoff approached, I was a mess, a quiet little mess unwilling to let anyone know how afraid and uncertain I really felt. Was I running away from my life as one friend had suggested? Should I have been satisfied and worked at making it better? Was it silly to travel to different countries because currently my heart was not fully alive, not in full gear? What did I expect to find in other countries that I could not find at home? And what if my budget wasn't correct and I ran out of money? Plagued with last-minute angst, my Stable Predictable Self continued taking potshots at my Adventurer's Spirit, tormenting it with fear and insecurities. What about my safety traveling alone when I had only two solo trips in my past? How would my real estate business survive over a full year? It had been my career, my source of financial support for the last 16 years. Would I be able to pick it up when I returned or would it be deader than a door nail? And what if that business fell apart?

Then there were more practical problems. With only 10 days to go, I had no idea where I was storing my furniture or the rest of my stuff. Looking at my giant backpack, I was again filled with self-doubt. Was I really capable of doing this for a year? Had I packed enough clothes? One project said to bring old clothes that I wouldn't mind getting dirty. Exactly how dirty was I going to get? Would I be too hot, too cold, too old? Would the fashion police take me away because my clothes were too ugly? Would my new quick-drying underwear advertised to last for 16 countries only last for 5? And what about the sleeping arrangements? Weighed down by way too much to organize and not enough time, I lost my ability to cope. Why did I even want to go? What was I thinking? Silently screaming, overwhelmed, tears fell in massive amounts as my self-doubt created a giant meltdown. I fell into bed crying myself to sleep.

But the sunshine of a new day brought a strong resolve to follow my dream, to honor myself, to be bold. The risks were enormous but there really was no choice. I was not content to stay and be comfortable. It was time to find my place in the world. It was time to let my heart take charge and open the door to change. It was time to use my Get Out of Jail card. It was time to be free. To escape the ordinary to create my life. As I imagined leaving the old behind and allowing the new to develop, a smile came to my face with a burning sense that I was doing exactly the right thing.

With the final internal battle won, my curiosity for my first destination, a restoration project in Altamura, Italy, resurfaced and I wondered what I would do there and what the other volunteers would be like. Was "restoration" just a lovely word for construction work in the hot sun in a small town in Italy pounding nails, throwing a sledgehammer, and digging ditches? Well, whatever it was, this adventure was beckoning me and I was ready for whatever came my way. Change was on the horizon. With a smile and an overwhelming sense of freedom, I shut the door to my empty houseboat not to return for 365 days.

One Plane and Five Trains to Italy

Leaving Seattle on July 1, 2004, I arrived in England at 8 am on July 2. Little did I know I was about to begin the "train insanity" part of my journey. What had looked easy on paper and had saved me lots of money was, in fact, way too much traveling without resting. First a slow short train ride from the airport to London in a crowded-with-commuters train. Leaning forward to keep from toppling backwards, I schlepped my giant backpack, wobbled through narrow train compartment doors, and bumped into people. In this reserved quiet British atmosphere, my bumping, groaning, giggling exhibition was acknowledged with just a polite nod. I knew these observers were full of dry bits of humor about the middle-aged American woman almost capsized under the weight of her pack but they just watched me. Planting my feet solidly, I lowered myself slowly and ungracefully into a vacant seat. I sat on the edge of my seat balancing tentatively, the pack ready to tip me over. Surrounded by businessmen in perfectly tailored suits and women immaculately dressed for work in black and white, I felt completely out of place.

Arriving at the train station in London, The Pack and I wobbled down the corridor and searched for my next train. Down a hall I went, around a bend, reading signs, while all around me everyone was full speed ahead. Jet lag clouding my brain, I wandered down halls looking for my next train, already regretting the size of my pack, which felt like a 65-pound barnacle clinging to the side of a ship. Finally I found where I needed to be and took the short train ride to the Eurostar station for the Chunnel train that I was anxious to ride.

I boarded the Eurostar with a bit more ease as my proficiency negotiating the pack improved. Exhausted and happy to be on board again, I sat near a lovely white-haired 60ish couple who began the trip by opening their picnic basket filled with champagne, lovely glasses, bread, and cheeses.

Curious, I asked, "What are you celebrating?"

"It is Friday afternoon," the man said as he smiled at his wife.

I sighed to myself as I watched them enjoy their picnic. My ideal love scene planted smack dab in front of me. Silver-haired love. Stronger now than it was in the beginning. Eyes full of trust and vulnerability. Romance. Caring. Would I ever look into a man's eyes and have him return the gaze as our love grew stronger over time? Tired and drowning in a melancholy coma from a 10-foot wave of loneliness, I fell asleep not even noticing the train's 150-foot descent under the English Channel.

Arriving in Paris with no time to linger, I grabbed a taxi to the next train station. The speedy taxi ride flashed memories of romance, of museums, of lovely dinners in Paris six years before with a man I loved. I smiled remembering the time we had spent together and the promise of love forever. But the taxi ride ended and the memories flew off as I arrived at my next train, the sleeper to Rome. Trains are usually my favorite way to travel but not now. Lugging this enormous pack, squeezing through narrow corridors and tiny doorways, I fantasized about leading a loaded pack mule with me around the world.

Lonely and tired, I crawled into bed early wondering how I would do without my friends for a year.

I was rested after a solid night's sleep, and morning brought a fresh attitude with coffee and croissant served in my berth and lush green rolling hills flying by as the train sped down the track. Vineyards ripened in the sun as a farmer drove his tractor around collecting cylindrical bales of wheat. A large tree grew out of the center of an old abandoned stone farmhouse, its branches thrusting out through the crumbling roof. In the distance, white houses with red roofs dotted the landscape. I was rested and feeling good. The trip had really begun!

Arriving in Rome, I stepped off the train and instantly felt the jolt of Italian energy as if I'd put my finger in an electric socket. Rome was fired up, full of noise, energy, and life. Sexy people walked in a million different directions. Everywhere in the station Italians were shouting, stiletto heels were clicking, and everyone was rushing past me. I was stunned by the activity and struck by the fashion.

Then there was the heat. The high temperature, the high humidity, the lack of even a tiny breeze—a sauna surrounded me. I tilted forward balancing that damn pack, sweating from the temperature climb, wide-eyed and wobbly. I looked for the ticket window.

Standing in the long line reeling from the weight on my back, I arrive at the window sweating profusely. "I need a ticket to Bari."

The answer comes back in rapid-fire Italian "Non c'e la finestra per le corse internazionali." Pointing and a gesture towards a hallway. Where is the ticket window, who do I ask, how do I get food? There is no one to ask. No one speaks any English. It's incredibly hot and I must look like I am suffering from a terrible disease with sweat running off my face. Exhausted, hungry, hot, lost, tired of schlepping the backpack, I am mad at myself for scheduling so many trains and this is only the third day of a yearlong journey! What was I thinking?

Wandering around, I finally join the correct ticket line. "I need a ticket to Bari."

The man is gruff. More rapid Italian I don't understand.

"What did you say?" I hold back a tear as sweat twirls down my cheeks.

Ah, now he tells me in English. "Ze train you want she is full. You musta wait for da next one."

Riding the train to Bari, I admired the sexy feminine women with gorgeous olive complexions, black hair and eyes. They were wearing tight skirts on narrow hips, tight blouses clinging to breasts, great shoes, lovely makeup, and perfectly coiffed hair. Young men also in tight shirts showing off buff, trim bodies and flirting continuously with their dark eyes and low whistles. They looked lean and hungry. The women ignored them. The men stayed with the hunt and the dance of flirtation continued as the train flew down the track.

I wondered how they saw me. Three travel days. Five trains, no shower. Bad hair, wrinkled pants, crumpled shirt, hiking boots, and no makeup! In my 3-day travel outfit, I felt grimy, fat, and embarrassed by my lack of style. In the middle of these lovely, sexy well-groomed women, I felt like a thorn bush growing amidst graceful willow trees.

What's more, no one talked to me on this train either and loneliness, my new travel companion, settled in. Traveling alone was quieter than I had imagined and I wondered if I could really manage a full year. All right, Mr. Loneliness, you've barged in on me before in the last five years since Joe and Dan went to college. When you come, you put a strangle hold around my neck squeezing the happiness out of the top of my head like toothpaste escaping the tube. Even though I was strong enough to weather the storm of being a single mom for 19 years, you still managed to sneak in at my most vulnerable times. But look, mister, I've been lonely at home and I'll be lonely out here in the world but you are not the background music to this new musical called Joyce's Dream. I will learn how to travel alone without you nagging me continually. I will learn new tricks.

Arriving late in Bari, I needed one more train to Altamura, my final destination, but it didn't run that late so I needed to find a hotel. Bari, according to the guidebook I had with me, had a dangerous reputation and I had no hotel reservation and no idea how to find one! Weighted down by the pack, I tilted unsteadily and hoped not to ram anyone as we gathered in the train corridor waiting for the train to stop. As the train slowed, I imagined getting off in the dark, lugging my pack, uncertain of directions and frightened of being mugged. Left for dead in a lonely train station, my passport and money stolen, my airplane tickets gone, my trip had become a disaster. Snapping out of my terror vision, I asked out loud in English, "Does anyone know a good hotel for me to stay in?'

No one said anything.

Again, looking very pathetic, I said, "Does anyone know a good hotel?" I was determined I would not cry. This was my big adventure. I knew it was dark out there in a dangerous city, I had no hotel, and I was tired, alone, and hungry but I would be okay.

Finally a monk with a long flowing brown robe and very kind eyes spoke, "Yessa, there are hotel nota far from this station."

Saved! We left the train together and he said, "Go thisa way under thisa tunnel (Under the dark tunnel, is that where he wants me to go? Oh dear.) Go thata way, then thisa way." I watched his hands flying around in what must be the direction, but I was unable to move to the dark tunnel on my own. I must have looked sad and helpless, for he took pity on me and walked me to the hotel! He was young and handsome in his robe (are they supposed to look handsome?), and I wondered what had made him choose this life. Thankfully, he took me right to the hotel door. I was safe!

"Grazie, grazie," I said as he walked away.

Hotel, safety, food, a shower, and a bed. I spent the evening curled up watching Italian TV and listening to laughter and music in the streets below. But the following day, Sunday, I found that everything in the town, including the trains, was shut down. The very noisy Saturday evening was now a silent morning with no cars, no people, and no noise. But it was my first day in Italy, the 4th of July, and I had a huge smile on my face. Eating my first Italian breakfast of fruit, hard rolls with crunchy crusts, soft cheese, strong espresso, and blood-orange juice, I was quite content. After breakfast and a nap, I headed down the boulevard toward the Mediterranean.

In the nearby park, people were sitting and chatting to each other and staring at me as I wandered past. Why were they staring? I was doing my best imitation of an Italian woman. What could be wrong? And then it dawned on me. First, I was walking way too quickly to be Italian! I had no wiggle, no bounce! I needed to slow it down to a saunter, add a hip swing, a sexy look in my eyes. But then, there was another huge problem…my sandals, American Teva sandals, utilitarian, sexless, comfortable! The women here wore sexy, strappy, feminine shoes with thin high heels as they sauntered down the sidewalk. My sandals were hiking sandals, not girlie-girl sandals, a dead giveaway and fashion violation number one! The stores were closed but the window-shopping was divine with glamorous, creative styles, sexy cuts, and interesting lines in colors not seen in Seattle (the official home of urban black).

I was already missing my houseboat on Lake Union in Seattle, so the harbor beckoned. Strolling down, I realized it looked more like an artist's canvas than reality. Bright red and blue wooden fishing boats were anchored along the coast bobbing up and down in the gentle waves of the calm sea. Sunday strollers wandered down the cobblestone walkway lined with palm trees and shade trees protecting them from the scorching sun. The hot breeze carried the salty smell of the sea as I gazed at a few daring swimmers jumping into the waves. Looking at the old stone houses, I felt that I was walking inside a landscape painting, as everything was much too beautiful to be real.

Then the heat became brutal on my Seattle temperature gauge and I strolled home to a good number of whistles sent my way. This flirting communication, unacceptable at home, was commonplace here. A constant reinforcement from males to females, the whistles and the eyes seemed to be saying, "Ah, you there, how lovely you are." A flirting culture was refreshing after the stoic men of Seattle who could barely look at a woman, let alone flirt. Women here walked with their hips swinging, feeling their femininity, and men answered with flirting eyes and whistles. A beautiful form of communication between the sexes.

Back at my hotel restaurant, my waiter was the beneficiary of all my pent-up communication needs. Four days spent without any conversation created a rush of words as I spoke broken Spanish to him, waving my arms around, pantomiming everything. "Yo soy de America y me gusta su pais. Tengo dos hijos y un gato y ahora viajando para un ano." (I am American and I like your country. I have two sons and a cat and now I am traveling for a year.) I chattered away like a mad woman who had been locked in a closet for a year. Amused by the wild American woman waving her hands and speaking Spanish, he joined in the conversation! The accent, the sounds, his hands moving in the air, we continued our Italian-Spanish pantomiming conversation throughout dinner for he stood by my table while I ate. In my little notebook, I started making notes of the Italian words he was teaching me. After that first Italian dinner, my waiter smiled as I left him saying, "Arrivederci. Arrivederci. Buona notte. Sogni dolci." (Good-bye. Good-bye. Good night. Sweet dreams.)

The next day my adventure would really begin. I would take the train to Altamura to meet the head of the Restoration Project, move into the volunteer house, and find out if construction in Italy was as I had imagined it. Excited and nervous, I fell asleep quickly and woke early, ready to find the right train. Looking out the window of my hotel, I saw that the Monday morning city was full of life. What had looked like an empty Hollywood set on Sunday had changed as the director shouted "action" and the actors hit the stage with cars zooming by, people rushing, and the small train station a flurry of activity!

"Where do I catch the train to Altamura?" I asked. I followed the hand signals pointing me around a bend until finally I found the correct train track. Luckily, the young woman I was following spoke English and acted as my guide because the train stop announcements were in Italian! Of course, how silly of me to think the announcements in Italy would be in any other language but Italian.

CHAPTER 2

A Restoration Project in Italy

ARRIVING AT THE TRAIN STATION in Altamura was like arriving in a deserted town with one lone building, sand-colored earth covered by the kind of arid bushes that grow in the desert, a few trees, and fewer people. The small empty train station had one outside phone booth that only used phone cards, which I did not have. Consequently, I couldn't call Tonio, the Program Director, to let him know I had arrived. A young Italian man saw me staring hopelessly at the phone and asked if he could help. He used his phone card to call Tonio. "Grazie! Grazie!"

Sitting in the empty train station waiting for my ride, I noticed a sign on the wall in Italian with an English translation that said something about snakes. Snakes? I started looking around the floor certain I would see a large poisonous Italian snake slithering past. The countryside here looked like snake country to me, but seeing no snakes on the floor, I walked over to the man who was working behind the counter.

"What kind of snakes do you have here?" I asked warily pointing to the sign.

He turned around to show me: "barre di caramella, gomma, fagioli di gelatin," pointing to the candy bars, gum, and jelly beans. I realized that the sign was telling me to look out for the snacks, not the snakes! Roaring with laughter, I pantomimed to him the difference between snakes and snacks, and we shared a big laugh.

Some minutes later, I noticed a very handsome well-built short man with olive skin and dark, laughing eyes enter the room. As he approached, I hoped that it was to flirt with me but instead, it was Tonio Creanza, the program director of the grass-roots nonprofit organization Sinergie Cooperativa. With his charming accent and devilish smile, he welcomed me and introduced me to the two women with him: Sam, a beautiful young woman ready to start college in the fall, and Jen, a soulful artist from Canada, both volunteers.

Loaded up in the car, I am full of anticipation as we drive to the Cappuccini Monastery, home to the Capuchin monks during the 16th century and now my home in Altamura. The long narrow tree-lined driveway hides Cappuccini as the old VW bus bounces down the driveway. When we arrive and I stand in the paved stone courtyard looking up, I am struck by the austerity of the weathered brick and stucco walls of the two-story monastery. This building is serious. Faded grey paint and black mold cover the outside walls with one thin line of sculptured detail over the door. A small rectangular bell tower on the roof above the doorway is the only detail. No architectural artistry to take away from the original purpose of this monastery: prayer. As I slowly push open the heavy carved wooden doors, I enter an alcove with a stark wooden cross facing me. Musty odors of four centuries of monastery life waft to my nose. Immediately aware of the drop in temperature inside the thick brick walls, we wander through the long dark hallway past unembellished grey walls and barren tiled floors.

But gloomy and cold fly away quickly when a new aroma greets me and almost brings me to my knees: garlic, onions, and spices. Entering the small old kitchen with its tall ceilings, I see one wall is filled with hanging pots and pans and cupboards for dishes with a long counter for chopping and mixing. On the opposite side, a refrigerator, a sink, and a large stove with sauces bubbling in giant pots and heavenly aromas filling the air. Adjoining the kitchen, a large room serves as a pantry filled with boxes of fresh tomatoes and vegetables. Rosanna, our cook, is flying around the kitchen like a miniature Julia Child shouting a welcome at us in Italian, hands flying. "Benvenuto, tutti!" She is maybe five feet tall, very petite, with dark hair and eyes, and as she talks to us, her hands are grabbing eggplant and onions while her knife is madly chopping vegetables. She is a bundle of energy moving around her kitchen shouting commands to her assistant. I find myself eager to try her cooking.

My group is the last to arrive and we introduce ourselves to the rest of the group who are sitting in comfy old stuffed chairs and couches in a lounge off the large dining room. A group of 16 volunteers has gathered from the States and Canada, Britain, and the Netherlands, ranging in age from 18 to 65 and volunteering for many different reasons. We are all curious about the restoration project asking each other if anyone knows about the work we would be doing. Looking around at the group, I feel really comfortable with the mix of ages.

As we are checking each other out, Teresanna Loiodice, an archeologist who works on the project comes into the room. Before she even speaks a word, we all feel welcomed by the warmth of her big brown eyes and her genuine smile. That smile and warmth would help form us into a hard-working but happy work party in the weeks to come. In her late 30s, very pretty with dark hair covered by a red bandanna and dressed in a T-shirt and shorts, Teresanna gives us a brief background on the project she has been working on for the last few years.

Sinergie Cooperativa, made up of archeologists, scientists, and artists, is dedicated to revitalizing historic sites in Puglia, a province in southeastern Italy in the heel of the boot. With local government support, they invite volunteers to Altamura to work on restoration projects for a minimal fee in return for room, board, and educational tours. Twice yearly sessions have been conducted since 1995 with international volunteers happy to work to restore the historical sites. The volunteers stay in the monastery with either one or two roommates. Rosanna cooks lunch and dinner daily but we serve ourselves breakfast.

Our first workday at Masseria Jesce, we learn, will be tomorrow. Everyone bombards Teresanna with questions about the project but she just smiles, "Tomorrow is soon enough to explain the work of the project. Now you can settle into your rooms and then get ready for lunch."

Heading up the staircase, I walked down a dormitory style hall to my new room anxious to see where I'd be staying and to meet my roommate. Our wing had about seven bedrooms for the dozen volunteers and one bathroom with only three toilets and no shower. Seems the two showers that we would all share were in another wing. Did they say two showers? I walked into my small bedroom with its institutional green walls, low cathedral ceilings, a window alcove looking into an empty field, an old armoire with mirrors and twin monk-like beds with iron headboards.

My roommate turned out to be Antoinette, a tall healthy 18-year-old from the Netherlands with enormous blue eyes and long blonde hair. We immediately started talking like long-lost friends. Antoinette's openness was wonderfully refreshing. A student studying architecture and possibly archeology, Antoinette had returned here for another summer project fueled by a strong work ethic and a desire to contribute. But she also had fallen into the love connection with an Italian fellow, Antonio, last year, and she was back to see if he was as anxious as she was to fall in love. Love became our favorite bedtime topic in the coming weeks as we fell asleep talking when she wasn't out with Antonio.

The first evening, the group took a walk with David, a returning volunteer and archaeology student from England, who acted as our guide through the 12th-century streets of Altamura. David was a wealth of information couched in dry British humor. Altamura, once the local capital, had been destroyed in the 10th century and then refounded in the mid-13th century. Surrounded for protection by walls of rough blocks of stone without mortar, the town fathers built narrow roads going out in concentric circles almost like a maze. We wandered past old houses made of stone, each with a black iron grill balcony. The streets were paved with cobblestone and small cars raced by somehow navigating their way through the narrow streets.

While walking past historic sites learning about the life in the 12th century, I noticed that people quite obviously retained the culture from the old days. At around 8 pm, the town, as in the entire town, went for a walk, almost a promenade around the inner square of the village where the large stately stone Romanesque cathedral with chiseled carvings depicting Bible scenes served as a gathering place. Older men in short-sleeved blue shirts and immaculate dress pants walked to the town square to chat. Teenagers stood talking in groups, flirting with each other, while young parents wheeled their baby strollers. Everyone was eating gelato—cool, fresh, and light. My first lime gelato on a warm summer evening in Italy was a sensation that woke up my mouth, my senses. Away from the square, the old women were sitting in wooden chairs outside their houses and talking to each other. I felt a long way from my home where families close their doors, watch TV, and rarely talk to their neighbors. Communication was not an effort here but rather like eating, a part of life. It was an amazing nightly custom! How wonderful to see people out of their houses visiting with each other. Excited to see tourists, they greeted us with smiles and "Ciao" or "Buona sera" as we joined their promenade.

Returning to Cappuccini after our walk, we sat out on the stone patio outside the back of the monastery excited to be living in quaint Altamura, with the buzz of new friends and still anxious about our project. Tonio surprised us all by pouring wine for everyone and then serenading us in his strong tenor with beautiful Italian songs as he played his guitar. It was an enchanting first evening sitting outside with warm breezes, stars in the sky, music and wine.

I looked around at the volunteers wondering who I would become friends with, then up to the sky and the stars, and was thankful to be there. This group of strangers had been brought together by a desire to do volunteer work in Italy. One American man, John, who had brought his 20-year-old son along was quite handsome, tall and dark with curly black hair. A fireman, he seemed interesting though probably too serious, while a Canadian woman, Vivian, was full of life and laughter. A California woman was there with her two spunky adult daughters, both teachers. Four people from the Netherlands in their 20s were reserved but friendly, and Paulo from America in his 60s, a good-hearted man with his roots in Italy, sang along with Tonio. After our three weeks of manual labor together, friendships would form and even some romance between us but now we were just at the start of our project. Teresanna finally joined us out in the patio sitting alone on the steps smiling quietly watching us all. Tonio's passion, we would learn, drives this project but it was Teresanna's laughter and caring that all of the volunteers would remember.

The next morning we drove to our first day of work in the classic old Volkswagen bus bumping along with no springs but a good loud sound system. Tonio cranks up his favorite music and sings along for us all to enjoy. When we turned into the long driveway and arrived at Masseria Jesce, a massive old farm building built between 1400 and 1550, the site looked abandoned and deteriorated. Leaving the car, my immediate worry became extreme heat survival when a wave of hot air covered me like a sweltering blanket. As my Pacific Northwest-acclimated body reacted to entering the sauna of the Italian countryside by pouring down sweat, Tonio and Teresanna explained the history of our work site. Walking through the farmhouse looking at old bedrooms and fireplaces, we saw that the ancient interior walls were decorated with early Christian frescos deteriorating from moisture in the air. Outside near the front of the farmhouse, we walked through a musty smelling underground crypt that had been used as a church by the local peasants. Decorated with more fading frescoes, one at the entry dating from 1350 was of the Madonna holding the baby Christ and further inside another dating back to 1664 was of the Archangel Michael piercing the devil with a pitchfork. Still visible though fading, these frescoes must have been very dramatic as I imagined a subterranean church sermon held here 700 years ago. Sinergie also wants to help preserve and restore these frescoes.

Two natural caves at the back of the farmhouse dating back 4000 years were used as habitation sites in prehistoric times, again in medieval times, and by agriculture communities for both people and their livestock. These caves smelled dank, musty, and old but cool like the basement of my childhood house. Masseria Jesce, our restoration project, had once been a medieval agricultural center with fortifications to defend against invasions. Many of these old farm structures in the region have crumbled from the ravages of time and neglect, but now the city of Altamura was supporting this project as a possible site for exhibitions, festivals, cultural and education events, and tourism as well as for its archeological significance. Tonio, Teresanna, and Giovanni Ragone, a geologist, and past volunteers had been working on restoring this farm for years.

So now it was time for our team of volunteers to find out exactly what restoration work means. The aim of our restoration project was mainly conservation through the protection and preservation of Masseria Jesce with a goal of authenticity. Restoration here would be the process of making repairs with the intention of restoring it to its original form by either adding the missing parts or replicating them, which is new work but done in an old style. If this project is not completed, the history of the land, the architecture, and the frescoes will be lost over time to a slow continual deterioration process leaving Masseria Jesce in crumbles.

Our restoration project meant days of manual labor: smashing rocks, laying bricks, and hauling dirt, using the original methods from the 15th century with very few tools, mostly natural materials found on the site, and human labor. Our team would work on three separate areas around the farm. We would restore the crumbling two-foot-thick stonewall lining the driveway. This turned out to like working a puzzle. First we found and hauled by hand large rocks that fit together from the surrounding land, then we balanced these big rocks on each other forming two outer layers, and then small rocks filled the inner chamber. Another project was to complete the landscaping of the yard. The yard crew hauled dirt from one area to another in wheelbarrows, restoring the courtyard area by laying stone tiles. The final project was to level the floor of the cave that would be used for small concerts or lectures. Unable to adjust to the July heat of the Italian countryside, I wondered how I would survive working on this project without melting. And then I walked down the 12 narrow, steep stone stairs through the concave opening into the cave. Its interior was cool, damp, musty, and dark. I had found my project. The walls of this natural cave were uneven and curved covered with mold and dirt, with dark crannies and a low ceiling. I reached out to feel the old cave walls, my mind boggled by the fact that it was 4000 years old. I imagined living underground with my sheep and cows, pigs and chickens living next door.

The floor was very uneven and our job was to level it to support chairs. Using pick axes, we hacked away at the dirt called *tufo* to level the floor. My new favorite tool was a big pickaxe used to loosen the tufo and I found swinging this axe incredibly satisfying. At one point, I realized it could have saved me thousands of dollars in therapy after my divorce. Gripping the handle with firm hands and my knees bent, I held the axe head behind me over my shoulder. I took in a deep breath and then bam! I breathed out and whirled that thing down with all my might. I could smash anything! I was amazed at my ability to destroy, to smash rocks. Manual labor is both physically and emotionally satisfying. The rhythm of the swing and the power I wielded as Queen Rock Smasher brought a new joy as the first stage of decompression from my old life unfolded with each swing of my trusty pick axe. I released pent-up feelings with each smashed rock. The power of the axe transferring energy to my spirit. The rhythm of each stroke like a meditation. The cave team all started feeling the satisfaction of mindless destruction. David, the Brit, and I sang songs to keep our rhythm steady as together we broke up the floor. Sam, the lovely high school graduate, sang with us as well. My roomie, Antoinette, seemed surprised by all of the silliness as she hauled buckets, four at a time, out of the cave. But pretty soon the entire cave team was singing, heaving our pick axes into the ground, and hauling the tufo out of the cave and having a great time.

While the volunteers working above us got tans, the cave people stayed pale but as the floor leveled, friendships began to form. John, the handsome man from Chicago, worked on my cave team and we flirted with each other in that smart-ass teasing sort of flirt. If I had put in an order for a sexy man to be on this trip, it would have been within shooting range of John's tall, dark looks: rosy complexion, broad shoulders, great ass, good legs, and a teasing manner plus charm and intelligence. Game to get to know him and perhaps do some "holidating," I chatted with him about life while we worked. He teased me playfully and yet underneath the glib banter he seemed cranky. I wondered where he had lost his smile. I reminded myself that handsome, glum men are nice eye candy but difficult. Sensing trouble, I put him into the sexy-with-issues category and decided to keep my distance.

However, one day at break time John walked me to a fig tree in the neighbor's yard, picking me a warm, ripe fig. Taking my first bite of a fresh, sun warmed fig, my eyes rolled back as I savored luscious mouthfuls of warm, soft, pink flesh, a sweetness and texture unlike any fruit I had ever eaten. Against my better judgment, my daily treat became flirting with John (ignoring my own warning) and eating one of the wild warm figs. In Italy, as I would later find out, figs are a man's way of showing his interest.

By the end of each day, I was hot, dirty, and tired from tough manual labor. Tufo smashing became a daily chore, hacking it into pea gravel bits, putting it into small buckets, and then hauling it up the stairs out into the sun. Each day we worked hard at this task and I gave it my best. Load two buckets, one for each hand and then schlep them up the 12 stairs that get steeper as the day wears on. Antoinette, my roommate, looked like she could carry one hundred buckets up the stairs. I was cool inside the cave but hauling all of the buckets up the stairs into the hot sun was wearing me out. But I looked around and everyone was still working hard. Was I the only wimp here? At home I played a lot of squash, rollerbladed, and kayaked, and though I could lose some weight, I was not fat. I thought I was in good shape but I was totally unprepared for lifting weights on a Stairmaster inside a sauna. But anxious to become fit, I continued the work with the hope that it would get me in better shape. Humming the theme from Rocky up the stairs and 'I am woman, hear me roar' while smashing rocks, I encouraged myself while testing my mettle and my will. Unwilling to cry uncle, I kept lugging buckets up the stairs though my knees were wobbly and my spirits low. I wanted to be a good team player, not a tired old woman who quits when the work gets hard.

Finally though, one afternoon, the heat takes every last bit of strength out of me and I am just too beat to work anymore. I drag myself like a wounded animal to a cool corner inside the farmhouse to lean against an interior wall, to hide and to recuperate. Teresanna, noticing my absence, follows me into the farmhouse and comes to sit by me. Seeing my exhaustion, she gently tells me, "Joyce, I think that you have been working too hard. Why do you push yourself so hard?"

"But Teresanna, everyone else is still working. I can keep going. I can." Looking into her soft brown eyes, I see compassion. Gentleness.

"Joyce, you must take tomorrow off. You laugh and smile here but now you are tired. You are not singing. I think you have overdone it. Look: your legs are wobbling and your hands are shaking. Don't you see how tired you are?"

"But I feel like a loser having to quit. I need to get stronger but hauling buckets in the hot sun is wearing me out."

"Joyce, it is okay to be tired. It is okay to need a rest. Tomorrow you are taking a day off!"

"Okay. Okay, Teresanna."

On my day off, I sleep and sleep and sleep. It is afternoon when I finally awaken to the sounds of the other volunteers returning from their labors. Embarrassed to be found still asleep, I slip out of the monastery and head to the town. Returning later, everyone is kind to me, asking how I am feeling and if I am okay. Uncertain how to respond, still feeling embarrassed by being a wimp, I mumble that yes, I am fine. I am just fine.

Now how do I keep up my tough guy front now when I have already shown weakness, vulnerability? Is this the first layer to be peeled away on my journey then, being tough, being strong? Is my habit of never asking for help or admitting weakness the first place to be challenged on this journey?

Teresanna finds me after dinner and we walked to a quiet place to sit down for a long talk that evening about life and work and rest. Again she uses her eyes to disarm my usual protective devices. She is looking at me as if she can see right past my strong woman act, right to my vulnerable marshmallow center. The "act" becomes unnecessary as I lose my protection to Teresanna's perception.

"Rather than concentrating on being a hard worker Joyce, I encourage you to enjoy yourself. Your work here is to keep laughing."

"Teresanna, you are so kind to me. You seem to understand. No one has ever told me to keep laughing and to rest when I need to stop."

"Joyce, here we have the siesta. I want you to know that we believe that it is good to rest."

"Ah, Teresanna, you don't know how great you are making me feel, so accepted."

With an arm around me, Teresanna says, matching the tears in my eyes with tears in hers, "Joyce, I know your spirit. We are both strong and we are friends. You and I both know it is good to laugh and it is also good to cry."

And then a hug. A gentle, compassionate hug absolving me of guilt for not being a hard worker, encouraging me to be vulnerable, allowing me to be weak but still honoring that I am strong.

"Teresanna, no one has "mothered" me in a long time. It feels great to have a break from being strong and to have your acceptance! You see me as I am."

"Joyce, your happiness is important here. Now you must tell me whenever you need a rest but I will be watching you."

Later that evening I think about Teresanna's gentleness and my vulnerability. How good it felt to be real and to be safe. Could I learn about my power pounding tofu with a pick axe in a 4000-year-old cave and how to balance it with my vulnerability admitting to feeling tired and weak?

The next morning I awake early, eating bread with coffee for my first meal. I have lost the need to eat cereal, pancakes, or eggs and bacon. Thinking that I am the first to rise, I am startled by the beautiful singing coming from the kitchen. Tonio is up and he is singing his heart out. Is his singing the influence of Italian opera on the culture? Again, I think back to my life in Seattle searching for a memory of a man singing in the kitchen but am unable to find one. Do men sing in their kitchens at home? When and where do men sing in Washington? What does my culture think of men singing in the morning with breakfast? I smile listening to his voice not understanding the words, sipping my coffee and waiting for everyone else to wake up.

My energy level returned. After working all morning, we drove back to the monastery covered in tofu dust, racing down the halls to see who would get into the shower first. After our showers, we all sat down for a magnificent lunch at our long table full of liters of red wine made by Tonio's father, baskets of fresh bread, bottles of rich green olive oil, and amazing dishes that Rosanna had prepared. How can something as simple as grated carrots with just a hint of lemon and olive oil taste so good? Or her pasta dish with eggplant, tomatoes, olives, mozzarella cheese, and garlic? Our salads dressed with olive oil are simple, fresh, and crisp. Do you remember when tomatoes had a taste? The smell of these tomatoes flashed me to my childhood garden with red globes fresh off the vine. The aromas filled the air. The flavors were fresh and simple, the wine robust, and everyone talked.

We were eating the food of Apulia, often referred to as cucina povera, the cuisine of poverty, but it was delicious. The bread with a thick crust is baked in masonry ovens in town and served with green olive oil, a gift from heaven. Never had I tasted olive oil so rich and fresh. I was in love, seduced by tomatoes, garlic, bread, and olive oil. I could stay here and live, forever happy. The first couple of lunches here I consumed huge helpings of the pasta, thinking that it was the complete meal. No, that was only the beginning of the meal with fried eggplant, whole fried fish, and other warm dishes to follow. For dessert we had sweet, juicy watermelon. Was I destined to waddle out of Italy, I wondered.

Clean, well fed, and happy, in the afternoons, we took on another Italian custom, the siesta! Feeling a bit like a kindergarten student, I headed to my room as I was told to do, to nap after lunch. I surprised myself by falling asleep every day along with everyone else in town for two hours. So let's review: Work hard in the morning, come back for a three-course meal with wine, and then a long sleep. Camaraderie, good food, wine, and laughter are essential elements of this Italian culture. Easily adjusting to all of these, I am quite certain that I was meant to live in this culture!

Altamura seems to be cut off from the rest of the world with families living here for generations. A move away from family to a neighboring town is considered a tragedy. I was happy here. One sunny, hot morning in town as I walk home having finished my chores, I notice that all the shops are closing for their afternoon meal. Walking down the street, I am enthralled by the sounds I hear inside the houses. Young voices of children jabbering away mixed with older voices in animated discussions. The clanking of forks and knives keeping beat like the percussion section at the symphony. The everyday sounds of families eating lunch together in the middle of the day. In a couple of hours, the streets would be empty, the sound of voices replaced by the peacefulness and quiet of families resting after their midday lunch. Perhaps this is why I only heard one child cry during my stay here.

Flash to my life in Seattle at lunchtime. What lunchtime? Often eating alone in my car, how often do I stop to enjoy lunch with my friends? I drive my car and eat a sandwich on the way to another appointment with barely a clue as to what the food tasted like. When do I take the time to taste my food if I am always rushing to somewhere with no time to eat? How would I get any of my friends to slow down long enough to enjoy lunch? An hour break for lunch at home means lunch with a client, business then the only acceptable reason for sitting down to eat and talk. Otherwise, that much time eating is considered a waste of time. Yet, I am easily adapting to sitting down to long meals with lots of conversation followed by a siesta. Why is this so easy for me? Everyone here has time for each other at lunch eating at home as a family and even able to take a siesta afterwards. I resolve that as I travel, I will ponder how different cultures spend their time and how my nature adapts to each culture.

In the evening, different groups of volunteers took walks through Altamura and the maze of still remaining narrow roads that always end at the center and the cathedral. The younger group seemed to be having a lot of fun on their own leaving the over-40 group to get to know each other in the evenings. One warm evening we stop at a restaurant for a drink, and the locals begin talking to us. But since I am only able to speak some Spanish and none of us speak any Italian, we can't really talk to them. How I wish I spoke Italian! The group of locals wanting to introduce us to a local custom buys us a round of limoncello over ice served in chilled glasses. This bright-yellow lemon liqueur is produced in Southern Italy from lemons trees that grow overlooking the Mediterranean Sea. Made from fermented lemon rinds, alcohol, water, and sugar, the taste is cold, sweet, lemony, and refreshing on a warm summer evening. We all toast each other in English and Italian as we learn to appreciate the national drink of Italy. Because of my deep appreciation of limoncello and gelato, I am certain that I have Italian taste buds on my tongue and a natural affinity for Italian customs on warm summer evenings.

Our new friends invite us to a party but we all pass. Then, the other volunteers head home and I take a walk with Mr. Serious, the handsome man I have been flirting with. Eye candy, chemistry, and limoncello are clouding my good judgment. We stop at the park to people-watch, to talk, and probably to test the connection. I suppose it doesn't matter what country I am in. A handsome, charming man is interesting to talk with. However, talk of warm figs turns to a few tender kisses in the park and I sense that our chemistry could get me in way over my head. The man is definitely sexy. Exactly how smart do I want to be on this yearlong trip? A question I need to quickly ponder as we walk back to the monastery. Returning late to the monastery, which in itself is a funny place to be thinking about sexual energy, we find that everyone has gone off to bed. We cozy up on a big stuffed chair and talk and kiss.

And then after a few more kisses, I know it's time for inner wisdom. Kisses or laughter? Would I want to spend more time with this man who has no apparent light side but really warm lips? A moment of bliss vs. moments of regret. Is he worthy? I withhold that decision until the monks would have shuddered deeply, covering their eyes and saying their thousandth Hail Mary. Finally and with difficulty, I say no. Not this time. Warm kisses without belly laughs will end poorly. I go up to bed shocking John, who thought we were moving in an entirely different direction. An unintentional blow to his ego. I'm not sure we'll be eating any more warm figs.

With all that I was learning as a restoration worker, walking in the quaint town of Altamura meeting people gave me the greatest joy. I loved the old houses, the friendly people walking along narrow streets with colorful clothes hanging out on the line, the fresh bakeries, and the vegetable man who shouts in the streets when he arrives with his old truck full of fresh produce.

One day when I am walking back from town, an older gentleman sitting on a wooden chair in front of his house motions me to come over to see him. He speaks to me in Italian, moving his hands, smiling, chatting. I recognize only two words, Bologna and vivere, which sounds like vivir, to live in Spanish. I try to understand, answering him in broken Spanish. "No, yo estoy de America."

He looks into my eyes for what seems a long time. In his white cap and clean-ironed shirt, with his tanned face with deep wrinkles, a good-sized nose, and a twinkle in his eye, he puts his hand out to me and he speaks again in Italian. "Dami la vostra," and then many Italian words ending with *per buona fortuna*. Not understanding his words, I put my hand in his and surprisingly he draws me in, kissing me on each cheek! And so we connect in a warm, wonderful way not with language but with a small kiss and warm eyes. Overwhelmed by his sweetness, I wished I had been able to speak to him. Italy is full of warmth. People linger on each other's eyes much longer here and when they talk, they seem to really feel comfortable looking into your eyes for a long time.

On each of our afternoon field trips, we learned about the archeology of the surrounding area. Dinosaur imprints have been found near Altamura and at one stop at the Lamalunga Station, we have a view of an ancient limestone cave that was recently discovered containing a 400,000-year-old calcified Homo erectus skeleton nicknamed the Altamura man, who was found by a group of spelunkers, cave explorers, including Ragone on our team. He said they were completely flabbergasted by this find. Today the site is protected and tourists can only "visit" via a camera with remote control monitoring. Staring at the old bones, I just couldn't fathom life for this man. I had no idea what the earth was like 100,000 years ago.

Usually at dinner I sat with the younger volunteers and Antoinette, Teresanna, or Vivian as the conversations are much livelier. As I'd expected, John did not appreciate getting turned down and moved from feeding me figs to flirting with another American woman, who seemed very happy with all of his attention. My instincts about men are reliable if I pay attention to them. Guess now I'll have to pick my own figs.

The entire group seemed to get along really well. Maybe people who take a vacation to volunteer by their very nature have an ability to work together and live together. Or maybe we are all really lucky to be having fun together while we work. The delicious meals also give us all a good chance to get to know each other better with time twice a day to enjoy good food together. Everyone is pleased with the progress we are making on our project, and our educational outings are going well, too. But I believe that the tone of the group, the camaraderie and patience, have to do with Teresanna's warm nature and Tonio's nightly serenades.

On another day off, I decide to have a pedicure and manicure because my feet after working daily in the tufo dust resemble those of a hippo: all dry, crusty, and nasty from the restoration work and the too short showers. Bring me pampering! I find a small shop in town where the young shop owner is thrilled to have a tourist come to her store. I pantomime what I want and then she starts working on my nails while speaking Italian a million miles an hour with no way for me to answer her. Understanding a few words, I reply in broken Spanish. Frustrated with no answers, she calls a friend on the phone who speaks English. She then proceeds to pass the phone between us with each question so that she can find out the answers! It is so much fun! Not very many tourists come to Altamura and those who do cause quite a stir. Suddenly in the middle of this conversation, four women appear at the door of the room staring at me. They have been told that an American is having a pedicure and they come to see me! They all start talking to me at once in Italian. Smiling from ear to ear, I leave the beauty shop with more than lovely hands and toes.

Back at the monastery, my laundry was hung out on the clothes line along with everyone else's in the land where dryers don't live. My quick dry underwear was holding up its end of the bargain though lighter materials in shirts would have been better for keeping me cooler. I needed another bandana for cool control as every day I soaked it in cool water and wrapped it around my neck, and I needed more socks as the ones I brought seem to be embedded with tufo dust that had dried to a hard crunch. But so far the rest of my clothes are just right and almost everything has been worn.

One of our field trips takes us to the coast to see the beautiful city of Trani. Looking out at the sea, I experience my first bout of homesickness, sighing continually at the beauty of this city clashing with memories of my home. With their wooden fishing boats anchored in the harbor, the fishermen construct small wobbly stands, selling their catch of the day. As I walk by them, smelling the fresh fish, I remember Pike Place Market in Seattle where I buy my fish. Moving on past quaint houses and cobblestone streets, we stop to rest at a grand towering church on the water's edge. In front of the church is a football-field-sized courtyard filled with uneven cobblestones. Sitting on the sea wall waiting for the sunset, we watch children kicking soccer balls and people strolling by but the real surprise is yet to come. Because this church is good luck, brides come from all over Italy to get married here and as we sit on the seawall, we are treated to an Italian wedding fashion show. The first bride approaches the church wearing a flowing white dress with layers upon layers of the skirt forming different hemline lengths floating gently in the breeze. Wearing red stilettos and a red shawl and carrying red roses, she glides gracefully on thin heels over the uneven cobblestones. The next bride flies around the corner, spectacular in a cream-colored airy gown with a fitted bodice and a skirt designed to move gently in the breeze. Her handsome groom in a dark tuxedo, with dark hair and dark eyes, is dashing. They seem to have walked out of a fashion shoot as they rush to enter the church. The fashion creativity in Italy is breathtaking, and this is definitely the place to be a bride.

Wandering around the city, we stop in at another church but feeling "churched out," I sit on a bench watching people. A nicely dressed, very elderly woman walks toward me crouched over, leaning on her cane with her eyes looking up at me. She stops to talk to me in Italian, reaching out for my hand. Luckily Antonio, Antoinette's boyfriend, is with me and he interprets. She tells me that I have a magical spirit and she wants to kiss my cheeks for good luck! She also wants me to walk with her. As she holds my hand, looks into my eyes, and kisses my cheeks, I feel blessed and honored.

Back at Masseria Jesce, the restoration work on our project was coming along beautifully with the outer wall almost complete and the garden patio area finished. Our cave floor was leveled, filled with a layer of hand-crushed pea gravel and covered with a final, level layer of cement. After three tough, hot weeks of everyone working hard, we had completed the project.

To celebrate, Tonio and Teresanna organized an outdoor barbeque at the site. We ate an amazing feast with at least 20 different dishes all beyond description. I heaped my plate full of delicious food and enjoyed the wine, the music, and the camaraderie. By now, our group was full of laughter and fun, as we all had gotten to know each other. The celebration was a huge success but we were not done with the party.

For our grand finale, Tonio and Teresanna planned an overnight camping trip at the beach though some of the older volunteers decided to use the time for sightseeing rather than sleeping on the beach. I was game however for a night on the beach of the Mediterranean Sea. Circling around the roaring campfire, we ate warm lasagna, garlic bread, salad, and even dessert, Rosanna's parting gift to us. Drinking wine and singing songs with Tonio, we were a happy bunch but Teresanna was not ready to go to sleep. Racing into the sea, throwing off her clothes, she shouted to us to join her for a late night skinny-dip. An irresistible invitation! We followed her lead throwing off our clothes and running in for a swim in the warm Mediterranean Sea. After our swim, warming by the campfire, we continued singing late into the night.

Lying down on our bellies looking at the happy faces gathered around the campfire and talking to Teressana, I thought about Italy. The warmth of the people, the closeness of the families, and the openness of emotions had touched my heart. In two days all the volunteers would leave, boarding the train moving on to our next adventures. Who knew if we would meet again? But I was happy. My first volunteer job had been a success. I had lived in the culture, eaten delicious food, and learned about some of the history of Altamura and the surrounding area. I had lived with a group of volunteers and enjoyed myself. I'd eaten warm figs but refused the fruits of passion. I was sad to leave but it was time to move on.

More importantly, my first volunteer project had made a direct hit on an old pattern. I now had a clear physical lesson about my internal imbalance between strength and vulnerability that I had been completely unaware of. My affinity for strength as the good and my resistance towards weakness as the bad had kept my true spirit hidden by a continual act of strength and control. The pick axe and Teresanna had taught me that indeed both strength and vulnerability are present inside of me regardless of how thickly I plaster on the Invincible Woman Act. It was time to take this new knowledge into action. Now able to swing a pickaxe and rest when I was tired, I was ready to head to Greece to begin my month-long volunteer project at the Lesbian Wildlife Hospital.

CHAPTER 3

From Athens to Lesvos

I SIT ON MY BED LOOKING around the hotel room while a dog barks outside. A scooter goes by and again I wonder how I got here to the Plaka district, the oldest section of Athens. My inexpensive clean hotel has a godsend of an air conditioner keeping me cool; I vow to stay here till sunset. Adventure beckons, however, and I wander through a maze of hot, cranky tourists along narrow windy streets lined with look-alike shops selling leather goods, gold, and clothing. I wonder if I should be dropping bread crumbs like Hansel and Gretel.

Hawkers stand at the front of each store aggressively telling me, "Come in! Look! We have the best price."

"Come in. Delicious food. Just what you want."

"Come in. See our jewelry."

Tourists jam the brick-lined streets as the heat of the day crushes me. Frantic for quiet, solitude, and shade, I walk quickly not paying attention to where I am. Gazing up a street, I see a large shade tree by a quiet, empty courtyard offering peace and quiet and the beginning of a love affair with a frappe called *metrio*, a whipped iced semi-sweet coffee with milk and sugar.

The scenic taxi ride from the airport past Hadrian's Arch and then the Temple of the Zeus had gone sour quickly. The driver pulled to the curb and told me to walk down the street to find my hotel. The spot just didn't feel right to me and I refused to leave the taxi. "NO, I am in this taxi because I want to be driven to my hotel so drive me there!"

Athens and I were both boiling with heat, and I was tired and nervous in this new city and refused to be lost on foot. When the taxi finally stopped, we had gone another eight blocks and I would have been struggling in the heat with the giant pack melting me into a large puddle. Sometimes it pays to be a bitch.

Exiting the taxi, I noticed a man get out of his car and head my way. Traveling alone in a strange city burdened down with luggage, I felt apprehensive as he approached me.

"Hello, where you are coming from?" he said with a charming Greek accent.

"I am here visiting from America," I replied, gripping my bags tightly.

"Ah, I would love to show you around Athens as I am lazy and have time. We could meet for coffee today or perhaps tomorrow. Let me give you my number. My name is Christofis."

With that he went back to his car and wrote his number on a piece of paper. "Be careful. Don't keep your belongings out in plain sight for a thief will come and take them."

"Okay, thanks for the warning. I'm off to my hotel."

Christofis with his stocky build, silver hair, and tan skin seemed like a safe bet for coffee but I doubted that I would ever call him.

As I entered my hotel, I expected an enthusiastic greeting from the very friendly hotel clerk (well, that's what the web site advertised!), but he barely managed a hello, showing me the miniature elevator obviously built for tiny people with tiny luggage. I squeezed into it with my pack feeling like the Jolly Green Giant.

I started to plan my days in Athens but suddenly I felt very lonely. With pangs of homesickness, I pulled out pictures of my sons, my cat, Seattle. The person in this hotel room and the woman in the pictures still did not seem to be the same though I was almost a month into my adventure. It still felt like I was walking in a postcard. How could I be here when I was just in Seattle living my life full of work, friends, and time-honed habits? How long would it take me to adjust to this trip?

My next stop at the wildlife hospital was scheduled for the month of August. When I had first found it on the Internet, I had laughed at the name, the Lesbian Wildlife Hospital, thinking about a hospital for gay wildlife. But after checking the location, I had realized that because it was on Lesvos, it would obviously be called a Lesbian hospital. Having traded many emails with Ineke, one of the founders who worked at the sight, I was looking forward to helping with the birds, dogs, and cats on what appeared to be a gorgeous island in the Aegean Sea.

In Athens for those days before taking the ferry to Lesvos, the cool evening breeze encouraged me to wander through the narrow brick streets. Each restaurant had an outdoor patio, a menu stand, and waiters beckoning me to come in and eat. Choosing a small restaurant and sitting at a table out on the patio, I was instantly joined by a feral cat with long legs, long ears, and a very narrow face.

The waiter was full of good cheer as I ordered tsatziki and sampled my first batch of Greek yogurt mixed with cucumbers and garlic. Reveling in the difference between this thick, plain, sour yogurt and the sweeter, runnier yogurt at home, I became an instant fan. Next I bit in to my first soriatiki salata, a Greek salad, and again as in Italy, I really tasted the freshness of the tomatoes, the richness of the olives, and flavor of the olive oil. My third taste treat was spanakopita, a flaky pastry with spinach and feta rolled between sheets of filo dough, then deep fried to a crisp until the spinach and feta were warm. As I watched groups of tourists wandering past the patio, I realized that I was going to need to learn how to eat alone without getting lonely. I'd spent the entire day by myself and my sense of adventure kept colliding with my need for companionship.

Getting the blues, I decided to retreat and hibernate inside my hotel but my waiter had another idea. "No leave. You must stay, you must stay."

"Oh, I'm tired. I think I'll go back to my hotel."

"No. You sit. I bring you watermelon. Free, on the house." He brought me sweet watermelon and finishing every juicy bite, I again got ready to leave.

"No, no, have ouzo. Free, on the house." Ouzo in Greece is irresistibly delicious and fast-acting. Suddenly after just a few sips, my anxiety and blues disappeared as I started enjoying the music and myself.

I relaxed. I made friends with the cat who was begging at my table while hoping that Harley, my cat at home, was safe and happy. The perfect antidote to loneliness, my waiter continued to bring me more ouzo and started teaching me a few Greek words. The ouzo greatly improved my pronunciation but did nothing for my head the next morning.

Waking to cooler weather, I decided to walk to the Acropolis, first stopping for a tall metrio to counteract my fuzzy head from last night's ouzo. Looking up the road, I gasped in awe at my first view of the Acropolis. It has a mystical beauty, something almost beyond my grasp. I stood stunned, completely overwhelmed by this magnificent structure over 2,000 years old. I am here! I am really here! I thought. Looking up at this famous archeological site, I wondered how they could have built it without machinery or modern tools. How did they carry the granite and marble up this steep hill? Who designed this structure and who built it? As I climbed the hill to the Acropolis appreciating the magic of my journey, I had a sense of contentment in the path I had taken and felt good that I was pushing myself to travel the world.

I arrived at the *propylaea*, the entrance, and walked up the concave marble stairs showing the wear of thousands of steps, each foot leaving its mark over time. Surrounded by pillars built out of enormous circular marble chunks stacked on top of each other, I breathed deeply, taking in the wonder of this place. The mystical feeling in the air that I was sensing was beyond words. Built to honor gods and goddesses, the magic of the history lingered. Each column, each statue, and each building was a work of art. Was it the sheer number of souls who had climbed these stairs that gave me a feeling of wonder? There was a sense of power here.

As I looked out at the wall that surrounds the Acropolis, I imagined life here thousands of years ago. The Parthenon is enormous with details that took my breath away. Within these walls, each building in the complex was more beautiful than the next with intricate carvings along the tops of the buildings decorated by exquisitely carved statues, statues with a small secretive wisp of a smile. What did the smile mean? Inspiration, thoughts, and dreams all seemed to grow easily on this mountaintop with the gods weaving in and out of each intricately decorated column. Were the spirits and gods still here?

And at the very center of the Acropolis, I spun in a circle looking out over Athens in every direction, filled with happiness to be here. In the harbor at Piraeus, I could see enormous ships, distant islands in the sea, and the mountains of the Peloponnesus beyond. Turning to the busy city though, I was jarred by the sharp contrast between the details of the Acropolis and the modern Athens. I saw only tasteless architecture, buildings constructed one on top of another with no place for aesthetics and beauty. Blanketed completely by densely polluted air, the Athens of today is a mess. Thousands of years ago, a single rider could be seen coming for miles and miles but today there is only smog.

After a farewell dinner with my waiters once again plying me with lots of ouzo, I woke foggy-headed and took a taxi to Piraeus to board the Lesvos ferry, an enormous 3-story ship divided into cabins at the front, hundreds of airplane-like seats filling the back, and a gigantic smoke-filled lounge open all night. My cabin was spacious with two beds, a window, and a bathroom with shower, perfect for the 11-hour overnight trip. Walking through the smoky lounge, which was irritating to both my eyes and my spirit, hearing a roar of voices from talkative Greeks, I escaped outside to quiet and fresh air to sit on a ledge to watch the sea, the waves, and the distant islands. As the sunset painted the sky with red, orange, and yellow, I wondered what the animal hospital would be like. Would Jorvis and Ineke be as warm as Tonio and Teresanna?

Then, curious to meet my roommate, I headed back to my cabin. Opening the door, I see an old short round Greek woman dressed in a black dress with big black shoes, grey hair tied back in a bun, a rather large pockmarked nose, dark eyes, olive complexion, and a large stomach. Unpacking her many belongings as if she is taking a 10-day cruise, she starts chattering with enormous enthusiasm…and chattering…and chattering at me in Greek. Stationing herself about four inches from my nose, she looks up at me talking continually. Smiling, I say and pantomime, "Sorry, I don't understand a word of what you are saying," but she keeps talking. She speaks rapidly with lots of emotion waving her hands and oblivious to the fact that I don't speak Greek.

31

She goes on talking. Unable to interrupt her, I keep saying, "I don't speak Greek. I only speak English."

But she keeps talking.

I say, "Hey, did you hear Anthony Quinn is on board?"

She keeps chattering.

I say, "No understand."

She still keeps chattering and so I listen. Maybe it's like some SOS message that I will understand if I learn the rhythm. With one hand on her face moving her head from side to side and the other pointing to her huge stomach with painful expressions on her face, she seems to be telling me that something is wrong with some part of the lower half of her body. Does she think perhaps that I am a doctor?

Opening a black case, she removes some "equipment," a small injection thing, pointing at her stomach then to the bathroom. I think this is way more information than I'll ever need and I get the feeling that she wants me to help her. As she readies her medical supplies, I move swiftly. I am not shooting injections, not helping with large belly problems. I am gone!

"Good bye, I have a date with a hot Greek man for dinner," I say, leaving the cabin trying not to laugh. She is still talking as I leave.

Unable to spot Anthony, I arrived in the dining room, ate tasteless spaghetti, and read my book until the restaurant closed, still unable to solve my eating dinner alone dilemma. Heading down the corridor towards the lounge, I squeezed around families sprawled out on every spare inch of floor. But the lounge is thick with cigarette smoke and unbearably loud, and I have no choice but to head to my room where luckily my roommate is fast asleep and snoring loudly.

Awake with the dawn, I packed up and went out to the deck to watch the golden sunrise fill the sky as the ferry glided past mysterious islands arriving into the harbor at Mytilene on Lesvos, an untouched, untouristy Greek island, the third largest of all the Greek islands with a history dating back more than 3000 years. The birthplace of poets Sappho and Pittacus, Lesvos during ancient times was second only to Athens in its cultural influences but now it is known for ouzo, olives, and fish. Mytilene was still asleep as we docked. The dawn light reflected from the clusters of white houses stacked up the hill onto the still water in the harbor. The fishing boats anchored for the night moved gently from the ferry wake. An empty boardwalk ran along the sea.

As the ferry docked in the harbor, 1600 passengers burst out of the ship in a mass exodus like rats fleeing a fire. I fumbled from taxi to taxi unable to find a vacant one to take me to Agia Paraskevi, the town where I would volunteer at the Lesbian Wildlife Hospital. Luckily a driver took pity on me, squeezing me in with a family of three, a mother, a grandmother, and a daughter in her 30s, who all had the wrong luggage. Upset with the luggage problem, the daughter began crying hysterically. The driver quickly retrieved the correct luggage but now the daughter began arguing with the driver pointing at me and yelling. I sat quietly in the back seat next to the little grandma and listened to the daughter and mama yell at the taxi driver. He listened and listened patiently; then finally he caved and starting yelling back at them. Two Greek women and one Greek man arguing sounded like a war between percussion instruments, and I squirreled down in the back seat hoping to become invisible. Grandma fell asleep on my shoulder unfazed by the fight and finally peace was declared for the hour-long ride. When Grandma awoke, she was surprised to be sleeping on an American shoulder.

"Σας ευχαριστούμε" (thank you), she said with a sweet smile and a grandmotherly pat on my leg. Winning points for helping the grandma, I am now okay and in English the daughter asked me, "Why are you going to Agia Paraskevi?"

When I explained my volunteer work at the Lesbian Wildlife Hospital, she seemed pleased. "May your stay here be a pleasant one," she said when they dropped me off in the center of Agia Paraskavia.

CHAPTER 4

The Lesbian Wildlife Hospital in Greece

AGIA PARASKEVI IS QUIET this morning on the small main street. All of the tavernas are closed and there is not a soul in sight. But I am excited to see that it is just a small village. This is exactly the type of town I wanted to live in: no hotels and no tourists. I spot a small sign for the Lesbian Wildlife Hospital pointing up the hill and lugging my pack up the steep cobblestone street, I follow the signs and their arrows. Walking up the hill panting from the weight of the damn pack, I arrive at a tall green wooden fence with a sign for the hospital. I wonder what I will learn behind this gate and what type of work I'll be doing. I knock on the door anxious to meet Ineke Peeters-Lenglet and Joris A. Peeters, a 50ish couple from the Netherlands who have set up a wildlife rescue in their home.

Ineke opens the gate. She's in her late 40s and looks like she hasn't showered for days. Her short, dishwater blonde hair is cut severely around her face and it has that just woken-up look with uneven clumps sticking out in different directions. No makeup. Fatigue written all over her face. I wonder if there is a problem at the hospital that is dragging away her energy. Dressed in a white sleeveless blouse and shorts, an unidentified tattoo on her upper arm, she greets me with neither smile nor fanfare. But entering the courtyard, I am enthusiastically greeted with lots of barks and yips from about ten dogs in all different sizes and all clamoring for attention. They seem really glad to see me. Perhaps they know that Cinderella has arrived to clean up their messes.

The courtyard smell is horrid, putrid from all of the pet urine. I would later learn that none of these dogs ever went for a walk. Ducking

34

my head as I walk into the small door of the house, I enter a dark hallway. The smell is even worse here, a combination of dirty litter boxes and dog pee and animal fur. My nose feels assaulted and I try not to gag wondering how I will survive in this dirty environment.

All of the dogs follow us inside, the younger ones jumping on my legs. As I crouch down to pet one dog, nine more surround me jumping on me from all directions. I give them a "Get down." command but they are too excited to obey. Arriving in the kitchen, Ineke introduces me to the eight cats scattered all over the kitchen. A small table at the center of the room with four chairs each with a cat, a fireplace ledge with books and a sleeping cat, a window ledge with two sleeping cats and one asleep on top of the small refrigerator. Only the mounted wall TV is without a sleeping cat.

Joris, her husband, comes flying down the stairs to meet me. A tall lean man maybe 60 or 65 years old with hunched posture, he wears a white shirt, high tide pants coming to his ankles and big black shoes. His long white beard and long straggly white hair flying away from his head made him look like a skinny Santa Claus after a lengthy diet of Subway low-fat sandwiches. But there is no jolly about Joris, no smile and no "ho ho ho" out of him.

"Hello. Let me show you to your room." Somber, stoic Joris leads me into the attached house next door without comment. Walking through my gate into a cluttered, messy courtyard, I see lumber, wire scraps, and junk. I have a small smelly toilet room with rat droppings on the floor and off the courtyard a separate dirty kitchen with a working refrigerator and large sink but there is neither tub nor shower here.

Walking up the stairs to the house expecting the worst, I am surprised when I enter my house because it is quite nice. There are a couple of bedrooms upstairs, and a living room and my bedroom are on the main floor. My only roommate is named Myspoos, a rescued blind cat, who meows loudly in greeting. Outside my bedroom window, a neighbor's pasture has two horses, four goats, and a whole flock of sheep.

"Be sure to close the shutters when you leave. Otherwise Myspoos will escape and be killed," Joris says as he leaves. After unpacking my things, I go next door to talk to Ineke about the hospital and my chores.

Planning on being here for one month, I am anxious to get to work but Ineke invites me inside to join them for breakfast. Sitting down at the small wooden table in the kitchen, we are surrounded by the entire gang of the cats and dogs. Ineke pulls out a tray from the refrigerator with cheeses, meats, and cucumber, and places it at the center of the table with a loaf of bread.

"Make yourself a sandwich, Joyce," she tells me.

But as we begin to eat, three cats jump up on the crowded table in between our plates and the tray. With tails flying and cat butts in my face, Joris proceeds to hand-feed each one. I make myself a cheese, meat, cucumber, and cat fur sandwich and we all eat in silence while Joris and Ineke watch the BBC news on the kitchen TV, neither talking to each other nor explaining my volunteer work to me. I feel a deep wave of disappointment.

When I had first searched for volunteer projects in Greece, I was excited to find the Lesbian Wildlife Hospital on the gorgeous island of Lesvos. The turquoise waters, the photographs of quaint Agia Paraskevi, and the romance of a Greek island appealed to my fantasy dream of life in Greece. In my many emails with Ineke, she was always kind and welcoming and sounded anxious to have my help. The hospital sounded very busy and in need of an extra set of hands. I hoped to learn about the care of injured wildlife and domestic animals with hands-on experiences and possibly even observing surgery. Looking up information on the Internet about Lesvos, I found that birders all over the world know Lesvos as a fabulous site to watch migrating birds. Growing up my sister Norine and I had rescued dozens of injured birds feeding them with eye droppers, building them little nests, and working desperately to keep them alive though we rarely succeeded. Maybe at the hospital I could finally learn how to keep rescued birds from dying. When I read copies of their old newsletters on their website, my long-ago dream of studying to become a veterinarian resurfaced with this project.

But as we sit at the table, I feel my energy drain. Perhaps they are both very tired from a lot of hard work. Or maybe they are just a quiet and reserved couple. My excitement and hope for the project are definitely dampened but as this is only the first morning, I hold out hope. Maybe I'll get used to cats on the table and there is still the work with the wildlife, my reason for coming here. Ever optimistic I eat my sandwich and watch the news trying not to let the initial disappointment overwhelm me. I try not to get too negative. But what a drastic change from the animated conversations at Altamura, the warmth of Teresanna and Tonio, and the delicious meals cooked by Rosanna. With no conversation, cats on the table, and the smell of urine in the air, I fight to keep an open mind.

But after lunch comes an insurmountable challenge to my optimistic attitude as Joris puts one of the cats in his lap and begins picking off ticks, then drowning them in his water glass. "You need to be very careful of ticks here," he says, taking one off the cat and plunking it into his water glass. "They carry a lot of disease like encephalitis and Lyme disease."

Ah, there goes another one into the glasses we drink out of.

"You especially have to check the warm areas of your body every night. (Is that an evil smile?). They are very dangerous."

I attempt not to scrunch my face in a giant grimace as I watch him pick around the cat's body, and I hold my feet firmly in place to keep them from bolting out of the room as I choke down the rest of my sandwich. He has to be putting me through some initiation process, I think. I calmly listen to him and then ask to help wash the dishes after lunch. However, washing dishes here involves a quick rinse in dirty water without much soap. Even the "tick water glass" is just rinsed. After seeing this, I decide to drink from my water bottle rather than their glass and I use my hands to hold my food rather than their plates.

Ineke, who is pleasant to talk to, tells me that my first assignment is with Joris. Driving with the still silent and gruff Joris to the wildlife rescue area just outside of town, we park the van in a wooded park and walk up the hill. Joris has leased this land from the city and has constructed seven large cages to house recovering wildlife. Each day Joris feeds and waters the wildlife here checking on their progress with a goal to release them all back into the wild. "Your job is to freshen the water bowls in each of these cages. I will go in with you the first time to teach you. Be careful to always lock the cage door when you enter and when you leave."

Our first cage has several very large perches made from tree limbs and an enormous owl. As we enter the cage, Joris tells me, "Show no fear when we approach the owl."

And in we go, walking straight up to an enormous owl to within a foot of his talons. The injured owl turns his head slowly and stares at me with serious slow-blinking eyes while I tell my heart to slow down and for certain to show no fear! We are having a staring contest. His markings are gorgeous but with just his eyes, this predator conveys a "Who the fuck are you?" attitude as we change his water and bring him food.

"Back out of the cage now as we are ready to leave," says Joris.

In the other cages, there are recovering hawks, gulls, 14 turtles, a cute miniature owl, and other birds. All need fresh water and food. Joris cares for all injured animals, domestic or wild. Entering the barn owl enclosure, he shows me how to hold them to feed them with the tweezers. As he feeds the injured animals, he tells me, "I cast a spell on these birds to keep them calm. This is what you need to learn, Joyce."

Intrigued by his rapport with the birds, I try to adjust to his demeanor. Without miscellaneous chatter, this grumpy man goes through his chores and I do mine. I want to learn, but his sullen silence is so different from our boisterous chatter in Italy that the disappointment washes over me again. We drive in that silence to the house where Ineke tells me to mop the floors upstairs and down in their house. She also wants me to clean the litter boxes. Cinderella's life has begun at the crazy Animal House.

The stench of the floors in the house is horrible as some of the younger dogs are not housebroken. The outside patio where all of the dogs pee is even worse. After washing the floors inside, I take it upon myself to wash down the patio. I have come to volunteer, and adjust is the name of the game.

After lunch, I do some more cleaning and then decide to take a break and head down to town to use the phone, have something to drink, and get away from Animal House.

In town the narrow main street is lined with groups of men sitting outside the tavernas in blue wooden chairs playing cards, drinking beer, and chatting with each other. Seeing a foreigner walking down this street is like an alien sighting for the villagers and suddenly all eyes are on me as I walk self-consciously down the street quickly ducking into the grocery store, which has the only public phone in town. After a short conversation with my sons, my mom, my sister, and my friend Bob, I walk back through the street of staring eyes and head straight home. I'm just too uncomfortable to have a drink on my own at the taverna.

Wandering back up the hill close to home, I notice a man sitting on the large patio of a beautiful gated home. As I walk by, he says, "Hello."

English? Did he say hello in English, I wonder? Then he walks down the steps to open the tall iron grill gate to invite me inside. Demetrius, born on Lesvos, has worked in Canada and the United States for many years but he and his family always return in the summer to Agia Paraskevi, where both he and his wife were born. This year his wife had suffered a stroke and she was now slowly recovering both her speech and her mobility. The villagers bring them food and are helping her learn to walk and taking care of her. Both of us are incredibly happy to be socializing and our conversation goes on for hours while he serves me ouzo and Greek pastries. He invites me back for dinner with him and his wife the next evening.

I leave their home feeling happy and really lucky to have met him because this friendship is exactly what I need. Now my journey starts feeling alive and as I dreamed it would be. One of my goals is to meet the local people from this town and to learn about their culture. I don't want to be isolated by the language and Demetrius is someone whom I will be able to question about life on Lesvos. His warmth and congeniality is also a welcome addition to the still reserved atmosphere at the Wildlife Hospital. Smiling, I walk home with a bounce in my step knowing that this project is starting to work out.

When I arrive back at Animal House, Joris and Ineke tell me to join them upstairs in the living room to talk about the day. There is no dinner planned and I'm glad I had snacks with Demetrius. Joris is sitting in the corner chair like a captain of a ship. All the while, he eats chips and drinks beer and discusses wildlife updates. Ineke obediently takes notes on everything Joris says keeping a detailed log of every animal that they treat. That first day he criticizes Ineke harshly for her work when she reports something inaccurately. She puts her head down, rewrites the information, and stays quiet. I sit on the sofa feeling uncomfortable watching their interactions. I am really having a hard time understanding the dynamics between Joris and Ineke and find myself being unnaturally quiet, timid, and reserved.

After the data is discussed and correctly recorded, the conversation becomes more personal. Joris tells me some of their history including his early life as a soldier of fortune for many years in South America. Perhaps this wildlife hospital was a penance for rougher times? He seems to love animals but he has little tolerance for humans, particularly the Greeks on this island. He harshly criticizes their lifestyle, their religious beliefs, and their lack of care for dogs and cats. In a belligerent tone, he says to me, "The people who attend church in this village are 'church rats.' They are all hypocrites wearing fancy clothes but knowing nothing."

Seeming to thrive on conflict and anger, Joris and Ineke had chosen to come to Lesvos to retire and help animals but in fact they hated the Greeks, their neighbors.

But shortly after this intense conversation, they return to the TV. I excuse myself to my room to read, think of ways to adjust to this project, wonder about escaping as a better alternative, and talk to the blind cat, Myspoos, who bumps into walls, chairs, and my bed and loudly meows "OWW" after each mishap. We cuddle but he cannot sleep in my room because I like the window open and he would jump out. Blind cats, 3-legged dogs, tar-covered hawks, and injured barn owls just another day in my adventures.

The blind cat and I have a rather restless first evening as throughout the night he bumps into things yelling "Oww" and I listen to sheep grazing, their noisy bells clanking loudly. Whoever said counting sheep was a good method to fall asleep has never been around a flock of restless sheep. Each one with its bell assaults the ears till you think that Quasimodo is swinging from the ropes at Notre Dame. I finally fell asleep only to be awoken by a rooster crowing at 5 am.

Washing up in my posh kitchen sink, I walk next door to start Cinderella's morning of sweeping and mopping the floors. I am happy to fight the stench on the floors but my work stops at their bathroom. When Ineke says, "Joyce, this morning can you mop our bathroom?" I twirl around to see whom she is talking to.

"Ineke," I say, "Sorry but I am not here to clean your bathroom. You'll have to do that one yourself." They must be from another planet if they think they can get me to wash their frigging bathroom. It's not going to happen...ever!

But Cinderella did such a good job that at breakfast, Ineke tells me to go to Skalla Kalloni, the nearby beach town, find the Internet café, and enjoy myself. Packing my stuff quickly, I decide to walk rather than bike the 14 km because the roads here are narrow and the drivers insane.

As I walk along the road, I discover that the large buses have a pedestrian prank. Just as they come up right beside you, they honk loudly to see how high you can jump. Each time they honk at me, I scream and jump off the side of the road into the brambles giving everyone on the bus a good laugh! Tired, thirsty, hot, and uninspired, I arrive in town to find that the Internet café will not open until 6 pm. Rather than go back to Animal House, I decide to spend the day at the beach until the café opens. I also check out hotel prices in case I decide to make a break from my less-than-inspiring job.

Effortlessly adjusting to an afternoon on a lounge chair under an umbrella at a topless beach, I decide to stay for dinner and choose a beach restaurant with small tables covered with white tablecloths, blue wooden chairs, a large canvas canopy overhead, and a wooden floor. When my waiter arrives, my heart stops. My dream of a gorgeous tall Greek god with thick, wavy dark hair graying at the temples, deep nautical blue eyes, olive-colored skin, and a muscular build is standing in front of me at my table asking me something in Greek. I am speechless and, to be honest, surprised that I don't fall out of my chair.

Gazing into those blue, blue eyes, I sigh hoping that he understands English. "What shall I eat? What should I go see? Where are the good sites on the island?"

"What are you looking for?" he asks. (A long slow night with you?)

Sighing again, I say, "I love the beach but am pretty open."

"Then you should go see Molyvos Castle at night when lights are on. This place is much magical from the bottom of the hill but no climb to top. For just like most people when you look at them up close, the castle too loses its magic."

My eyes open wide on this bit of wisdom as my philosophical waiter walks away. When he comes back to check on me, he asks, "Did you put the olive oil on your salad?"

"Yes, do you put olive oil on yours?"

"Yes, olive oil cures everything that is wrong with you. Eaten raw before cooked even better. I like show you my island. If you give me phone number, I take you to Molyvos to see castle. My name Makis. What your?"

And so our first meeting ended with me giving him my phone number though I doubted he would ever call. But the cab ride home was quick and filled with dreams about a Greek god and a castle. It seemed the only thing I didn't like about Lesvos was the Wildlife Hospital!

Before falling asleep, I did a tick search and was happy to find zero ticks. However, I had 24 bug bites! What was biting me here? Ticks? Fleas? Mosquitoes? Bed bugs? I shook out my sleeping bag and fell asleep wondering how to change my rotten attitude concerning my current project. But the following morning I was still Cinderella unhappily mopping and sweeping the stinky floors and by afternoon I knew that I must escape. Finished with my chores, I walked to town to buy food and call home. As I walked down the main street, a tall grey-haired man approached me. "What are you doing here?" he asked.

"I am volunteering at the Wildlife Hospital."

"Ah, you are there with Joris. Everyone here afraid of him and think if he angry he put curse on town and snakes come."

"Well, he is a scary man but I hope not a witch."

"At other town he lived on Lesvos, he left because townspeople made him leave. There was much anger. Are you married?"

I marveled at this sudden switch in conversational direction. "No, I am not." I said.

"How does woman like you be single and how you travel alone? Are you not afraid?"

So suddenly I was telling him my business. "Well, a long time ago I was married but it ended in divorce. Now I am happily taking a trip around the world to learn new ways."

"Ah, well, welcome to Agia Paraskevi. I will explain to other men what you doing here."

"Thank you. Goodbye for now." Smiling, I walked away thinking about that brief interchange. I had been feeling really self-conscious and isolated walking through the main street unable to communicate with anyone. Now a man who knew that his fellow villagers were curious about me had asked his questions and could clue the other men in on my stay in town. Perhaps, I would feel more comfortable now when I walked through town. It was a good opportunity to feel like I was more than a tourist just passing through as I would be able to say hello to him again tomorrow. And I had learned an interesting piece about Joris and the town's attitude towards him. At least I wasn't the only one feeling intimidated by his gruff manner.

About three blocks from home, two women sitting on their porch were busy making pasta, their hands moving quickly. Their smiles encouraged me to stop to ask in pantomime what they were doing. With devilish smiles, they explained the pasta and then started teaching me words in Greek, laughing as I repeated them. With my little notebook handy, I wrote down the words they taught me. Laughing they pointed to body parts saying the words for face, eyes, nose, mouth "στόμα, προσώπου, αυτιών, ματιών" while I repeated them the best that I could. Next, they both put their hands on their arms and legs: όπλα, πόδια. Next they put their hands on their rounded breasts, smiling as they said "θηλές στηθών." Cupping my hands on my breasts, I repeated the words and they both fell over with laughter. I felt like a small child being taught dirty words. While we were laughing, a handsome man walked by and I rolled my eyes. They taught me a long sentence: "αυτό το άτομο φαίνεται τόσο καλό εσείς θέλει να τον φάει." And then laughing more they pantomimed what their words meant. (He looks so good you want to eat him.) And so we continued my funny Greek language lesson until the pasta was all made.

When I walked by my neighbor Demetrius's house, he was sitting on his deck and invited me inside. Thankful for an evening away from Animal House, I happily jumped at the chance to visit with him as he gave me a history lesson. Serving ouzo with delicious pastries filled with spinach and feta cheese, Demetrius explained, "Four hundred years of Turkish rule brought Greece's culinary heritage appetizers such as tzatziki and octopus pickled in lemon juice and olive oil. After the years of Turkish rule, the occupation of German troops followed during the Second World War, which was followed by a civil war, which was even bloodier. No one was really aware of what the Greeks on Lesvos were going through during the WWII or the civil war but people were starving and the standard of living was very low. For this reason, we have never had time to take special care of the stray cats and dogs but at the same time we wouldn't harm them. Joris hates the people in this town because of the stray dogs but he fails to understand the history of the culture. He has no friends here."

"Yes," I replied, "His attitude toward the town seems strange for a man who left his home country to retire here. He has nothing good to say about Lesvos."

"I love Americans. They are the sweetest people and would give you anything. The Italians are very warm, the Greeks can go either way, the French, now the French think they are superior to everyone, but there is no city like Paris."

I noticed his beautiful eyes, a brown so deep it could hold the world and I compared the expressions in his eyes with the eyes of the world, noticing how differently each culture uses eyes to express feelings.

"What does it mean when I walk through town in the evening and all the men sit playing cards, drinking beer, but there are no women with them?"

"Ah, this has been going on from the days of ancient Greece."

"Hmm…wait a minute, you say ancient Greece like it's yesterday!"

"Yes, it is a part of my heritage and the culture of Agia Paraskevi has grown out of this original culture."

Suddenly, the men in wooden chairs playing cards become philosophers in togas discussing the world, life issues, and mathematics. What do men in the United States do when they want to talk to each other at night? I wondered if men everywhere have this need but no way to express it. I thought of men in America and pictured a man on a couch with a remote control in hand watching sports. Would he rather be at an outdoor café drinking beer, playing cards, and discussing the world?

"Men long ago came together to discuss business or to find answers to questions or to discuss philosophy," Demetrius said.

"But where are the women?" I asked.

"Ah, the women are home both because they want to be as there is work for them there and so they can talk to their friends and also because it is very expensive to go out every night. The cost of living is very high in Greece. Things that cost me so little elsewhere are two or three times as much here. A couple cannot go out every night together. My wife Alexia is next door visiting neighbors and getting help recovering from the stroke she had last year."

We continued to talk until his wife returned home with the neighbors helping her up the stairs. I was struck by how fortunate I have been to be healthy. Sitting down slowly, she said, "I am working hard to control my legs and arms but it is such a slow process to recover."

"You are doing well. I have a friend who had a stroke and I think that you are making good progress."

"Oh, thank you. I have exercises I need to do every day. It is slow progress. It is hard on my family."

"Thank you both for inviting me to sit with you. I really appreciate your kindness."

"Oh, it is nothing. Come visit anytime you like as we are always home."

I thought about this couple. Demetrius, a vibrant successful man who had traveled the world for work but now stayed home quitting his job to care for his wife because it was the right thing to do and Alexia, fighting hard to regain her ability to walk. Her husband was fighting hard to support her but I could see he had his own struggles. For me, talking with them was a delightful chance to speak English and learn about Agia Paraskevi as well as be rescued from the crazy Animal House with the cats on the table!

Returning home I decided to "take a bath" and wash my hair using my outdoor kitchen sink. Stripping down, I gave myself a baby bath with a wash cloth laughing at the sight I must present in my little kitchen. With no choice but to keep going, I washed my naked body in the little Greek kitchen wearing only my hiking boots. Washing my hair in cold water with no water pressure, rinsing and then rinsing again, I wrapped myself in a towel, walked into the courtyard up the stairs hoping only the sheep saw me.

Myspoos greeted me with "Meow, meow' and then "Oww" when he walked into the bed. Following my nightly ritual of searching for ticks, my body bug bite count was now at 35 but for the first time since arriving in Lesvos, I went to sleep happy after talking to my neighbors. My list of friends in Lesvos was growing, allowing me a chance to escape the solemn environment of the Lesbian Wildlife Hospital.

When the rooster woke me, I wanted to just roll over and keep dreaming but Joris and Ineke wanted me at work at 6:15 a.m. I dragged myself out of bed, put my shoes on, and walked to my filthy, outdoor toilet noticing the fresh rat droppings on the floor. And so started the day as Cinderella...sweep the floors and mop the floors, wondering why I volunteered to be a maid. Outside I continued to scrub the patio to remove the urine stench but it seemed permanent. When I finished, I was given a promotion to Bird Cage Cleaner inside the small hospital built off the courtyard of their home! Hoping to possibly impress Joris enough to actually help with the birds, I cleaned the cages dutifully as he tended to the birds.

The Wildlife Hospital has a separate surgery room, a pharmacy room with medicines and special food, and another room filled with cages for injured birds and some small injured animals. My job was to clean all of these cages while Joris fed them and checked their wounds. My first assignment was the baby barn owls cage filled with six owls less than a foot long clinging to their perches. They had the cutest white faces almost in the shape of a heart, each one with different eye features giving them a different expression. They had been rescued about a week before when they had fallen out of their nests, and Joris hoped to nurture then till they were old enough to be set free. When barn owls are nervous, they move their heads back and forth like the backup group to a rock star but somehow Joris's presence calmed them. The first day we worked together, Joris held each one in his hands, explaining and showing me how he hypnotized them to calm them while dropping food in their mouths. This was an amazing process to observe. While he fed them and told me their story, I cleaned the cages in bird crap heaven. Fascinated by Joris's abilities with the birds and hoping to learn from him, I congratulated myself on moving from dog pee to bird droppings. Perhaps what had started as a difficult project would turn around and I'd actually feel like I was a contributing, welcomed member of this project.

Next Joris fed a young crow, then a baby bat the size of my thumb that was fed with an eye dropper, a sparrow, and a miniature owl. The tiny room was filled with cages full of recovering birds and a large aviary outside housed the "graduates" of his program.

The day before I arrived, Joris had released three rescued barn owls that had recovered from their injuries. When he told me about them, he was actually smiling and happy. For rescued dogs, he and Ineke have developed an excellent adoption program shipping them to new owners in the Netherlands. Travelers from the Netherlands come to visit him and it is truly the only time he seems to be civil to anyone.

One cage held an enormous hawk that had become trapped in tar after diving to capture prey that was trapped in the tar. Joris brought him home with wings and feathers completely covered in black tar and unable to fly. Joris and Ineke worked for hours removing the tar from his talons and feathers trimming what they could not clean. During his 6-month recovery growing new feathers, the hawk with his HUGE talons and powerful beak sat in a tiny little cage unable to soar in the sky. Joris mysteriously cast his spell on the enormous injured hawk and picked him up to sit calmly in his lap while he handfed the hawk raw liver. This hawk could have ripped a huge hole in Joris's hand but now he sat as calmly as a pet. Perhaps Joris was a bird whisperer or a witch as the village believed.

As I scrubbed to make the hawk cage spotless, I was struck by the similarities between the hawk's "illness" and Alexia's stroke. Neither saw it coming. Neither knew how drastically their lives would change. Both were now completely dependent on others and it would take months for them to heal. The hawk sat in his small dark cage blinking at me when he used to fly and hunt. Alexia could only walk if someone was helping her and each word of conversation was an effort. Both were in the middle of life and both were stopped short. Again I was grateful to be healthy and able.

One afternoon more Dutch visitors arrived at the hospital for a visit and it was a perfect time for me to sneak away down the hill to enjoy an afternoon break at the corner taverna sitting under a magnificent 100-year-old maple tree with leafy branches so broad and full that the entire stone patio was cool in the shade. Ordering a metrio from the friendly waiter, I reflected on the problems I was encountering at the project: I didn't enjoy the work though I loved watching Joris with the birds. I hated the dull, stoic, serious life around the hospital but the friendship of the neighbors and the people in the small village was blossoming. My body bug count was now up to 52 and I set 65 bug bites as my limit!

Glancing up, I see a Greek man my age standing at my table. He is dark and tall, his brown eyes have a twinkle, and the shawl over his shoulders looks like he could be doing a dance using it as a prop. "Hello! Where you from?"

"I am from America."

Questions and answers follow. "I seaman for 20 year and I go many ports in America. Would you like go beach for coffee?"

It's a short drive away and he looks safe enough. Besides, I am ready for a change and I say yes.

On the way there we laugh and try to communicate, which is difficult but not unpleasant. Arriving at the beach, we go to a restaurant that one of his good friends owns, a man originally from Australia. We order beers and watermelon, and Johnny, the owner, interprets for us. "George wants to drive you all over the island as he does his work. You will see our beautiful island and keep him company as he drives and enjoy each other."

"Sorry but I work every day at the Wildlife Hospital until 14:00. I may have a day off now and then but I am not interested in this trip," shaking my head no to George. Little did I know that in Greece our no headshake is their yes headshake! Confusion to follow!

Smiling, or rather leering at me, Johnny says, "George says that sometimes you and he would need to stay in a hotel while you are traveling."

I was suddenly thinking, Slow down there, Jackson....What does he think he is lining up here? I'm not going anywhere like that with George! NO, definitely NO.

Finishing my beer and feeling really uncomfortable, I suggest we head back to Agia Paraskevi. I feel very "done" with George.

However, the conversation from George goes like this, all layered in a heavy Greek accent. "I like you. I like you very much. You like me?"

"Sure. It was fun to go to Johnny's. Now it is time for me to get back to work."

"I like you too much. I like sex. You like sex?"

"What?" I say, shocked by his words.

"You like me?"

"Yeah, sure, no big deal."

"I like sex very much. Very much I like sex. You like sex?"

He has now stopped his truck about six kilometers out of town near the woods. Angry at myself for being naïve, I look around planning my escape if it all goes south. Now there aren't enough words between us to really explain to George that he's NOT getting any nooky so I say firmly, "No, no sex."

"You no like? You say you like me now you don't like me. I like you too much."

I repeat, "No sex, no, no, no sex!"

He says, "Ah….you no like me. I have now a bad heart. It is black. I have a heart problem."

"Ho hum, no, no sex, not now, not ever."

He isn't listening to me and just keeps saying, "Ah, you no like. You say you like but now you don't like. Oh, my heart. You no call me ever."

Trying very hard not to laugh, I say, "Okay, home now."

Okey dokey…cowboy. Go home and work on your pick-up lines. It's not that easy where I come from! Or maybe it is that easy, just not that direct. Perhaps George is saying what most men in America are thinking on that first date and he's just taking the shortest route to what he wants. Silently, he drives me back to Agia Paraskevi where I hop out of the truck and return to the taverna patio.

When I got back to the wildlife hospital, Ineke told me that because things were slow, I could take the next day off to visit another part of the island, perhaps a different beach. With no chores to do, I headed back to my now favorite tavern.

Once there, the owner comes over to introduce himself, "Hello, my name is Anchises. So, what are you doing here in our little town?"

"I am volunteering at the animal hospital."

"Ah, yes, I get along well with these people but it is not true of everyone. They do not understand Joris and Joris does not understand the Greeks. A love of wild animals…is strange to the Greeks."

"Yes, Joris seems to be angry at the town but Ineke is gentler. I am a little scared of Joris."

"Ah, the people in town scared too. They think Joris a witch and if he angry he cast evil spell on town and snakes come."

"Wow, now that is too bad."

"Oh, I think townspeople see Joris handle hawks and owls and no get bites. He storm in town not speak to anyone. People here know there was trouble at village he arrive at first. The mayor want take away the land where he keep rescued birds. Joris very angry at this."

"I have seen him do amazing things with wild birds and with them he is very gentle. I think when he was younger he was a soldier of fortune. He has told me a little about this. He is a strange character."

And so the afternoon goes. A group of British tourists sits under the tree and orders what looks like wonderful omelets. Seven young Greeks in their 20s sit together at a table talking and laughing with each other reminding me of my sons and their friends, bringing a wave of homesickness.

But Anchises interrupts that thought and tells me a funny story after the Brits leave. "Americans have Viagra but me I has my chickens more powerful than all Viagra. Those Brits just eat omelets of these eggs so tonight…look out! They must be ready. Tomorrow they back for more omelets. You will see."

I laugh and shake my head.

I decided to go to Molyvos for my day off because it is so popular with tourists and to see the castle. Seems my handsome waiter was never going to call me to take me to see it! Hopefully, I could spend the evening with Demetrius and Alexia. In the midst of planning the day, I realized that this big trip had finally become real. Somewhere in the middle of the misery of mopping floors and planning my escape, I had become the trip and I no longer felt like I was looking at a postcard. Was this a function of time? I had been on the road for just over a month. Or was this a function of being uncomfortable at the Wildlife Hospital? Had figuring out how to adjust to the unpleasant routine here brought me into the reality of my journey?

Morning finds me flying through my chores followed by a quick walk to the taverna to eat one of those spectacular omelets. It is undoubtedly one of the best omelets I have ever eaten with or without the Viagra effect!

Anchises tells me, "There is a shortcut to walk to Molyvos. You can always hitchhike if you get tired. There are no problems here with hitchhiking. I will draw you map."

Following his directions, I walk about 200 meters out of town looking for the asphalt road but the road I come to is dirt. Thinking this is not the correct road, I walk another 45 minutes but with no luck in finding an asphalt road. There are hills, olive trees, a few cars but no asphalt road. Finally flagging a car down a car I ask, "Is this the road to Petra?"

"No, NO," he says, shaking his head and then pointing back the way I came. Okay, walking back another 45 minutes I take the small, little traveled dirt road in the middle of olive trees and start walking and walking and walking.

In the rising heat and with a water bottle almost empty, there are no villages, no houses, and no cars for hitchhiking. Discouraged and thirsty, I pray for a car as I have been walking for almost three hours now. Amazingly and thankfully a car comes down the bumpy dirt road heading in the opposite direction and stops when I wave. "Is this the road to Petra?"

They only understand a wee bit of English and reply, "No."

"What, what, what? I am not on the right road? How can this be?" They say they will give me a ride to the next town, which means retracing my now wasted three-hour walk.

Dropping me off in the small town of Skala Sikamiras, they say, "Take bus to Molyvos." But there is no bus. I drink a coke in a small café, head down, tired and discouraged though still determined to get to Molyvos.

The café owner rescues me by calling a cab driven by a hysterical Turkish driver who speaks a little bit of English. He chatters continually making me laugh and asking me questions about President Bush as we wind along the stunning coastline on narrow roads through the mountains. Driving like a madman taking the blind, narrow curves wide with a honk at the start to warn the driver on the other side, he points out Turkey and the clear turquoise waters of the Aegean Sea. "Are you from Texas like Bush?"

"No," I laugh, "Why do you ask?"

"Because you wear a big hat like a Texan!" he laughs like a madman. Even with his broken English he communicates his lack of respect for Bush, a theme I will hear wherever I go.

Following the coast we round a sharp curve and I see Molyvos, one of the most beautiful harbors in Greece. It is truly breathtaking with boats anchored in the turquoise water, stone houses with red tile roofs, and olive groves separated by old stone walls held together with uneven chunks of mortar winding down the hills. The town is situated on a small mountain and the town architecture board has allowed only the old-style stone houses with wooden painted shutters and tile roofs to be built here. The houses climb the hillside like vines with foundations three stories high to make them stable enough to stay on the steep hill. The narrow, windy cobblestone street whose mortar has long since sunk between the rocks creates a bump, bump, and bump sound as my taxi and nearby scooters race by.

Walking down to the beach, I am surprised to see that it is composed completely of small river rocks. There is no sand anywhere on this narrow strip of beach forcing everyone to wear clear plastic shoes with grips on the soles into the water and to sit in lounge chairs rather than lie on blankets. The crystal clear water beckons me to take a long swim and afterwards a nap. Waking up hungry, I head up to a gyro shop where tender juicy lamb roasts slowly on a vertical spit. I order an inexpensive gyro filled with lamb, Greek yogurt mixed with garlic and mint, and French fries all wrapped up in pita bread. Undoubtedly the best gyro of my life.

Not wanting to get lost on my way home, I took a taxi back to Animal House. After another standing kitchen shower, I went inside to bed for my nightly tick search and bug bite count. At 64 bites, I only need one more bite to qualify to escape! But I had told Ineke that I would be here to help for the full month. It would feel wrong not to honor that commitment. Before I left Seattle, I hadn't really thought about what I would do if I were miserable someplace. When I called my sons to tell them about my difficulties with this project, they both had advised me to leave as they could tell that I was unhappy. But maybe with a little more time, I could adjust to the atmosphere here and for certain, the people in town were friendly. I was enjoying meeting the villagers but being a maid to a gaggle of dogs and cats in a somber environment was making me miserable. My belief in keeping my commitment to stay here to help for a month was colliding into a question of how long I should endure an unpleasant project that was teaching me little. Maybe if I stayed, I'd have a chance to work with some of the birds. But bugs were eating me alive and there was never any laughter or joy here. The call of freedom was beckoning me to leave. As I debated whether to leave or to stay, little did I know that fate would take care of that without any planning!

The next day Cinderella woke up to a day just like the day before, mopping the floors, watering down the pee-ridden patio, and then breakfast on the little table with the same tray of cheese meat, cucumber, tomato, and bread. We had been eating from the same tray for breakfast and lunch for my entire first week. Joris continued feeding the three cats on the table and the only conversation was from the BBC announcer. What was it with these people? What was with me staying? Finishing my breakfast as Joris plucked ticks off the dog and put them into his water glass, I thought, I need the beach. This place is horrible.

My first job of the day is bird cage cleaning and I give it my all because the small hospital is grossly dirty with crap on the tile walls, filthy cages, and a floor that seems to have been never washed. I decide to attack everything to fight the smell even though there are no windows and it reeks from stale air. When I am done, it's spotless and smells clean.

In the afternoon, I head down to my maple tree to read but stop instead to talk to Demetrius and Alexia. Hearing that I have the next day off, Demetrius offers to drive me wherever I want to go. We agree to meet in the morning and I am thankful for his help and impeccable timing. As we talk, suddenly I hear Joris yelling from the Animal House, which is about a block away. "Myspoos, Myspoos, Myspoos" he is shouting.

"Oh, shit." I say. "My blind cat must have escaped from my house. I hope he is safe. Maybe I should go help find him but I'm scared of Joris. What to do? I don't know what to do, Demetrius."

The shouting starts to sound closer and closer scaring me. Next I see Joris flying down the street, his white hair and beard splaying out in the wind, his body curled over as he stomps his long legs down the street looking like a madman yelling "Myspoos, Myspoos, Myspoos."

Luckily he doesn't see me behind the iron grill fence surrounding Demetrius's patio. "I am in big trouble now," I say. "The blind cat has escaped from my house. I feel so bad. What if something has happened to Myspoos and it is my fault. What then? I'll feel terrible."

Demetrius says, "It is a cat. Even blind, it will find its way back home."

"No, I am in trouble. Big trouble." Afraid to go home, I stay and talk to Demetrius until it is very late.

When I finally get back, Animal House is pitch black inside and out. No light has been left on for me. I slowly open the gate to my courtyard hoping it won't creak too loudly. I squint into the darkness certain that Joris will be standing there in the shadows ready to yell at me. I tiptoe up the stairs to my room and find a note taped to my door. "Your irresponsible behavior almost cost Myspoos his life. It took 30 minutes for me to find him. Be out of this house tomorrow by 7 am!"

Shocked by the note, sad about Myspoos' escape but relieved that he is safe and that I am leaving, I apologize to the cat, who seems happy to see me.

I sit on the edge of my bed holding Myspoos and crying. Things are not going well at all. I cannot believe that at 57 years of age I have been kicked out of my second project. I am feeling really bad. My goodness, what if the rest of my volunteer projects end up like this? What then? What guarantees do I have? Well, I guess I am one for two right now and I'll just make the best of this and head to the beach. While I pack my things, I go over in my mind what had gone wrong here and what I could have done differently. I really felt like I had chipped in and done my work whenever they gave me a new chore. I only took breaks when my work was done. But for me, Joris's attitude was too difficult with all his sharp criticisms of the people in the village, his inability to smile or laugh, and the lack of conversation. Mealtimes were torture and though I wanted to learn how to be a bird whisperer, it just wasn't in the cards. Luckily Myspoos was not injured because of my carelessness, but I didn't suppose I'd ever know why those people didn't like me here.

I decide to say goodbye to Ineke in the morning and thank her but not Joris, who has enough anger for three men. No wonder the townspeople are frightened of him! I am too! When I get in bed, my body bug bite count is at 72 bites after just one week of life at the Animal House. Yes, I am definitely ready to go.

Afraid of seeing Joris in the morning, I hide quietly in my room until Demetrius is ready to drive me to the beach. Leaving my bedroom door open while I finish packing, I talk to Myspoos, who purrs and stops crying whenever he sees me. We cuddle and I explain that I am leaving. I apologize again to him that he got out last night. He must have been very scared, too.

Suddenly Joris stomps into my house, grabs the door handle to my room, and with a face full of anger slams my bedroom door screaming, "Keep this door shut!"

Insulted and hurt by his screams at me, I walk to my door and calmly open it. He returns standing in the doorway with eyes bulging screaming at me, "Close the door so the cat doesn't escape again. Leave my house NOW!" and he slams the door shut again. My old stubborn nature kicks in and I am unwillingly to be intimidated by a mean bully. I open the door and say, "I am leaving soon but for now I need the door open."

He yells back, "Leave my house NOW!"

I yell back, "Go blow yourself!" Yes, just a nice friendly volunteer job.

Gathering my belongings, I walk out without saying good bye to Ineke.

Demetrius is shocked to see that I am carrying my enormous backpack and hand luggage for just a day at the beach! "Why are you taking so many things with you today?"

I explain that the wrath of Joris has struck and I have been booted out of the house! He sympathizes with me while reminding me that I will have a great time at the beach. Little does he know how right he is! Cinderella is about to meet a prince!

We drive to a hotel in Skalla Kalloni, and I book a lovely white-on-white room with a garden patio for only 40 euros a night. Little do I know what a magic room this will become and how happy I will be that the wildlife hospital didn't work out. Thanking Demetrius for all of his help, I turn to say good-bye to him and am shocked by a giant smooch. Pushing him away I say, "Hey, we are friends. Don't do that ever again."

"But don't you like me?"

"Liking you and kissing you are light years apart. Have you forgotten that you are married?"

"Yes, but my wife will never know."

"But I will know and there is no reason in the world for me to deceive your wife. You are way out of line here. Thank you for helping me today but you need to leave now."

"I apologize for my actions. I thought you liked me and I thought it would be good to make love."

"Well, you were wrong about that for certain. Goodbye."

"Goodbye. Again I am sorry. If you need anything at all, please call me. I will be happy to help."

Shaking my head over yet another stupid male encounter, I unpack, walk to the beach, jump into the Mediterranean, and realize I couldn't be happier to be gone from Animal House. After a long buoyant swim from all the salt in Skalla Kalloni bay, I shower, lie down on a lounge chair under an umbrella, and fall asleep for hours waking up with a craving for fried sardines, Greek salad, and my favorite restaurant! I've got another three weeks here on Lesvos and I'm going to have a great time.

CHAPTER 5

The Beach and Love

Dressed in a summer frock and with a ravenous appetite, I head that evening to the restaurant where gorgeous Makis comes over to wait on me. Though he never called me, he does remember me!

"Would you like sardines again and a Greek salad?"

"Yes."

"Anything to drink?"

"Ah, some ouzo, please."

"How have you been?"

I fill him in.

"How long you stay in town?"

"I will be in town for a couple of weeks."

"Would you like see castle tonight?

"Yes," I say with a big smile.

"Come back in hour and we go together."

Yeah, baby! A castle and a prince, things are working out for Cinderella! Finished with dinner, I prance through town to the Internet café for another glass of ouzo while I wait for the hour to pass, which seems to drag on forever. Finally, it comes but I think I need to be a little late so I don't appear too anxious.

As we drive to Molyvos, we talk.

"How you like this town?"

"It's small, which I like, and being on the beach is great."

"How did you decide to take this trip?"

I launch into my story.

"You seem a wise woman. Where is your man?"

"I do not have a man."

"How can this be? I see in eyes passion and yearning."

Oh, dear, if passion and yearning are showing and he can read it that could be dangerous! Must be some animal sixth sense.

"What is wrong?," he continues, "your heart been broken?"

Now there is something about being in a foreign country speaking to a Greek man knowing I will probably never see him again that brings out the truth. Here with Makis, I open up, letting go of my need for secrets. I tell him the truth, from my heart, fully vulnerable and knowing that if he was an American, I would give him an answer that wasn't the full truth protecting my privacy and past mistakes.

"I have two problems," I say. "One is that I love to laugh and I have a very hard time finding a man who will laugh through life with me and enjoy the way I see things. Men seem very serious."

"And the other?"

"The other is that I am afraid. I am afraid of trusting someone with my heart and giving up control though I ache for a best friend. I want to enjoy someone. I want a commitment but I want to have a life as well. Not just the man's life. When I find a man who loves my laughter and gives me my freedom, then I will love him with all of my heart. And yes, my heart was broken badly but it has been a long time ago. I think hearts do heal on their own but it is not until they are tested and rewarded in love again that they truly heal. And you, how did your eyes become so soulful? You have sadness in your eyes as I look at them. And longing."

"Ah, you are perceptive, I see. Yes, a woman broke my heart. I thought she was one way and she turned out not."

"What do you mean?"

"Ah, we used to spend hours talking about our dreams and our hopes but it turned out that she just talking, not from her soul."

"What does your soul say?"

"Ah, that is complicated. I want a woman who lie next to me and be quiet. She understand the peacefulness when two souls want to be together. I want woman who understand I need to be alone and cannot always talk. I want woman who accept love. I want give kindness."

"What do you mean?"

"I want no walls between us but I want us separate."

"Do you think you are too much of an idealist when it comes to women and love?"

"Perhaps, and you?"

"Oh, I am an idealist," I say, "a romantic and unrealistic too. With all of my emotion I know that I am tough to get close to, that I don't give my trust easily. Like a deep river, I have changes of current, dangerous eddies, and pure calm. I feel life on a very sensitive level and a man needs an appreciation of the river called Joyce. I know that I can feel deep joy and deep sadness, cry big tears and roar with big laughter. With my heart open, I have the ability to love a man deeply. A shallow relationship doesn't thrill me, not in friendship nor in love. I would like to feel safe enough to allow someone into my most vulnerable places and to have him allow me there as well. To be sad and have a shoulder to put my head on. To work through anger and disappointment. To learn how to grow love and keep it alive and yet to still have two people, together and yet separate."

I am amazed. This is the most real conversation I have had in a long time. In the silence that follows, I think of Bob, my best friend, and all the times we have talked and talked. Always freely, always with acceptance and not judgment. I had been missing him deeply, wishing I could talk to him for longer than a three-Euro card allows and here was Makis, whom I had just met but with whom I felt comfortable talking. Maybe being in isolation at my Cinderella site was helping me move outside of my walls.

"How long you be here, Joyce?"

Oh how cool is it to hear my name spoken with a Greek accent by a Greek god! Okay, Joyce, pay attention. I believe he just asked you a question. "I'll be here two to three weeks before I leave for my next assignment."

"Then maybe we spend more time together. It feels to me like we have feeling between us. Perhaps more than just body heat."

Okay, did you hear that? Body heat? More than that? Well, calm me down and tell me to breath. The man is saying a lot by Western standards, an enormous amount, and I'm just thinking "Hot!" Slow down, Joyce, slow down.

"Yes, I want to talk more. (I am a liar about the talking, but ho hum). I feel drawn to you and want to speak to you from my heart." (Nice cover, eh?)

And so the night ended with a gentle kiss.

Back in my room, I think about fast changes: tortuous days as Cinderella and now the beginning of a friendship with a soulful man. In my mind I will never understand how chemistry works but when it does—Woo! The fire lights up. I see this evening as an opening, a heart opening about honesty and feeling safe and comfortable enough to talk and listen to a man about feelings.

As I lie in bed thinking about men, through the open patio doors a cool breeze is blowing through the trees, relieving a day of stifling heat. Soothing Greek music drifts from the pool and in the distance a conversation in Greek. Perhaps it is an advantage not knowing Greek as the sounds without meaning are like music. The music soothes me as do the rustling leaves and the smell of the sea. It seems so natural now to be here on this journey not knowing anything or anyone. When people talk, I watch their eyes and pay attention to my senses while I learn about the world, about life, and about myself.

Later, walking by my now favorite restaurant, Makis stopped me. "Will you be at the beach today?"

I nodded and smiled.

"Good. I come later and take swim with you. I meet you at three o'clock."

"Great!"

Oh, dear. Greek god on the beach. Jeez....a bathing suit date? Terror of all terrors! I wear a two-piece, definitely not a bikini, because I lost my bikini body somewhere in my 30s and can't seem to find it. However, all size women wear bikinis here and I walked to a little shop to see if anything will fit me. In pantomime I asked the owner for help, and she sized up my body by cupping her hands on my breasts and feeling my hips. She then chose five different swimsuits for me. However, there was no place to try them on. Feeling optimistic, I bought one and amazingly, when I brought it home, it fit! How can that be? At home I would shop and shop and shop and go home depressed about my body, feeling fat and ugly. Here I walk into a shop, the woman feels my body, and she hands me a suit that fits and looks good! Perhaps I have a Greek body living in America? Or perhaps I need to rethink my self-image.

My next dilemma is the topless issue. Women go topless here on the beach. On my own that is not a problem as the sun feels wonderful on my breasts and the water feels better. BUT swimming topless with the Greek god Makis? Now that is an entirely different story. How in the world is that going to work? Shirt off, and then bingo, top off, and gosh, hi, how are you with my boobs just smiling in the sunshine? How am I going to pull this off? Wear my top and feel like a prude? Take my top off and feel like a wild woman?

Well, I find a spot on the beach and when he arrives, I am incredibly uncomfortable. What is it about greeting a man with my nipples out that just throws me off? Okay, he sees breasts at the beach all of the time and perhaps, this is just like seeing my face or my feet? I act cool.

Makis has wonderful deep eyes and he does that long look thing that the men here do. No words, just eyes. His voice is deep and with his accent, well, it just makes him sexy, delicious, and great to flirt with but he's also intelligent and I like it when he tells me about Greek life.

"I know beach we walk to. More private. Let's take walk there."

Okay, protocol here, please. Does one walk to another beach with a top or topless? Bouncy boobs and intelligent conversation…do these go together? I decide to fasten my top and we walk to a quiet beach with just a few other people. There is a small restaurant across the street for an afternoon cocktail. We lay the blanket down and arrange things. I take my shirt and shorts off and then start fumbling with the clasp of my top.

"Do you need help?" he says.

Oh gosh, now what…yes, can you help me take my top off so you can see my big brown boobs? I will remember this when I am 80 for sure!

"Yes, can you help me?" Gotta love a woman who needs help getting her top off. So, he takes care of the latch and then vavavoom vavavoom, my breasts are free!

Yes, he is European. Yes, he has grown up seeing breasts at the beach. I'm not expecting a reaction but he says, "I think you are very beautiful."

Wow, baby! How fun is that to hear! "Thank you," I say demurely both embarrassed and proud.

"Gorgeous really! Shall we swim?"

"Yes, let's go in." Now the thing about the bay is that the water is shallow for a good long time. So I suck in my stomach, stand up, and start walking, breasts out. But it's really shallow for a long time and it's hard to talk holding my breath and my stomach in and then of course, with the shallow water, my breasts are still shining in the sunshine. Finally the water is deep enough to dive in but there's a catch, salt water. Everything, I mean everything. floats better in salt water. Suddenly I have two natural buoys in front of me with lovely nipples all nipped out. Let's have a meaningful conversation now.

Well, he does a great job telling me about Greek mythology, Greek conquering, the land and power they had for so many years. I vaguely remember some Greek history from school but swimming topless in the Aegean Sea with a Greek man talking about Greek history is a much better way to learn! While we talk soaking in the water for over two hours, he explains, "Salt water is very healthy. It is a custom here to soak in the sea."

Finally out of Greek history, we shower off at one of the handy outdoor showers they have along the bay and head over to the restaurant patio with music playing and a cool, sea breeze. Makis is a charming man but I am unable to get him to laugh. Men need to be so serious. Do they feel they are in charge of the world? What I wouldn't do for a hearty belly laugh! Intellect is appealing to a point for me and then I just want to be silly!

After lunch he drops me off at my hotel with a gentle kiss and a promise for more.

The next day at the beach I plopped down on my lounge chair, which I rented for 2 ½ Euros, to read and nap. But it was too hot to read, so I gathered my courage to walk topless into the sea by listening to Ravel's "Bolero" in my head and throwing my shoulders back into my best Bo Derek imitation! As I was doing My Walk in the perpetually shallow bay, I noticed a man in the water looking at me. Since nearly all the men in this little town seem to be either husbands or dads, I just continued with The Walk but getting closer I noticed that he was deliciously handsome. I did my dolphin dive to get in and when I came up, he had moved next to me!

"Where are you from?" he said, his accent French and sexy.

"I am from America. Where are you from?"

"I am from France." And we began talking though I was completely mesmerized by his gorgeous blue eyes and not thinking too clearly.

"I am here on business. Why have you come here?"

I explained my trip and he encouraged me to open up, to talk more. He was easy to talk to and laughed as I joked about my time at Animal House. I became totally infatuated within seconds. As we talked, I realized I was physically drawn to him and he to me. Neither one of us could keep our eyes off the other.

If I read about this in some stupid romance novel or heard some friend retell this experience, I would shake my head and say, "Yea, right. Give me a break." But there I was talking to a man I didn't know, listening to his every word, infatuated. Was it the accent? Was it the blue eyes? Was it the way he was drawn to me?

I have had other men enraptured by me before and just let it go. How could this man be different? As we talked, I learned that he had been an Olympic athlete and now was an Olympic coach here with his team training every day for a few weeks. He had come to the beach with one of his coaches to swim and relax.

Suddenly he held out his hands to me and for some unknown reason, magical mystical magnetism, I put my hands in his. He drew me to him, wrapping his arms around me in a tight hug. Two people in the water like dolphins finding each other after a long, long time.

A first kiss is always telling. With his hands on my face and looking into my eyes and the sun shining down on us, that first kiss took my breath away with a deep sigh, an intensity that surprised us both. His soft lips kissed me with gentleness and then a long gaze into my eyes. Lips with perfect communication. My mind was lost to the sensations. The warmth of his body next to mine, the cool water moving around my back, the heat of the sun on my face, and these long, gentle kisses: the magic of the moment.

Taking his lips away, he looked to the sky smiling and said, "Thank you. Ah, you are my dream. You have dropped out of heaven and now you are here. How could I be so lucky?"

We kissed again. Never, ever in my life could I have imagined this. Swimming in the Mediterranean, kissing a man I had just met and wanting the moment to go on and on.

"I want to see you tonight," he said. "I must see you tonight, my dream. I want to call you. What is your number?"

"My hotel room has no phone."

"Ah, but I must see you tonight."

As we kissed again, a man came over to us. It was his assistant coach, Misha. "Robert, tell me, who have you found in the sea? Is this a long-lost friend?" He smiled at us all wrapped around each other.

"Ah, this is Joyce. She is my dream. I must never let her go." Then turning to me, he said, "But, my love, I must go back to my team."

And so we held hands walking out of the water. Grabbing his towel and then running back to me, he said, "Here is my number. Will you have dinner with me tonight?"

"Yes, yes, yes!" I said.

"Ah, my love, do not forget me. I will be at your hotel at 9:00. But you must call me, okay?"

"Yes, I'll call. And yes, dinner. And goodbye Robert." I'm sure I was gazing with soft eyes in wonder as we kissed again. What had just happened to me? To us? A delirious smile covered my face as I lay down on my lounge chair hoping never to wake up from this delicious dream.

When I returned to my hotel later in the evening, I called him.

"Ah, my love, how are you?" he asked. "You are my dream. How could it be that I would be so lucky to find you in the sea? But, my love, tonight the mayor of the town is having a celebration in my team's honor. I want to be with you but I must go first there but then I come to you. If it is too late, you will be very hungry. I don't want you to wait too long. Is this still okay, my love?"

"Yes, Robert. Enjoy the celebration. I'll get dinner and I'll see you when the celebration is done. I can't wait to see you, Robert." Disappointed but still ecstatic, I tried to figure out what to wear and how to calm down. I had hours to deal with before seeing Robert again.

When he knocked on my hotel room, I opened the door to warm kisses and sweet words. "Ah, my love, I am sorry I am so late. All night I want to see you but the mayor he wants a big celebration. He gives me ouzo, much ouzo, and we all dance together like Greeks. It was a big honor but now I am happy to be here with you."

"Ah, Robert, I know about ouzo here."

"But, my love, we are out of balance now. We must go get balanced."

"What is that?" I did not understand what he meant.

"Ah, I have too much ouzo now. We must go somewhere and you will drink and I will have a cola until we are in balance!"

"Ah, now I understand. Let's go to the bar by the pool." I laughed at the logic. Sitting by the pool, listening to music, drinking coke for him and zambuca for me, we talked.

"But, my love, how is it that you take this trip?"

"Robert, I think my soul felt too confined to keep selling real estate. I needed a bigger dream."

"What you are doing is very good. You have a very good heart. I see that."

"And you, have you always dreamed of being a coach?"

As we got to know each other, I learned about his life as an athlete, his humbleness, and his zest for life.

"You are beautiful both in your heart and in your eyes, Joyce. I must see you every day. Is this good for you, my love?"

"Robert, do you see this smile? I am in wonder that we have met. Yes, every day. I can't believe that I left the Animal Hospital and now have a grin across my face. How did this happen?"

"Ah, we must be thankful. But for you, this smile must always be there. Your nature is to smile. And now another zambuca for you and I will have another coke. We are getting balanced."

Laughing together, I asked him more questions. "How long will you be here?"

"Ah, we will be here till the opening ceremony. Each day my athletes work hard training and I am with them. But we must meet for a swim. In the evenings we will spend time together. Tomorrow, my love, I will take you to dinner. I am sorry that I didn't take you tonight."

"I am here for the rest of the month. I am so happy!"

We sat in the lounge chairs talking and laughing till we were even...me a little tipsy and he a little less. Leaving the bar, we walked to my room.

"Ah, my love, shall we say good night now?"

Appreciative of his manners but hungry for kisses I said, "Oh, come in and we can sit on my patio and listen to the breeze together."

In the morning, looking into his happy eyes, I smiled and giggled kissing him and appreciating our romance in full bloom.

"Ah, my love, I am late for my athletes this morning. They will wonder where I am and why I am so relaxed. Greece is good. Who needs to go to the Olympics? I will stay here with you, my dream. You are my dream. Last night was wonderful. I will see you later today. You must call me."

"Yes, I will call you and we can meet for an afternoon swim. See you soon, Robert. Last night was wonderful. Kisses go with you."

He hurriedly left to get back to his athletes while I got all mushy thinking about my new romance. How did this happen? He's dreamy with all of his compliments and he is so happy to be with me. What if I had stayed at the Animal Hospital or not gone swimming yesterday? Robert, who are you?

Robert and I met for a wonderful afternoon swim.

"My life began in Armenia. Do you know where this is?"

"I am embarrassed to say no."

"Ah, well, it was my home till the earthquake that killed so many people including my father."

"Ah, how sad! How very, very sad!"

"Yes, my family will always miss him. But now I live in Paris."

"I love Paris."

"Yes, it is beautiful but it is not my home, my roots. My soul is not there."

"I have lived in New York, outside of Chicago, and now in Seattle. Seattle is by far the most beautiful place with mountains and trees and water but I don't know if my soul is there. Maybe when I am out on the water or hiking in the woods, maybe my soul is there."

"When I am with you, I am so relaxed."

"And when I am with you, I smile all the time. We are good for each other, Robert." And then a hug and a kiss and a swim.

"Now I must go back to my athletes. But tonight, tonight I want to take you to dinner. Is this good, Joyce?"

"Yes, I'll be ready. It would be lovely."

I raced into town that afternoon after our swim for a new dress or skirt or something sexy. My year-long volunteer-trek packing had not included What-You Wear-on-a-Date-with-a-Handsome-Man. In this little town with only two clothing stores, I found a sexy cream-colored dress with spaghetti straps and a small green embroidered design running down the sides. With deep slits, it looked casual and sexy but there was nowhere in the store to try it on. Feeling lucky, I bought it and took it home and voilà, it fit!

When Robert came to pick me up, he was dapper in a tropical shirt and perfectly tailored linen trousers. We drove to a cozy restaurant on the beach with small twinkling lights hanging from the canopy of vines. Looking out at the Mediterranean, up at the stars and the moon, listening to the music from the restaurant, and holding Robert's hand, I was filled with happiness.

Throughout the evening he kept telling me, "Eat, my love, eat. To be strong for our love."

Do Frenchmen take a class in romance? How to Make Women Swoon 101? He held my hand, reached over to my face, and kissed me throughout dinner. "Ah, my love, feel the breeze that is flowing from the sea. It is so fresh and gentle. Everything feels stronger when I am with you. The stars, the sky. Eat, my love. Stay strong."

"How did I meet you? How is this all possible?"

"Ah, my love, you are my dream. You dropped out of heaven. Where will you go from here? How will I see you again?"

"Oh, Robert, my trip takes me around the world but if there is a way for me to see you, then I will."

"My love, I will see you again."

In my heart though, I wondered if I really would ever see him again. It seemed impossible.

We talked about his life in sports, his coaching. "It is very important to me that my athletes will do well. They work hard and I want them to succeed but there is such competition at the Olympics and mentally they need to prepare. Mentally I was always very tough during competitions."

I told him about my life, my sons, and more about my trip around the world. "Do you hear the rustle of the leaves? I love that sound."

"You are close to nature. Outside you are happy. We must spend our time outside."

How could he sense me so easily? How did he understand me so easily? I felt myself get very calm and peaceful with this man. And to be looked at like that with wonder and love? Being a woman felt really good around this man.

"You have beautiful eyes. I love you, Joyce. You are my dream. I do not want to work. I want to be with you."

"Oh, Robert. I am so happy with you."

Maybe the Greek gods decided to give us to each other. The next day, Sunday, would be his day off.

"My boss, he comes to town tomorrow evening. Afterwards it will be crunch time getting the team ready. We will not be able to see each other as much. Tonight we will love each other and smile. Tomorrow I want to spend the day with you. Can you do this, Joyce?"

"Yes, that would be wonderful. I'd love the whole day together."

"Let's drive around the island. Have you seen much of this island?"

"No, only here, Molyvos and Agia Paraskevi. I'd love to see more with you."

And then a gentle kiss and a loving gaze from those gorgeous blue eyes.

We woke up in the morning ready to play together all day. Without a map to guide us, we started our drive. "Joyce, I do not think we need a map. We will drive until we see where we want to be. Is this okay?"

"Mmm...okay, Robert, that sounds perfect." I loved his spontaneity.

"You say 'mmm, okay' to all my questions. You say yes. I love your attitude. I love you!"

"Our natures are really happy together," I replied. "We can relax." Driving together in the car, we spent more time talking about our lives. Everything he had done had been around sports.

"I can't imagine what it is like to devote yourself, your life to a sport," I said.

"This sport has given my family opportunities. I am always grateful for this. And the people I have met have taught me many things. I am very fortunate to have this sport."

"You have a sense of lightness about you, Robert. Your heart is light and happy."

"Ah, I am with the woman who says okay, yes to everything and so I feel that I can do anything!"

As we drove along the coast, he told me jokes in English and smiled when I laughed. "My English is improving. Now I can make you laugh at a joke! Are their dirty words in English that you can teach me?"

"You're serious, right?"

"Yes, Joyce, teach me these words, words about sex." And so we drove along the windy roads of Lesvos with me saying words and phrases while he repeated them with his French accent leaving us both laughing hysterically.

At a nearly deserted beach with not a grain of sand but only river rocks covering the shore, we decided to stop and swim in the crystal-clear water. Running in after each other, dunking each other under the water, splashing and playing in the water like children, we twirled around in each other's arms filled with happiness.

"We are good together." he said smiling at me with those dreamy blue eyes.

"Yeah, I can't remember when I've been so happy and so free. It feels so natural to be around you all day."

"It is good if I come to Seattle?"

My heart dropped thinking that I must have misheard him. "Good? Yes, good!" I said, twirling around in the water.

"What will we do there? Can a coach find a job there?"

"I don't know but with your skills, I am sure you can find a job."

"But what will it pay and what does it cost to live there? Where I am now, I get a very good salary."

"It is expensive to live there but you can come and live with me while you find a job."

"We must stay in touch. Email, phone."

"Yes, I will call you and write you," I said, grinning.

"Maybe I can come to see you."

"Oh yes! Oh yes!"

"Maybe South Africa. Whatever it takes. You must tell me where you are and when."

After we swam, we lay down on the hot rocks warmed by the sun, the original hot rock massage with the stones heating my muscles.

"I will show you how I break a rock." He walked the beach and brought me back a rock, not a pebble, a rock. With concentration and a swift chop of his hands, the rock split in half.

I was flabbergasted. "How do you do that?"

And he did it again. "Bring me another rock. I learned things when I trained for the Olympics."

I watched him focus his energy and then crack a rock. "How did you learn how to do this?"

"Ah, to be an athlete you must train your mind. You must learn to control your thoughts."

"Oh, my gosh, I am flabbergasted. I have lost my heart."

"No, Joyce, you have found your heart," he said.

"What a beautiful thing to say, Robert." And probably true, I thought. It had been a long time since I just let myself go with a man.

After our swim, we continued adventuring around the island and headed to Eressos, a big tourist town that reminded me of California. It had beach volleyball, a boardwalk along the sea with lots of restaurants and tourist crowds. Eressos was the hometown of Sappho, an ancient Greek poet, who was believed to have been a lesbian based on interpretations from her poetry. A portion of the beach is reserved for lesbians. Robert's curiosity about lesbians compelled us to walk to their section. He watched them talking, playing volleyball as if he wanted to understand what it means.

Finally he said, "I understand now. I have never seen this before."

"In Seattle, we are pretty comfortable with lesbians and gays. This beach seems very normal to me."

"Ah, never have I seen this but now I understand."

We found a restaurant on the beach and ate a romantic dinner while the sun set.

"Tomorrow I will work longer hours. My boss will need attention too."

"Robert, can we see each other each day? To swim or to talk?"

"Yes, my love, this we can do each day. I will make love to you each day. I will hold you and kiss you and thank the heavens that gave you to me."

It had been a perfect day, one we both knew we would remember. But I found myself caught between being in the present and enjoying a soul connection and dashing off to the future wanting him to be my forever dream. It's a girl thing, I think…dreaming about the future, wanting forever.

But I was leaving and he was leaving. How could our love ever work out? Could I learn to accept my destiny and whatever it brought?

This love had opened my heart, filled it with joy and laughter. I had seen myself in his eyes filled with love and tenderness. I had seen into his heart and I had felt love. Now destiny was in charge.

As the countdown to the Olympics approached, Robert's time was spent with his team and his boss. I understood. He had worked towards this goal for four years and it was a week away. Love would have to wait. I wondered about this love thing and me. My long-ago marriage had started as a big strong love affair. But then over time, it had slowly leaked out love like a tire carrying a nail until a dangerous blowout left us both riding on the rim. Since then few men had grabbed my attention; usually I bailed before a relationship had a chance to grow roots. I was unwilling to make a commitment. But sometimes love turned her back on me when my arms were wide open, slapping me in the face and sending me for cover. Was holding on to love like holding water in my hand? Was love always slipping past? Now my heart was full of love for Robert. We shared laughter, touch, listening to each other, and an innate understanding. I was ready. But love forever was my elusive butterfly.

Our last week I vowed to spend in the moment gathering every ounce of happiness from our time together. When we swam or met at night by the pool, I stopped worrying about the future and enjoyed the sparkle in my life. A little while love is for certain better than no love at all.

"Joyce, I want to see you. I want to spend all my time with you. But my team needs me now. Can you understand, my love?"

"Robert, if I had my dream, I'd spend every day with you. You are in my heart now. I understand your work. I don't understand how love plays with me but I'm okay."

"Be strong, my love. I ask you to be strong."

Another evening after returning from the Internet café, I sat in my hotel and decided to call Robert hoping to see him.

"Je te verrai bientôt, mon amour," he said.

An hour and a half later he still had not come so I called him to wish him goodnight.

"Where are you, my love? I'm here in the phone booth at my hotel, my little office!"

"Look up! I am here with Misha!"

Looking out the window, I saw Robert and Misha walking up the driveway. Sitting down by the pool, we ordered drinks and started talking.

"I love this beauty. This woman is wonderful," he told Misha.

Tickled by his gush of love talk, I was unable to speak. My native language had me tongue-tied.

Misha, a Russian, was devoted to Robert and sprinkled him with praise. As they spoke Russian to each other, I remembered my father and how I used to hear him talk to his mother in Russian. So I tried it out on them. "добрый вечер как вы оба?" (Good evening. How are you?)

They both stopped talking and stared at me. Dead quiet. "You know Russian?"

I explained my heritage, "My father was born there. My grandparents, too."

"Both sides?" asked Misha

"Yes."

"Why have you not told me this?" asked Robert.

Suddenly I was not an American; I was a Russian and had become infinitely deeper, with more soul.

Misha wanted to know more. "What is your family's name?"

And I realized that I needed to know more, way more about my family and my Russian heritage, not just for Robert and Misha but for me. When I take the Trans-Siberian Express next year, I thought, I'll spend the night and day in Moscow. Maybe this will be a beginning.

"When my father came over from Russia with his parents, his mother left five brothers, all doctors. She never heard from them again. Hopefully at least one survived the Revolution and maybe I still have family there."

"You have this Russian soul in your heart. It is there," said Misha.

"Now I understand your soul," said Robert.

"But I don't know about this Russian soul," I said. "What does it mean?"

"Большая русская душа means the great Russian soul," answered Misha."It is a strange, mystical quality that Westerners think they can feel when they read Tolstoy and Dostoevsky. But in my Russian language, the soul is the key to a person's identity and behavior. I do not know if any kind of soul exists in your young country on the scale that it exists in Russia. Maybe as you Americans drown in materialism, we Russians drown in our feelings of soul. Our hardships, our tragic history, our land stretches from the arctic wastes of Chukotiya to the balmy Black Sea shores. We have been challenged by Mongols, Poles, Lithuanians, Swedes, Napoleon, and the Bolsheviks and more. People have starved there. People have been murdered on the streets. This long tragedy is part of our soul as is the connection we feel with it and each other. With your family born there, you too are a part of the great Russian soul."

They started to teach me Russian words. "Your pronunciation is very good, Joyce. It is in your soul. You must find your family there."

This feeling is one I have never known: a connection to Russia. Growing up during the Cold War, the mere mention of the Soviet Union brought looks full of suspicion and worry. As a child, if I said my background was Russian, I heard "Ah, you are a Russian spy?" in reply. I stopped talking about it and certainly never thought about my roots affecting my soul. I didn't even read Tolstoy until I was in my 30s. But now talking to these men, one from Russian and one from Armenia, listening to their opinions about my heritage, answering their questions about my family, I realized there was a piece of me that needed to be discovered.

Watching the friendship between the two men as they talked about love and happiness, I was grateful for this moment.

"This woman was sent from the heavens for me," Robert said to Misha.

"You are the sun and the moon coming together for love," the Russian smiled at us.

"Today, when my athlete wants to jump, I am thinking of you," said Robert." I say, you jump, you fly, and you do what you want to do. He jumps very good. I say 'Ah...' This morning I am at breakfast and I am thinking of you. The boss asks, 'What is wrong, Robert?' I say, 'Oh, I left something in my room' but ah, I am thinking of you, my love."

That moment right then I was living and loving exactly as I had dreamed, full of emotion, love, laughter. Maybe that was why it felt so natural here. Having dreamed this for so long, it could only feel like home. I couldn't remember if there was any stress in my life. I was overwhelmed with my good fortune at being there on that journey and with these expressive men.

"I do not like Paris where I live because the houses are big and everyone is very rich but at night they close their doors and stay inside," said Robert. "My family has barbeques where we all sing and talk and laugh."

I suddenly realized that Robert was talking about one of the reasons I was taking this trip. Everyone is too separate where I live, even in the houseboat community where I hoped neighbors would drop in to talk and to laugh. But the culture is directed towards work, towards the dollar, and there is only so much time for life outside of earning a living.

Now for the first time, I wondered if my trip was about my time. Changing how I spend time and rather than using it to look for dollars and possessions or doing what everyone else wants me to do, using my time instead to enjoy the warmth and magic of people. Are my travels meant to teach me how other cultures deal with time, love, women, and emotions? I was looking for a home where I could be loving and kind. In Seattle, children give me this love and some of my friends do for certain, but it is always overrun by another theme: trading time for work, work for money. But big houses and pretty things cannot dance, they cannot sing, and they cannot love. Is it my big Russian soul that moves me along on this journey? I wondered all this as we sat in the beauty of that balmy evening.

Because we were having a grand time, Robert and Misha ordered me one more zambuca, my fast-acting crazy-making drink. Encouraged by Misha, Robert showed me how he could dance to the Greek music as I watched in amazement. Graceful and light on his feet, singing along with the song. If I hadn't already been in love with him, I would have been then.

Misha joined in with the dancing and the two circled around the pool arm in arm, legs kicking, both men singing. And I was next as the three of us, an American, a Russian, and an Armenian danced around the swimming pool to Greek music singing as we went. We collapsed in laughter, and the magic got stronger as the zambuca wove through my head. We continued for hours laughing and singing with Robert and Misha telling stories of their friendship.

I woke up early when Robert headed back to his team but I rolled over to sleep with a head caught between a night of laughter and too many zambucas. When I finally woke up, I was starving even though my head was pounding. My stomach wanted a hearty meal to balance all of the love. Walking down the road, I felt a strong breeze off the Mediterranean blowing through the trees, through my heart, through my hair. Greece. A place with magic. A place with soul. Here, listening to the music and feeling the breeze, the pace of this place had gently come into me. I breathed in thousands of years of life. Of love. Of war. Of people being here on this planet. I was filled with joy. I remembered that in my dream the night before I had been with Robert in a fight with arrows or spears. He was fighting one man, then he jumped into the air to fight another, and I saw a man who had a poison arrow. Though I ran to stop it from going into his heart, I could not. I felt heart-broken.

And then there it was. The day I had not thought about but knew would come. We had to go our separate ways, Robert and I. Our time together was over. I knew that when we first saw each other, there was nothing for us to do but be together. The day before when we played like dolphins in the sea, I imagined what it would be like to have this man in my life forever…laughing, making love, listening, and talking… taking care of each other. Our natures were so very happy together, so compatible. He was happy and joyful and full of life. He understood this in me.

Today will be our last time together swimming in Skalla Kalloni. We go to the sea, our home. We kiss and dive; we laugh and talk. I see from his face that the stress of work is getting bigger. He uses the sea to relax…floating upside down, ducking under the water, and then looking at me with those eyes of love. Again he holds out his arms to me like he did that first time. I reach out for his hands and he pulls me in looking into my eyes and we kiss. He says all of the sweet things I love to hear. We swim and then we make love.

"Joyce, we can lay down by the pool at your hotel and take a nap, yes?"

"Sure, okay, that's fine. Last night was a late, late night for us both."

Holding hands lying in the lounge chairs, I watched him sleep marveling at how incredibly handsome he is. After he wakes up, he says, "I want to stay. I want to be with you, my love."

"Oh, Robert, I would love that. Believe me, I would love that."

"Ah, but you have your trip and I have my team. My love, my dream, now I must go." He has stayed as long as he can stay. We walk to the car as I fight back tears. I want him to leave seeing me smile but tears start to fall.

"My love, my love, I cannot leave while you are crying." He makes me laugh with his silliness. And as we are laughing, he says, "Now I must go while we are laughing. Stay positive. We will be together. I love you, my love," he says. "Be positive, my love. We will see each other again. Whenever I talk to you, I will always say: See you soon."

"Robert, can you pack me in your suitcase so that I can come with you?"

"No, my love, a suitcase can be lost. I will hold you tight close to my heart so I never lose you."

We are from faraway places and we are heading in different directions. What can I say again fighting back tears in my eyes with so much feeling that I think I will burst? Inside I am screaming, "Stay, don't go. I hate the Olympics. Stay with me!"

But aloud I say, "I will see you again. You have come roaring into my life taking my heart by storm with your sweet tender words of love, your passionate kisses, and your laughter. I am overwhelmed with the sheer joy of being with you...the silliness, the passion. You relax when you are with me. I smile. And those hot memories: our first walk into the water, our talks, your eyes and the way you look at me, your hands reaching out to mine, our kiss, looking into your eyes, and the feel of you."

"Ah, my honey, honey baby, I kiss you, I miss you, I miss you so much. You are okay? I love you, you are my dream. I can only leave when you are happy. We must always be happy when we leave, no tears, my love."

"Okay, Robert, for you I will smile and say that I will see you soon."

"Kisses, my love, I give you kisses. When your mother and father made you, they must have put in too much sugar, for you are so sweet. Never in my life have I met a woman like you. Ooh là là. Now we say 'see you soon, my love.'"

And so he drove away while there was a smile on both of our faces. Now destiny can blow our love away with the wind or maybe not. As I turn away, tears flood my face. And as I walk to my room, I wonder what will happen now.

CHAPTER 6

Adjusting to being Alone

THE REST OF THAT DAY, I was deep into love's afterglows remembering words of tenderness and our laughter. As I walked through town unaware of the outside world, my mind replayed tapes of all of our times together. With a vague memory of a woman who didn't trust love, I wondered who this woman was now. Where was her edge? Where were her protective devices?

But after dinner, any post-gushy feelings of love were replaced by the reality of being alone without Robert. Now what? Where did I put all these gushy feelings for Robert? How did I adjust to being alone and resume my journey? Would I ever see him again? Was it just a beautiful little-while romance with no forever-after fairy-tale ending?

Back at my hotel, I called him to say goodnight.

"Ah, my love, I am thinking of you all day. You are fine?"

"Yes, yes, I am fine, Robert. I miss you already though."

"Ah, I miss you, my darling."

But he had to keep working and we said goodbye.

"Je t'aime, my love.

Je t'aime, Robert." I fell asleep both happy and sad.

In the morning knowing that I needed a change and way more activity, I packed up and took a taxi to Molyvos, the busy tourist town I had visited on my day off. Inside my room in the two-story white brick hotel, I saw the castle on the hill and remembered Makis, who first told me about it and took me to see it.

Whatever had happened to Makis, the handsome Greek God? Without a phone in my hotel room, he had no way to contact me and

I had been so full of Robert that I had not stopped by the restaurant to see him. I had loved talking to him and would have seen him again, but then Robert came flying into my life. Well, I'm sure I was just another tourist to him.

Opening my balcony doors, I smelled the nearby sea and the air rich with the fragrance of roses and jasmine. With its white walls, white bedspread, and white gauze curtains that flew in the wind, my soul felt light there. The curtains filtered the light giving the room a blue hue, almost spiritual in its glow.

Unlike quiet Agia Paraskevia, which was devoid of tourists, this town has a buzz of energy all day and through the night. Walking to the other end of town, I found the harbor filled with painted wooden fishing boats anchored for the evening and one glamorous yacht that looked completely out of place. Fresh octopus hung from the line along the shore and cats prowled the patios at each of the restaurants along the harbor begging for food. People on holiday filled the streets but I didn't hear one word of English. I hoped that the energy of this vacation town would help me adjust from the intensity of my love affair with Robert to being back on my own.

Leaving the harbor, I walked up a very steep hill that climbs away from the beaches at a 60-degree pitch. All of the mortar between the rectangular stones in the narrow streets has settled leaving a bumpy, uneven path for scooters and pedestrians. The stone houses with red clay tile roofs and wooden shutters to keep out the heat are painted in red, blue and dark green, which adds to the quaint charm of the town.

Walking up the winding path under a thick canopy of twisted vines shading the walkway past stores selling jewelry, handcrafted items, books, souvenirs, and ultra-feminine summer clothes made out of flowing material in soft summer colors, I found a tiny book store that was more like a cave crammed with hundreds of books in little nooks and crannies with an old shopkeeper who looked like he had grown out of the walls. Desperate for either a history book on ancient Greece or a mythology book to learn more about the land I have become so enamored with, I searched the shelves until a book by Plato, *Symposium,* jumped out at me, and reading the introduction, I decided it would be perfect: *"Symposium* is fun and should really be read in the first place at a single sitting….*Symposium* is about love. Actually, it is about eros, which is the Greek word for passionate love…sexual desire."

I laughed to myself wondering who was guiding me through this island adventure, thanking them. Out of every book on the shelves, I had found one written in 400 BCE full of Plato's thoughts about passionate love while I was in recovery from a steamy love affair! It was beginning to feel like I was being led through my experiences here.

Reading taken care of, music was next and I wandered into a CD store anxious to bring some Greek music home with me. Without the ability to listen to music on this journey, I wondered if I should buy an ipod to travel with to bring sound back into my life. It felt like a huge oversight on my packing list but I wasn't sure if I needed one more thing to schlep as I already had a laptop and a camera. I had decided to bring music from each country home with me as my only souvenir knowing that each time I listened I would be transported to each country by the magical musical carpet.

"I love the music here. I want to bring some of it back with me and also give my mom a CD."

"Let's listen," he said. "Our music has passion."

I spent the next hour listening to music not understanding the words but able to completely lose myself in the feelings. What is it about Greek music? Their emotion is natural for me.

"Do not mail your CDs to your mother from here. There may be a problem with it. Greek mail cannot be trusted."

"Okay, thanks for the warning. I can wait till I get to England next month."

Walking further up the hill, I noticed restaurants precariously built on the edges of the steep slope with a flimsy foundation supported only by thin beams. It looked like a big crowd eating out on the deck would tip them over the cliff. But reaching the top was well worth the walk. The views from the cliff were gorgeous out over the bay to Turkey and the Aegean Sea. Further over crowning the hill was the enormous 500-year-old Byzantine castle that is romantically lit every evening by golden spotlights.

Suddenly hungry, I walked down the hill to the main street and a small café with friendly owners for a hot gyro on fresh, warm pita bread. I ate it slowly relishing the flavors as tourists walked by. But everything was bittersweet. Delicious gyros, missing Robert. I was having a tough time figuring out where to put my feelings for Robert. In between juicy flavorful bites, I did a lot of sighing. Did I now regret falling in love? Was I spending all of my time wondering what would happen in the future? Was my present now going to be spent remembering my past? How could I convert these expansive feelings of love for one man into productive energy to fuel my trip?

My philosophical nature was not yet up for the challenge. My physical body, my emotions were still tingling from the earthy sensations of love. The abrupt silence of being alone was brutal. Restless and uncomfortable with my thoughts, I decided to take a swim to move my feelings through the water. Clear water, clear thoughts? More salt treatments for my joints and my soul?

On the beach, the water looked much clearer here than at Skalla Kalloni. The deepest parts were turquoise. Renting a lounge chair for a relaxing afternoon, I settled down with Plato wondering if he could shed any light on my current frame of mind. Taking myself back to Athens 400 BCE, I joined a dinner party of ancient men to listen to their speeches on love. After filling themselves, they leaned back on couches, and the speeches began. I settled into Paedrus's speech, "Love is one of the most ancient and venerated gods, and one of the most effective in helping a person during his lifetime, or after it, attain goodness and happiness."

Goodness and happiness. I started to sense a seed of thought that was quite different from thinking about Robert and love as taken away and leaving me empty. Was he rather a catalyst for my heart opening?

I didn't want to put the book down but I was getting too hot, so I surrendered to the sun and headed in for a swim. The Molyvos beach is not white soft sand but rather filled with rocks, thousands of rocks mostly two to three inches and worn flat from the waves like those on a river bed. Entering the water can be painful when a rock edge presses into the tender part of your arch or disastrous when a group of rocks slips out from under your feet and you crash backwards onto your bottom. Most of the tourists here wear clear plastic Mary Jane sandals with grippers on the bottom to keep themselves upright and to avoid the pain of a natural reflexology treatment, but I toughed it out the first day.

As the gentle waves roll onto the shore, they bring life to the rock beach changing their dull grey colors to shiny and vibrant silvers, browns, and reds, bringing all the rocks to life. As the waves retreat back to the sea and abandon the spaces between the layers of rocks, they create clicking sounds as the rocks strike each other. Rock chatter fills the entire expanse of beach, and the sounds continue as the waves retreat and the process begins again. Each wave reflects the connection between the sea and the land.

Everywhere they came together, I felt the exchange of energy. The sea brings life to the rocks. They shine, lose their rough spots, and chatter. Caressed by calm waters and battered by crashing waves, a constant ever-changing romance exists between the two. The rest of the afternoon I spent reading Plato, napping, listening to the rock music, and swimming in the clear turquoise water daydreaming about Robert. When I swam, the water glowed all around me, and I could almost see the bottom when I dove, all the while asking the water to care for me as it did the rocks.

In Greece, evening brings everyone out for a stroll along the narrow cobbled streets while the moon reflects on the still waters. The twinkling lights of the cafes along the beach and the music in the air added to the pleasure of this cool summer evening. Tonight was the opening night of the Olympics being, which were held here in Greece, and all I could think about was Robert and his team and hoping they would do well.

A hush came over the town in anticipation of the Opening Ceremonies. Sitting on the patio of a café, I was surrounded by Greeks watching the outdoor TV together. I could hear the man near me breathing for the crowd was quiet, enraptured by their country's creation. They sighed and they clapped after each performance but there were no conversations. They were riveted on the performance and their faces were filled with pride. The only voice heard throughout the entire town was the Greek TV announcer followed by cheers. Even the scooters were quiet tonight. Not a soul walked through the town. I looked around at the faces watching the Olympics and realized that this was a magical night that I would remember forever.

When the ceremony ended, an enormous party broke out all over town with shouting and singing till 5 am. I headed home early all alone wondering what steps to take to readjust myself to solo travel. Plato and I spent a quiet evening together while outside the entire town was partying.

In the morning I returned to my favorite café enjoying the cool shade from the roof of thick ivy vines. The large, green leaves twisted around each other provided a cool, natural cover for my morning frappe. Feeling content and peaceful, I was glad that I listened to my soul and decided to go grab my life. In the grips of doing, going, getting, there wasn't time to hear my soul. I was living a life accomplishing things yet knowing that it was not what I was destined to do. Listen to your heart. Look at yourself. Breathe. Pause from working and dream. Get quiet or get noisy. Get happy or sad. Whatever it takes to bring in dreams. Leave what you are doing long enough to make space for something else.

Question. Yes, question my entire existence. And then listen to what my soul says. There are answers and there are dreams. Somehow, between the coming and going, the getting this done, the worrying about that, the crying about this, the being afraid, the keeping of a schedule, the being busy, the phone, the chores, the successes, the business, the wondering, somehow in the midst of all that, there was a dream full of desire that was filled with the passion of my heart. I listened and agreed to change everything. Now I was on Lesvos Island living each day in my dream seeing things I had never seen before, absorbing the energy of another culture.

Greece was flooding me with feelings soaring into my soul. I breathed very deeply here, belly breathing, deep and slow. Did I learn to breathe deeply in Greece? Was it a result of taking time away and giving myself a full 24 hours in a day to be me? Did Greece hold the key to my soul flooding me with beauty and philosophy? Or had my heart opened from my magic love affair with Robert, flooding my soul and opening me up to bigger dreams?

This country comforted me. I didn't understand the language and I was unable to adjust to the sweltering heat yet I was comfortable here. Do all dreams feel like this when they become real? Is this what happens when a person listens to her heart? Breathing with nature to find my soul. Loving a man to feel my soul. Greece was my soul food. Maybe this country allowed more sensuous feelings than mine did. Could that be it? When I am home, I smell the air and look around but the energy is electric, life linear, and the pace frenetic. Things are done in a wonderful orderly fashion but it is hard for me to find the poetry of the day there. In Greece, as soon as I awakened, the poetry flew into my window with the breeze.

That morning on the patio of the cafe, there was a butterfly in the flowers, a yellow monarch. I looked at the butterfly and remembered that my big sister, the sister with all the magic, had had a pet monarch. No one would believe that. She would walk outside to our backyard holding her arms out like clotheslines, and the orange monarch would come and land on her hand. Slowly she would bring her hand to her mouth and the monarch would give her butterfly kisses. I thought all big sisters did this. I didn't know I had a magic sister. And she taught me how to do it, how to be still as the monarch walked from her hand to mine, to slowly bring my hand to my mouth to feel butterfly kisses. When she wasn't home, I would go out in the yard with my arms out and wait and wait and wait, but the butterfly knew my sister wasn't there so I just stood there alone. Here a Greek butterfly reminds me that magic isn't just for childhood.

But a moment of fear came to me then. How would I ever go back? How would I buy a car, fill my office with paperwork, greet clients and cheerfully find them houses every day? How would I breathe in Seattle? Where would I put my creativity when I went home as time sped up with no way to linger or to create?

Relax, Joyce, breathe, I told myself. Your dream is just beginning and part of the wonder is that it comes not from fear but from joy. Fear and lack sometimes sneak into my brain, old habits from an old life. I allowed Greece to bring me back, to comfort me, teaching me to return to joy.

That day at the beach I started talking to the woman sitting near me, Bettina from Germany. We were both alone here, both in love with the water, and after two days of exchanging hellos, we started chatting and decided to meet for lunch. What an unexpected treat! With her blue eyes and blonde hair, her reserved but warm nature, she reminded me of Terri, my best friend from high school. She was 41, a single mom on her first holiday alone...recharging.

She was a gift for me, for we found so much in common. We talked about our lives and our sons. As single moms, we both hoped that we had raised our sons to be confident, to know they were loved, and to have happiness in their futures. We both lived with the guilt of divorce, which had forced our children to go through difficult times. I could feel the intensity when Bettina talked about the love she had for her son and her sadness that he couldn't have a mom and dad in the same house. We recognized our similar feelings and somehow it was comforting to talk about it. We both prayed that somehow over the years of growing up, the love we had given our children had balanced their tough times. Mothers from around the world sharing common concerns and love for our sons. Love is love. We decided to meet for dinner that evening.

Our dinner conversation moved to men, her boyfriend and my love affair with Robert. We were amazed at the similarities between life as a single woman in Germany and in the United States. Do women from all over the world talk about men? Men of the world, do you talk about us? Generally, we are confused by your behavior. We wish you would take classes about what to do with emotions, how to find them and how to talk about them. We want you to talk to us so we don't have to spend time talking to each other about what we think you are feeling. Okay, men from around the world? This is a universal plea. We are desperate to know what you are thinking.

Walking home after our dinner, it started to rain. I rushed home and opened my doors to my patio and my window to let the cool air in. I wanted to feel the rain. I sat on my bed with the wind whirling my curtains, the rain pelting down, the lightning and thunder putting on a display. It rained and rained and rained. It was a fabulous night with clear, cool, fresh air. I slept to the sound of raindrops just like in Seattle with cool breezes blowing all through the night.

In the morning when I arrived at my coffee shop, the waiter approached in his crisp clean shirt, black pants, and slicked back immaculately combed hair. "How are you today?" he asked, his Greek accent thick and lovely.

"I am happy today but I was very surprised by the huge rainstorm last night. It blustered, blew, and flashed lightning with big rain drops for a very long time reminding me of my home in Seattle."

"Ah, this is money rain. Ninety percent of Lesvos make its money off olives. Not tourism. I works here three months during growing season and make $3000. When I go home to family olive orchard, I make $30,000. The rain yesterday was raining money to olive farmers. It has not rained since May and this is August. This weather is usual but when it rain hard like yesterday it mean bigger olives, bigger money for olive groves."

"I am so glad that I was able to be here for the big storm. In Illinois where I grew up, I loved to curl up in my bed and watch the lighting storms and listen to the thunder. It was so exciting. Your storm reminded me of being a little girl."

"Yes, it is always good to remember life of the child. Here in Lesvos my child learn about olives as I did when I was boy. He too will help in the harvest. In late December, January, the olive growers put on machine on back, gas-powered engine, and it shake olives from tree. Put nest on ground to catch the olives. But cool weather make it okay to work hard. My family all work together, each one a job. The olive price stay about the same. If goes too high then hard to market."

"But I don't understand. Good olive oil at home is very, very expensive. Is the farmer not making any profit, only the manufacturer? The farmer needs to make more money, too."

"Yes, but farming is our blood. My family and olives are good together."

Long daily swims in the turquoise waters were soothing to my bouts of missing Robert as I dove to the coolness of the bottom letting the buoyancy of the salt water slowly bring me to the top. When I rested on the beach, Plato brought me more wisdom about love.

On the beach, Bettina and I were kindred spirits swimming constantly, talking for hours, and enjoying life.

"Your name is perfect for you. You truly bring joy to others and find so much joy in life," Bettina said to me.

"Bettina, I think that is the sweetest thing I have ever heard. Thank you. I am in the midst of pure joy in my life with the adventure of a lifetime. If somehow it is contagious, that's even better!"

In the evening we decided to go out to eat again as Bettina would be heading back to Germany the next day. Our restaurant deck was high on the cliff with a stunning view of the bay, the twinkling lights below, and the sunset.

After dinner we headed to a taverna to listen to music. There we met two Greek men, Gregorios, medium tall, dark hair, and shy, who seemed quite taken with Bettina, and Alexious, tall, dark, and a bit dangerous-looking. The men were old friends who had grown up together on the island. Gregorios started singing a song to the music that was playing.

"What was that song you were singing? It is lovely," I said to him.

"Ah, s'agapo, s'agapo, s'agapo. It is the most important word in the Greek language."

"What does it mean?"

"It means I love you. Love is the most important word in the Greek language. Love is everything to a Greek."

Transfer to America. I meet a man for coffee with a girlfriend and he starts singing without being drunk. Okay, stretch your imagination. What are the chances that he is singing about love? And what is the most important word in the English language anyway? Men of America, when you are singing to yourself, what is it about? There is more freedom here for men...they sing and they dance. Maybe it makes it easier to sing about love if you can sing and dance in public and not be considered a wuss.

"For a Greek, health number one and love second. Money you need for life but it is not what you style your life around. First, you are healthy. We are outside. We eat outside, we sit outside, all simple things. Then you love."

"I hear that the diet here is what makes Greeks healthy."

"Ah, we only eat fresh. No cans. No frozen. If you give this us, we no touch it. Must be fresh."

"What do you eat for breakfast?"

"Ah, maybe bread with olive oil. Maybe fish soup. Maybe cheese and bread. Nothing set. The big meal at two."

"And siesta?"

"Ah, yes, always at least an hour. Must be siesta. It is slow here, yes?"

"Yes," answers Bettina. "It is slow."

"Is it true the way they show America in the movies? Life in the suburbs with a garage, a yard, and for everyone?"

"Yes, the suburbs are full of yards, garages, and cars, but there is more to America than what you see on the movie screen."

"Does everyone smoke there?"

"No, fewer and fewer people are smoking, especially not students."

"Ah, so America stops their bad habits and gives it all to children of the world instead? The tobacco companies continue advertise here and make our young students feel smoking cool."

Feeling his anger and my own disappointment at what he was saying, I said the only thing I could meeting the intensity in his eyes, "I am so sorry."

Graciously changing the subject, Gregorios said, "People are buried for four years and then their coffins are opened"

"Wow, wait a minute, did you say opened, really?"

"Yes, each one of their bones is washed with wine for the sweetness of life and with vinegar for the bitterness. Holy water is used to bless them. The bones are then put in a box, pelvis first, all the little bones, then skull at the top and the humorous bones in an x below the skull.

The head will always be in charge and the X will ward off evil spirits. Does this remind you of something?"

"Yes, it's the Skull and Cross from the pirates' flag! I wonder how that custom came to be."

"You like it here?"

"Yes, we love it here," Bettina and I answered in unison.

"The life here is slow. Here at the sea with the mountain behind us, we Greeks say that our thinking is clear, with a vision outward but protected from the back. This is a good place for you to come. But as things get more expensive, the life will move faster. It is the way. Can you stop it from moving faster? No, is the way of life."

"Does everyone here speak naturally of philosophy?"

"Yes, probably so. You like philosophy?"

"Yes, I find your culture very interesting and comfortable for me, but I would like to talk to more women to find out about their lives here."

"I think that you belong in Greece. It suits you; your passions are at home here."

About then, we all decided to move to a different taverna with live music.

"The Greeks will start to come out after one, after dinner."

"After one? No wonder everyone needs a siesta!"

At the taverna, a trio composed of an incredibly talented violinist with dancing fingers, a guitarist, and a Greek guitarist played the old songs, pouring out melancholy sounds. Watching the fingers work on the instruments, listening to the music, I looked around the dark taverna and noticed that some of the old men in the taverna were singing along with the trio. With their sun-parched faces, deep wrinkles, dark eyes, and stocky bodies dressed in white shirts and dark pants, I imagined them fishing each day off the wooden boats that are anchored in the harbor.

As the ouzo flowed, so did the music and before long the men who were singing were dancing together. I watched them remembering Robert and Misha dancing around the pool. Legs kicking, arm in arm, they circled around the taverna as friends, smiling and laughing while Bettina and I clapped along.

"Hoopa, hoopa" we all shouted.

Gregorios and Alexios joined the dancers, a custom that hopefully will last forever. As 3 am approached, Bettina and I decided to call it a night and walked home together to make sure our Greek friends didn't get the wrong idea.

A gentle, cool breeze was blowing from the sea as we walked the narrow street that overlooks the water. The castle on the hilltop glowed a golden shade from the spotlights, and I thought I saw a knight looking down at me. Maybe I needed to watch how much ouzo I was drinking! Arriving safely at my hotel room, I saw the wind blowing my curtains around like white ghosts and beyond my small balcony stars filled the quiet sky, but my mind was full of song, hoopa, hoopa and s'agapo. Warmth. That was it. I need more warmth. More open affection. More time. I do not want to struggle to spend time with people I love. I want to live in a place where the culture allows time for love between people. So is this what I am looking for?

Though it was very late, I called Robert.

"Ah, Joyce, how are you? You are up very late."

"I'm great!"

"Great? How can you be great? You should be missing me, sad because I am not there. How can this be?" he said jokingly.

I laughed and said, "Okay, okay, I am miserable. I really, really am."

We talked about his team, my night, our love, and then said goodbye. I missed his smile, his laughter, his touch. He missed my calm, my laughter, and the heat.

The next day, with just a day left here, I found myself getting sad to be leaving this mystical island where so much had happened, an amazing sequence of events taking me through intense feelings. I had taken this island into my heart. I was mistreated and misunderstood at the Animal House, wanting only to help injured animals and ending up as Cinderella in a filthy, unhappy place where not only the animals were injured but the people in charge were as well.

After a long first week, I was sprung free into Robert's arms filled with love and laughter. And after our glorious time together, Molyvos gave me a grand finale of a Greek Salt and Soul Treatment. How much salt would it take to fill my bathtub at home to bring back the magic of the sea?

The Mediterranean Sea. I read about it being the cradle of civilization when I was young and had no interest in such things. Now I understood. This environment nurtures souls with heat, earth, and sea. We become like olives. Olive trees are beautiful with small leaves of green on their sun side and a silver lining on their down side. A seed can germinate in the crack of a rock growing into a beautiful tree. And souls do the same.

I cried today. It was the first time in a long time. Was it leaving Lesvos? Leaving Robert and wanting to be with him? Was I scared to change my life? I knew that I didn't want to chase time any longer. I wanted to be in the present moment not thinking about the past or planning towards the future. But why tears? Maybe they were farewell tears to the life that I had before I started this journey. As I learned about myself on this journey, my safety net was being dropped away. I was like a child hidden under a blanket now peaking one eye out to take a look around at my new life, slowly absorbing my new view of the world and my place in it. I wanted to be open, vulnerable and to express myself and what I was feeling. Tears helped me make the transition. Tears helped me find the root of my feelings.

On my last trip to the café, my friends told me, "See you again. This is what we say."

I smiled hoping they were right as I walked to the big bus to Mytilene. It arrived on time for the 90-minute journey along narrow, curved roads, and at each sharp curve the bus driver honked in warning to oncoming traffic. Arriving in Mytilene, I took a long walk around the harbor, then joined an older woman sitting on a bench waiting to board our ferry. Dressed all in black, thick stockings, heavy black shoes, her thick silver hair pulled back in a bun, she was quietly working on a word puzzle. We smiled at each other and she spoke to me in Greek.

Of course, not understanding her, I smiled and tried to understand. She really wanted to talk to me though so we settled on sign language. She counted out with her fingers the number 81. And then she made some motions to show that she would not be strong enough to carry my bag. Then she grabbed my arm feeling my muscles and said something in Greek for strong.

I laughed and said, "Oi vey, not so strong for this heavy big bag." I counted out my age with my fingers and we both smiled.

Somehow we talked about children because she signaled the universal sign for pregnancy with a swoop over her belly. I showed her a couple of pictures of my sons. Out of her purse in a little folder with a rubber band around it came all kinds of little black-and-white photos. In her purse was a 70-year history of her life and we looked at each photo. There were pictures of her kids when they were young and grown, pictures of herself as a little girl and as a young woman. Pictures of her mother. Of herself as a mother. When we were done, the little rubber band wound back around her little book full of her entire life. Traveling with her life wrapped in a book. Next time I traveled I wanted to bring a little book full of pictures of my life. Yes, I was looking for a new view of myself but I too wanted to carry love from my past with me. Without a word in common, I felt a strong message from her for my soul in one of those little sparkly moments that I loved about this trip.

Upon boarding the ship, I found my cabin and wondered who my roommate would be this time but to my surprise I had the cabin to myself. As my eyes closed, I imagined sitting in a hotel lobby in Athens. Robert would arrive rushing to my arms, sweeping me off my feet in a passionate kiss. Falling into a coma-like sleep, I didn't wake up till we docked in Athens.

Remembering my fairy tale dream, I decided to give it a try. Maybe I could see Robert one last time. I had six hours but I had no idea if his team was on that day. I told the taxi driver, "Take me to a large hotel in downtown Athens."

The cab driver seemed at first not to understand that I didn't know where I wanted to go. "I just want to sit in a lobby."

Still no help.

Finally remembering Plato, I said, "I am in love. I have fallen in love with a man who is a coach at the Olympics and there is a small, small chance I can see him before I fly out of Athens. I just want to wait for him in a hotel."

I must have sounded desperate for love, the sound of hunger, passion.

"You must go to a hotel, rent a room for a few hours," said the driver. "It will cost you not so much."

Hmm…spend money on a chance to see my man. I was still mulling that over when he stopped at a hotel and started talking and talking to a man standing outside a hotel. Oh gosh, what have I gotten myself into? Does he think I'm a hooker?

Talking and talking in Greek, he turned to me and said, "Yes, you can stay here for a few hours for just a few euros!"

How could I resist? I rented the room and called Robert. "Robert, I am here in Athens and I have rented a hotel room. I have four hours before I have to leave for the airport. In my dream you come here to be with me."

"Ah, my love. My love. Ooh là là! I must see how I can do this. But it is very difficult. The village is far. The security takes a long time and there are meetings but my love, I will try. I will try. I want to be with you. I will call you back in one hour."

But when he called, it was bad news. "My love, are you there? Ah, this is not good. I cannot. I cannot, my love. Will you keep me in your heart? Will you call me from the airport?"

"Yes, yes," I said and I left for the airport, so sad that my pretty romance was over and that my imagined meeting would not take place. I cried. Before boarding the plane, I called him one last time.

"My love, you are in my heart. Have a safe journey. We will talk again, my love."

"Good luck with your team, Robert. I'll take you with me in my heart. Goodbye."

Tears fell down my face as the plane ascended. What would happen now? Was it all a beautiful dream to keep in my memory box? Destiny, destiny, where would this love go?

But change was on the horizon. Now it was time for me to travel to Looe, England, in Cornwall where I would be volunteering for the month of September at the Monkey Sanctuary.

CHAPTER 7

On the Way to England

TRAVELING ALONE AGAIN on the train from Rome to Paris to London after five lovely days touring Florence with Sue, my friend, I was thinking that travel affects our lives in different ways. We could observe scenery and people, keeping them outside of ourselves and simply enjoying the experience a bit like watching a movie. Or we could bring a culture inside our centers forever changing our internal scenery like adding new ingredients to an existing recipe.

Some people traveled happily walking around looking at stuff like statues, buildings, rivers, towers, and churches or driving around in double-decker open-topped buses with a guide telling them the same things they had said a million times to a million other people. People taking pictures of themselves in front of these statues, buildings, rivers, towers, and churches.

But if you walked around a new country surrounded by people from your country listening to your tour guide, would the culture you are visiting ever reach you? Or was this tour more like a really good virtual slide show with you in front of the scenery? Would this type of travel give you new ideas and allow growth? Or would you return home to say, "This year we went to France." An accomplishment, something to tell others.

Maybe we all live within a shape that determines how we react to traveling away from home. Some people live in squares, everything forming neat grids inside with order and rules, a life planned out. For those folks, travel experiences get classified under existing categories.

Some people live in a circle and travel round and round revisiting everything again and again, forming habits to take them through the 24 hours in a day. Still others live inside free-forming amoebas, creating new spaces as the experiences of travel bring new thoughts.

Do some people live in open shapes with a door or a gate to freely allow experience to move in and out as they travel? Is taking this journey moving me away from my shape and giving it a new form? It takes courage to leave the gate open and allow new ideas to enter without a filter. If I stand here looking at the world with my gate wide open, am I offering the world an open invitation to come inside my world? Is a locked gate a sign of being old? Is it this closed gate of aging, this static shape what I fear most? A fear of being able to recognize everything within my world with no surprises? To have stopped growing with nothing left to learn?

In this journey on my quest, I crave to understand life in different countries. How do you live here? How do you feel? How do you love here? How do you care for each other as a country, as individuals? How do you feel about work and life? When your mother gets old, who will care for her?

With this desire to feel each country from the inside out, I was volunteering in each country to get behind the buildings, the landmarks, and the churches. I wanted in. I wanted to learn. I wanted to help. And in this process, I wanted to be affected. I wanted to shake up what I had established as 'Joyce.'

And the shake up was definitely taking hold flooding my psyche with unrest and agitation like a mosquito bite that I couldn't reach. Was I ready to let go completely? Obviously some part of me was grabbing my old life clinging tightly to my old style of thinking nervous about letting go like a child on ice skates gripping her fathers hand unwilling to fall. Could I trust the part of me that had created this journey and jump off the Land of Safety into the Land of Discovery?

Agitated about love, I wanted to know the ending of the story of my romance with Robert. I was not content to let it unfold naturally. Maybe it was already over. What then? Would I be frustrated and mad that it hadn't continued or smile remembering the feelings? Could I learn to see this romance as one type of love and go on to fill my heart with more love? Keep the door open rather than shut it all down? Could I learn to understand love as a feeling much greater than what one man and one woman can create? Was I ready to fire up my heart to its true limitless abilities? No, not yet that lofty. I wanted to know if our romance was the beginning of a love story or an ending and I wanted to know now!

Arriving in London, I took a cab to the next train. My cab driver was very muscular, dark with a mustache. He was a talkative man with a deep voice, his white shirt neatly pressed. From Victoria Station to Paddington Station, he asked me a million questions all the while apologizing in case he was asking too many.

"I really like your tan but I don't understand your giant backpack. Why are you traveling with such a big, heavy pack?"

As we talked about my trip, he told me about his college years, his travels, and the people he meets as he drives his cab. "I read that 80% of Americans do not have a passport."

"Wow, I had no idea the number was so low."

"And when an American travels, he just heads south, north, east, or west within the United States. When I was young, I went with some friends to America. One was black, I am mixed, and I was worried that I might find trouble being black back in the 70s. But we were safe everywhere we went. But now tell me about your Bush man? Will he win the election? I have no respect for the man, an inability to speak, his philosophies."

"Oh," I said, "I pray that America snaps out of her trance and realizes the harm that another four years of Bush will do."

"Well, I think if he wins, then it is the fault of the Democrats. Surely he would be easy to beat. It is their own damn fault if he wins."

THE FOUR-HOUR TRAIN from London to Liskaard, a fishing village on the southwest coast of England, was stiflingly hot. Sweat dripped off my face and I found it difficult to breathe; the air conditioning system was broken. Everyone in my car was dying of the heat but the conductor waited till the end of the trip to explain that we could move to the other cars where the air conditioning was working. I was furious that he had not spoken earlier, but in reserved England, no one grumbled at him except me and even then I just muttered at him under my breath. I couldn't believe that no one complained to him.

At Liskaard I walked over to the next train, a small train with just a few cars. It resembled a Disneyland ride. I was excited to get to Looe and the Monkey Sanctuary.

Looe looked more like the movie set of a fishing village than a real town. There were dramatic cliffs at the shore, surfers riding waves crashing onto a sandy beach, swans in a harbor filled with small wooden fishing boats starting to float as the tide rolled in, Victorian houses painted in classic colors built close together up hills on either side of the quay. As I walked through town, almost everyone seemed to be eating something called a pastie, a delicious pie with thick crust and a filling. Signs along the sidewalk advertised English tea with Cornish clotted cream and scones.

I stopped for a cup of coffee and after writing a few postcards, I was ready to find a place to stay for a couple of nights before starting my volunteer work at the Monkey Sanctuary. Approaching the waitress I said, "I think I need to pay."

She stared at me blankly, looking rather startled.

I repeated myself saying it louder this time thinking that she hadn't heard me, "I think I need to pay."

Then a smile crossed her face and she started to laugh. "Oh, I thought you said, 'I think I need to pee.'"

This set us both to laughing as my American English accent and her Cornwall English accent met for the first time.

Looe has a quay. It is not pronounced like quack as some laughing Brits explained to me but rather like key. There's a small ferry crossing the narrow harbor at high tide; it costs 60 pence if you don't want to walk the bridge connecting East and West Looe. The village was full of tourist stores, Victorian houses, and lots of stout people. Remembering

Italy with its thin bodies and healthy olive coloring, I found the Brits pasty white, very round, and more serious. There was nothing sexy about their walk, their shoes, or their clothes. My travel outfit fit in completely.

Searching for a book from my new country, I stopped into an old bookshop with an incredible collection of old children's books including *The Bobbsey Twins* in old bindings. The owner was wearing a black derby hat too small for his head. He explained his love of books. "It started, mind you, when as a child I read all of the books in the children's section of the library starting with the A's and going all the way through! I was given special permission to read in the adult section when I ran out of books. I retired in Looe and started the shop with many of my old books."

Picking out an old book from an author I didn't know I asked, "Where would you suggest I go to sit and read?"

"The Southwest Coastal Path passes through this village and they say that if you walked the entire route, it would equal five times up and down Mt Everest! Find a spot along the path at one of the many benches."

Before starting my walk, I paused to watch surfers in their wetsuits riding the small waves. Along the way, I was amazed to see palm trees in England.

A few minutes later, a man joined me. "Hello, there! Name's Rudy Parthington."

Rudy was about 10 years my senior with white hair, a dark tan, blue eyes, and the strong facial features I see here in Looe. He also had the local beer belly. Rudy moved closer and closer as we talked until he was backing me into the parapet. Could he be deaf? He seemed too old to be amorous.

"I am going to take a walk along the South Coastal Path tomorrow." I said.

-"Might I join you?"

"Sure. I'm starting out at 9:30 and I can meet you here."

"Would you like to sit on the bench for a bit?"

"Sure, Rudy."

"I was born and bred near here." he said. "Never been more than 20 kilometers away either. My wife died a couple of years ago though and now I am getting lonely."

"Oh, I'm sorry," I said and turned to look at him. And then out of nowhere, he tried to kiss me! At some point I will figure out this kiss thing. Has there been a memo going around Europe that American women traveling alone want to kiss?

I jumped up although he seemed harmless enough and said, "Goodbye. See you tomorrow for the hike to Polperro."

The next day as Rudy and I headed out on the path on a crystal clear morning, he told me the name of every plant we saw and what it is used for. Rudy pointed out gorse, which had been mentioned in every English novel I had ever read or so it seemed.

"Those ponies were introduced to the land to eat the gorse to prevent it from overrunning the land. Here you see the sloe gin berry, the elderberry, big beautiful rose hips, lupine growing wild, and watercress." Rudy was a walking Discovery Channel.

"I saw a show on foxes," he went on, "where the fox went to the willow tree and took off all of the willow fuzz balls until they formed a big ball in his mouth. Then mysteriously, he went into the lake and submerged his full body except for this ball of willow fuzz. After a little while he came out, shook off, and went on his way. The man filming went down to the lake and took a stick to the ball of fuzz. It was swarming with fleas! That smart fox had figured out how to get rid of his fleas!

"Now, Joyce, look up at the hawk. It can hover like a helicopter not moving at all while looking below for prey."

"See that bird sitting out on the rocks. He has no oil on his feathers because he needs to dive into the ocean for his prey and the oil would make him too buoyant!"

We took a break midway for ice cream. Suddenly, he tried to draw me into a kiss again! I pulled back.

"Can I just have one kiss?" he asked, almost shyly.

Geez, what is this...everyone wants a kiss!

"Please, just one kiss."

"Okay, Rudy, one kiss and then that's it."

As he kissed me, I thought that if this was Cornwell kissing, the women here must be very grumpy. It was like kissing a wall and it went on and on. I finally pulled away. Charity kissing was over.

"Thank you, Joyce."

When we returned from Polperro to Looe, the sun was setting, filling the sky with yellow, orange, red, and blue that reflected on the rocks, the trees, and the sea. I think sunset light is a gift from nature. It invites me to stop my busyness for a deep breath, a chance to feel my heart, my soul, and the power of nature. Sunset begs me to comprehend that I am not looking at nature but rather that I am a part of nature. To allow the beauty of the light, the colors of the sky, and the magic of the sea to bring harmony inside, to reflect on my soul.

I think the light of sunset and sunrise must be the time when all things spiritual come together to give inspiration. As I drank in the colors, the rhythm of the waves danced with the rhythm of my body. I feel alive as the wind brings me life. Is there any better air than the fresh air at the sea? A light more mystical than sunset reflections?

As I returned from my reverie, Rudy was staring at me.

"I was dreaming about nature. I really love it out here," I said.

"Yes, I can tell you do. You were lost, I thought. Do you want to take another walk tomorrow?"

"Oh, tomorrow I begin volunteering at the Monkey Sanctuary but thank you for a lovely day."

"Might I ask for one more kiss?"

"Oh, Rudy, now just go home. No more kisses! Thank you for a nice day."

CHAPTER 8

The Monkey Sanctuary in England

MY TAXI DROVE A SHORT distance out of Looe to the Monkey Sanctuary. We drove down a hill on a long, private wooded driveway to an enormous dark Tudor house with white trim that sat on a large expanse of property overlooking the Atlantic Ocean. As I left the taxi, I looked around at the beautiful gardens at the front of the house and at the enormous cages around the back.

Excited to be here, I went inside and was reminded of hippy housing in the 1960s. The walls were painted in bright yellow and orange, and there were comfy old couches in front of a TV, a big wooden dining room table, and a large kitchen cluttered with remnants of breakfast and lunch, all the signs of a busy household.

"Hi, I'm Joyce, here to volunteer," I said to one of the people eating at the big table.

"Oh, hi. I will get Mickey. She is the volunteer coordinator."

Mickey came around the corner with an enormous smile on her freckled face and her short spiked orange hair matching her energy. "Hi. Welcome! I will be showing you to your room and introducing you around. Follow me to your room, unpack and then you can come back here."

My September bedroom had three sets of bunk beds. "You share the loo. The lower bunk is yours and there are a couple drawers for your stuff," said Mickey. "Just come back to the kitchen when you are done. There are four other volunteers sharing the room. You will meet them later."

How did I come to volunteer at a monkey sanctuary in England? Monkeys, of course, are not native to England. This sanctuary was started in 1964 by Leonard, a man living in London who was given a woolly monkey by one of his friends. Deciding that London was no place for a monkey, he bought this 8-bedroom, 3-story home on this vast piece of waterfront property, and he and his monkey moved in. Next, figuring that his monkey was lonely, he placed an ad in the paper offering a place for any monkeys living in the city who needed a change. Apparently there were many people who had the initial idea that a cute little monkey could be trained as a great pet but in reality found that they were unprepared to deal with a wild animal.

That was the informal beginning of the Monkey Sanctuary, a trust now run by 12 permanent keepers who are totally devoted to the welfare of the woolly monkeys and capuchins. The sanctuary rescues the animals from lives of isolation giving them a home where they can safely socialize with other monkeys and live as naturally as possible. The trust also campaigns to stop the primate pet trade in the UK, believing that captivity will always be inadequate for the needs and lives of these animals. They work to promote alternatives such as rehabilitation and to improve conditions within zoos. They also seek to protect primates from exploitation in the advertising, research, and entertainment industries.

The primate trade is still legal in both the U.K. and the United States, where monkeys are sold as pets. The horror of this primate trade is that in South America, Asia, and Africa, primate traders shoot the mothers, steal the babies, and transport them across the sea, selling the ones who survive the trip as pets or for experimentation. Taken from their mothers before they are weaned and denied the company of their own kind, the stimulation and diet they need, many monkeys die on the trip across the ocean and others suffer for years.

Here at the Monkey Sanctuary, the keepers educate the public about the monkey colony that lives here. Throughout the season, 200 people a day visit the sanctuary to see and learn about the monkeys through school programs or as families and tourists. The keepers walk groups around the grounds educating them about the various personalities within the troop while explaining the reality of the primate pet trade.

As a volunteer, I was going to help with cleaning the grounds and the monkey enclosures, working in the art project room when children came to visit, helping in the visitors' café, which served vegetarian food, preparing food for the monkeys (gathering wild leaves and berries), and helping out wherever it was needed. The keepers tend to the monkeys' health and monitor the politics of the troop working through conflicts between monkeys in captivity and providing a socially stimulating environment.

This first day I am anxious to learn my tasks and headed back to the main room. Mickey was there to greet me.

"Okay," she says, "everyone makes their own breakfast and lunch here. Just help yourself to whatever you want to eat. You can go to the store for treats. We all try to clean up after ourselves but with 20 people sharing a kitchen you can see that does not always work." She smiled at the mess in the kitchen. I frowned when I looked at the fresh fruit and vegetable bins. Everything seemed rather old.

"Each night," she continues, "one of the keepers cooks dinner for everyone and we have both vegetarian and vegan food. On Sundays, the volunteers cook dinner for us!" Walking me over to a chart on the wall, she explains, "Here is the chart of all the volunteers and their work for the week. There is a computer that you can use for short periods as well as the phone if you get a phone card."

Hmm, I think, this organization is much different than where I have been.

"Your first task is monkey food. You'll do that with Jade, one of the other volunteers, but I'll take you through the first time. It's really important for the health of the monkeys that it is done correctly. Because the monkeys are not native to England, their systems are more susceptible to disease. Okay, you have about 30 minutes to walk around. Just make sure that when you look at the woolly monkeys, you don't look into their faces. That is a sign of aggression and it will upset them. Use your peripheral vision."

With some free time, I immediately dart in to use the computer desperate to write Robert, whom I hadn't spoken to since I boarded the plane leaving Athens. Without a cell phone, he had no way to call me and his Greek number is no longer working. It feels like a lifetime ago that we had been together in Greece. I send him a quick email packed with love letting him know the phone number here. I am anxious to hear from him though he seems a long way away. Little daydreams dance in my head wondering what will become of our love.

Love mission completed, I walked outside to watch the woolly monkeys in their enclosures. These monkeys are big with gorgeous thick gray coats, strong tails used to swing through the enclosures, and small black faces each with distinct features. Their builds varied from linebacker to delicate princess. An endangered species because of the pet trade, woollys are actually the largest primate in South America.

Spread out over the property, there were six large enclosures with hanging ropes, big tree limbs, and heated sleeping huts for the woollys to cuddle together, take naps and sleep. The sanctuary had one enclosure with an enormous tree that all of the monkeys loved to climb. The different enclosures were connected by overhead runways used to move monkeys around when they needed a change of scenery or different playmates. There was one big indoor playroom with a loft, swinging ropes and shelves to sit on. Coming from a sunny, warm climate below the equator, the colony had to adjust to Cornwall winters with rain forcing them inside their heated huts for most of the day. Walking around I found it hard to watch them without looking at their faces but they naturally turned away from me if I mistakenly caught their eye.

At lunch the other volunteers help me gather fixings for my lunch as I made the first of many grilled sandwiches.

"Get water from the tap and a tin of soup from over there. Would you like something savory?" Laura asked me.

"Did you say savory? All right, what does savory mean?"

They explain.

Laughing, I said, "I believe that in my entire life I have never had any American ever ask me if I wanted to eat something savory. We are specialists in sweet and salty." But it isn't just the new words. Their accents are throwing me for a loss, and I cannot understand most of what the Brits say when we sit down at the table. Consequently, I am a step behind on their humor, which is usually my strong suit. I would guess that I appeared to be rather slow as I just stared whenever they burst out laughing.

After lunch I tackle cleaning the fridge, apparently the most dreaded chore at the sanctuary based on the crude that was in there and then wash the kitchen windows earning me a new nickname, Mom! With all but two keepers in their 20s, Mom is definitely the right name and I like it! But I had to laugh at myself taking on the dirty refrigerator when I had balked at my cleaning chores at Animal House. What was the difference? Definitely the warmth and vitality here. Instantly I felt welcomed and there was a sense of comradery. There was laughter and I was part of a group.

With free time after lunch, I went outside to listen to one of the keepers talk to the visitors about the monkeys. Each keeper has a different style of talking and different stories to educate the public. Matt told his group a story about a dominant male who didn't like to baby sit much.

"He had one of the babies on his back for a ride but he was getting tired of babysitting. He moved too quickly and the baby fell off on the ground. The mother ran to her baby and luckily he was just fine. However, she wasn't done with the incident. She gathered the aunties together, took one strong male, and they spanked the dominant monkey reprimanding him for not taking proper care of the baby. Afterwards he was ousted out of dominant position and the male who had helped the females was installed to replace him."

Ah, we could learn something from these primates.

After my first vegetarian dinner with the group, my mantra became adjust, adjust, adjust. I swear the food was mostly just different versions of Kill the Vegetable. Carrots, broccoli, and cauliflower soggy beyond belief to the point of no taste, then mixed with lentils with just a bit of seasoning. I was a vegetarian for 6 years but even my tastes were struggling getting used to British cooking. Adjustment looks like a slow process.

The conversation around the table was also an area of adjustment. It was so fast like watching a professional ping pong match with lots of laughter from humor I couldn't follow and words I didn't know. "Bung the salt over mate." Someone was being wicked, someone else buggered and someone else was going to get their jumper. I told them that in American English wicked was only used when describing Cinderella's evil stepmother.

"Too bad about your language, Joyce." Lou said smiling at me with the dickens in her eyes .

"You cheeky monkey," Matt told her smiling "Are you taking the piss out of her?"

"No. I think she's brilliant."

Bushed from the stimulation of so many people and my brain fried from translating British accents to American words, I fled to my room before anyone else even thought of sleep, escaping to my bottom bunk and a bathroom that needs a good cleaning. With woolly monkeys and capuchins and lovely British accents jumping around in my brain, I fell fast asleep but with each of my four young roommates coming in at different times and with lights going on and off and too much rustling around, I woke up and lie awake.

Those night goblins that start work around 2 am decide to start me fretting rather than letting me fall back to sleep.

First thought: my sons Joe and Dan. I hadn't seen them for over two months and though we talked on the phone, I really missed them. I wonder how they were doing. So far, it had been impossible to have a long, meaningful conversation on the phone. Tossing and turning with a classic mother fret, I finally calmed myself. Joe and Dan are strong and independent and fine. Just fine.

Then I moved to worrying about sweet Harley, my great cat. I believed that Autumn would take good care of him but still I worried about him. I wanted him to be safe and happy and not to miss our great life together. Now completely wide awake, I decided to call Autumn in the morning to check on Harley.

Still awake I moved on to Robert. Here just a week away from him, I had hoped to find a gushy lovey dovey email from him professing his love. But there was nothing. This long distance thing was not going to be easy. I replayed his words a million times. Why hadn't I heard from him? I was sure he would write me. Long sigh. Have faith.

IN THE MORNING, it was time for work and the Brits were nothing if not organized. My first official chore was "routine," which translated to cleaning out the monkey enclosure picking up the old food and scooping up poop. In the bunk houses where the woollys slept, we washed all of the wooden surfaces with soap and water and then rinsed them thoroughly. A team of volunteers and keepers work together every morning wearing one-piece red or blue work outfits, Wellingtons, which are tall rubber boots like our fishing boots, and rubber gloves. All of the cleaning gear was kept well away from the house to keep us safe from monkey germs and to see if we could keep the monkeys safe from our germs as well.

Whenever I walked inside the enclosures, I got a feel for what it would be like to be a monkey confined in a cage with lots of ropes and tree limbs to play on with their friends. But it was not joy as I had expected, rather sadness inside this confinement. I kept looking at the fence. It felt like jail.

"Lou, how hard is it on these monkeys to be confined like this?"

"A monkey in the wild would travel four miles a day through the tops of the trees barely touching down on the ground. But here they are confined to enclosures with ropes, trees, and overhead walkways, and they spend much more time on the ground than they ever would in the wild." Lou was one of the keepers. "They sleep in heated bunk rooms and though we move them around each day for variety, life at the sanctuary is a far cry from freedom. Their confinement here is bloody all man's doing. We tried to rehabilitate them to send them back to Brazil but because of different viruses, Brazil had to turn us down." She looked both angry and sad.

"But at least every effort is being made to make their lives as comfortable as possible. For certain, it is better than being someone's pet with no socializing with other monkeys." I said.

"Shite. Joyce, the primate trade is still going strong and it pisses me off!"

"It is still legal in the States then?"

"Yes. Sometime Google primate trade. You will be really shocked by photographs of capuchins dressed in stupid outfits. Then you will know sadness."

Later I did as she suggested and I was shocked by what I found on the Internet in the UK and the US. There was a long list of monkeys for sale and Lou was right. Most were dressed up in stupid outfits! I was outraged. They loved socializing with each other living in groups. They weren't meant to live alone as a pet. Why would people believe that monkeys were pets or were ours to use in advertising or TV shows or to run experiments on? Why were there no laws protecting them? I hated this selfish attitude of using nature to suit our whims. How did we get so disconnected from nature and our feelings?

"I didn't know. I just didn't know." I told Lou later, beginning to get a sense of the mission here. Would there even be a need for this sanctuary if man respected the animal kingdom?

After Routine was completed, I took a quick lukewarm shower. After breakfast Laura, another volunteer, and I prepared the monkey baskets washing leeks, lettuce, bananas, apples, pears, and other fruits and vegetables being very careful to get all of the dirt off. The keepers worked as a team and everyone had separate responsibilities always putting the monkey's welfare first. Passion drove this sanctuary.

I thought about Animal House. Joris's passion too drove his work, his caring focused completely on the welfare of the wildlife and his anger towards people who misused their power. Lou was pissed at people who forced these monkeys into a life of confinement. But here the keepers had each other to depend on and to work with. Joris and Ineke were alone and felt they were against the entire island. Joris lacked the compassion that I saw here in everyone's eyes and the laughter.

After completing my chores, I went to check the computer. No email from Robert.........argh! Frustrated by my inability to get in touch with him and his total lack of communication, I grumbled to myself not sure if I was more sad or mad. Exactly what was going on here? Had it been just a really romantic version of holidating? I had fallen in love. I was still all gushy and soft and dreamy eyed sighing as I replayed memory movies smiling to myself, vulnerable, trusting. Robert, how about you? I sent another email wondering if they were reaching him.

Better to watch monkeys than think about this, I went outside to listen to another keeper talk to the visitors. Brian, tall and lean and about my age, explained about their life spans.

"Because woolly monkeys live 20 years in captivity and capuchins 40 years, the keepers decided in 2000 to stop them from breeding as they felt they would be breeding them for a life of captivity, a life sentence in jail. Also, many of the monkeys are related from the past years, making a limited gene pool. But the contraception method did not work and there you see the result. We have Ollie, a sweet little baby monkey born in 2004, who roams around freely. He is the favorite of everyone in the troop and certainly all of us. His birth brought new energy to the troop and changed the dynamics in a very positive way."

On my first full day off there still had been no email from Robert. All right, where was this guy? Steam coming off the top of my head my teapot boiling. Damn, was I ever going to hear from him? Nothing like a frustrated woman left with no communication!

I decided to Google him. Me, Stalker Chic! And there he was…a million sites with information about his athletic accomplishments but nothing at all about his love for an American woman!

Was he married? Stalker chic continued her search. All I could find was his date of birth and that stopped me cold. The man was born when I was in eighth grade! Oh, my gosh! How could that be? He had grey chest hair! I was stunned and then I started chuckling. I could have been his babysitter! I had fallen in love with a man 14 years younger than me. But after a minute of recovery, I started feeling rather smug. It was actually pretty damn hot. Miss 57-year-old had attracted a hunk of 43. Feeling rather cocky about myself as the femme fatale and still unable to Google my way to a wife, I decided to remove him for the day from the Prime Time of my thoughts and spend my day off in pursuit of non-vegetarian food. I could think about Robert, The Young Stud, another day.

I walked to a nearby town to buy some snacks taking the small road leading away from the Sanctuary. It was classic Cornwall, so narrow only two small European cars could pass each other if one tucked into the bushes. Over my head, tall thick dense hedges lined both sides of the road full of brambles, shrubs, and thorns. They were used as fences for the cows and sheep in the fields.

As I entered the first town, I had a choice of shopping at a surf shop, a post office, or a small café. Eager for a great cup of coffee, which was a silly thought in a country that loves tea, I walked into the café ready to get to know the people there. But British reserve was in full gear. My coffee was served with no hello, no warmth, and no conversation. I sat in silence missing the Greek waiters.

With just a small selection of snacks there, I decided to move on to Downderry, a larger town a couple of kilometers further down the road. I was excited to find three restaurants, a post office, and a grocery store. At a beach café, I ordered a meat sandwich, which came as two giant pieces of thick, dry grilled bread with two slices of dry, flavorless roast beef. Disappointed, I also knew I wouldn't starve here but so far England overcooked all vegetables and dried out beef.

One of our work projects was a beach cleanup just down the hill from the sanctuary. Afterwards, we all stopped for a beer and a chat. When it was time to head back to the sanctuary, I decided to walk home for exercise. I asked if anyone wanted to join me but everyone else hopped into the van. I walked up the hill alone.

Walking up the hill suddenly a big wave of sadness hit me hard and tears fell fast. Thank goodness I was on an empty country road! Sometimes at home when I get overwhelmed, I cry and it lets all my frustrations come to the surface like the door that holds everything in collapses and all of my real feelings flood out. Crying I walked alone. I missed my sons, my mom, my sister, my cat, my houseboat, my buddies, and my life. Long-term traveling meant that the only "my" was "my backpack." No, that wasn't it. More tears brought the truth.

Robert tears were falling. Tears for love. His phone number no longer worked. He had forgotten me. I had emailed him but hadn't heard anything back. There was no way for me to call him and the chances of me being inside the sanctuary if he ever called were slim. But where could I put my still in-love feelings for him? I was a soft, gooey marshmallow unable to believe that I had been played. He did not seem to have a player's heart. Or was I just gullible? Not talking to him made me kind of crazy. Would I ever talk to him again?

Then listening to my sappy self, another thought came along. Order in the court!   Am I taking a trip around the world for me and tears are falling for a man? Get a grip! Obviously there is a lesson here but it's not about heartache. I needed to move up the emotional food chain, clean up some old baggage. I could stay home if I wanted to do a man mope! Was this trip about a man or me?

Maybe the tears were about the disappearance of my romance but I was also adjusting to a change of cultures and communal living. Living with a group of young people was after all an extreme change. I wondered how to make myself adjust to the differences faster. As I gave myself a pep talk, I saw someone walking down the hill towards me and quickly dried my eyes. Laura, one of my roommates, had decided to come down and meet me on the road.

"Hi, Joyce. I did not want you to walk alone."

"Wow, that is so sweet. I was actually having a bit of a melt down."

"But you always seem so calm and steady," she said.

"Ah, well, I guess I am calm and steady and emotional too. I left a love in Greece and haven't heard from him at all. I am wigging out about fitting in here and who knows what else."

"Oh, Joyce, all of us volunteers love you!"

As we talked about love, boyfriends and her life, I felt much better. Being open and vulnerable was a better way for me to go. I didn't need to be perfect. Earlier Teresanna had encouraged me to tell the truth about how I was feeling. I had not really needed to be Wonder Woman of the Cave armed with a pickaxe and endless energy. Now Laura was making it easy for me to be talk about my emotions by accepting me, listening without judgment. She didn't expect me to be In Control Woman. I was getting small glimpses of walls coming down as I learned to express myself from my center and accept being loved. A paradigm shift. Ice was melting somewhere.

In the second week, my first chore was to get the place ready for the public, which included cleaning the public toilets...yuck! Did I really need to go around the world to clean toilets? I swept leaves off the long driveway appreciating the physical outdoor work and cut food for monkey dinner baskets.

Then it was my turn to try something new making monkey cake. There was no set recipe, just a list of good carbohydrates and protein sources that need to be in the ingredients.

Asking Lou for more of her sage advice, she explains, "Start with two layers of bread. Stew together apples, blackberries, and raisins, and spread that over the bread. On top of that sprinkle sunflower seeds and raisins and covered that with slices of bread. Bake for 30 minutes and Bob's your uncle."

"Bob's your uncle?"

Laughing, Lou explained, "That just means that's all!"

"Ah, how very British!" I followed her directions but had no idea if this monkey bread pudding was any good, monkey-good. Monkey cake was served as a bedtime snack.

Lou said that if the woollys really liked something, they start trilling really loudly and singing to each other. I had my fingers crossed that they would like my first cake. In the dark night unable to distinguish the woolly shapes, Lou started distributing the monkey cake to each of the woollys. And then I heard it: trilling, loud and clear from one enclosure to the next. It sounded like they were letting the other monkeys know that were waiting for their cake. "Hey, this is really good. You're gonna love it!" The sweet sound proved that they loved it! Next to baking for Joe and Dan, it was the most satisfying baking I had done in a long time.

A BUNDLE OF ENERGY, Lou had me in awe of her spirit. Ready to joke at any time, good for a tease, and absolutely committed to the welfare of the monkeys, she was ferocious when it came to the primate trade. I admired her tremendously. Her commitment and passion forced me to look at my life and challenge my choices. Where were my passion and my commitment?

As the second week came to a close I had developed my own schedule of sitting near the enclosures in the early morning before routine even started. A chance to study the monkeys and a time to be alone. I sat quietly by myself listening to different sounds. The most frequent one was "eeolk," a sweet soft musical sound, which meant "I'm all right. How are you?" from one enclosure to the next. But then I heard giggling. I moved quietly and watched two of the woollys tickle each other making a laughing sound! I was amazed! Normally I'd say that the best soul brightener is a baby's laugh but the sound of these monkeys giggling was a close second. A sound that made me feel the energy of innocent joy.

Watching the monkeys cuddle, I realized that I probably needed some warm bunk time with a gentle monkey too. I was a little lonely here. I had not found anyone to really chum up with. The kids were all sweet here but still kids. After dinner they were drinking, smoking weed, or watching TV. At night it was a lot of chatter and loud music and even as Mom, I didn't fit in.

Out on the patio one night with Matt, we had a great talk.

"How are you doing Joyce? Are you adjusting okay?"

"Yeah, each day seems better. One of the biggest adjustments is being around all of these people constantly. This lifestyle is definitely communal living, which is something I always thought I'd enjoy. Now I am seeing both the good and the bad. I'm doing better now."

"Here's an idea for you. Put your towels or another sheet around your bunk to make a little room, a cave, to give yourself more privacy. That's what I used to do. I think you'll like it. Kind of like your own little room!"

"Okay, I'll try it. Hey, Matt, here's a question. When I walk around the sanctuary at night near the enclosures, I get waves of sadness. Sometimes I even start to cry. Am I crazy?"

"No, no Joyce. There is sadness here. We have had deaths here and it is after all a jail. As hard as we try to make their lives good, there is still a lot of sadness. You are feeling that sadness from monkeys kept in captivity."

"Is there nothing we can do to help?"

"Well, I guess we do what we can but it is still jail for them. Their instincts tell them to sleep up in a tree in a jungle but they're here because man is more powerful and took control of their lives."

"Aw, Matt, that makes me so sad. They should be sleeping in the forest in Brazil. What are humans thinking to allow the killing of monkeys, the capture of their babies for a life away from their natural environment?"

"Yeah, I know," said Matt. "Me, too."

Tucked into bed, I admired my new "room." Following Matt's suggestion, I had put up a sheet around my bed. Feeling like I had my own private space, I snuggled down for the night. Matt watched the monkeys to understand what they needed. I had the sense that he was watching me and knew what I needed even before I did. He had no idea what a spectacular person he is. I watched him be kind to people, quietly get things done, support people, and smile at all the pretty girls who generally smiled back. I'm not sure he is totally appreciated here or that they recognize how integral he is to everyone's health and welfare at the sanctuary. Perhaps Matt's instincts of caring for the monkeys had made him very sensitive to people as well.

Ready for a new experience, I moved to the capuchin routine, a totally different experience from the woollys. Capuchins, considered among the most intelligent monkeys, are named for their "caps" of hair, which resemble the cowls of Capuchin monks. Agile and lean, these capuchin monkeys were about a third of the size of the big woollys. Their brown fur was thinner with cream around their face, neck and shoulders. Their faces were adorable. Their enclosures were filled with small trees and their bunks were like children's play rooms with things to jump over and play in.

Like the woollys, they came from the rain forest and usually lived in large groups from 10 to 35 and stayed hidden in the trees in thick forests eating fruit, bugs, leaves and even small birds. In the wild they were great at catching frogs and cracking nuts and only came down to the ground to drink. Able to jump up to nine feet, they sprang around their cages quickly.

Different from the woollys, they loved to look at us seeing if they could catch our eyes for some attention. We were supposed to let the monkeys socialize with the other monkeys and not interact with them to wean them away from humans and encourage them to form their natural groups. But I found that tough.

"Lou, it is almost impossible for me not to communicate with the capuchins, who seem so anxious to interact. Do you have suggestions for me?"

"Monkey enrichment. They need things to keep them occupied. Rather than talk to them, design things for them to work on."

"Okay. Monkey enrichment it is."

"Go pick dried up hogs weed stems," she suggested. "Don't use the green ones. They are poisonous. Can you do that? And pick dock leaves, blackberries. And when you come back, I'll show you what to do next."

When I came back from my walk with an enormous bag of stuff, Lou showed me how to put little holes in the thin stems of the dried up hogs weed tucking sunflower seeds, raisins and leaves into the holes all the way up. Once I finished the bunch, Lou passed them out to the woollys. They grabbed the stems in their hands like kids offered a favorite snack of fruit leather. Then they sat twisting the stem methodically picking all the treats out of the stem a slow enjoyable process.

But then we gave the same thing to the capuchins. Their little fingers picked through the stem so quickly it was hard to tell if they liked it or not. I was going to have to design something different for enhancement for the clever capuchins. They were like teaching accelerated classes!

After routine, I asked Lou for more suggestions for capuchin enrichment.

"Well, they are really smart and anything you design will take them just a couple of minutes especially if Peppy gets a hold of it. He's the smartest of the lot. They like opening boxes."

So I designed a box filled with newspaper. Inside I hid a sock that was filled with newspaper and tied it up tightly with string. I made two other boxes with different surprises inside each one and we put them in with Gary and Peppy.

The keepers said, "Peppy will work through those really quickly but still they'll enjoy it." Peppy went flying to the first one, tore everything out, and it all ended up on the floor reminding me of a young spoiled child tearing through presents at Christmas.

But when Peppy opened the box with the sock, he and Gary were instantly alarmed. They thought the stuffed sock was a snake. They started attacking it and working together to kill it. He and Gary threw it around the cage for a really long time trying to kill it working as a team. Finally, the paper fell out of the "snake" and it died.

"Joyce, that was great! It is good to see them working together, really involved. You kept them busy a long time. Can you make more?" Lou asked.

I set my mind to other ideas for the clever capuchins.

When I went in for dinner, Jill, a keeper, told me, "Robert called while you were out on routine. He seemed very disappointed not to be able to talk to you. I told him to call you back in the evening."

"What? Robert?"

Everyone looked at me sensing my concern.

"Well, mate, tell us about Robert." Lou asks.

"Robert is a man that I fell madly in love with in Greece but I have not heard from him in weeks. I missed his call. Crikey and bloody hell. I'm gutted." amusing myself by using their words.

"He said he would call you back."

"Okay. Okay. If he calls, come get me. Thanks."

But evening came and went with no call back. Argh........men!

At the end of the week my day off found me dying for exercise missing squash, rollerblading, and sweating. I needed a big walk and a new adventure. Though it was pouring buckets with big gusts of wind, I decided to walk the coastal path. At the same little café, I stopped in for a cup of tea hoping to have some conversation with the owners if I ordered the national drink. However, British reserve was still in effect and halted any possible conversation. The British culture had an initial coldness but that changed to witty conversations with friendship. Adjust, adjust, adjust, my mantra for this trip.

I walked a couple of kilometers to Downderry and then decided to keep going. The coastal path was carved along the edge of bluffs with steep stairs up and down giving me a great workout. Breathing in fresh air looking out at the ocean with rain, fog, and wind was exhilarating! At times, I couldn't even see down to the sea through the fog but the clean cold wet air was cleansing. After so little exercise these last few months, the steep climbs were tough. Panting up the stairs, I realized that I should add daily walks to my life here.

As the rain turned into a downpour and the wind became powerful gusts, my red raincoat had a waterproofing breakdown. I cold feel both the wet and cold seeping through to my shirt. Sideways whirling rain gave me a sopping wet face. I was hungry, tired, cold, and wet and ready for the next town to appear. Adventure over. Had the sign been correct for a town in six kilometers? Finally at the top of a hill, I saw a small town in the distance.

Dreaming of a little snug café with a bowl of hot soup and hunks of bread, I quickened my pace. The streets were deserted. I walked into town like a gunfighter looking for the saloon but saw nothing but rain and wind. Maybe I should have asked about a café before coming this far. I wondered if I had enough energy to walk back the 10 kilometers. I looked in the windows of the houses along the street at people warm and dry. In my imagination, I pictured sitting with a sweet older woman for tea with warm homemade scones and clotted cream.

As I walked along dreaming of food, I saw a large building on a hill that looked more like the Munster's house than a hotel. A somber-grey wooden box of a building with no landscaping. The sign said it was a golf club and hotel.

My hair was dripping, my raincoat was completely saturated a small river forming at my feet. My shorts and big hiking boots were sodden. A drowned rat. Starving, freezing, an orphan in the storm, I hoped they would let me in. I pushed open tall wooden doors and walked into an entry with cathedral ceilings and wood-paneled walls. I shook myself off like a wet Irish setter. Then I opened the next set of doors into a stately room with upholstered furniture with wooden arms, oriental rugs over hardwood floors, and landscapes hung on the wall. Tiptoeing past the lounge and leaving a path of raindrops, I was anxious to find the restroom before anyone saw me. I crept past the very proper British people dressed in tidy conservative clothes sitting upright reading their papers sipping tea.

Ducking into the bathroom, I was shocked to see myself in the mirror and burst out laughing. Mascara was dripping down my face in black trails, and my wet hair was clinging to my head. I was a total disaster! When I removed my red raincoat, I started laughing again. My shirt had red streaks running down the front from the dye off my raincoat. I dried my hair under the hand dryer and wiped the mascara off my face. I still looked like a drenched rat.

I slinked into the bar hiding in the corner like a fugitive from the law keeping my eyes down, a trick I learned from the woollys. A group of men were having a beer at the bar and watching golf on TV; a few other groups were scattered at tables. The waitress walked over and took my order neither gasping in horror at the wet mop sitting in her bar nor asking a single question of the totally wet woman. Ah, the British reserve, saved me from embarrassment. Even the other customers kept from staring at the wet Irish setter who had entered their proper establishment.

Steaming tomato basil soup all hot and creamy turned the day around for me. Warm and well fed, I decided to walk home in a damn good mood appraising my progress at the sanctuary. Midway through my month here, I was pleased. I liked my new cocoon bed, loved talking to Matt and Lou and even understood their accents. The word usage here was definitely more descriptive than at home, storytelling more of an art. The humor was still difficult for me and when I watched TV, I missed the funny bits but things were definitely on the rise.

As I walked, I scanned my Robert feelings. No, he had not written. No, he had not called me back. But I had a feeling that I would talk to him again. Somehow I believed that with certainty. At least I was stubborn enough to be sure that I would talk to him again. There were a few questions that I'd like answered. But I no longer felt we were destined to live in a castle somewhere forever and ever. At the same time, I wasn't ready to turn it into a rocking chair memory for my old age just yet, but I felt both my sadness and anger softening.

Almost back home, I stopped at the café ordering tea and scones and clotted cream. I loved this rich 55% fat cream and lapped it up like a happy cat. The owners still weren't talking to me even on my second visit in one day but it was okay.

ONE NIGHT AFTER DINNER I brought out a sheet of paper. I wanted to make a list of all the British words that differ from ours including their great slang. My ear had adjusted to the fast-paced accents now and the words they used like wicked, brilliant, blokes, mates, knickers, and bollocks made sense to me now and were definitely more descriptive than American English. I got some of the Brits to sit down at the dining room table to make a list of words different from American English. *Todge and tool, stiffy and willy, sod, snog and sorted, smarmy and scrummy, naff and narked, jammy and khazi, daft and dodgy, wind up and wanker, tickety-boo and squidgy, blimey, and stonker.* I filled two pages.

In the other direction, two words totally cracked them up: *fanny and fanny pack.* In crossing the ocean, our *fanny* describing our backside had mysteriously turned into vagina on this small island. So, each time an American said anything about her fanny being big, sore, wet or hurting or looking for her fanny pack, the Brits were gutted keeping themselves from falling in a heap of laughter. And in Britain, "pardon me" is saved for when someone farts in public or at the table. We sound like we have an enormous problem with gas when we continually excuse ourselves with *pardon me.* By the end of the evening, we were all laughing hysterically and each day I was more comfortable living here finally adjusted to communal living.

But I hadn't learned all of British English. After morning chores, I walked up the hill for a bit of a workout. Brian, the keeper, was also starting out on a walk. He doesn't talk to me that much but I stopped to chat.

"How are you getting on, Joyce?"

"Oh, I feel better now about the quality of my help here. But gosh, I just don't think I brought enough pants on this trip."

He said nothing. I figured the man was painfully shy or just not interested in small talk. I walked in the opposite direction.

But when I told Helen, my new roommate, about the conversation, she burst out laughing. "Joyce, *pants* in England is our word for underpants. Brian thought you were telling him that you didn't bring enough underwear! No wonder he was quiet."

"Oh, my gosh. Poor man! Now he'll never talk to me."

A NEW SCHEDULE gave me two days off in a row. Everyone told me to take the train to St Ives, a beach town on the Southwest Coastal Path for a weekend away. Anxious for seafood after three weeks of marginal vegetarian food, I ate a delicious grilled mackerel served with beet relish on warm lettuce with great bread and then seeking local music I attended a classical guitar solo by Neil Smith held in a stately 600-year-old church. But tired from fighting the British reserve, the best part of the day was a long hot shower and a big fluffy bed in my own room.

After smoked salmon and eggs for breakfast, I toured the town walking to the surfing beach that looked like California with big sand and big waves though everyone wore wet suits in the cold water. Starting out on a sunny walk along the coastal path, the cold wind sent me back to town to the protected bay at St. Ives to eat fish and chips on the beach and then a stop for tea, a scone with jam and clotted cream. Full and warm but definitely lonely here, I was more than ready to return to all the liveliness of the sanctuary.

On the train ride back, I talked to a vacationing couple from Kent happy to be speaking with anyone after two days of silence. She was an estate agent which was the career I had left so we compared notes on our careers. "I work about 11 hours a day and my commission is 1½%, of which the company keeps 96% and I earn only 4%. Listings are kept within the company and you can only sell the houses that your company has listed."

"Oh, you don't want to know how real estate works in the United States. It is much more lucrative. I make 3% and split it with my company till I meet my plateau and then keep 100%. It is very lucrative."

"That explains being able to take a trip around the world. I could never do that here. Well, here if you do not make your quota, they kick you out of the company!"

I commiserated with her. "It sounds very difficult. I must say that on this trip I haven't missed selling real estate at all."

"Do you think you will go back to it when you return home?"

"Well, I am leaving that question unanswered because I don't know what the next thing is that I'll do to replace it. However, I am getting a sense that I won't be selling real estate any more. I don't miss my career. It was great for raising my sons but now my heart wants to do something that I love instead."

Remembering real estate and driving in my car most of the day, I realized that I had been outside almost the entire day every day since July. I walked everywhere I wanted to go. I had not driven a car in months and I didn't miss it at all. How could I go back to making money to support my lifestyle when I had seen first-hand that there are people who care about the rest of the planet and are willing to live their life devoted to helping? I also realized that I was really excited to return to the sanctuary and happy to have everyone at the sanctuary to go home to, to talk to and laugh with. I would only miss the big bed, fluffy pillows, and hot shower from my day off.

THE KEEPERS WORKED very hard throughout the tourist season and to celebrate they planned a vegetarian feast at one of the pubs in Looe, their traditional end-of-the-season party. On what would be my final day off, I walked to Looe to stay at a hotel. I was craving a bubble bath after a month of lukewarm showers. My plan was to walk to the pub after a long, hot bubble bath.

When I entered the restaurant, everyone from the sanctuary was already seated and they spontaneously shouted a cheer for me, "MOM!"

I was overwhelmed by their show of affection. I knew we had joked all month about me being the resident American mom, but seeing their smiling faces looking at me was really sweet. After three weeks, I was totally comfortable and with just 10 days left, my time at this project seemed too short.

A rather drunk local man sat down to talk to me. I was with the group from the sanctuary but he wanted to know if I would dance with him. He wasn't totally obnoxious, just tipsy or "pissed" as they say here. I could feel the others watching him, ready to step in if he got out of line with Mom. I felt like body guards were protecting me.

"No, thanks."

Mickey asked, "How are you getting back to your hotel?"

"I think I'll just walk."

"No," she said, "We will give you a ride. You are not walking alone here."

Protection. How sweet!

"I was going to punch that bloke if he did anything wrong," one of the fellows said.

I liked being the resident American mom!

Back in my hotel after the party with my heart happy from friendship and celebration, I remembered walking home from the beach-cleaning and feeling so sad about Robert and that I didn't fit in here at all. Looking back I realized that it was the turning point. Now adjusted, I liked living with a large group of energetic people, eating together, talking and laughing. Communal living had definite advantages and just like the monkeys, I did better in a group. Volunteering here and being a part of passion and commitment had restored my faith in people's goodness, in their ability to work together to improve conditions. Robert was fading into my hot adventure category. My sadness over him had been pushed out by the friendships at the sanctuary.

Love traded for love. A man and now a sanctuary. Not a loss at all then in the love column. Maybe love came in many different flavors and I had fogged my thinking by believing that the only worthy love was the man-flavored version. The Eskimos have 52 words for snow distinguishing subtle differences. Perhaps I had been using only one word for love and now I was learning about the subtle flavors feeling them in my heart.   Perhaps my heart was coming alive opening up.

Happily living in this group, I thought about my lifestyle at home. For the last five years with Joe and Dan in college, I had lived alone. Before that as a single mom for 17 years I lived with my sons but no other adults. Yet I liked group energy and felt accepted and appreciated. This trip was peeling away the layers of habits that no longer served me. Maybe living with caring people, gave me a different sense of self. My mirror was reflecting a different Joyce. Things were definitely changing.

I loved the philosophy of the sanctuary recycling everything possible, caring about the environment and helping the planet, not living just for themselves. I found their attitudes inspiring, life-changing. The keepers in creating a safe place for the monkeys had also created a colony for themselves of caring people with very different styles. What I found at the sanctuary was acceptance. People had learned to manage their frustrations living and working together in this big house. Monkey politics, people politics, no matter where you go there had to be some conflicts and disagreements, but the team of keepers worked well together, helping each other with patience.

Before coming to Looe, England, I had no idea there was a primate pet trade business. I knew there was a monkey on the TV show *Friends,* but I didn't really think about it. Now I knew that currently in the United States, it was legal for people to sell monkeys and breed them for pets. But I had watched monkeys tickle each other in glee, giggling. I had seen them groom each other, wrestle and chase, cuddle together and care for baby Ollie as a troop. I had heard them call out to each other, trill with delight, and get angry. They were beautiful wild animals that should never be forced to be a pet or lose their life in the wild. Hopefully someday the primate trade will be stopped and monkeys will live only in the wild.

Do we have the right to capture an animal from the wild and force it to live as we choose? Is man's arrogance sufficient reason to inflict harm on a colony of monkeys, killing the mothers, stealing the babies? How can we rationalize the brutality of the pet trade because individually we want a pet monkey? Is the belief that we are separate from nature accurate, that harming monkeys is not ultimately harming us?

Could we all become more conscious of our stewardship of the planet and put our energies and efforts into protecting and caring for all wildlife? Could we learn to take our responsibilities seriously for the health of the earth as seriously as deciding what car or a big screen TV to buy?

But it was time to fly to South Africa. I left a romance in Greece and now a different kind of love in England. Both were difficult to leave and yet the experiences were alive in my heart. I boarded the train heading away from the sanctuary with tears in my eyes. One foot back and one foot forward. A heart growing stronger. Now to turn that heart to my next adventure to my volunteer job monitoring a troop of wild baboons that were causing chaos on their raids into town.

CHAPTER 9

A Brief Encounter

DEEP IN MY OWN THOUGHTS, I was looking out the train window but not really seeing anything when someone came and sat down—a man. I stopped writing, shut down my laptop, and looked out the window lost in thoughts about leaving love. Leaving the love of people at the sanctuary and the love of monkeys and comparing this feeling to leaving the love of a man and a culture in Greece. It seemed that as I left each place, my right foot wanted to stay but my left foot wanted to head off to a new adventure. Drifting from my thoughts, I was pulled into listening to an amusing conversation.

The man, who had sat down next to me, was talking to the old woman across from me. She wore a plain white blouse with a brooch at the neckline and a plain blue skirt that fell past her knees to her sturdy black shoes. Her grey hair was pulled back in a bun, her bulbous nose was very large, and her face was of pasty white and wrinkled, but there was a twinkle in her eye as she talked and a warmth.

I turned to see the man seated next to me who was babbling on in a charming Scottish accent. He was long and lean, his complexion tawny, his jaw line well defined, his eyes sexy and blue. He looked like Liam Neeson, masculine in a neatly ironed denim shirt and jeans. With that irresistible accent and a very deep voice, I found him charming as I listened to him speak to the old woman. He was playing with words, saying witty, caustic things about the British government. They were obviously enjoying the banter. His use of the English language was beautiful and he expressed himself clearly.

When he saw I was listening, he moved on to the American government, turning to me with the dickens in his eyes as he mocked our government and the coming election. Each brutal statement about Bush and the American way made me laugh and the woman across from me was definitely amused. He was testing me, I thought. He wanted to know if I could laugh at being American and understand his dry humor, a British specialty. Luckily my month at the sanctuary had my ear up to speed on accents and wit.

Traveling Joyce was thinking about Seattle Joyce. In particular about men. In Seattle I could catch a man looking at me but if I looked at him, his eyes darted away quickly as if he was frightened by my eyes like the woolies actually. I wondered if Seattle had developed this strange culture that viewed direct eye contact between the male and the female as a sign of aggression to be avoided at all costs. In a town so politically correct, did the men there feel that flirting was socially unacceptable? Is that why so many wonderful women in Seattle were both frustrated and single? For certain I was getting much more attention out in the world than I would at home.

As we started talking eye to eye in a very connected way, I sensed that under the bravado was tenderness. The four-hour train ride to London flew by with laughter and questions in a very intense conversation. He was off to a dreaded family business meeting that he would rather not go to. I imagined a castle for the family meeting, rather stuffy aunts and uncles sitting on their titles discussing where next to invest their funds. Cinderella meets a prince, an ongoing fairy tale permanently lodged in my child's mind.

Because he was getting off at the same stop, I asked him to help me with my backpack and then as we were leaving the train, he said, "Well, we can't very well end this here. Would you like to go get a drink?"

"Of course! I knew we were going to see each other again." I was not sure how I knew this but there was just something about him that felt very familiar to me. And I loved listening to him play with words. A retired English professor, he was very intelligent and a little zany in a creative way.

As we entered the pub in the train station, he said, "I do not understand what is happening."

"Well, we are having fun so we are going to spend some time together."

"But I do not do this. I do not talk to women on the train and then ask them for a drink," He shook his head in bewilderment. "Shall we sit here at this table away from everyone else?"

"Yes, it looks quiet here. By the way, what's your name?"

"Leonard. What's yours?"

"Joyce."

We ordered beer and both took a long drink before looking at each other. There was intensity between us that caught me off guard.

With tenderness in his eyes, he looked into mine. He said, "I guess it is silly to talk to you because you will be leaving tomorrow. Would you stay? I think we would have a lovely dinner together. I will joyfully abandon the family meeting."

Smiling at the now nervous Len, I said, "Oh, I'm sure we would but I have my plane ticket and my next volunteer project starting right away. Would you come visit me in Cape Town?"

"Hmmm, I was not planning on it," he said smiling.

"Well, can we email each other and stay in touch? I will be in Ireland for two months in May and June volunteering as a newspaper reporter. We could surely meet up then."

"That is too long to wait."

"Then come see me in South Africa."

Looking like he was about to burst, he confessed, "I am a bit too nervous to do much plane travel. I am surprised that we are even talking, as I am normally shy. I have not spoken to a woman in quite some time."

When I looked at him, I saw his nervousness and his tenderness. I put my hand on his back and told him to just relax and to calm down. There was something very delicate about him. He was given a huge amount of creativity that was apparent from the way that he interpreted the world. He talked to me in beautiful detailed pictures with his words coming alive. He used his voice like an instrument changing his tone, speaking quickly and then slowing down, using his hands weaving together a story. I was mesmerized by his words and the feelings behind them. He loved poetry and literature. His sensitivity was a new experience for me, his passion for words enchanting. Like a musician composing a piece, Len could feel each word both the sound and the feeling. I felt like I was being taken along with him on a ride full of new ways to experience the world as he drew me in with his words.

We talked about romance and former loves. He told me about a girlfriend who had wanted to be with him but he hadn't wanted forever with her. And then the last one, a former student with a child but it was just too much for him to cope with.

"I have been alone for about a month," he said.

With his charm, his wit, even with his tenderness and sensitivity, I felt certain that he would have no trouble finding a woman who would love him and nurture him to make him strong again. But did I want to be that woman? Hold it. Stop everything. What was it that made me meet a man and immediately try him on for life? Here I was having a perfectly intense lovely flirt and within moments I was already testing out our compatibility looking for leaks in the balloon. Joyce, Joyce, Joyce get a grip. Enjoy yourself. Stay in the moment.

"I have been married two times," he said.

"Oh, me too but each time I married the same man!"

"Will you marry him again?" he asked smiling.

"No, I think we both have decided not to give it a third try! "

We continued a very personal conversation about our feelings, our lost loves, and our worries, both of us open about things normally kept a secret so early in a meeting.

"Of all the things I understand and of all the things I have learned, relationships still elude me. I keep thinking that the only way I can learn about it is to be in one but it never feels right. It is always like being given a book to read that is written in Greek. All I can do is hold it in my hands and look at it. I don't even know when I missed the class on Greek either! And for a long time I thought I could find love if I just learned one more thing or changed or got a new haircut. But now I think if I am meant to be with one man, he'll find me. Now I love the world moving from culture to culture. All of my senses are alive now more than they have been in a long time. I have burst out of my emotional jail and want to be free." Len was watching me intently as I talked. "You are really easy to talk to Len. I like the way you listen."

Leaning towards me he asked shyly, "May I kiss you?"

Thinking that a sign reading "I want a kiss" must be painted on my forehead, I said, "Yes."

Len leaned over to kiss me gently and then nervously apologized afterwards. "Oh, that was terribly rude of me. To ask for a kiss here in a pub, barely knowing you."

"I'm glad we kissed."

"I just wanted to kiss you. I don't know what has gotten into me. Usually I am with ectomorphs."

"Hmm...doesn't sound very soft to me. Aren't they the no fat girls like Twiggy all bones and skin? You aren't calling me fat are you?" mustering up my face ready for a fight.

"No, no, not at all. I think you would be wonderful to cuddle with. What is going on with me? I am way more forward than I would expect."

When he said "cuddle," I was transported to an old English study with books around the room, a big old leather chair big enough for two, Beethoven playing in the background, rain falling on the windows of our third-story love nest, the two of us breathing together peacefully now and then kissing gently while we read.

Now I wondered the same thing as Len: What in the world was happening here? On the one hand, I saw myself having a wonderful time with Leonard completely engaged by his wit and intellect and I definitely was attracted to him. Could he give love in big lovely doses? I loved the way he used words, his descriptions. He was wonderful at understanding my feelings when I told him something that had made me sad or happy. We had a really nice click together in our sensitivity in a very short amount of time. I found his voice hypnotic. And yes, those gorgeous blue eyes. I was sure nothing would come of it. But we traded emails, both of us insisting that we would write and see each other again. Hugging him and giving him a kiss goodbye, I watched him go to catch his train.

The next morning I flew to Cape Town, South Africa, to volunteer as a baboon monitor for the month of October. As I flew towards Africa, I thought about my journey through Italy, Greece, and England.

Passion. Teresanna's passion towards her project and her caring protection that she had given me. Robert's passion for me in Greece and falling in love. The passion of Lou at the Monkey Sanctuary fighting for primates. And now Len's passion for words and poetry. Each stop gave me a different view of myself in relationship to new surroundings with passion always in the background. Heart set the tone. Like holding a diamond in my hand and turning it slowly to see each new face. My reflection, my heart.

If I got quiet and listened to my inner self, I understood that a man right now would slow me down. That I would perhaps be stopped on my quest and not dig deeply enough into the core of my being so that I could take away the parts that were not really me. To unwrap my heart and free the passion.

CHAPTER 10

Baboon Monitoring in South Africa

OH, WHAT I WOULD GIVE for a business class ticket! I hated trying to sleep all scrunched up for hours in a seat made for passengers 5'2" tall. It was torture finding a place for the other 7" of my body in the 12-hour flight from Lisbon to Cape Town. I moved around like a washed-up contortionist no longer able to put my legs over my head, the only place they'd fit. But flying over Cape Town and seeing the beauty of the coastline brought back my excitement, if not the circulation in my legs. What would my next volunteer experience bring and how quickly would I adapt to new surroundings?

My driver met me at the Cape Town airport and we started out on the hour-long drive to the volunteer house in Komentije. Leaving the airport, I was immediately overwhelmed with sorrow. Miles and miles of land as far as my eye could see were filled with millions of shacks built on top of each other. It was the starkest view of poverty that I had ever seen. My stomach tightened.

"Can you tell me about these people living here?" I asked the driver.

In a very serious tone and with a straightforward honesty that I would come to respect in South Africa, he explained. "These are people who are mostly unemployed. Over a million people live there. Many have come from other parts of Africa in the hopes of finding work. South Africa has a 40% unemployment rate now. Even for white people it is very difficult. The ANC gives the best jobs to blacks. There is no solution. I have had a very tough time finding work."

"How do these people survive?"

"I don't know. Pinched into the city electrical line, the shacks provide free housing and free electricity. Crime is an enormous problem there."

As we drove past the area, I was unable to comprehend the size of it. People were not living here like people. Their shacks were made from pieces of metal and wood put together to form a tiny little box. I didn't know what they did for running water, for cleaning up, for cooking, or for toilets. I didn't know how many people lived in each shack. And the solution, what was the solution? How does a government create housing, low-income housing for one million people, with more coming in every day from all over the continent? I fought tears back from an overwhelming feeling of despair.

There were problems of the same nature in the United States, but I guess I didn't see them in Seattle. I didn't drive past them every day. I didn't believe it was as bad as here but maybe it was just not so evident. Maybe I was desensitized to my own country's poverty. How could I live my life of plenty and ignore others' needs? Compassion was demanding that I pay attention. This was no newspaper photograph. I was here with these people. How do we provide enough education and a decent lifestyle to allow people to improve their lives?

"How have things changed since apartheid or have they?" I asked.

"I grew up during apartheid," he said, "and it was much easier then for white people to find a job than it is now."

"But how did you feel about an entire group of people not being allowed the same freedoms that you had?" I was being rather direct here and hoped he understood that I wanted to understand, not judge.

"It was just the way," he said. "Everyone was doing it and so I suppose no one really thought about it. As a child, I was taught that black people were different from us and I really didn't think about it."

"And now, how do you feel now?"

"Now, it is the economics. I need to earn enough money to feed my family. Now I am at a disadvantage being white because the good jobs go to the blacks. I had nothing to do with the situation that created apartheid but I am paying the price now. I resent the changes but I don't resent black people."

"This housing and poverty is beyond anything I have ever seen. It makes me feel sad. But I know that back home where there is more money available, we still allow people to live in poverty without education or health care."

After that, we rode in silence.

Leaving the slums, we drove past areas with lovely houses and then past areas with very expensive houses. The extreme differences were incomprehensible because they were so visible, so unhidden. An in-your-face reality of extreme poverty just miles away from wealth. I wasn't used to it and couldn't settle my emotions down. Full of questions, I needed to understand the culture here.

The volunteer house was in Komentije, a small town outside of Cape Town. The neighborhood could have been somewhere in the Midwestern United States where I grew up with its modest houses and well-kept yards. When we pulled into the driveway, there were five volunteers relaxing out on the lawn. The house was about 10 years old. It had a big living room lined with cushioned wall benches, an open dining room and kitchen, and one big dorm bedroom filled with four bunk beds, then two other bedrooms with bunk beds, and two bathrooms. Upstairs was a loft supposedly for the volunteer coordinator but she must have had other things to do as she was never there.

After putting my pack in my room, I started meeting the group, all in their 20s and only two males among them. They were from England, Ireland, Canada, Australia, Scotland, and Cleveland. Many were traveling and volunteering as part of their "gap" year, a year of travel before starting college or "uni," as they call it. Most of the rest of the volunteers living in the house were out on a garden tour of other parts of South Africa.

"Joyce, do you want to see the beach? It's just a few blocks and you can watch the surfers and the little black flies!" asked Aaron, who was from Cleveland.

"Sure, I'd love to."

Different from the Monkey Sanctuary, here there wasn't anyone on site to really keep things organized, and I immediately heard about their frustrations with the group, i-to-i, which had booked the trips.

"We are having a problem with getting enough food. What they give us is crap," Diane, a blue-eyed blonde from Britain told me. She had worked at a zoo in England and on a farm and had a lot of experience with animals. "The meat they buy us looks like thin strips of fat with just a bit of meat. We get terrible soft, rotting veggies and very little fruit but there is lots of white bread, peanut butter, and jelly."

"Have you complained?"

"Yes, but they don't do anything about it."

"Well, that's going to change! I said feeling like the mom again. Checking out the kitchen, I found the ingredients for some cookies and decided that a batch would cheer everyone up. I was mystified as to why there was so little food and decided to put proper groceries on the top of my list!

"We are all going to Cape Town for the weekend," Ian told me. "Do you want to come with us? We are going to Table Mountain and Robben Island where Nelson Mandela was held prisoner for 27 years. We'll stay at a hostel."

"You know I think I'm getting a cold and it would be better for me to rest up for the start of my project on Monday," I replied.

"If you're sure," he said slowly. "You'll be here alone. Alison and Louisa, the volunteer coordinators, probably won't stop in."

"No worries. I'll just read and relax and get better."

But my cold got worse overnight, and Saturday dragged on for me. I was unable to breathe well and coughed constantly. In addition, I had a miserable headache and the full agony of aches and pains. All alone and sick in a foreign country, I moaned and groaned and then put myself to bed wrapped in lots of blankets even though it was not cold outside. I read a book, drank a cup of tea, and finally had a sympathy cry for myself. I looked for cold medicine in the bathroom. Rule number one that I hadn't known: Always pack cold medicine when traveling!

I hadn't had a cold for over a year back home and being sick took me by surprise. I guessed that I should have packed some vitamin C or some Emergen-C or something for a cold or flu. Had I taken a positive outlook too far perhaps? Well, at least I was armed with Imodium and prescription Imodium if I was struck down by diarrhea! There were no other American drugs that were traveling with me for wellness, just antibiotic creams for scratches, creams to stop bug itches and sunburns and oh, creams for the phantom yeast infection. I realized that I was dependent on good luck. Lesson learned for my next trip around the world.

But the evening improved as I ate a peanut-butter and jelly sandwich in bed and read Cosmo. Better that was until the lights went out. And not just in my bedroom. The entire house was pitch-black. I waited for them to come back on while I searched my pack for my flashlight, and then remembered that I had left it in England at the Monkey Sanctuary. Now what? It was already dark out. Without any lights, I couldn't read the numbers on the phone card to call Louisa for help. Sick and alone in a dark house in a foreign country with a reputation for violence, I strained my eyes to adjust to the darkness. I decided to just take a nap and figured the lights would come back on later.

But then the burglar alarm went off. Not only was I sick in a foreign country cut off from everyone without electricity but now there was a loud shrieking alarm going off continually. My imagination went wild frightening myself till I curled up in the corner of my bed watching the door and straining my eyes, listening to every noise. I wondered how I would die and the tears fell down my cheeks.

Eventually, however, when no murderer entered my room, I calmed myself down and wrapped up in a blanket to brave a trip out of my room to check the damn alarm. Even with all my years in real estate, I didn't have a clue how to stop it. Surely the neighbors must hear it, too. It must be disturbing their sleep. Wouldn't they come help me? I went back to bed and for the next 8 hours listening to the alarm scream "Beep beep beep beep. I was exhausted.

At 7:30, I called Louisa at i-to-i to tell her what had happened.

"Oh, sorry. I'll take care of it, Joyce. We forgot to renew the electricity." But apparently she was not particularly concerned about me because it took another three hours for her to come fix the electricity.

When Alison, the other i-to-i volunteer coordinator, finally came to turn on the power, she said, "Gosh, you look terrible."

"Well, I was up all night without electricity unable to make even a cup of tea. The alarm went off all night and I was as sick as a dog. You knew I was sick on Friday but never even called me to see if I was okay. One phone call last night to check to see if I needed anything would have solved the entire problem. I look terrible? I think you and your program look terrible right now!"

Shocked by my blast of temper, out she went in a hurry, "Well, I don't want to catch what you have. Hope you feel better."

I spent the day in bed recovering.

BY THE TIME ALL of the volunteers returned from their great weekend, my cold was on the mend and they were full of stories about the trip to Cape Town. The other group of volunteers who had been on the garden tour also returned home. It was a good evening spent getting to know them and the house was filled with chatter and laughter.

When I had searched for wildlife volunteer programs in Africa, baboon monitoring sounded interesting and a bit funny. The information said that I would be helping to keep the baboons out of the towns when they went on their raids. Wednesday, garbage day, was particularly difficult because the baboons loved all of those trash cans brimming with delectable treats. Because of a fascination with both Jane Goodall's work and Diane Fossey's, I saw this project as an opportunity to learn more about primates.

I did some research on baboon life in South Africa. In nature, baboons spend about 40% of their time foraging for plants and insects, though some are able to get protein from shellfish and sharks' eggs found at the seashore. Even though the adult males have large canine teeth, they are not predators; however, sometimes they will kill rodents and birds. Large canine teeth sounded frightening.

In South Africa, their territory had once been the entire Cape Flats but now they were forced to share land with humans, who took more of the land for housing. However, adapting easily to change and encouraged by tourists who fed them, the clever chacma baboons had discovered that raiding towns was a much more efficient feeding method than foraging in the forest. I supposed that they regarded their hunger as a time-management problem. Why spend long hours foraging in the woods when a half a loaf of wheat bread found in a house or garbage can equaled about the same nutritional value? Human food was a fast-food solution for the baboon troop. All the houses needed were the golden arches sign!

The baboons conducted house raids by scaling the walls of a house looking for open windows. When they found one, they all climbed in and headed right to the refrigerator eating whatever they liked and throwing out everything they didn't. When the troop was full, they left the kitchen in a complete disaster with food thrown everywhere. It was no wonder that some people would rather see them dead. These constant house raids had created an ongoing conflict with the other Kommetjie primates, some of whom had guns, poison, traps, and dogs at their disposal.

In the early 1990s, the baboon-human conflict problem reached a low point when a government conservation group, Cape Nature Conservation, shot 18 baboons exterminating the entire troop near Kommetjie. As a result of this slaughter, residents, led by two South Africans named Wally Peterson and Jenni Trethowan, staged a protest and formed the Kommetjie Environmental Action Group (KEAG) to help protect the remaining baboons. But seven years after the troop extermination, things improved dramatically when Proclamation 12 was passed. It declared that baboons could no longer be hunted or removed from the area—the first such baboon-protection legislation in Africa. An endangered species threatened with extinction because of their conflict with humans, there were now only 360 chacma baboons remaining on the Cape Peninsula.

But what would my work would be? I was anxious to begin! On Monday, Louisa drove me to Da Gama Park, which borders a small town near the ocean about 30 minutes from the volunteer house. I was introduced to two baboon monitors: Johnny, who spoke English, and Rodney, who only spoke Khosa. Johnny was in his 30s, just a bit taller than me, with a lean build. His long pants, long-sleeved shirt, and jacket told me that he was obviously better adjusted to the heat than I was! His face was the color of coal and was lit up by his welcoming smile and the twinkle in his eyes. Rodney was a bit younger, of medium height and with a muscular build. He seemed very relaxed when he shook my hand and smiled warmly, a handsome man.

Their job was to keep a troop of indigenous chacma baboons in the hills of De Gama Park. On my first day, Johnny explained, "You mustn't think the baboon is an animal that you can outsmart or overpower. You must learn about the baboon to understand what they will do next. Every day we must climb up the mountain; there is no holiday or weekend for the baboon. Only work. If the baboons try to go to the houses, we chase them. We do not ever hurt them. It is a war every day. Some days we win and other days the baboons win. I love this job and the baboons."

Off we went, walking up a dirt road that wound through the hilly park in the beautiful Slangkop Mountains with a view to the ocean. It was beautiful, fresh and green.

"The baboons are safe here but only if they stay in the park." Johnny told me.

The green hills were layered with large flat white rectangular rocks that seem almost stacked on top of each other. The ground was covered with tall grass, groves of skinny trees, purple and white wild flowers.

"It certainly is much different than the environment I come from, which has an abundance of rain and tall evergreen trees. I'm really not used to the heat here."

"Tell me about your home, Joyce," Johnny said.

And so I did.

Within five minutes of walking, I was astounded to see my first baboon troop sitting high on a hill. Unbelievable! After seeing the woollies and capuchins in captivity at the Monkey Sanctuary, I was thrilled to see the lovely troop of baboons running around the mountain as free as could be. Two young baboons frolicked in the tall grass jumping over each other. They picked bugs to eat from the fallen trees a field of orange and yellow wild flowers.

"Baboons spend most of their time on the ground. The males can weigh from 50 to 100 pounds and the females can weigh from 30 to 50 pounds." Johnny explained.

Two enormous adults sat on a large flat rock at the top of the hill above us grooming each other and watching us. In another area in the tall grass, baboons were shagging. But what I kept noticing was their freedom. Freedom to forage for food, to play, to mate, and to enjoy the perfect blue sky and summer day. How different the life was here for the baboons compared to the monkeys at the Monkey Sanctuary!

"We can sit in the shade and watch the troop now," said Johnny.

It felt great to escape the heat of the sun and watch the troop. Cute young baboons chased each other, jumping from tree to tree, falling and then getting back up. Large baboons groomed each other, or shagged, which took about two minutes tops.

"They are always trying to lull us into thinking nothing is happening and then they try to sneak away."

Then a few minutes later. "Up now. We need to move. They are making a break for it. Let's go."

Quickly we rushed off to another side of the hill. They had sneaked off so quickly. Johnny and Rodney yelled at them in a loud "Aaah! Aaah! Aaah!" Figuring that I was in training, I watched the monitors. When their sound didn't work, the men loaded up their slingshots shooting rocks at the ground, which blocked the baboons' paths and the baboons returned up the hill.

We found another place to sit in the shade to monitor the troop. Johnny was full of questions about my trip and my life, but again those sneaky baboons were off and we moved every time they did.

"So, Johnny, how can I help you?"

"Well, we don't have a sling shot for you but you can yell at them. Stand your ground and make the same noise we make."

He went on to explain the social structure of the troop. "George, the dominant male of this group, is the enormous one with the big shoulders and arms. Can you see him up there? He supervises the troop and he watches us to see when we aren't paying attention. He'll move the troop as soon as we aren't looking. If any of the males step out of line, he screams and yells at them, chasing them all over the valley leaping from tree to tree. But he has a sweet temperament generally and has never killed a baby. However, if one of the lower-ranking males tries to shag one of the higher-ranking females, George comes screaming. At some point when George gets older, another male may get strong enough to challenge him and win but for now George is very secure as the troop's dominant male."

He smiled. "Every day but Wednesday, garbage day, our watch is pretty calm."

My volunteer work was over around 2 pm, but Johnny and Rodney kept working till dinner. Tuesday was the same routine as Monday. Talking to Johnny and watching the baboons made for a great day but I wanted to know about life here for a black man. All of the monitors were black. "How is your life here after apartheid? Has it improved?"

"Well, I never know how long I will have my job. This money supports my whole family here and in the Eastern Cape, too, where I am from. The pay is not too big. If the money runs out, there is no IU and when I am old, there is no retirement. I will just not have any money."

"What is IU?"

"Unemployment insurance. I have no guarantees. As my age increases, my knees ache from walking these hills to protect the baboons. I only think about my family and being able to work. Apartheid was a time of hatred and even more poverty than we have today. Tell me, Joyce, can you help me get a different job? Could I get a job on a ship? My English is good."

"Oh, Johnny, I wish I had some contacts for you. I would love to help. I promise to think about it. I know it must be tough for you, but you all do a great job here helping the baboons survive."

He smiled again, a little sad this time. "Tomorrow is garbage day, Joyce. Let's hope we get them before they get the garbage!"

We talked until 2:00 when I left for the volunteer house.

143

When I woke up Wednesday, I was really excited to get to the site wondering what kind of trouble the troop would have gotten into. For their sakes I hoped none. When I arrived, Johnny had not found the troop in their usual sleeping spot and he shouted, "They are already raiding!"

We got into a car to see if we could find them. When we arrived at an apartment complex, the sight of more than 20 large baboons on a garbage can raid was so outside of my comprehension, I had to work hard to stifle my laugh! Emptied cans rolled in the parking lot and garbage was thrown everywhere. The parking lot was a disaster. Each baboon had his head in a can throwing out anything he didn't want to eat. The young ones picked through the scraps eating what they liked. A Garbage Day Picnic for the Troop. With no locks protecting the contents, the baboons were having a great time stuffing their mouths with leftover bread, vegetables, junk food, and salads. But how, I wondered, did they know it was Wednesday, garbage day?

Johnny flew out of the car, yelling and arming his slingshot. Some of the baboons seemed to recognize his voice and were afraid and immediately left for the hills, but others ran into the open hallways and stairwells of the apartment buildings. How strange to see baboons standing on a staircase!

"Joyce, go around to the back and start moving them out!" Johnny told me.

Ah, finally, work! I thought. Excited, I jumped into action and ran around the back of the building where many baboons were hiding from Johnny and Rodney. For sure I was scared of them but now how to make them scared of me!

"Aaah! Aaah! Aaah!" I yelled.

No reaction.

"All right, you baboons, get out of here! Aaah! Aaah! Aaah!" I yelled in a ferocious voice imitating Johnny waving my arms around.

Still no reaction.

Then Johnny came around the corner shouting and every baboon took off. Rodney and Johnny continued yelling and using their slingshots while the aggressive American woman screamed.

Memories returned of my first year teaching school with a math class completely out of control. These baboons were misbehaving just like my students! Fed up by my inability to help, I turned to the small young ones, who were absolutely adorable. I started yelling like a mother of two sons on a rampage! I gave them my strongest and deepest "Aaah! Aaah! Aaah!" and they ran! Finally, success!

For the rest of that day, we stood like sentinels, protecting garbage cans from marauding baboons until the garbage truck came. The garbage collectors had to sweep up the entire mess.

"Johnny, I'm sorry. I tried my best but only two little baboons were scared of me."

"Oh, don't worry. They are male-dominated and only fear male voices. You might never get a male to do what you want."

"Ah, I see. What's new?" I said, laughing with Johnny.

"You know," he said, "a woman who loves these baboons gave padlocks to the people in this apartment complex to use on their cans but most of the people don't use them. Many local people view baboons as menaces that need to be either moved or shot. They have been maimed from people shooting them, beating them, poisoning them, or sending their dogs after them."

"You monitors are the only relief of tension between the baboons and the community," I said.

On another day, the baboons worked their way down the hill and one broke through our line. Both monitors went to retrieve the escaped baboon leaving me as the only guard. However, they didn't tell me I was in charge and didn't give me instructions. They just took off as fast as the baboon had. I looked around in all directions and saw that I was all alone, the sole defender against the Great Baboon Raids. When the baboons started to make their way down the hill, I picked up a stone and threw it yelling, "Aaah! Aaah! Aaah!"

Noticing that their real monitors were gone, they looked at me in defiance as if to say, "Hmm...is that really your best shot?"

I put my hands on my hips yelling, "Hey, you baboon, get your ass back up that mountain now. Don't mess with me. This rock means business. Move it, buster!" I said all this in a gruff, deep voice but the baboons didn't even flinch. I started laughing at myself. Here I was alone in a park in South Africa armed with a rock and a mediocre throwing arm, yelling at enormous baboons in a screechy female voice. The substitute monitor and a troop of baboons. The entire troop quickly figured out that I alone was guarding the gate to their freedom.

George, the enormous muscular, football-shouldered George, started ambling down the hill very close to me! He stared right at me. Completely intimidated, I lowered my head and looked away. Dominant male baboon wins staring contest with independent American woman on quest for adventure!

He was way too big and too powerful (think big teeth in strong jaws!) for me to start yelling. As he walked past me, I said sweetly, "Oh, hi George. Have a nice visit in town. Troop looks great. Love what you're doing with your hair. Bye, bye, now."

He turned and walked away. A cheeky young baboon came down the hill quite close to me following George. Not frightened by him at all, I picked up a rock and pretended like I was going to throw it. I yelled, "Aaah! Aaah! Aaah!" although I had to try hard not to laugh at myself. But the little one was frightened and walked back up the hill! Yea, the Amazing American Baboon Monitor has stopped one baboon from heading into town today!

But the joke was on me. The monitors had been hiding behind a tree watching me, enjoying their prank. They had already sent the escaping baboons up the hill into another area and now came back to laugh at me about my lack of authority! I couldn't believe it!

"Oh, you rascals! How rude! I thought I had let all the baboons escape and felt terrible!"

"Yes, but we had a good time watching you!"

Johnny told me stories about the baboons he had been tracking for six years. "George will probably only be in power for another 3 years" (Hmm...does he mean Bush or the Baboon?) Then one of the other young males will challenge him and win. Erik is another dominant male. He heads another troop nearby. He is George's father and actually bigger than George!"

"I can't imagine that," I said. "George is enormous."

"Erik is one tough dude, meaner than George by a long shot with even more powerful shoulders."

"I'm glad I'm here with George, who would rather watch the youngsters play!"

"Yes, but George is in danger from the villagers, who want him shot."

"Oh, Johnny, such a sad thing! Your job is so important here."

Back at the volunteer house, the group was really gelling with shared meals, baking cookies, reading books in the evening, and walks to the beach. Each time they were in the mood for cookies, someone helped me bake and we even got chocolate chips. Jade, a spunky vet student from Ireland, told me, "I like having an American mom here to bake us cookies. It's just like in the movies!"

"Well, I love having your help!" I replied.

The volunteers all took turns cooking dinner for the group. I had spoken to Louisa and Allison about how disappointed everyone was with the quality of the food they were buying for us. I suggested that they let us shop for ourselves but they promised to upgrade our groceries. Since that conversation, the food supply had improved though it was still tough to cook without many seasonings. We ate dinner together around the table at night, which was turning into one of my favorite parts about volunteering. I liked the chatter, the fun, and sharing chores.

Again as in England, I felt like the "mother" of the group and I loved it. I liked reading quietly in the living room with Aaron and Ian, who were always there to help out with chores. It seemed like they were getting more comfortable living in the midst of a sea of women. In the daytime, they all volunteered at Tears, the dog and cat rescue or the Buffalo Park, on maintenance work. We regrouped in the early evening.

One day from our lookout point, the baboons escaped our watching eyes and we scampered down the hill to find them. A pretty blonde woman dressed in jeans, a casual shirt, and hiking boots was at the bottom of the hill waiting to talk to the monitors.

As I reached the monitors, the blonde turned towards me. "Hi! I'm Jenni Trethowan," she said, reaching out to shake my hand.

"Hi, I'm Joyce. I've heard about your work with the baboons."

For the last 13 years, Jenni had protected the baboons by keeping the monitor program alive and helping injured baboons. She was considered magical by the monitors for her ability to communicate with the baboons and by how much the animals loved her.

Jenni asked, "Would you like to go with me closer to the troop? I am going to take some photos."

"Yes!" I said and we walked over to the trees where the troop was gathered.

As we walked, she told me, "To feel whole in our souls, we must connect with animals. I don't know how to explain this to someone who feels animals are just something to entertain us. I don't know how to explain this to someone who doesn't cry when we damage our earth, our air, our water."

Her words touched my heart. She understood the connection between humans and nature that I was here experiencing eye to eye for the first time.

"When we get to the baboons, move quietly. Don't be nervous and don't stare into their eyes."

Ah, I remembered the woollies who also felt that staring into their eyes was an act of aggression. I was nervous as we approached the baboons but I was really excited to be there with Jenny.

We walked over to an area where a few of the baboons were sitting. "Hello Crook, Thamsanga!" Jenni said, calling them by name in a sweet way. Sitting down, she gave me directions. "Joyce, just follow my lead. Come here and sit down."

The baboons who were near us came closer. One was staring at me, looking in my eyes, and out of the corner of my eye, I saw him and felt his presence. I had been around lots of dogs and cats but these eyes, even using only my peripheral vision, were deeper, more intense, more questioning. Was it the wildness? They all stared at me. Did they remember me as the rock-throwing baboon monitor? Should I apologize now? Could they sense who I was?

Jenni reminded me, "Be calm, Joyce. They are just getting to know you."

Wild animal. Stay calm. My Jane Goodall moment. Breathe.

Being stared at by the baboons, I wanted to gaze back into the small golden-brown eyes and thank them for letting me be there. But I didn't want to alarm them or be viewed as an aggressor. I sat calmly while I was sized up and hopefully given a thumbs up. With a mix of joy, wonder, anxiety, amazement, and fear, I thought kind, gentle thoughts and trusted Jenni that I was safe here.

Jenni noticed that the babies were all down playing at the river and she suggested we go down by the river and watch them play.

There was an enormous male near us spread-eagled on a large rock showing off his erect penis. We would need to walk past him to get to the river and I imagined him taking a grab at my ankles when we walked by just for kicks. I wanted to ask Jenni if this erection thing was a good or bad sign but decided to be quiet instead, as this definitely would be the wrong time to start laughing.

"Now, just walk right behind me and don't look at him," said Jenni. Her voice was calm and serious. So, maybe he's like the baboon version of the guy with the raincoat? Hey, girlies, look what I got!

I didn't ask Jenni what would happen if I did something wrong. It seemed better not to know. I walked in Jenni's exact steps not even breathing, just feeling the mix of excitement and fear coursing through my body. I got past the male safely and sighed deeply. Perhaps as he watched me walk clumsily down the steep hill through the fynbos, he figured that I was too ungraceful to bother with! Baboons are light and fast on their feet, pure grace flying over the terrain.

Arriving at the river, we sat under a big maple tree. "George," Jenni said, "is sitting up in that big maple tree with some of his females watching the youngsters and us. If anything endangers them, he will fly into action."

I had not forgotten enormous George and I prayed for a calm day. Watching the young baboons was just like watching children play. Most of them sat at the river's edge with one or two bravely walking into the river splashing around and beckoning the rest to join them! They were adorable and obviously having a great time.

However, while we were busy watching the young baboons splash in the river, more and more baboons circled around us until we were really sitting in the middle of the wild troop! I looked behind me and a mother on a log was nursing her baby while grooming a male. A lovely family having cuddle time together. On my left, two little males like Mutt and Jeff sat staring at us with the same curiosity I had about them. I wondered if these were the ones I had scared back up the mountain. Their young eyes touched me, a feeling of so much conversation waiting to happen.

"Jenni, they seem like they want to talk to us," I said.

"I have a friend who studies interspecies communication and she is helping me learn to communicate," she replied.

"Jenni, I think you are already understood by this troop. They seem very comfortable having you here."

"Yes, but I want to understand more."

Upon hearing her speak of interspecies communication, I tested out a bit of telepathy sending a loving, kind message, thanking them all for letting me sit among their troop, I sent them a love offering, a signal that I was a friend. It also helped calm my panicky nerves as I sat there amidst so much wildness. Sensible Joyce kept asking herself what she was doing sitting with a bunch of wild baboons with large sharp teeth and strong arms!

Breathing slowly I was starting to feel a little bit calmer and then things changed dramatically. "There is a male approaching you from the back. Just relax," Jenni said quietly.

I gulped and held my breath. How could I relax when a wild male baboon was coming up behind me? What exactly does that mean anyway? But Jenni was calm. Okay, breathe, Joyce. Send out more than fear. Send out gratitude.

Suddenly I felt a warm body lean against me! Warm like a child's body, his full weight leaning into my back. And the feeling of connection was absolutely amazing, someplace between complete awe and a sense of spirit. My fear was gone.

"I have never seen them do this before to a complete stranger." Jenni laughed. "Hand me your camera."

As I was handing it to her, the male's little hand reached around and gently grabbed my upper arm. I looked down and saw his furry hand holding my arm, his little black fingers with little black fingernails much like a child's hand holding onto my arm in a gentle, warm caress. I was getting a baboon hug as he rested his head on my back. Jenni was taking photos and I kept looking at the little hand on my arm in utter amazement. How could this be happening to me? Soon he moved his feet resting them on my back and I could feel the heat from the soles of his feet. Baboon hug. Baboon love. In South Africa under a tree sitting in the middle of a baboon troop getting hugged by a wonderful wild male baboon.

As baboons do with each other, soon my new friend started grooming my back, his tiny fingers moving gently over my skin skimming the surface looking for ticks. The sensations were thrilling like gentle tickling until he found a mole on my back and thought it was a tick. Slowly he started picking at it to see if he could pry it off. Terrified that he would bite it off, I told Jenni, "He is picking at a mole and it hurts. What do I do to get him to stop?"

"Say 'Ow!'"

"Ow!" I said praying at the same time that he would understand. "Please stop."

He stopped but I couldn't be sure why.

"Jenni, he stopped!"

"Well, that's good."

But the young baboon had more in mind for me. I froze, my heart pounding, when Jenni said, "Joyce, he has a bunch of your hair in his hand. Relax but let me know if it hurts."

My heart skipped a beat. Now what? I figured that he was going to yank my hair out and braced myself. I wondered how much it would hurt and how long it would take to grow back. But no, he was only grabbing it to start grooming my hair! His little fingers darted quickly and lightly through the bunch of hair he had grabbed, separating the hairs, and when he was done, he grabbed more checking every hair for ticks and bugs! His fingers felt like human fingers gently braiding my hair. With my fear appeased, I relaxed while the baboon meticulously went through every hair on my head. What a lovely custom! What is better than a date who brushes your hair?

My affectionate baboon finished grooming my hair and returned to hugging me bringing me an entirely new joy in connection with the wild. I felt honored by his approval, grateful for this experience. I would never forget the feel of his little hands and feet on my arm, those little fingers and nails, the warmth, and the connection that I felt sitting quietly, surrounded by the troop. I had a sense of what it was like to be a part of a baboon family and vowed to keep the small piece of harmony with nature that I felt here within me. This was truly the beginning of a new sense of awareness about my place on the planet, my responsibilities beyond my immediate family.

"Say goodbye to your friend. Get up slowly and quietly. Some of the older males are getting jealous and we need to leave now," Jenny said. Her voice sounded nervous, and a large male was coming up the hill, perhaps disgruntled by all of the attention the other male was getting.

"Goodbye, my friend. Thank you for our time together. I love you." I touched his fingers and walked away. The baboon coming up the hill intimidated me and I kept my eyes down as I tiptoed behind Jenny, leaving the baboon troop feeling exhilarated and ecstatic about my experience.

To experience this connection firsthand was to understand the need to protect our earth, to protect all creatures. "Jenni, I thank you for the most amazing experience of my life. If there is some way for me to help, please let me know. What would have happened to this troop if you hadn't followed your passion? Seems like my journey keeps putting me in front of people who are following their hearts helping the planet. That experience back there with the wild baboon made quite an impression on me."

"I want more people to understand that the baboons are much more than a nuisance," said Jenni. "Most people will never see what you just saw."

"I am honored to have gone with you. Maybe other volunteers here could take a walk with you, too."

"I would be happy to do that."

"Thank you again. I am forever grateful. If I can ever help you, I will." As I walked away, I sensed that my life was changing forever.

Hopefully, the baboon-monitoring program would always continue and the public funding meeting the next month after I left would go well. Understandably, when the troop raids garbage cans and houses making a mess, the baboons become more than a nuisance. But they are scavengers finding food in the most efficient way. Man must understand that we share the planet, and as we encroach on wildlife, we must provide for their protection. We have come too far, and know too much, to act with primitive instincts toward our wildlife protecting only the cute ones or the ones that bring us money. We have an obligation to protect all creatures we share the planet with.

The monitoring program affects people here, too. The monitors that I had met were devoted to the baboons as they kept them from raiding the villages. Johnny had worked hard here for six years walking up and down the hills after the troop with no job security. If the funding was not found, the monitors would lose their jobs and their families would lose their income. A future problem was the worry of aging for the monitors. When the monitors were too old to continue hiking all over the mountains after the baboons, they had no retirement plan, no social security to help them in their old age. South Africa, a country rich in beauty and resources, was young in developing an economy that allowed more people to have a shot at the pot of gold.

BACK AT THE HOUSE, I took a walk through my neighborhood, passing the pretty "white man" houses here in Kommetjie with the neat lawns and fences of an average neighborhood in a developed country. About a mile down the road, I passed Ocean View, the cement block houses painted in blue, pink, and green, where the "coloureds" (an apartheid term for those of mixed race) lived. Uprooted from their homes in the late 1960s, these people were forced to live in this neighborhood.

Walking another few miles from my house on the way to the Long Beach Mall, I passed the township known as Site 5, another apartheid term for the area that blacks were also forced to move to during the late 1960s. We had been advised to stay away from this area at night. As I walked by and looked in, I saw an overcrowded area with dirt roads and tiny ramshackle dwellings like the ones near the airport. Shacks without plumbing and certainly not enough room or protection from the cold, only big enough for a bed for a family to share. I could see that this represented years of prejudice. Apartheid had been incomprehensible to me, but what was going on now to improve conditions?

The volunteers had all gone on tours with Duncan, a local chap who was about 50, and I called him to take me on a tour through Site 5 and Ocean View. I wanted to understand. Duncan arrived at the volunteer house to pick me up, and it was obvious that he spent a lot of time outdoors from the leathery tan of his skin.

"I'm a surfer," he said." I surf every day here and also work on projects that help children in the area. I like to take the volunteers out to show them South Africa. We'll take a drive and I'll fill you in on our culture here."

We drove through these two areas, stopping to talk to the local people.

"You wouldn't want to walk through here on your own but the locals know me," Duncan said. Within Site 5, small stores were set up in some of the shacks for hair cuts or selling fruit and other goods. We stopped to talk to a man who was designing iron works. There was a vibrant spirit here that would have been hidden from me if I had only walked by looking at the shacks or by calling it Site 5 or by being afraid of the people inside.

"I don't know how they patiently wait for the ANC (the African National Conference political party), to help them. Duncan, it is amazing to me that this lifestyle is accepted both within and without."

"The real name for Site 5," he said, "is Masiphumelele, which in Xhosa means 'We will succeed.'"

"Why are the volunteers taught the degrading apartheid name of Site 5, not the Xhosa name and its meaning?" I asked.

"Masiphumelele is an expression of hope, of endurance dating back to the early 1980s when a group of 400-500 black people started the first informal settlement close to where Masiphumelele is today. The police chased them away telling them that they must live further away in Khayelitsha Township because of apartheid laws. When apartheid finally ended, about 8000 people from Khayelitsha and from the Eastern Cape formed their community again in 1991 at Site 5."

"Walking by wouldn't help me learn about this township of 26,000 people." I said. "The baboon monitors live here. We talked about life here while we watched the baboons."

"There is no police station in Masiphumelele and just one private doctor with a staff of nurses plus a few visiting doctors in a day care clinic. The primary school here has 1000 students and the high school more than 600. Crime, hunger, and AIDS are the major problems with an estimated infection rate of HIV/AIDS and TB at 30-40 %."

I was silent a moment after his description. Here in South Africa, Nelson Mandela came to power bringing peace, not revolution, and the people respected him and followed him. South Africa is considered a "miracle nation" because of its peaceful transition to democracy in 1994 after a brutal history of apartheid that had ruled the country since 1948.

Duncan explained, "My wife and family moved to Australia because we couldn't accept apartheid and it was very dangerous here."

"But you are here now. What happened?"

"This is my home. I wanted to be here."

"Are you scared now?"

"My house is one of the few that isn't surrounded by a tall fence. We want this country to heal."

"The patience of the blacks slowly recovering from 46 years of apartheid is something I marvel at, Duncan. I can go surfing at the beach, eat at a nice restaurant, enjoy the Cape Town waterfront, go to Boulders Beach and see a cute tourist town with adorable penguins, take a ride up Cable Mountain and completely ignore the dire poverty, the problems here. There is so much beauty to see, so many wonderful things to do that as a tourist, I might overlook the problems here. But the drastic, shocking differences in the quality of life for the people in need of decent housing sadden me."

He nodded. "With half of the population living below the poverty line, the lack of opportunity for change is discouraging. That contributes to a lot of the crime, as does the enormous unemployment rate."

I thought about my own country and her problems. The next week Americans were going to vote for the President of the most powerful country on the planet. How could it be Bush? How could we as a country believe that he was the best man to help us when we had gone backwards the last four years? How could we believe that we were safe when he was making such strange wars? How could we feel our economy would improve when it had only gotten worse? I would never understand the thinking if he got reelected.

Now as for me, where was I in all of this? I had been out in the world for four months neither working nor making money. I had not had this much freedom in my entire life! Going back to selling real estate would only do one thing: provide income. I did love the freedom that real estate gave me to roller blade, play squash, kayak, and hike when I wanted to. However, not feeling passionate about my work was no longer acceptable. If I pictured myself back at the office sitting at my desk, figuring out where to get a new listing or how to find someone the perfect house, I found myself asking why? For the luxury of making great money in trade for losing my soul? Could I remove my fear of change and create a new dream for my life filled with passion?

What would the dream be? What did I miss from my old life? I missed my sons, Joe and Dan, right now! Talking on the phone was not the same as seeing them. I felt very disconnected from their lives and though they were independent and capable, I missed cooking them a big breakfast and eating together. I wanted to ski together. Being at such a distance and out of touch with them was very difficult for me. I missed long talks with my mom, my sister, and my friend Bob, who had helped me every time I got the blues. I missed my sweet cat Harley. But I didn't want to go back to being responsible, predictable, knowing when I was going to wake up and what the day would bring as a realtor. Perhaps as

I continued to travel, the dream would unfold as my passions were free to grow. Unfold. Allow. Dream.

My last day with the baboons I waved goodbye to the troop that had given me the most amazing experience of my life. Johnny and Rodney wished me well. I left wondering what I could do to help the baboon monitor program stay funded and to keep the chacma baboon troops safe from harm. I had not been a successful monitor keeping the baboons at bay. Though my volunteering didn't help the monitors, maybe meeting an American who cared opened their eyes to another side of my country. Certainly my education about life in Site 5 had opened my eyes and my heart.

My last weekend there, Ian and Aaron and I went to the movies. Afterwards at the Internet café in the mall, I checked my email just in case Robert had written but there was nothing. With his phone number no longer working and no returned emails, I was adjusting my emotions to an ending rather than a beginning. I still had curiosity about him though and hoped that someday I would talk to him again. I didn't think he could completely forget me but only time would tell.

Most of the volunteers in this house would be heading to Johannesburg together to volunteer at the Lion Park, which we were all very excited about. I was looking forward to living with them as part of their team and we were all really excited to feed lion cubs! I flew to Johannesburg wondering what my next volunteer project would bring.

CHAPTER 11

The Lion Park in South Africa

FLYING INTO JOHANNESBURG I was afraid. Crime here was not the simple warning of "Beware, pickpockets" as it had been in Italy. Johannesburg had 5000 murders a year, twice as many rapes, and it was the carjacking capital of the world. Fear quickened my heartbeat, a nervous system already hyped-up by an overactive imagination that pictured an airport teeming with criminals ready to pounce. Okay, I chose to volunteer in this city. I tried to calm myself. On a planet with many different forms of violence, South Africa was rated the highest, and on a continent of violent cities, Johannesburg, was, so they said, the worst of all.

But John, my very tall, very buff, very white driver was waiting for me when I landed, calming my fear of imminent death. After four months of solo travel, I still had a very active imagination, which was fueled by nervous anticipation whenever I landed in a new country.

As we drove to the Lion Park, where I'd be volunteering I was shocked by the sight of another township even larger than the one around the Cape Town airport. Soweto has 3.5 million people living in shanties, many without water or electricity.

"Why are you coming to Johannesburg?" John asked.

I explained about my trip.

"You must have a lot of money to make this trip. I don't think I will ever be able to leave South Africa."

"I'm hugely grateful for this trip and my real estate business that has been good to me but I'm a long way from rich. I just decided to spend money to experience the world rather than save it. It's a huge risk that things will go all right," I replied.

I looked out the window. "I cannot get used to the shanties in these townships and in Cape Town. Does it seem impossible to find a housing solution for everyone with toilets, water, and electricity?"

"Our unemployment is high. There is no money to build houses," he said matter-of-factly.

"How do you feel about apartheid now? Isn't it about 12 years since Nelson Mandela was elected?" I asked.

"When I was young, apartheid was just something that existed, and the belief was ingrained in white young people that if the blacks came to power, communism would win over the country."

"But didn't it seem wrong to treat blacks without equality?"

"When you grow up with something, I don't know that you question it. And now all of the good jobs go to blacks. The whites don't get these jobs so everyone is suffering. Your country's election is this month. Who will win?"

"I haven't been home for four months but I'll be crushed, defeated, and angry if Bush wins."

"So then you know that what a country does and what you feel about it can be very different?"

"Ah, I get your drift there. I guess you have questions about my country too."

"I thought everyone loved Bush and what he stands for."

"No, no, definitely not loved by everyone but the outcome of the election...well, who knows."

Driving through the wealthy white northern suburbs that looked like homes from Miami Vice, I saw high walls and electric fences hiding every house from view. Signs advertised burglar alarm systems, metal grilles, and infra-red sensors. Some of the fences had barbed wire on the top while others had crushed glass embedded in the walls. The architecture of fear.

"I see all these walls topped with barbed wire and broken glass. Does this work?"

"No, it is never safe here no matter what type of fence, what type of burglar alarm system. Maybe guard dogs are the only thing. Even driving in your car, carjacking can happen. There are signs that say "Dangerous area, carjacking", and you don't have to stop at the light if no one is coming."

When we finally arrived at the Lion Park, which was located on a rolling piece of farm-sized property, I saw an enormous township directly across the street. My heart sank. I was just not sure how to reconcile my life of plenty and all of the poverty I saw.

Driving to the middle of the park, we saw four green safari tents and a short distance away a cement block building with showers, bathrooms, and a shared kitchen. Each tent had four beds with cozy duvets, and electricity for reading at night; it had the feel of camping and yet the comfort of a bed.

The volunteer grounds were completely surrounded by a thin horizontal rail fence that hardly seemed sturdy enough to keep out the wild animals that freely walk through the park. At the same time, it was a landscape straight from the movie Out of Africa. Beautiful acacia trees had their leaves eaten off at the height of a giraffe's head, jacaranda trees were full of violet blooms, and out in the distance grazing peacefully was a herd of springbok, an ostrich, a herd of zebra. I heard the distant sound of a lion's roar!

When I had found the Lion Park online, I was enthralled with the chance to feed baby lion cubs. I thought they would be small cuddly little lions to hold in my arms, something exciting but definitely not frightening. I had no idea that I would be working with lion cubs up to 6 months old. The Park is not a sanctuary for lions as none of these lions had been rescued or were endangered. All of the wildlife here were protected, loved, and cared for, but the idea behind the park was to give people an opportunity to see wildlife up close. Busloads of local children who would never get to Krueger National Park came here to learn about their country's native wildlife: lions, cheetahs, giraffes, ostriches, warthogs, hyenas, springbok, wildebeest, gemsbok, wild dogs, and more. The park also had a restaurant and a gift shop though the volunteers would all be cooking communally as we had done in Cape Town.

My friends from Komentjie were all here, but there was bad news. When they had arrived Sunday, Helga, one of the most magnetic animal trainers, a pretty young white woman in her early 20s and full of spirit, had asked the volunteers if they wanted to go with her to the cheetah enclosure. Of course, they said yes and off they went. Diane, a very capable Brit who had worked at a zoo in England as well as on farms, drove the jeep. As they entered the enclosure, Helga got out and told them all to get out even though wild cheetahs were in the enclosure. But when Diane got out from the driver's side a cheetah attacked her, biting her backside and refusing to let go. Even with those sharp teeth biting into her, Diane stayed calm trying to pry the cheetah's mouth open, saying, "He's got me." The volunteers were scared to death.

Diane ended up going to the hospital and getting nine stitches! So, when I arrived at the campsite instead of smiles, I found everyone very sad. Thank goodness, Diane was strong but her first week here was spent recovering from her injury and the trauma of the attack. Her wonderful, exuberant nature was also crushed by the attack. With her laughter gone, we were all feeling the effects of the cheetah attack. We made a pact to be extremely cautious and wary of trusting anyone at the park even when they said it was safe.

After this crazy introduction, my fear was at the forefront and lion cubs suddenly seemed very dangerous, but Jade told me that I was going to love them! Julie, Jade, Shona, and I walked to the nursery to see the youngest cubs; they were only four weeks old, little fuzz balls with cloudy blue eyes, who were unable to walk. Adorable, absolutely adorable bundles of fur! I couldn't wait to bottle-feed them. But to protect their health, we were not yet allowed to feed them.

Jade and Myra walked me over to meet the 3-4 month-old cubs, the size of a cocker spaniel but with wiry fur, alert eyes, and giant paws. As we entered the enclosure, they watched us with curiosity ready to play. Though they were small, their paws and claws still looked big to me and I was timid, but Myra happily sat down and got tackled by two of the cubs, way more contact than I was ready for!

"These are the cubs we work with. We feed them, sit with them, and play with them. There are larger cubs that we can also sit with that I'll show you next."

"Oh, these are quite big enough for now, Myra," I replied.

We spent the entire afternoon sitting with the cubs before heading back to the tent at dinner time to help cook.

We had a porch with a table outside of the kitchen where we all sat around and ate. Dinner was great fun until two giraffes walked right over the fence and headed towards us. I was petrified as they approached as I had been warned to stay away from them because they can kick forwards, sideways, and backwards. But Diane put a piece of white bread in her hand and the giraffe called Gambit lowered his head to eat, looking her right in the face. He had big dark eyes with long lashes, a black tongue attached at the front of his mouth, and an amazing coat.

Purdy and Gambit were obviously quite tame and used to visiting the volunteer kitchen for handouts. I did wonder what other wildlife could climb over our "protective" fencing.

Appreciating a cool evening after a hot day, I went to bed early and snuggled under my cozy duvet admiring the big tent and enjoying the quiet. But nighttime brought an amazing surprise...a lion concert. Lion concerts start after sunset with enormous full deep roars. I could feel the vibrations in my chest. The roar is impossible to describe, a powerful hollow sound like a baritone gone wild. I imagined his face as the King of the Jungle announced his presence. The long roar started low and then built as he opened his mouth wider, bellowing with a force and intensity that I could feel in my cozy bed. A sound of boldness, of strength! How close was he? I wondered. Another long roar, then shorter roars that gently petered out to nothing.

What was he doing? Was he having sex? I lay in bed wondering what was going on just a half-mile from where I was sleeping. Were we safe? While he was roaring, another lion began a chorus of overlapping roars. The sound of lions roaring carries five or more miles declaring for all within earshot that the lion owns the land. I lay there eyes wide open listening to every sound while figuring that a lion claw could easily ripe the canvas of the tent if he escaped. And as the night deepened, a lot of different wildlife made their presence known: hyenas, wild dogs, and other unidentifiable creatures.

I finally fell asleep. But in the early morning I awoke to munching outside the tent! I could tell that whatever it was, it was close. But what was it? The curiosity killing me, I unzipped the tent flap to see what was on the other side of my bed. Peeking around the tent, I saw four zebras grazing and an ostrich poking his head into the earth making an odd sucking sound! Who cared about sleep! I was in Africa.

After breakfast I was ready for chores but my only job there was to play with cubs. When I asked Charne, a young white woman who was also a trainer, if there was more that I could do, she replied, "We are lazy here, very slow, very lazy. You must work to learn our culture."

"No worries, I will do my best to get into this South African lifestyle!"

Thinking about the organized Monkey Sanctuary and the weekly list of chores, I felt I would have no problem adjusting to this change to a culture of laziness, especially with the heat factor. No chores, play with lions all day, and take a nap in the afternoon!

Sitting under the shade of a tree for our orientation, Ian Melass, the manager of the Lion Park, walked over to welcome us. In his 50s, a tall lean man with the weathered tan of one who has spent most of his life outdoors, his deep voice, his South African accent, and his amazing ability to tell a story had us immediately riveted on his every word. Listening to him, it was apparent he loved lions. He had spent years researching them in the wild and he mesmerized us with fascinating tales.

Ian especially loved to talk about his precious white lion. "I brought Thor, an elderly lion, from the Johannesburg zoo in 2001 to breed, but he wasn't interested in the females. So I waited and waited but still nothing. The five gorgeous lionesses all licked him and fell over him but no, he ignored them, much to my chagrin. But finally, the white lion got the idea of what he was supposed to be doing and started shagging the females. And yes, now there is a happy ending with white lion cubs.

There are only about 2700 lions left to roam free in South Africa. Most of them live in Kruger National Park but bovine tuberculosis is a growing threat there to the lions. If you go, you may see some of the lions affected with this disease. Their fur is in terrible shape, and they are thin. Lions in the wild live for up to 12 years but lions in captivity live twice that. They are fed and loved here. If you talk to my lions, they'll tell you that they're never going to leave!"

He smiled at us. "I'm so privileged," he said. "Not many people get up in the morning and love what they do. But I'm cautious. You can't just walk around these lions like you are taking a stroll on the beach. Lions are very forgiving. They will warn you a couple of times if they have had enough of something. If you listen, there is no harm. But you must always be listening, always alert.

"Every day I go and talk to my lions to see how they are and to make sure they know that I love them. One night I was working in my office and one of the lions escaped his enclosure (Escaped? Do I want to know this?). He wandered to my office to say hello. There he was filling the doorway and I was alone. I was alone and afraid but I talked to him and then we walked back to his enclosure."

Ian has been working with lions for a long, long time and listening to him was like listening to someone talk about dear friends.

"You are welcome to join me when I go talk to the lions but I can only take a few of you."

From then on whenever Ian drove into the enclosures, we all tried to tag along to watch him and listen to his stories.

One of our best chores was the jungle walk where we marched the 4-month-old cubs from the nursery down into the park. As we walked along, they would run after us getting into a bit of mischief along the way, playing in the garden area, tackling each other, or investigating the grounds.

We sat on the ground watching them eat but I was still wary of them. One came to my lap to cuddle like a giant version of my cat Harley! Rather afraid and timid, I stroked his fur, which was thick and coarse, and when he flipped over, his belly was soft and warm.

"Let him suck your finger, Joyce." Myra said showing me how.

"Really?"

"Yeah, it feels cool."

The lion cub looked at me with sweet eyes but suddenly the sweetness left and in its place was pure mischief. He was ready to play rough, pouncing on a stick and wrestling with his brother.

Myra, Jade, and I spotted Ian and we hurried over to talk to him. "Are you going out to the lions? We want to listen to your stories."

"Okay, quietly, quietly," he said. "Let's go talk to the lions. Don't tell anyone we are going. I will take the rest of the volunteers tomorrow. Quick, let's go!"

And off we ran to his buggy driving through the gates right up to a large beautiful male, his thick mane surrounding his regal face. Ian stopped the car and took a spray bottle full of a liquid that keeps the flies off of their heads. Trainers raised the lions in this enclosure.

"Hello, the lion. And how are you today?"

The lion with his huge mane, enormous head, and enormous feet, just looked at Ian as if to say "Hi, old friend, good to see you."

I was in awe.

Ian walked right over, sprayed him, and scratched his head! Truly, he scratched his head and patted his body. Friends with an adult lion! After their chat, Ian drove a bit further to talk to more of his lions.

Did the lions feel as we did about this charismatic man? Was it his voice, his temperament?

We drove to the enclosure where the wild lions lived.

"That lion is Big Boy. A couple of years ago Big Boy ate two tourists! An Asian couple got out of their car thinking the lions were either drugged or tame and approached Big Boy to take a close photo. Big Boy answered by killing the man, gnawing off his leg and dragging the woman off to kill her too."

"No, that can't be true, Ian."

He nodded. "I'll show you the photo."

Later in Ian's office, I saw the gruesome photo of the chewed-up bodies.

But now Ian was calling Big Boy over to us for a spray on his ears. "It's a hot day. The female he is with is in estrus but maybe he will come see us. The only time lions and lionesses are together are during mating. They will mate every 20-30 minutes for two to three days until the estrus cycle is over, exhausting the male," explained Ian.

No wonder lions need to sleep up to 20 hours a day!

We then drove to the spotted hyena encampment. Kevin, the assistant manager at the park an athletic-looking fellow with dark hair, was sitting down talking to three hyenas, three wild hyenas! A man face to face with this ferocious beast that could chomp his leg off in one bite. Some say the spotted hyena have the strongest jaws of all mammals. Yet here he was rubbing the female's back and tummy and putting his face right in the hyena face for a cuddle!

I held my breath.

"These hyenas are very smart, very misunderstood," Kevin explained. "They are female dominant with an interesting twist by Mother Nature."

He showed us the dangling clitoris, which looked just like a penis and balls on each female. Some joke by nature, perhaps to test out what a female dominated animal group would be like. Add a fake penis and you get to lead the group? It seems to work. Spotted female hyenas are vicious, even killing their brothers or sisters immediately after birth!

We drove to Ian's beloved white lions. A pride of pure white lions was stretched out in the sunshine, a breathtaking vision.

"They look spiritual, Ian," I said.

"Yes, indeed, they are named for spiritual things."

Words like "of the gods" and "mystical" convey only a partial sense of the feeling of seeing them. It was as if I were in a dream. They were inspiring. Beyond description. The pure white color. Their inherent power. These white lions bridge the gap between nature and God.

"Ian, it feels almost religious being here in their presence. Does that sound strange?"

"No, you are experiencing the beauty of nature and how it connects to your spirit."

"Is that what nature brings to us? God, faith, dreams, wonder and the sense that we are a small part of the earth?"

"In the eyes of these creatures we see simplicity, love, and the wild unspoiled."

I thought about this for a moment and said, "And by trusting and being with wildlife, I can better know myself, honor nature and feel love."

In my recognition of the beauty of trees, the sunset, in each moment I care for a garden, a baby animal, I think I am coming closer to my true nature and closer to what God or spirit wants me to feel here on earth. Man uses nature like a tube of toothpaste, giving her a squeeze when more resources are needed with little thought to protecting her. How can we not notice our carelessness? How do we miss the connection between our planet and ourselves?

I looked at the enigmatic white lions and knew that my life could not just be about taking care of my sons and myself but rather about a more conscious protection of the earth and her resources.

At the next enclosure Ian stood at the fence and the lions jumped up to kiss him: love between a man and lion.

"Go ahead, do it as well," he said. "The lions will kiss you, too."

With my heart pounding but trusting Ian, we all leaned our faces on the fence. A full-grown lion jumped up and his rough tongue glided up my cheek from the other side of the fence. Licked by a lion. Absolutely amazing!

Another day after our morning duties were finished, Helga surprised us by saying that she wanted to take the cubs and Homer, the hyena, for a walk. I was really curious how we would do that. She told us to load up into the minivan. The minivan?

Six of us got in although we were still cautious after Diane's experience. We drove to get the bigger cubs and Homer. Helga opened the doors to the van and the six lion cubs, the 5- and 6-month-old cubs, the size of golden retrievers but with much bigger paws—and claws, jumped into the van with us! It was totally insane! No wee little cutsy cubs here. A minivan with six volunteers and six lion cubs jumping all over excited to be going for a walk. Homer, the hyena, was on a leash in the front seat. Completely surreal!

I sat way in the back hoping no lion cubs would find me. I was still getting used to being around the older cubs. Wrong! The lion cubs were too excited to sit down and buckle their seat belts. They jumped over the seats, from seat to seat, from the front of the van to the back. It was pandemonium! I leaned over covering my head in my lap saying silent prayers. But the lions thought I meant it was time for a game of leap frog over my back. They all started jumping over me! Thank goodness we finally got to the walking area.

"Just start walking down that path and the cubs will follow. Their instinct is to stay with the pride," Helga said. Sure enough, we walked and they followed. Sweet lion cubs going for a walk with Homer, the hyena. We walked for a little while and then stopped and rested while the lions jumped over each other. Homer played with all of them.

While they were playing, Helga spotted a giraffe in the distance. "We need to walk the cubs back to the van. See that giraffe? The cubs will run after it out of instinct and could get kicked. Let's walk quickly back to the van."

Earlier I had had quite an experience with the giraffe. Purdy had been very naughty eating the leaves off the trees right near the lion enclosure. Because visitors to the park were nearby and someone could get kicked, Purdy was supposed to stay in the fenced area but apparently she was hungry or curious. Jones, one of the keepers, tried to scare her into going away but that just made her run in crazy circles dangerously close to the visitors. Next he went to the kitchen for white bread but when she was full of bread, she walked back over to her favorite trees. Jones was totally frustrated and left to get three more people to help him round her up. They were shushing her along rather nicely getting closer to the gate but she had a change of mind and bolted, running with her legs flying in all directions. Charne and I ducked quickly behind a tree.

Charne and I tried to get Purdy's attention but she was deep into a thorn tree, her favorite, and not interested in white bread. Three maintenance men came to help and it looked like they were going to get it done. All three men were behind her walking her forward. She looked like she was going in and then, one more time, she bolted and ran around scattering everyone again. I don't know if giraffes have a sense of humor but this was all hysterical to watch! She found Charne behind a tree and ran around the tree after her!

Finally when she calmed down, I thought I'd try the bread one more time. I raised my hand with the bread and slowly walked to her gate calling her name. Purdy, the very naughty giraffe, followed me like she had not caused any trouble at all. Once she got in her enclosure I fed her the bread, but she had the last laugh. Looking up too late, I noticed a long slobber of giraffe saliva drooling out of her mouth, a long string of the stickiest, slimmest piece of saliva floating out of her mouth into the air landing all over my face. Yuk! I started dancing around trying to get it off but it was sticky, nasty stuff and when I tried to wipe it on my sleeve. it spread all over. It was everywhere. Jade, who was watching me, started laughing so hard she cried as I jumped around, making faces and noises and swiping at my face. I picked Jade up from where she had fallen over from laughing too hard.

WITH ANOTHER COLD coming on, my birthday coming up, and a Brazilian visa needed for my next stop, I decided to go to the Brazilian embassy in Pretoria. I could spend the weekend relaxing at a hotel with ironed sheets, fluffy pillows, and a bathtub. After a thorough birthday pampering including a bubble bath, a facial, and a pedicure, I went to a restaurant to eat kingklip fish that was fried like fish and chips.

As I ate my lovely dinner under the restaurant awning, huge raindrops started falling, loud thunder cracked, and lightning streaked across the sky! The smell of the fresh air was invigorating and I ran to my hotel before it started again. And start again it did. Lighting, thunder, and torrid rain pelted us for five hours. Everything in South Africa is extreme. But I hoped this rain would end the drought at the Lion Park. When I left there, we had run out of water in the showers and bathroom. Hopefully that situation would be fixed as eight women without showers or a toilet was not a good thing, not a good thing at all. But back in my hotel bed, I only heard city noises and I tossed and turned. I missed the lions' roar.

In bed I thought about my birthday. I am having a birthday in South Africa by myself where I had opened the giant present of freedom. Celebrating my life and feeling really proud of myself for taking this trip. Happy Birthday, Joyce! You did it!

I could do whatever I want now....truly. I didn't need to please anyone. I could pay attention to what I wanted and learn new things. My birthday present was to live my life exactly as I wanted to. It didn't have to look good from the outside. It didn't have to be what anyone expects of me. I could find my own music and play it. The poetry of my soul.

It is so easy to follow the herd, which has such a strong pull. I am okay because the person next door is doing the same thing as me and he's okay and on and on and on. So, who is okay? Who is living life to their fullest and how did they get there? How do I break the chains when I can't even see them? How do I become the unexpected? Wind blowing through trees. Each country uncovering a part of myself.

Tonight at dinner the waitress asked me, "Would you ever come back to South Africa? What do you think of it?"

"Everything feels very alive to me here and direct but I have a hard time with the townships. At the same time, I love the wildlife."

"Oh, we take both for granted and don't even notice them," she said.

I went on to explain how I was feeling: "I would have to adjust to the organization here or the lack of it. It seems to me that a problem does not get a logical organized solution. Sometimes it gets solved and sometimes it doesn't though I've really only been two places in your entire country."

"Yes," she said "Yes, if there is a problem, we would rather just go get a drink. We are lazy."

"I have heard this word many times here used by South Africans to describe themselves. I wonder what it would be like to live where saying 'we are lazy' with a smile is just fine. Right now I miss the lions roaring and hyenas barking, and want to go back to the Lion Park."

I arrived to big smiles back at the Lion Park and joined Shona, Jade, and Diane to go watch the Ireland-South Africa rugby game, my first, at a nearby bar that had 30 TVs and a movie-theater-sized screen. Jade taught me the rules of rugby by filling me in on plays and telling me which guys she thought were hot.

"I had no idea rugby was such a great game with so many handsome chaps. I wonder if there is a senior league in Seattle." I said.

Later, a very drunk man asked me to go to his car with him, which made us all laugh.

After a disappointing loss to Ireland, most of the South Africans went home but we stayed and sat at a table with three brothers from Joburg. One had been dreaming of coming to Seattle for the head-bangers convention in October.

John, one of our tablemates, said, "I have a plumbing company that has five employees. One of them just died this year from pneumonia, which is the polite way of saying AIDS, and no one in the company even knew he was sick. And another of my employees was a black man, who was doing well, not a big success, still living in the shanties but starting to accumulate things, and then some of the people in the township killed him and burned his place down. They just couldn't deal with his success!"

I didn't know how to respond.

"I am upset about both of these," he went on. "One that I didn't even know my friend was dying of AIDS. It is an epidemic that no one wants to look at here."

With one out of four having the disease, he was right.

"My other sadness is that a man was killed for being successful."

I appreciated his openness which I had found was a big part of the South African culture. Not politically correct as in Seattle but real feelings and opinions. The straightforward honesty was refreshing.

We were ready to head home but at that late hour, no safe cabs were available. I decided to approach two couples who were having a beer to see if they knew a safe taxi company. The woman took out her phone and called for us.

"It will be 300 rand to make the trip," she said, "which is a complete rip-off. Are you okay with staying for another hour or so and we will drive you home?"

"Wow that would be great!"

"Well, let us buy you a beer and some Jägermeister shots to welcome you to Joburg."

Nick, the chattiest one, asked, "How did the four of you get together here as you are obviously different ages?"

We explained our volunteer project, which he found amazing!

Robin, the woman sitting across from me, asked, "How are you enjoying South Africa?"

"I find this a fascinating country with extremes beyond my comprehension, a raw power here, an edge but a straightforwardness that is very appealing. Where I am from people are not as direct. I appreciate the honesty of feelings here."

"We are the only country that has not had a civil war given the situation that has arisen. It would have been quite easy to have a war given the horror of apartheid and the hate from the past. When Nelson Mandela came to power, he said it was not time to linger in the past but to work together for the future of a bright and healthy South Africa."

"The passion and love for your country is beautiful to hear about."

"Where are you headed next?"

"I am going to Brazil," I said and then explained about my trip.

One of the women who had been very quiet just looked at me and said, "That is so amazing that you are doing this trip all by yourself. I think it is so wonderful. You are amazing and brave and I wish you so much luck on your journey."

Nick said, "I'll take all of you home if we are ready now."

THE YOUNGEST CUBS were now 6 weeks old and we were finally allowed to bottle feed them! All of us wanted to cuddle these adorable little cubs in our laps and feed them like babies. They were soft and sweet and holding a cub in my lap while he suckled the bottle was a beautiful experience. Between bottles, they licked us with big wet milk kisses that none of us could refuse. Thank goodness they needed lots of bottle feedings. I was completely smitten and spent hours with them letting them climb all over me.

One evening around 10 pm, we heard screams, horrible wildlife death screams coming from the park. An overwhelming fear gripped me. I ran to the park with Jade, Diane, and Kathleen, tears falling from my eyes listening to the terrifying screams. Though uncertain what was happening, we knew that the sound was coming from a killing somewhere. The screams were gut-wrenching. Following them, we arrived at the brown hyena enclosure where two hyenas, who had just been moved in together, were continuing a fight from the day before. The wounded hyena lying down in the dirt in agony was unable to move, her leg shredded. The dominant female stalked her, moving in for the kill, slowly crouching, head down, piercing eyes, the stance of a predator. These two hyenas should not have been in an enclosure together; even I knew the fight was inevitable between a stronger and weaker one.

Out of fear I yelled at the attacking hyena, screaming at it to stop the fighting. I was frightened that the wounded hyena would be killed. I put every bit of dominance into my yell like some wild ferocious animal, a sound from my depths that I didn't recognize. Miraculously, the dominant female backed away. Soon, Jade and Diane were standing by me and then Given, a trainer from the park, came out of his house aroused by the ruckus.

But Given said, "We cannot move the injured hyena till morning."

"But, Given," I said, "what if she is attacked and killed?"

He shook his head. "There is nothing we can do till morning."

I stood there feeling helpless. We were all crying. None of us knew what to do next. We decided to go back to our tents knowing we would be right back here if we heard another scream. We all said prayers through the night to save the hyena and by some miracle, there was no more fighting.

In the morning the injured hyena was moved to our nursery to heal her leg. She looked exactly like the big bad wolf in Little Red Riding Hood with her enormous head. Her legs were striped in black and white and she had a yellow collar of long fur around her neck. Her eyes were sad as she sat in the nursery alone most days while her foot healed. I stuck my fingers in between the wire to pet her long, bristly coat. Having watched Kevin talk to her, I tried talking to her in the squeaky voice that Kevin used and slipped her small pieces of liver throughout the day. I found out that Jade was doing the same thing!

Later when Kevin was checking on her he said, "Joyce, get her some ribs for dinner."

I told Charne, the trainer, about the ribs.

"Well, let's go pick up the meat now," she said, hopping into the truck to drive to the butcher's shack where the flies zoomed around continually. Picking up meat for the cubs was the grossest job at the park.

When we arrived, the butcher with hatchet in hand was carving up a dead horse, blood splattered over his apron and oozing over the ground. Horses that are close to dying from old age are donated by farmers in the area. The sight of the carved-up horse, the smell, and the swarming flies made me wretch.

"Joyce, are you okay?"

"Yea, yea, I'm okay. But I can't stand over there. Sorry."

The butcher put slabs of meat, liver and ribs into large buckets in the back of the truck. I vowed to become a vegetarian. Back at the nursery, I had the slicing job, which was beyond the worst job I could ever imagine.

I asked Diane to help me. When we started cutting up the slippery raw liver, a big, bluish piece of slime, we were both so completely grossed out that all we could do was laugh.

But back at our volunteer site, we discovered that we were without hot water. No showers! But after my nasty butcher job, I didn't care about hot water. I was hot and sweaty, a dirty mess of cub smells and horse blood. Freezing under the ice water shower, I scrubbed my body clean.

JADE, THE VOLUNTEER from Ireland who was studying to be a vet, asked me to make a traditional Thanksgiving dinner! We invited people from the park, 23 in all, and each volunteer got a job helping. Almost all of the meat in South Africa is barbequed and so the only oven we had was the tiny one in the volunteer kitchen, which was just big enough for a small turkey. Shona and I went shopping for all of the food including two small turkeys and found everything, even little jars of cranberries. We decided to eat at the enormous table at the park Braai, the South Africa word for barbeque, a large area with a big deck and a covered pavilion with a thatched straw roof.

No one in South Africa had a clue as to what Thanksgiving was all about. "Is it for presents?" "Is it religious?" "Are there prayers?" "What kind of music do you play during Thanksgiving?" And no one here knew what turkey tasted like.

Our Thanksgiving menu in South Africa included two turkeys, mashed potatoes, sweet potatoes, green beans, carrots, corn, and rolls with pumpkin pie, apple pie, and two South African desserts from Helga's future mother-in-law. The whole park was excited about the feast.

Shona and I cooked the first turkey in the morning at our camp kitchen, and when it was done, we started the next one. But in the middle of our cooking extravaganza, the volunteers came by and said they were going to take the lions for a walk. Shona and I jumped at the chance to get out of the kitchen and hopped into the back of the truck with five lions. How comfortable I was now with these lions and what an unusual break from cooking Thanksgiving dinner!

When the turkeys were done, we moved everything up to the big restaurant kitchen and since everyone was pitching in, our progress was smooth. The table design was gorgeous with flowers and an artistic wire giraffe that Jade had made and lovely place settings. We put everything out on a buffet but before we ate, we had a surprise.

Purdy, the giraffe, who never wanted to miss a party, decided to come for Thanksgiving dinner! So we ate deviled eggs and cheese and crackers with a huge giraffe looking on. My first Thanksgiving with a giraffe.

Sihke, one of the black South Africans who worked at the gift shop, had arranged for music during our meal because music is a part of all of their celebrations. Everyone went through the buffet line piling their plates full of food like they knew the Thanksgiving tradition of eating too much. Once everyone was seated, Jones asked us all to rise and he said grace in his own language, Xhosa. And then the eating began. I was going to stop everyone and explain the history of Thanksgiving but I was hungry and ready to just relax. Yet I wanted to share a part of our traditions and I asked everyone to tell something that they were thankful for. As I sat at the end of the table watching everyone eating and enjoying themselves and listening to their stories of gratitude, I felt very grateful indeed.

After dinner, Able, one of my favorite workers at the park, came to say thank you. "I am honored to be invited here. Big Mama knows how to cook."

He had a big beautiful smile with one front tooth missing. He was my age and every time there was something wrong at the tents, I would go find him and ask for his help. He would smile at me, then fix it. If I keep one memory with me, it will be of Able and his smile. I think it starts from deep inside and by the time it comes out, he lights up the sky. When I asked him how it shone so brightly, he explained to me that he was happy now, not worrying about tomorrow. The beauty of a sincere smile. The simplicity of his happiness. A lesson repeated for me here in South Africa: the beauty of living in the moment. My smile needed to improve permanently!

We all finished eating and the black South Africans immediately got up to start dancing. They danced with rhythm and moves that were impossible to copy. We all tried our version of this great rhythmic dancing but I for one could not get my hips loose enough to move the right way. Finally, we danced enough to make room for dessert. The South African desserts that Helga's boyfriend's mom had made were delicious, a yummy cake-like baked pudding with vanilla pudding to pour on top and a cold yogurt dessert. When we finished, we danced again. The music of South Africa combined perfectly with American Thanksgiving dinner and even Purdy liked it!

Beautiful, beautiful South Africa. One night, inside my tent looking out at the hills and the fields, I heard a thunderstorm rumbling loudly with just a few drops of rain to show for all the noise. With the tent window shades rolled up, the sounds of the storm surrounded us with loud cracks of lightning, rolling thunder, and then the crash of another strike of lightning. The inside of the tent lit up with each strike of lightning, which sounded really close to our tent, and cast a light on the springbok herds grazing over the range. A breeze blew through my tent. I was in love with all that I saw around me. Overwhelmed by nature's beauty. A herd of wildebeest galloped past moving to higher ground before the rains came. The zebra herd had just gone past as well. The air was suddenly fresh and cool after a very hot day. A crack of thunder. The ostrich was meandering around outside. The rain started, and the wind furiously swept the plains. A huge herd of blesbok ran past. Wow, I was lying in my bed watching the Discovery Channel outside my tent as the wind whipped our door flaps around, I thought about how everything in South Africa is extreme.

I loved South Africa. I wanted to remember the extremes that are here: nothing smoothed over, life, death, rich, poor, heat, coolness, the most beautiful smiles and strong souls like those of the lions. I was sad to be leaving the land, the people, and the beautiful lions that recognized me now, wanting to play or sit in my lap. I felt peaceful when I sat with the lions in a new unfamiliar way. It felt like I belonged here. But I would be leaving in two days and I cried thinking about leaving the beautiful lions.

How do I explain what I have found in South Africa at the Lion Park? A combination of the people working at the park, the lion cubs, and our great group of volunteers. I knew that I was looking forward to feeding the lion cubs when I signed up for this project, but I had no idea I would find so much joy here each day. When I went to see the little cubs, they would come over to jump in my lap and then crawl on our heads with sweet licks. The older cubs all came running to the gate to greet me, talk to me, and lick my hands. Love here in many different forms.

We volunteers had "endured" not having a phone or computer except at the distant mall, running out of water during the dry spell, broken hot water pipes, no roof over the shower and kitchen building when a wind storm came through, all with very few complaints. Our group of volunteers was tight and we had a reunion planned for next year when I would be in Ireland.

The last night at my going-away party, Rodney, a keeper I had laughed with many times, came to wish me well, giving me a hug and a South African handshake. Looking me straight in the eye, he said, "Continue to make everyone smile as you travel the world. You make everyone smile." He hugged me again. His words went straight to my heart, to my time here.

Early on my last day, I took a walk to say goodbye to the lions and walked away crying. When my ride came, I left everyone in tears. I was so sad to be leaving. My heart was full of lions and volunteers and Able's smile from living in the moment. But it was time to head to Rio for Portuguese lessons, a conservation project and a South America adventure!

CHAPTER 12

Conservation and Portuguese Lessons in Brazil

SHOCKING CHANGES. No transition from South Africa to South America except a long plane ride. Leaving customs in Rio, the passenger exit was lined with screaming taxi drivers who all seemed to want to reach out their long tentacles and grab me.

I searched the boards for my name. Where was my ride? Shit! How was I supposed to pick out the one taxi that wouldn't rob me? I didn't even know how much it would cost or where I was going besides the address and the area of town, Lago de Marchado. And it was nighttime!

With eyes down, my back pack wobbling, and a "Don't fuck with me" look, I left the street and found a quiet bathroom to settle myself down from my usual case of new country anxiety. Breathe, Joyce. Okay, my ride was not here. I hoped that everything was okay with my host family.

Taking another deep breath, I entered the chaos that was my new home, Rio de Janiero looking for a taxi. A young handsome clean-cut man my son's age dressed in a perfectly ironed yellow oxford cloth shirt, came up to me and said politely in English, as he would to his mom, "Do you need a taxi?"

Immediately calming down, I said, "Yes, here is the address I am going to. How much will it cost?"

He quoted me an amount that sounded fair and I followed him out to the street, got into a cab for the 30-minute night drive through Rio.

Arriving at night was always miserable and dangerous, a lesson that I would remember on future travels. The driver slowed down and then pulled over, saying something in Portuguese, which is close to Spanish but NOT Spanish. I looked out the window. Storefronts and a few streetlights. Nothing that looked at all like a condominium.

I sat scrunching my shoulders to my ears, hands in the air, head tilted with a puzzled look on my face, the international sign for "huh?" I was not getting out in the dark to put on my backpack and find this place. Figuring that he had a stubborn woman in the backseat, he got out of the cab and grabbed my backpack. I followed him like a little chick after her mother through a wrought-iron door down a dark wide hall to a door where he buzzed my host family and said something in Portuguese. He held up 10+1 fingers for the 11th floor, and I opened the door to my new life, which began with a slow ride up a small dark elevator with doors that opened onto a dark hall.

As my eyes adjusted to the dark, a door opened, shedding light into the corridor and silhouetting the figures of my host family, who were welcoming me in Portuguese.

"Boa vinda a nossa coass. Vindo dentro." They did not speak English. I did not yet speak any Portuguese.

"Obrigado" I said. "Thank you"

We smiled a lot. My host family was Alzira and Renato, a petite couple in their 70s. Alzira, her grey hair pulled back, wore a print dress and Renato was well-dressed in a short-sleeved shirt and trousers. Caio, their 40-something bachelor son, equally petite and with an equally warm smile, lived with his family and would until he married, the custom here. Marina, their adorable 9-year-old granddaughter seemed shy.

Everyone was tiny, less than 5' tall. At 5'9", I felt like an enormous Gulliver entering the land of the Lilliputians.

Alzira was holding Chuppa, a small scruffy dog with long tangled golden fur, and having just come from lion cubs I reached out my hand to pet him. Chuppa jumped into action fighting hard to escape Alzira's arms, his old dark broken teeth appearing behind snarling lips. He was ready to bite my hand off.

Quickly pulling my hand back I said, "Ah, meshugina."

"Tenha cuidado. Meu cão é porcas e tentará mordê-lo. Eu sou pesaroso," Alzira told me.

I shrugged my shoulders, able to understand only the few words that sounded like Spanish. She went to get a small slip of paper with the following message,

"Be careful. Chuppa the dog is dangerous and will try to bite you if you come near him."

"Ah," I say, "meshugina."

Besides the living room and dining area, there were three bedrooms and we all shared the bathroom. My bedroom had a twin bed, a closet, and a TV with a view of my new city neighborhood. Alzira walked me into the kitchen saying,

"Eu farei seus pequeno almoço e jantar. Você não necessita ajudar com qualquer coisa dentro aqui. Eu lavarei também toda sua roupa."

"Entiendo un poco de espanol. No entiendo Portuguese. Lo siento." I said in Spanish.

"Você deve somente falar o português, Joyce. Nao espanhol." she said disciplining me to only speak Portuguese.

Seeing that I did not understand her and still holding on to the crazy mutt, she used hand signals to explain to me that she would do all the cooking and wash my clothes.

"Obrigado."

Without the ability to speak, I signaled back that I wanted to unpack my backpack and go to sleep.

My first night in Rio I looked out my window at the city lights feeling the heat from the city wrap around my body like a heavy cloak. The ceiling fan barely moved the hot, humid, heavy air around my room. Lying in bed, my sweaty body sticking to the sheets, I listened to the sounds of the street outside, the cars, buses, and scooters. Where were the sounds of the Lion Park? I closed my eyes longing for lions roaring in the cool South African night.

WHEN I FIRST DECIDED to go to Brazil, it was to volunteer at an herbal medicine farm where I would learn about herbs and work at the farm. But they didn't respond to any of my emails and I was afraid that they were too poorly organized. At the last minute, I switched to a conservation project in Rio that included the study of Portuguese, which I saw as a test of my brain's ability to still pick up foreign words and accents. I didn't want to be one of the 93% of Americans who spoke only English. Besides Rio had always held a fascination for me. I was an avid watcher of carnivale on TV, I listened to samba music, and of course, I wanted to see the beaches. It felt exotic. I wanted to dance.

My month in Rio would be spent taking Portuguese lessons every morning for three hours and then working on a conservation project in the Tijuca National Park, which was on the edge of the city. Scheduled to begin classes in the morning that marked the beginning of the sixth month of my journey, I could hardly believe that I had been traveling work-free for five months and was now on my third continent.

Morning in Rio brought a cold shower. I waited for the water to heat up. I turned the dial in different directions but no, this was ice cold water and if I wanted a shower, I was going in. Is there anything more shocking than ice cold water on a hot body? Perhaps they had heard about the American custom of long hot showers and were keeping my time in the one bathroom short! Well, my journey was about new experiences and testing my flexibility and so far I had not had a hot shower at any of my projects. Let's go, Joyce, adjust!

Alzira had breakfast on the table for me and it was definitely a south-of-the-equator treat: fresh mango, a papaya smoothie, fresh bread, coffee, and a bit of cheese. I was in tropical heaven. The mango and papaya tasted like there were just taken off a tree. Little did I know that every morning Alzira would make me a different smoothie: mango, papaya, pineapple, banana, and my favorite, avocado.

"Você gostam do leite com seu café? Você quer mais do que este? Você gostam de mangoes? Como você dormiu? Eu sou assim que feliz você é ouve-se. Você comprende qualquer coisa que eu estou dizendo. Não se preocupe, logo você."

Wondering what she was saying, I tilted my head like a dog does when his master is talking.

"Mas lente por favor," I said hoping my Spanish for "slow down, please" would work.

"Mais lento por favor. Repita o que eu digo."

Ah, okay, she wanted me to repeat what she said and so my Portuguese lessons began with my 30 minute breakfast.

Alzira was a bundle of energy. Every morning for a month Alzira and I sat at the table while she watched me eat. She chattered away in Portuguese, patiently hoping that soon I would understand her. Alzira taught me that coffee was *café*. No more bread. *Não mais pão.* This drink is delicious. *Esta bebida são deliciosos.*

Chuppa rested at her feet and if I moved mine too quickly, he growled. I was pretty sure that I could boot him across the room if he came after my toes, which were exposed like sitting ducks in my sandals, but I couldn't believe that he would growl at me all month! After all lions, baboons, and monkeys seemed to like me. Little did I know that Chuppa was patiently plotting an attack on my big toe, just waiting for the right moment!

That first morning, Alzira explained that she would ride the subway with me and show me the school, which was great news as I had no idea where I was in downtown Rio. When we walked outside into my new neighborhood, the street was hopping, Rio chaos, and I was glad that my "mom" was with me. Vendors lined both sides of the sidewalk selling jewelry, hair bobs, shoes, CDs, chotchkes, and underwear either from a table or right on the ground. There were beggars all over the streets. A man with no legs was sitting on a small board with wheels attached selling and fixing shoes all day. Unable to take it all in, I was glad when we ducked into the subway entrance with the rush of commuters. Alzira motioned to me to keep a firm hand on my small pack as we entered the surprisingly clean and air-conditioned subway car, but I felt totally safe inside.

We exited the subway station into downtown Rio. Although skyscrapers blocked the sun, the heat hit me hard in the face and my senses were overloaded with smells from food stands and a whiff of stale urine from off the pavement. A cram of people from beggars to immaculately dressed businessmen filled the sidewalk. There were roaring buses, cars, and taxis, and everywhere someone was selling something. I was surrounded by Portuguese words, unable to either understand or talk. It was like being on some crazy Disneyland reality ride. The weather was humid enough to make my usually straight hair curly and to give my skin that permanent sticky feeling reminiscent of growing up in Illinois. I immediately noticed that everyone had a built in, sexy, rhythmic walk. Did the samba play internally for all of these people? Brazilian hips moved with freedom. If I followed someone, would I learn this hip walk thing too?

SCHOOL WAS INTENSE. Laura, a clever, fun-loving woman in her 30s from DC was in my class, and we laughed at ourselves continually. Val, a gorgeous woman in her late 20s and full of enthusiasm, was our instructor. From the moment we walked in until we left the building, we were not allowed to speak English, which considering that we knew no Portuguese was actually a form of mental torture.

My brain was living in Portuguese boot camp and screaming for help. My instructor demanded 100 pushups. Listen to new sounds, repeat them and form sentences. Speak Portuguese, not English, not Spanish. My first day of immersion took me to my knees. It was like learning to swim by diving into the deep end. My face was tired from all the facial expressions I used to communicate frustration, exasperation, laughter, and eye-rolling. Three hours of repeating words, listening, and staying focused.

Because my conservation project was not organized, my afternoons were now free. The head of the school told me to be patient. I was disappointed by the lack of organization and hoped it would improve. I didn't want a month of only Portuguese classes. I had picked this project to combine conservation work with learning a language in a city I had always been curious about. I was surprised that they were so poorly organized as the website had convinced me otherwise.

But there wasn't a problem to find a solution for free time. Laura and I jumped at the chance to go to the beach. We had hit it off immediately. I had been dying to see Copacabana and Ipanema since the mid-1960s when "The Girl from Ipanema" hit the radio waves. We arrived at Copacabana, an enormous beach with million dollar hotels and condominiums on Avenida Atlântica, a four-lane street with fast moving traffic. A cross between the beaches of Miami and southern California, this four-kilometer long beach had beautiful white sand and lots of action. Rollerblading, jogging, walking. and vendors selling things. *Futevolei,* a lightning-fast volleyball game using only feet, soccer, and a fast paddle-ball game. Music. Sugar Loaf Mountain and Christ the Redeemer.

Walking the beach looking for a good spot to soak in the sun and the atmosphere, I couldn't stop humming "tall and tan and young and lovely, the girl from Ipanema goes walking." I had always wanted to see this beach. Paranoid that my imperfect body would be an embarrassment for me compared to the gorgeous Brazilian women, I was pleased to find that it just wasn't so. Every shape was here at the beach and perfectly comfortable in their thong bikinis. Breasts were covered but cheeks exposed. I chuckled.

"Does every country have a favorite part of the female anatomy?" I asked Laura.

Cheeks smeared with suntan lotion were shining in the sunlight and bouncing along in small, medium, large and extra large getting a tan. The attitude here was liberating. Every woman wore a thong but Laura and me.

"Laura," I said, "I think I'm going to need to rework my body awareness here and my bum appreciation and be more accepting and stop being so self-conscious. If I got used to being topless in Greece, I guess I can change to a string up my bum and my cheeks getting a tan here in Brazil! Maybe tomorrow I will buy a new suit. What do you think?"

"Well, it looks like vendors who walk along the beach sell them. Maybe you could buy one right here!"

"Well, we are a dead giveaway as tourists with these cumbersome bottoms on! I feel conspicuous with my butt covered up!" I told Laura laughing.

The local guys wore skimpy Speedos as they did in Greece leaving no room for the imagination.

"I'm still not used to men in Speedos. I guess it's a cultural thing and it will take some getting used to before I think of it as sexy. Truth in advertising if you know what I mean. Are we the only country that has baggy swim trunks for men?"

"Good question. There is some nice scenery here though." Laura said, looking at a group of handsome fit men.

We sat down on lounge chairs and immediately ordered a caipirinha, the Brazilian national drink recommended by Ruarik, one of our teachers. It combines *cachaca,* a cane sugar liquor, sugar, and lime with sunshine. The second we hit the sand every peddler in the area converged on us and that meant constant shopping.

"Laura, if we trade in our swimsuits for thongs, they won't know we are tourists! They'll think we're Cariocas!"

Ruark had explained the term *Cariocas,* the name for people living in Rio. He had also warned us to watch for thieves at the beach.

"Well, with your dark skin, you look like a Carioca but I'm white as white and blonde. No way tan or no tan."

But after the second caipirinha, which had been brought to our lounge chairs, we were happy to meet everyone selling anything.

"I think my Portuguese is improving speaking to the vendors with the help of these drinks," I said.

"Yea, they're great!" Laura agreed. "I'm wondering what I should buy. Maybe some earrings."

And as the afternoon moved along, all of the peddlers, who sold hats, bags, jewelry, credenzas, tops, blankets, and henna tattoos, stopped at our chairs. A wave of food vendors came by selling grilled shrimp, prawns, and oysters but Ruark had warned us off them. Practicing my Portuguese, drinking in the sunshine, watching the endless games of speed paddle ball at the beach, keeping an eye out for thieves prowling the beach, and talking to Laura, I was really happy! At one point, perhaps after our third caipirinhas, we decided to have henna tattoos on our feet from the handsome young man who came by selling them.

"What beach do you want to go to tomorrow?" Laura asked. "Ruark said LeBlon is good. I think it's down by Ipanema."

"You know there's 45 miles of beach here. You are only here one week. Tell me where you want to go!"

"I just want to go to Ipanema."

WITH NO VOLUNTEER project to work on, my stay felt different here from the previous countries. I really didn't want to become a tourist here and not just because I hated walking around looking at stuff either. I wanted into the culture, the people. Though the four teachers were doing a great job of giving me their version of life here while we practiced the language, I wanted more. Living with a family allowed me into their lifestyle, but I hated that I was not actually helping on a project, spending my time on something that connected to my heart. I really missed my volunteer work. But I thought that I had a solution.

I decided to go on a hunt for a squash club, my favorite sport, in search of exercise and friendship and located a club not too far from the house. Arriving at the club, I found eight squash courts and the welcoming sound of a squash ball hitting the front wall and men, only men, playing squash and watching matches. Hmm, good move, Joyce. Way to get to know the culture! With my limited Portuguese, they still understood me and sent me to the front office for a one-month membership into this bastion of masculinity. The Pro lent me a racquet and I changed my clothes anxious to enter the court.

I entered an empty court and started hitting. The heat and humidity made the court feel like a sauna but I was immensely happy hitting the ball. A tall, handsome, very fit man in his 30s knocked on the glass door.

"Hi. I'm Markus. Do you want to hit?" He spoke English but with a German accent.

"I would love that!"

"Can I give you some pointers, Joyce?"

"That would be great. I haven't played much in the last five months. Point away!"

"Now Joyce, you must practice not hitting the ball hard but hit it precisely as I have told you. Move your hips (everything in Rio is about the hips)." Markus put his hands on my hips to show me the motion. "I will give you another lesson after you can consistently hit the ball 20 times as I have taught you."

"Thank you for your help!"

He left the court and I continued to hit wondering about the Lone Ranger of the Squash Court who was rescuing my backhand.

Another man knocked at the door.

"Hi! I am Rodriguez. Would you like to play a game?"

"Great!" I said, wondering if he would work on my forehand! But we were playing a match and I got my butt kicked. I was out of shape, unaccustomed to the heat, and just not as good as Rodriguez, who was probably 40. He had dark curly hair, dark skin, was fit and handsome. This squash club was turning into a great idea.

"Nice game." I was happy to be speaking English here.

"Would you like a beer?" he said and we walked upstairs to the lounge. "How do you know Markus?"

"Oh, we just met."

"He's taken an interest in your game."

"Oh, I guess so. It was great to have his help."

"He is a pro player from Germany who comes here every winter to work on his game."

"No way! Wow, how nice of him to help me. It would be great to improve my game. I love playing squash."

"Let's play on Thursday," Rodriguez said.

"I'm there." Maybe squash friendships would develop the sense of connection that I always found volunteering.

Back with my family, Caio and I talked about music from around the world in slow Portuguese and played my CDs from England, Italy, Greece and South Africa. We listened to his wide variety of Brazilian music, sambas, flute music, jazz, and blues in his bedroom, where shelves were stacked full of CDs. The music here was amazing with lots of energy.

"'Cada momento é bom para a música.' E um provérbio de los Cariocas." he told me. "Every moment is good for music. Você quer ir hoje à noite ao Largo da Lapa ouvir a música?"

Recognizing enough of the words, I said, "Grande!"

We were going to Lapa to listen to music. Happy to have a night out with a local escort, I jumped at the chance. I hadn't really thought about music when I left on my trip but it had become something for me to discover and enjoy in each new country. A highlight of my journey and the only constant souvenir. I knew how important music was to me at home but I hadn't brought an ipod with me and was starving for the sounds of music.

Sabrina, one of my teachers, told me that Lapa was a funky popular area for music, dancing, and late nights but she warned me that I was not to wander around by myself. Seemed there was always this warning in Rio...don't go alone, keep your hand firmly on your bag, watch out for thieves. All of these warnings made me uncomfortable to be anywhere alone past 9 pm though I walked the streets of my neighborhood in the daytime without reservation. But one time walking around the stores near my house, a man had run by me holding a gun! Shocked and frightened, I looked around to see if it was safe and suddenly a policeman pointing an automatic rifle ran by in pursuit of the thief. I walked home in a hurry.

We took a cab around 10 pm. That's when things start in Rio. We went to a boteca, a small club, with a live band. Caio played the tambourine with the band and then introduced me to Richard, a Brit with a graying beard and longish hair and ironed white long-sleeved shirt. Richard lived in our neighborhood and was around my age.

He seemed pretty serious but then he surprised me by asking, "Would you like to dance?"

"Great! But I don't know how to samba yet."

The dance floor was so crowded that it didn't matter about my steps and it was way too loud to talk. The heat was crushing. We danced until the heat was too much for me. He was there teaching at the University and seemed a quiet man for such a lively culture though he obviously loved dancing.

Luckily he was not a total night owl and at 2 am he said, "I'm going to take a taxi home. Would you like to share it with me?"

Happy to have an escort, we drove through Lapa, the people spilling out into the streets and music playing everywhere.

"It's like this from Thursday through the weekend until 5 am," said Richard.

Late nights and music. Party now like there is no tomorrow. Obviously, this Carioca culture understood something about the wee hours that I had not yet discovered but then they also had the siesta. I was living in a party city with dancing and music, a very important part of the lifestyle. How different from home! But with constant safety warnings, I was never relaxed here. Something needed to change.

The next night, I was content to stay home and watch novellas on TV. Every night when these overly dramatic soap operas came on the air, the actors in heavy makeup and dressed in gorgeous designer clothes, Alzira was glued to the set. Her friend Giselle was over watching and Rui, the ex-husband of one of the daughters, came over to visit, too. A handsome man in his 40s with a great smile, he asked me if I would like to go samba dancing with him. I looked at Alzira, not knowing if it was cricket to go dancing with her daughter's ex. She told me to say yes.

"Sim. Obrigado. Pero não samba."

"Eu ensiná-lo-ei." he said pointing to me and then to him and moving his hips laughing.

After he left, Giselle, who was close to my age, got up and started to give me samba lessons during the commercials. When she danced slowly, it was fine but I could only laugh when she cranked it up. Apparently most nights she was out dancing to samba clubs. "Eu sou um sambista. Eu amo ao samba," she said slowly enough for me to understand while she kept on dancing.

"Que ropa?" I asked.

"Que devo eu desgastar?" Alzira corrected me.

We went to my closet and figured out what to wear for my samba date.

I was really excited to go with Rui because of his smile and laughing eyes even though I couldn't really talk to him. We went to Rio Scenarium, a wildly popular place with three stories filled with old bikes, radios, and clocks. not at all what I had expected. The club was already rocking when we arrived.

"Você quer dançar?"

"Sim," I said, and we hit the dance floor.

Rui smiled a lot and danced the samba slowly, teaching me how to move my hips. The Cariocas around us were amazing samba dancers even on a crowded floor. Their moves reminded me of the dancing at the Lion Park after Thanksgiving.

Rui was patient teaching me the steps but the hip movement was not easy for me to learn. He put his hands on my hips to help me which felt very sexy but I wasn't clear on whether to be attracted to this hunk of dancing Carioca since he had divorced one of Alzira's daughters. We danced till 3 am with little time for talking.

"Obrigado, obrigado" was all I could say when we got to the door. He gave me a long tender kiss. Was I even supposed to be kissing the ex-husband of Alzira's daughter? But my Portuguese wasn't fluent enough to ask anyone.

My squash club was a good safe place for me to hang out and I went there most late afternoons. Without volunteering, I had decided to parallel my Seattle city life in Rio because squash was a big source of happiness back home. One afternoon, the director of the club invited me to enter the in-house tournament and attend the churrasco afterwards. I was tickled to be representing women squash players from Seattle and the only woman in the tournament, but I went out quickly in the first round. I cheered for Rodriguez and then Markus, who won the tournament in an exciting match with another pro player.

After the tournament, we all went upstairs to the patio for the churrasco, an orgy of meat. Delicious barbequed chicken, beef, and pork with each hunk of meat cooked slower and much further from the heat than at home. They brought a hunk of meat to the table, sliced it, and then returned it to the grill to finish cooking. No one sat down. Rather all of the men circulated around the small table eating pieces of meat with their fingers. There were a few little side dishes but really it was a meat and beer extravaganza. Talking to men. Perfect.

The men, who were mostly professionals, were welcoming, entertaining, and very polite though more reserved than I had expected. With my beginner's Portuguese, I listened intently and appreciated the men who spoke English with me.

"You need to be careful here in the streets of Rio," Ajose said. "Do not go home by yourself or walk alone at night. How are you getting home tonight?"

"Well, I was going to take the subway."

"Never! I'll drive you home," Rodriguez chimed in.

"We have a staggering problem here with poverty, crime, corruption, gang warfare, and drugs," Ajose said. "The criminals live up in the favelas and the police can never catch them. When there is a raid, the criminals leave and when the police leave, the criminals return and shoot off fireworks as a show of their strength. We constantly have to protect our children here from kidnapping."

"Do you think there is a solution in improving life for the people living in the favelas?"

Silence. Had I wandered into a Republican-like hornet's nest?

"Right now there are no solutions in sight." one of the men said with an unhappy look on his face.

I decided to listen rather than stir up trouble as the conversation moved to business talk until 3 am. How different it felt to be here with wealthy business men!

FINALLY THE CONSERVATION project was organized and I took a bus with Alcimar, the head of our school, to the Tijuca National Park, where I would be volunteering. We passed many different economic sections of Rio including the favelas that I had only seen in the distance before. The *favelas,* the slums located on the hillsides here reminded me of the townships in South Africa. Here too there was no water, no sewage, no toilets, no electricity. There were probably 800 favelas all over the city with maybe 25-40% of the population of Rio living there in poverty. Nothing was being done to change it. That same juxtaposition of my abundance and their poverty for me to deal with.

"These look like the townships in South Africa except they are stacked up a hill. Will they always be here?"

"Well, I don't see it changing soon," Alcimar said. "Joyce, this ride is not the safest. The favelas are home to most of our criminals. I wanted to go with you for the first time to show you how to board the buses and where to transfer."

We arrived at the top of the mountain surrounded by the thick vegetation, moist fresh air, and quiet found only in a rainforest. A wave of homesickness for beautiful Washington State hit me. Away from the over stimulation of Rio streets, my entire body relaxed as I closed my eyes and took a breath. Moments like this reconnected me to the Northwest, to home. Life in Rio was not my style and suddenly I missed my family, friends, and cat. How was my sweet Harley doing?

Tijuca National Forest is the largest urban forest in the world. The land had been heavily deforested, stripped bare for coffee plantations during the 1800s and sixty years later, erosion had created problems with Rio's drinking water supply. Looking for a way to protect that water supply, King Pedro II ordered Major Archer to expropriate a 13-square-mile area and hand-plant it with 40,000 species of native Atlantic Rainforest plants. Who was this man who in the mid-1800s had understood conservation solutions? Now over 150 years later, it was a lush blanket, a jungle garden that offered tree-canopy covered trails past waterfalls, caves, and mountain peaks though very few tourists ever visited. Thank you, King Pedro II.

"You are our only volunteer now." the project coordinator explained. "There really isn't much for you to do.

Upon hearing this, I was incredibly disappointed not to have work in this gorgeous park. I had come here to volunteer. Now what?

"Today you can choose between picking up litter or taking a hike with a park department member and some local visitors." he told me speaking in Portuguese. Passing on the litter to take the hike, nine of us took off along a gorgeous green trail. The trail was much more rugged and steep than those at home. I felt so at home here surrounded by shades of green, but our guide was speaking way too quickly for my beginning language skills.

I noticed right away that everything was more protected at home than here in Rio. Our entire American lifestyle is like a safe cocoon with the government looking out for us. Rules cover safety issues and lawsuits scream when the protection doesn't work well enough. Even paths up mountains are protected with signs, gravel, clearly marked trails, and switchbacks to protect our hearts from collapsing from too steep a climb. Have a problem? The parks department is responsible. It is easy to forget our own responsibility in a country that teaches us to always rely on someone else. American government was like a big mother protecting her helpless children, her citizens.

Rio had a different view, putting the responsibility on the individual. This path felt like we were the first people to find our way up the hill; it was more like a scramble than a hike. As we headed up, I noticed there were no signs and no switchbacks to help through the steep parts and the path seemed dangerously narrow, risky. But the vegetation here was gorgeous and it felt great to be out of the city.

Dripping from the heat and humidity and a bit timid on some of the narrow trails, I knew I was slowing the group down but I mustered my resolve and continued trudging upwards. We arrived at a solid mountain of rock and found our way to a dark, skinny tunnel. Apparently we were going to slide down on our backs to the other side through the narrow opening that had barely enough room for a person with a long nose. A cold, hard, narrow, dark, claustrophobic passage.

"No, no, não mim," I said, shaking my head.

"É divertimento grande. Você será fino. Vindo junte-nos," my hiking buddy says. Something about great fun, join us.

"Eu sou uma galinha," I replied, clucking like a chicken, which made everyone laugh. But they goaded me into doing it. First time for everything.

I lay on the cold rock and pushed myself into the dark birth chamber. The deeper I went, the darker it got, with only my hands and feet to push me along. What if my boobs got stuck? What then?

Did I know enough Portuguese to explain to the person below me that my boobs were hung up on a small crevice? As the light at the end of the tunnel came through my closed eyelids, I thanked God that I was getting out.

When the hike was over, I spoke with the project coordinator.

"I am sorry Joyce but there really isn't any reason for you to come here every day to volunteer. I don't have anything for you to do. You can come on the weekends and hike if you like."

Here I was halfway through my trip and now my second project was going sideways. Time for decisions again. I liked the school and my family. Could I find another project to volunteer at in Rio perhaps? I decided to study and play squash because a spectacular treat was coming my way.

My son Dan was coming to visit me in Rio! My mom had generously offered to pay for his airfare knowing how much I missed my sons. I was so excited to see him after after no hugs since June! But I was nervous too because we had only traveled together to Whistler, BC, to ski. I wanted him to have a great time. I was so anxious that I arrived at the airport an hour before his flight did!

We would have a week together to explore Rio and our relationship as travel companions. After we settled him into his hotel that was near my family, we went out to eat and for a walk around. Dan is smart, funny, and kind-hearted. He's also very handsome with olive skin and a tall, muscular body. With our dark skin and hair, the waiters gave us the Portuguese menu. Our natural camouflage made it easy not to stand out, a great thing when in a foreign country.

When I took Dan to my condo to meet Alzira and her family, she was ecstatic to meet my son and she couldn't stop talking about how tall (6'5") and how handsome he was. Dan was over a foot taller than her entire family as they strained their necks looking up. The more she chattered away, the more Dan smiled though he didn't have a clue what she was talking about. I was so proud of him.

The next day Dan and I rode the subway to school to meet the other students, who were all his age. He immediately made plans for the evening with some of the guys, and I was quite sure that Dan's experiences in Rio were going to be nothing like mine. He played basketball late in the evening with Cariocas and went to the bars with my classmates seeing Rio from a totally different perspective.

On the advice of my teachers, we took a weekend trip to Ilha Grande, an ecological reserve, which involved a long bus ride and then a ferry across the bay to a gorgeous island where the movie *The Blue Lagoon* was filmed. Only bikes, boats, and walking were allowed on the entire island. I hoped that on one of our hikes we'd see some of the monkeys, parrots, iguanas, and snakes that the island was known for. Dan hoped there would be some night life. We were adjusting to traveling together. I chose an inexpensive *pousada* on the beach for only 50 reais a night that included breakfast to save money and to expose Dan to that type of travel but I shocked him by booking only one room!

We hiked together through the dense forest to the other side of the island where there was supposed to be a gorgeous beach, Las Palmas. The hike through the rain forest brought me no monkeys, parrots, or iguanas and when we got to the beach, we were the only ones there. We talked about my journey and all that I had seen.

"I'm proud of you mom. But do you like it in Rio?

"No, not really. I always have to check my back for safety. How about you?"

"I like learning to play Rio rules at the basketball court but even those guys warned me not to walk home down certain streets."

"Well, you can go out with the kids from school, too." Somehow I had the feeling that Dan needed more than hanging out with his mom and luckily help was on its way!

John, a young Brit who ran the hostel and who had attended my school, took Dan under his wing for what I think must have been an amazing celebration. They took off after dinner and didn't come home until dawn. I worried about his safety but I was tickled that he was having fun.

On our trip back to Rio, Dan filled me in on a few of the details of his night out with John.

"I think your look at Rio is totally different than anything I'd ever see!"

Smiling at me, he nodded his head. "The girls here are pretty forward. They surprised me."

Dan moved hotels to the Copacabana section of town closer to the fun and the students in my class. His evenings were full of Rio nightlife. We seemed to have settled in after our weekend away. Our conversations were definitely more relaxed, giving me exactly what I was missing, time with Dan, a loving contact after six months on the road. Walking through the streets of Rio, going to a movie, eating together, we had hit our stride for traveling together. Walking with Dan was an entirely different feeling than being in Rio alone.

"So, do you think I've changed?"

Dan is very perceptive and I always respected his opinions. He looked at me giving me that smile of his. "You look tan and relaxed. Do you think you've changed?"

"Yes. I am learning good things about myself and feeling really good about world travel as a way to refresh my soul. But it is really good seeing you. I think there's this Mom thing that just breathes easier around your kids. It's heart-warming to be here with you, talking and listening."

"That's good mom. I like being here with you. Get what you want out of your trip."

Both of us were pretty laid back and not interested in doing a lot of touristy things. We enjoyed being together without needing a lot of extraneous conversation. An understanding of each other's hearts. I knew he had had a good visit, his first trip out of the country.

"Maybe you can come see me again in a different country." I hoped we'd get to travel together again. But his short visit was over and after I left him at the airport, I had a huge case of loneliness.

I WAS COMING TO the end of my journey here with only 10 days left. But those 10 days included two giant holidays to experience Rio-style: Christmas with my family and then New Year's. This month had been extremely different from the previous months because the volunteering never materialized. Without volunteering, I was more like a tourist with no friendships to enjoy. I was ready to leave even though my language skills were slowly moving up the learning curve, giving me a bit of communication. My buddies at the squash club were fun, but I was happier volunteering, that was for certain.

Christmas in Rio was wonderfully different for me than Christmas at home. There was no music in the stores, barely any lights, no huge push to buy, buy, buy, and nothing frantic in the air. Alzira had cooked for days and the house smelled delicious. She told me that 15 people from the extended family would arrive around 10 pm for the celebration and dinner. Alzira was the center of the universe. Her boundless energy, permanent smile, and delicious food made everyone comfortable. She was patient and kind at all times.

I had already met her two daughters, Vitoria and Beatriz, both very friendly, and Guilarme, Beatriz's very handsome husband, a black man who was built like a rock. They would be there and my samba buddy Rui, who was still treated like one of the family, plus Renato's family, all invited here for Christmas. Rui was my favorite of the whole crew, always laughing and joking with people.

A Christmas celebration beginning after 10 pm was a classic example of Rio's skill at finding more hours to party in each day. As the family arrived, each person in the family talked to me, and everyone was very friendly as we gathered together in the living room for family time with music provided by Caio. At midnight, they popped open the champagne and started making toasts, blessing everyone in the family. Each person offered a toast that I almost understood and with champagne bubbles bursting in my head on an empty stomach, my Portuguese suddenly went fluent. I gave a toast and everyone applauded.

Alzira had covered the table with the best feast I had ever seen. We had ceia de Natal (turkey) marinated in champagne, a braised tender meat dish like brisket, Alzira's version of feijoada, lots of other dishes that were completely new to my taste buds, vegetables and tropical fruit and, of course, beans and rice. Sitting around the living room, everyone balanced their plates on their laps eating Alzira's delicious meal, but the children were getting anxious to open their presents.

"Seja paciente. Nós abriremos os presentes após o jantar." Alzira told them all.

Ah, yes, in every country children are impatient to open their gifts.

Balancing my plate on my crossed legs, I sat on the couch eating delicious food happy to be spending time with these fun-loving people. I carefreely swung my left foot back and forth to the beat of the music. And then my serenity ended. The damn dog, Chubba, a senile 13-yr-old insane little grunt of a dog fueled with anger chose this moment to attack my swinging foot. He took a superlunge across the room leaping from Alzira's chair, and put a death grip on my big toe. I screamed. He hung from my big toe. Even with his rotten teeth, as his grip tightened, he hurt me. I was pissed! No one moved. They were all too stunned.

"Shit. What the hell is Chubba doing?"

(Oh dear. What did I just say? Now praying that no one understood English.) I screamed again not sure how to pry him off my toe. Still that scrawny, nasty dog hung from my big toe with the entire family watching him dangle afraid to interfere! Finally Alzira walked over and grabbed the dog and took him to the bedroom.

Everyone immediately gathered in a large circle looking at my toe, the children kneeling by my side. (Oh, why don't I get pedicures? My feet were way too ugly for an entire family Christmas spectacle. I was so embarrassed.) I put my head in my hand ashamed of my feet but they thought I was in pain.

"Você é ferido? É seu dedo do pé aprovado? Podemos nós ajudar-lhe? Oh é você feriu? Mordidas desse cão da nada todos nivelam o bebê! Por que é destilador aqui?"

Everyone talked at once. Beatriz brought me a cloth to wash my toe. I hopped to the bathroom to give it a good scrub and then we bandaged it up. So, I had been with monkeys, baboons, and lions, and it was Chubba who gave me my first bite. Luckily most of his teeth were bad, and though he clamped his jaw down in a serious vice grip, my

SMILING AT THE WORLD

American toe was tougher. I was not going to die of rabies in Rio and only had a black and blue the next day.

After dinner, the children opened their presents and the party continued until 4 am! Rio definitely had a different appreciation of the wee hours of the morning. And they would all be back the next afternoon for another Alzira dinner! But on Christmas Day everyone slept late and there wasn't a sound until noon when we all got up and did it again! After the two days of celebration, my Portuguese improved and I now easily stayed up until 4am!

CLASS WAS STILL THREE hours of conversation with no English allowed, but I didn't have an achy head when it was over any more. One day Val, my favorite teacher, explained flirting in Rio.

"Men here will stare at you. You must look at him moving only your eyes and then quickly look away. In a little while you look again and this time your eyes linger just a little longer."

As she explained, she showed me how she used her eyes.

"Val, that is so sexy. And coy. And feminine."

"Yes, we must never look too interested but we must show enough interest to keep the man curious."

"And how long does this go on?"

"Oh, it is a lot of fun. There is no time, Joyce. It is a conversation with the eyes."

"This is so different from what I am used to in my culture. It sounds GREAT!"

"Well, when you are ready, you look at the man and then smile just a little. This is his signal to get up and come over to talk to you."

THE TEACHERS GOT me very excited when they explained what to expect on Ano Nove (New Year's Eve).

"Everyone goes to the beach. All of the beaches in Rio will be packed. Young and old. Rich and poor. A beautiful sight. There are many different traditions for Ano Nove. Everyone will wear white, standing for the peace that they wish for in the new year."

"Wait, everyone wears white?"

"Yes, it is amazing. You must wear white, too. How do you celebrate American New Year's?"

"Everyone has a separate party at their home or at a hotel. Most everyone wears black."

"Black? So unlucky. Ah, that is why you have Bush!"

"You're so funny."

"People can accessorize with red if they want romance or yellow for prosperity or green for health. What do you want?"

With a little nostalgic memory of Robert, I said, "love."

"Then buy some red underwear if you want to find love, Joyce."

"A lot of people bring flowers and you should throw them in the sea before midnight. They are an offering to Yemanji, the goddess of the seas. Bring a bottle of champagne to pop and drink at midnight. If you are on the beach and you decide to shake the bottle and spray it around, nobody will complain. It's considered good luck."

"Okay, is there anything else?"

"Some people go into the ocean to wash away all the negative energy from the old year. You can do this too even up to your knees. If you go to the beach the next day, it's empty. No one goes to the beach the following day because there is too much bad energy there."

"I am so excited!"

Two nights before New Year's Eve I had an impossible time sleeping. There was always heat, humidity, sticking to the sheets, and the noise of the fan blowing the hot air around but I woke up and all I could think about was Harley. Suddenly I missed him so much that I started crying. Then I heard a cat cry but how could that be? We were 11 stories up. Missing Harley and feeling guilty for leaving him, I prayed that he was safe but nothing was working. I cried myself to sleep uncertain what was wrong. I needed to call Autumn, who was caring for Harley for the year, and my sister.

But I could not reach Autumn or my sister the next day, and that night after I fell asleep, it was the same thing. I awoke unable to sleep with Harley vividly on my mind. Other nights when I had missed him,

I sent him a message of love and then I calmed down, but tonight no sleep was possible. Again I called Autumn hoping to talk to her but there was no answer. I was a wreck. Something was wrong and I needed to find out what.

My Brazilian family was spending New Year's together and we all walked to the beach, Alzira and her husband, her two daughters, Guillerme, the two granddaughters and Giselle, all of us carrying bottles of champagne. My teachers were right. All types of families from all over Rio were walking to the beach, a mass migration overflowing the sidewalks and covering the beaches of Rio. Every inch of beach throughout Rio was filled with people and almost everyone was wearing white. It was a vision of beauty.

Peace. Here in Rio all 11 million people hoped for peace in the New Year. No individual resolutions. A wish for peace, then love, health, and prosperity. This city full of music, dance, crime, stealing, chaos, and late nights was praying for peace in unison. Standing on the beach with my family, I looked all around at the faces and I prayed for peace. If everyone in the world wore white tonight, would peace come? Is there magic when we all join hands in the same wish?

As for me, I wore my white outfit and red underwear. Robert thoughts. I had stopped sending him emails as they were never answered. I had even stopped Googling him. I had let him go almost completely. I could remember the fun with a smile now. Love. Would this red underwear do the trick then? Maybe I needed a red bra too to get the lasting kind of love. No, if I thought about it, the universe was sending me lots of love.

Standing on the beach, I was captivated by the music, the dancing all around me and the laughing as the spotlights shone on everyone's faces. It was an experience like none other. As the clock struck midnight, the famous Rio fireworks began lighting up the sky while champagne bottles popped off all around me in unison. The city of parties was revving up for one of their biggest! Everyone in Rio was toasting the New Year for peace, love, health, and prosperity. I took mental snapshots of all the love and happiness around me. As I turned around, I spotted an old woman with white hair all curved over leaning on her cane. In her right hand she was holding a bottle of champagne and slowly she brought it to her mouth chugging it down in celebration. I smiled at her beauty, her joy in the moment. All of the young children were here with their parents on the beach celebrating the New Year. The fireworks display was magnificent, filling the sky in creative new designs.

When it was over, Gisele asked, "Do you want to walk around the beach?"

"Yes, that would be wonderful!"

So we did. The entire city was there and everyone was dancing the samba. I followed Gisele as we partied through the night dancing the samba.

With the morning sunrise, Giselle and I walked home. I stopped to call my sister to wish her a Happy New Year full of samba and champagne and good wishes. But the news was crushing. My heart was broken. My cat, the best damn cat in the entire world, had died. I could not imagine that this was true. Harley was not dead because he could not die. But he was dead. He was such a joy. When I left on my journey, I cried and cried not knowing how to leave a cat that I loved for a trip that I needed. I didn't know how to rationalize that. But Autum seemed so very sweet and she loved Harley, too.

Maybe I should never even have gone on this stupid trip, I thought in despair. What had I gained in the last six months if my cat was dead? I had lost the chance to be with him when he needed me the most. I had lost his trust in me. It was his heart. The vet said it was congenital and it was a miracle that he lived that long. But I thought, no, he died of a broken heart because he loved me and I left him. I loved him with all my heart and I left him. What good was a trip to find myself if I couldn't be trusted to take care of my sweet cat? He didn't understand that I was coming back. Harley, wherever you are, do you know how bad I feel that you died without me to help you? Damn it! Damn it! Damn it! My heart was crushed. I couldn't stop crying.

Clearly Harley had come to me then those two nights to tell me he was dying. When I woke up and heard the cat cry, it could only have been Harley. And all the love I sent you then could not keep you alive. Oh please, tell me that you heard me. But how to forgive myself?

It was the first day of the year. My sweet Brazilian family was jabbering away in the living room and I was hiding out in the bedroom. I told them my stomach was not top notch after too much champagne. I didn't have the words to tell them the truth. Sorrow, gut-wrenching pain about the sweetest cat on the planet and me leaving him alone. Torn between being a good friend to him and being a good friend to me. What was the lesson here for me? Right at that moment, I would have thrown away this entire trip for the return of that one spectacular loving cat. Not the world not the life I was seeking not the adventure not anything was worth not having my sweet cat alive. My grief was profound and I found it hard to let it go, to let it be.

It was hot that day in Rio, hot enough to fry an egg on the sidewalk or in my room. Everyone was talking in the living room at the same time. The music was so damn loud. Jeez, if I could have escaped right then, I would have. I was in such a foul mood that I planned on staying in my room until the next day when I would leave Rio. Distraught and sad down to my bones, I was in a complete emotional energy drain.

Leaving Rio? Great! Rio was not my cup of tea with so much going on all over the streets at all times. I was tired of the constant reminder to be watchful, ever vigilant for thieves, the constant worry about things getting stolen. Hide your camera. Hide your purse. Hide your money. Hide yourself. I was not a Rio girl. Nope. No more big dangerous cities, please. No more million people everywhere. There was no beauty here for me, only buildings and the beach. No calm. No tranquility. No trees. I had worked very hard to feel the culture here, to enter it but I was glad to be leaving Rio. This was not my city.

Depressed and sad about Harley, I wasn't sure where I could be happy right now. My heart was home with Harley playing with me imagining him still alive. Only regret and sadness here in Rio. I still needed to talk to Autumn and to the vet again. What had really happened?

My next stop was Australia, a country I had wanted to visit for the last 10 years, though enthusiasm was tough to muster in my present state. My work would be in Melbourne with a conservation project, hopefully one that was better organized than the non-existent conservation project here. Yet with overwhelming sadness in my heart, I left Rio, uncertain of everything. My heart crushed.

CHAPTER 13

The Roo Gully Sanctuary in Australia

AUSTRALIA WAS A LONG way from Rio. I traveled for more than 20 hours and I arrived in Sydney foggy headed and heart broken, mourning deeply over Harley's death. I was like a big balloon with a slow air leak and getting through this without friends to sit down and talk to was a miserable challenge. Even with lots of time on a phone card, talking across the ocean couldn't come close to the hugs that I needed, the comforting. In fact, words coming through the phone from my caring sister and my buddy Bob made the distance and my isolation seem all the greater.

I had not considered how I would handle tragedy on this journey and now I was confronted with grief, guilt, anger, and regret. If being alone in a foreign city was a challenge, being heart-broken in a foreign city brought me to a new level of heaviness that I was not prepared to endure. My emotional reserves were depleted and I had no way to express my feelings. I walked outside of my bed and breakfast with a big cloud of grey hanging over my head. No matter what the vet had said, I felt that I was the cause of Harley's death. Forgiveness for abandoning my cat was not possible. And yet I knew I had to move on.

My neighborhood here could have been the Queen Anne neighborhood of Seattle. It had lovely homes and beautifully landscaped yards, the only sound the wind through the trees. What a drastic change from Rio with all its chaos and noise, apartment buildings, busy streets with cars and buses. From the cool evenings in Africa with lions roaring to the hot humid nights in Rio with people partying till 5 am to this pure quiet in a safe, civilized Australian neighborhood, changes in my environment over the last three months had been drastic.

Sydney was gorgeous, like Seattle on sunshine, and boarding the hydrophane ferry for the short ride to downtown Sydney, I wished that Seattle, my sweet city, ran these ferries for a fast commute. Homesick. Or maybe friendsick. I was walking around looking at stuff, amazed that I had finally made it to Australia. At the same time, my heart was on its own journey inward, looking for relief from an overflowing bucket full of sorrow.

I purchased a ticket for that evening's opera wondering if music could distract me or bring some healing. Mozart's *Così Fan Tutte* was playing, a story about women being as prone to infidelity as men. I pondered this premise curious that in 1790 this was an acceptable topic for an opera. Dying to discuss this with someone, I waited during the intermission on the outdoor patio, admiring the architecture and the Sydney Harbour Bridge and ready to talk opera to whoever came near me. But it was all couples, the men dressed more formally than in Seattle and the women sparkly in gorgeous designer dresses.

With no one to share my thoughts with, I started judging the women, deciding which ones were prone to infidelity. I amused myself greatly in between surges of date envy, watching what I imagined as happy couples.

Are we as prone to infidelity as men? Women moved to infidelity when their emotional needs were being ignored and they no longer felt treasured. Men were moved by the physical draw of another female, I thought, or their egos needed a boost. I would give men the edge on ease and frequency of infidelity though. Mozart, we aren't saints but generally a woman has to be miserable to the max to walk through the infidelity door. Men wander through more casually. Philosophy on a warm evening in Sydney surrounded by glamorous people and feeling quite alone. Traveling solo was sometimes lonely.

With one more day before heading to Melbourne and my volunteer project, I walked to the famous Bondi beach to swim and watch people, get hot and tanner with memories of the liveliness of

Ipanema and Copacabana. How tame this beach seemed with hardly a foreign feeling at all. Regular bikinis, tops on, bottoms covered, it looked like Huntington Beach in California. No edge. No danger. No vendors. No tall hotels. No caipirinhas or henna tattoos. There were better waves, but the beach was just a beach in my current downer of a mood and I walked to an Internet café to check my email and check in with my friends.

There were some emails from friends. Leonard, who I had met in England, continued to write me and I loved his poetic touches. His gentleness and emotions were beautifully expressed and it seemed like perhaps we would meet up again but who knew. There was also an email from the sea turtle conservation project I had scheduled for March in Thailand. Sadly, the massive tsunami had destroyed the project beaches in addition to thousands of houses and thousands of people. My project was cancelled. Where did I want to go instead? What project did I want to work on?

Knowing how much I had loved wildlife, I Googled sanctuaries in Thailand and after reading through all of the possibilities, I chose The Elephant Nature Park, which was a sanctuary for abused domestic elephants. Even though I wouldn't be able to cuddle with an elephant on my lap, I was fascinated by their intelligence and memory and I wanted to learn more. I sent off my application and hoped that I would be accepted as it seemed a perfect match.

I flew to Melbourne for my next project with the Conservation Volunteers, a group that worked all across Australia on various projects. My main motivation had just been to get to Australia because for years people had been telling me that my direct nature would be a good fit in the Australian culture. I was curious to see if they were right. Finding a project to volunteer at in Australia had been really tough. I had spent many hours of research with very few choices turning up, and though I wasn't sure what this project work would be like, I was anxious to put in time helping the earth.

The volunteer house in Melbourne was filled with a Brit, an Irishman, and eight Koreans all under the age of 26! Everyone welcomed me and I felt comfortable immediately. We had two coed bedrooms filled with bunk beds and one bathroom, much like the house in South Africa, and we cooked dinner as a group. Our house was within walking distance to town, to the beach, to the pool, and to squash courts, which was really exciting. But no one seemed very excited about our project work and I wondered why not.

Anxious to begin my volunteer project, I loaded into a van with others and we were driven to a park in Melbourne. We each got tools and gloves and then we were directed to begin weeding. No, I thought, say it isn't so. I hadn't come halfway around the world to volunteer with weeds in a park. Our mission was to dig up invasive plants that were not indigenous to Australia like prickly pear, which fought back by giving us nasty stings from its sharp thorns. These were not wee little plants but rather big shrubs grown out of control. The job was muscle work in the hot sun against plants with thorns that secreted some nasty juice that burned when it entered your skin.

Joking with the John, our park ranger, about the unexciting nature of the project, he tried to inspire me with a story about the history of prickly pear. Seems the Brits brought it here with the First Fleet in 1788 to plant as a food source for cochineal insects. What in the world were they thinking to bring a shrub halfway around the world because of a fascination with cochineal insects? Follow the money, as they say. These little bugs about the size of a match head when squashed produced a red color that was used in dye. In particular this dye was used for the British soldiers' red coats. (I didn't want to think about how many bugs were needed to dye one coat or who had the job of squishing them.) Seems that back then Spain, and Portugal had a worldwide monopoly on these little bugs and the red dye and England would have none of that. They planted prickly pear in groves and moved in the bugs, happily squishing away buckets of red dye, not realizing how aggressive the plant was.

By the late 1800s, it was out of control and more than a nuisance. In 1886, the first Prickly Pear Destruction Act was passed forcing farmers to destroy the plant. Obviously in the last 120 years, the plant had still been winning. The battle had now grown to one of international importance as the Korean-British-Irish-American team gathered to hack, dig, and attack all of the plants to let the natural vegetation take over. But the damn thorns hurt and I wasn't inspired to wage the Battle of the Prickly.

Back at the commune, Team Korea vs. Team United States were cooking up a storm. The group of Korean kids all worked together in the kitchen making us Soon-Doo-Boo, a tofu soup combination and delicious Korean-style pancakes and rice. On Team America night, they all helped me with cutting and chopping, so excited to eat a homemade American dish. My meatloaf with mashed potatoes and carrots brought them to their knees and I finished them off to win the competition with homemade chocolate chip cookies. Making cookies around the world had become my specialty.

But after two days of gardening in the hot sun, this project was not floating my boat, even with playing squash at night. I needed an emotional connection to my project, especially, I think, in light of my loss of Harley. I walked to the Internet café, I Googled sanctuary and hit pay dirt. The Roo Gully Sanctuary outside of Perth needed volunteers to feed and tend their joeys and young wallabies. After explaining to the organizers of the group about my problems with weeding the parks and getting their approval to leave, I applied and was accepted to Roo Gully. I was sky-high, when I booked my five-hour flight to Perth.

With one day free before my flight, I decided to take a guided hiking tour with a group of adults to learn about the local ecology before I flew west. Our guide Steve took us near a wild group of kangaroos and I explained that I would be heading to a sanctuary in Perth.

"Yes, many roos are orphaned from car accidents involving their mothers. If they are not found, the joeys die inside their mother's pouch. Perth is a lot different than the areas we are driving through. There aren't as many people there; it's still the real Australia."

Later we drove to the beach for a lovely hike through a tea tree forest.

"I've used tea tree oil for homeopathic healing of wounds but I never associated it with a tree. Is this river the color of tea from the trees?"

"Yes. The Aborigines were the first to use tea tree oil for healing."

At lunch, Steve took out his didgeridoo and played for us. The sound was startling. I had never heard one before and it was haunting, like the earth singing, mysterious, hollow, and beautiful reaching deep inside my soul to some new place that I didn't recognize.

"This flute may be the oldest musical instrument on earth and is played to accompanying Aboriginal chants. The Aborigine listened to earth in a way we don't understand. Animal sounds, wings flapping, their feet on the earth, water over rocks, thunder and wind. A becoming with nature to form the music of nature. By their own desire knowing that they were a part of nature, they found a tree hollowed out by termites and carved it into an instrument to express themselves in the same manner as the sounds that they heard from wind, water, and wildlife."

Steve passed the didgeridoo around the circle with each of us taking a turn to make the sounds, no easy task.

When Steve played again, I heard in the music a message that I had first heard in England. We are not separate. We are the same. What the tree feels when it stands strong is part of our being, and what the bird feels when it soars, we also know. Our fascination with nature comes from our unity, not our separation. We must tell everyone that to hurt the earth is to hurt your self. Mother Nature nourishes our soul. I was listening differently now than at the start of my journey. I wondered if soon I would hear the flapping of eagle wings as he soared about me.

After lunch, we hiked into a rain forest full of a million shades of green. The colors soothed me immediately. Tall fern trees that looked like umbrellas with wide lacey leaves filtered the light, bringing coolness and moisture to the air. The fresh, damp air was like breathing in the earth and the sound of my footsteps was muffled by the moss-covered ground. Complete surrender in a rain forest. Breathing in serenity. The quiet, the glow of green light, and the magic of a fern forest brought peace to all of my senses. It was so easy to breathe here. I was forest woman.

Steve walked us to a giant eucalyptus tree, 300 feet high with a wide trunk and a fence around it to protect it.

"These trees started growing in Australia 35 million years ago!" he explained. "The eucalyptus sheds its bark into piles that eventually create a fire. That heat opens the seed pods at the very top of the eucalyptus trees and burns only a bit of the tree. The other competing trees in the forest, which burn at a lower temperature, burn up in the fire that the eucalyptus trees start. Somehow these trees have figured out how to compete in the forest. The Aborigines understand when to start these fires if they are not started naturally, thus bringing new life to the forest in cycles."

I stood in the hollow of a burned eucalyptus tree that continued to grow very tall above the burned out space, wondering about tree intelligence that could start a fire to wipe out the competition, a concept beyond my reasoning. Walking further along, we saw koalas sitting and sleeping in the eucalyptus trees. They curled up like stuffed animals, cuddly and fat with the sweetest faces.

"The eucalyptus leaf carries a toxin that other wildlife cannot digest but the koalas are able to eat it." Steve grinned. "They seem to get stoned on it and then need to sleep as their body adjusts to the toxins."

The cutest animal that I had ever seen was curled up in the smallest fork of a very high branch completely stoned and sleeping for 20 hours a day! So the eucalyptus tree was almost successful keeping wildlife away except for the stoner koala bears!

"They have two thumbs on each hand giving them a better grip and they wedge their bottoms into a tree fork for solid sleep. They jump between tree tops but they are not bears. They are marsupials with pouches like the roos. About 8 million were killed in the early 1900s for their fur, but now their biggest problem is a disease that is going through their population."

Walking back to the van, Steve had a bit more information for us.

"Now before you head off on your own to your adventure, I want to let you know that the snakes and spiders here can kill you. But anti-venom has been developed for all of them and there are very few deaths. The enormous huntsman spider that jumps is not poisonous but it's big. You'll be scared. There is a white spider that hides under toilet seats and they are poisonous. Then there are the dreaded ants whose bite contains a poison that hurts like crazy, the nasty black flies that crawl on your face and bite your skin, and snakes of all sorts. When you walk in the tall grass, really stomp your feet heavily as normally the snakes will move away. Only occasionally will a snake be in a pissy mood and attack you. Generally if you run into a snake, stand still. If you're gonna be in tall grass, wear boots. Those might save you a nasty bite."

"Hmm…gosh! Thanks, Steve, for scaring me. Lots of ways to die in Australia, then?"

"Well, yes, and we haven't even talked about the ocean. But the good news is that the wombats who prowl around at night looking like round furry pigs will not hurt you at all." He smiled as he watched the fear in all of our faces.

When I arrived back at the house to say goodbye to the other volunteers, they asked me to make meatloaf. To my amazement, after dinner each one of the Korean volunteers gave me a present. I had no idea how I deserved this kindness: a gorgeous fan, a book ring, a mask, a small pin, a lovely key chain with a Korean instrument, a coin purse, and a sweet note from one of the girls telling me she would like to be just like me when she was my age. I felt honored.

I sat and talked with Kyoung-mi to thank her for her compliment.

"Oh, I wish you were my mother or that you could meet my mother and tell her about your adventure. I want to be just like you when I am your age. Independent. Strong. And a good cookie baker too!"

"I want to hear from you over the years. I've got lots of confidence in your ability to find adventure. We can email and stay in touch. Okay?"

"Yes. I wish I was leaving the weeding and going with you to work with kangaroos!"

"Next time Kyong-mi. Next time."

Perhaps my next career would be in international relations with groups of volunteers or maybe as an International Chocolate Chip Baker! I think volunteers from every country appreciated and needed a mom's love when they were traveling away from home.

Rereading Kyong-mi's note to me, I thought about being a role model. When I was young, I thought that anyone in their 50s was old, well past their prime and, for certain, lacking a sense of adventure. I judged them done and just playing out their years till they got really old. Not a very compassionate view back then. However, I was always really excited when I read about any woman over 50 who was an athlete or an adventurer or shaking up the world with innovative thoughts and actions. Their spirit was inspiring.

Maybe young women in their 20s needed role models of women in their 50s or older, women who were alive in spirit. Maybe we all needed to know that adding years added wisdom and a few wrinkles but was not an end to vitality, curiosity, and a sense of adventure. I do know that I looked at myself in a different way after seeing what she saw in me.

After the five-hour flight to Perth with its minimal snacks, I arrived starving at the small airport but ready to go to Boyup Brook. I asked a tourist guide and the shuttle bus driver how to get there, but I was surprised that neither had a clue. Then my ATM card failed to work and with no money and no food and no idea how to get to Boyup Brook, I decided to rent a car and find my own damn way there! But no, I could not rent a car with only a debit card. Another lesson for the world traveler. I had not planned on renting a car on this trip but I had not known that I'd need a traditional visa if I ever needed to rent one. Lesson learned.

Defeated, I went to buy a sandwich and the clerk yelled at me when I accidentally stepped behind the counter. I sat down on a chair put on my sunglasses and cried....quietly. I was not doing well. At what point on this journey would I have a smooth entrance into a new airport? A call to my debit card company cleared up the problem. The card was not stolen as they thought. I had called them before I left to give them my itinerary for the year as I moved from country to country but their system was set up to protect me and stopped usage of my card when I showed up in an unforeseen city.

With the train leaving for Boyup Brook in the morning, I booked a night at a hotel in Perth for a rest! Maybe all of the constant changes over the last six months were wearing me down. Time for the bubble bath/fluffy bed therapy that had proven so successful in other countries.

I had been asking a lot of myself with changes of country and culture every 30 days and barely enough time to adjust and then I was off to the next adventure.

But a big surprise awaited me. Walking back from the closed train station, which had no information about time schedules, I looked across the street and spotted a miracle. Shona, one of my friends from South Africa, was walking on the other side of the street. Imagine a Scottish lass and an American woman meeting up in South Africa and then again on the streets of Perth. Ecstatic to see each other, we took a 10 km walk around the lakes of Perth, a quiet city that reminded me of Spokane, Washington, and caught up on the last month of travel. We talked on and on right through the day and into the night over lunch and dinner. Finally I got the hug I needed when I told her about Harley, and my spirit felt rejuvenated, ready for the train and bus ride to the Roo Gully Sanctuary.

My first impressions of Australians were that they were very relaxed, informal, unaffected, and straightforward, all qualities that I admired. As I traveled, I wondered if I was becoming more real and unaffected. These Australians were bound to be a good influence. I still had faith in this journey as a wise choice for my spirit to grow, but at times I was fearful, thinking that this path was too radical. Was leaving everything behind unwise? Was the future that I wanted possible? And then instinctively I felt the answer: Be strong in your dreams.

But habits were hard to break. Old ways of doing and practiced ways of thinking and being were sneaking into my thoughts like those damn prickly pears, and I needed some mental stump removers or else old habits would keep me confined for a lifetime and I'd never break free of imaginary bars. The freedom to dream. To give birth to a Joyce beyond what I knew now. That's what I was doing. Throwing myself into other cultures, stirring it around a bit, hoping to pop out the real me. Getting really good at smiling the smile of my South African friend Able. Being present in the moment.

I was on my way to work with joeys. Who else would be there besides Carol, the woman who started the sanctuary? Would working with joeys be like working with the youngest cubs and would I like the work? What would the small town of Boyup Brook be like? I was full of questions when the bus stopped in a sleepy little town that could have been small-town America with one small grocery store, a large beautiful swimming pool, a pub, a gas station, and one doctor from the Netherlands, whose salary, room, and board were paid for by the town because no local doctor would work there!

Carol, the owner of the sanctuary, turned out to be a wiry, lean woman with short brown hair and straightforward eyes. She wore a plaid cotton shirt and jeans when she met me at the bus stop with a warm welcome.

"Howdy, mate. Was the trip okay?"

I felt at home instantly as we drove to Roo Gully Sanctuary through the dry hills of the countryside. The big brick rambler home sat on a hill and the property flowed down into a gully with a river that ran only in the winter during the rainy season. But this was summer, January, and everything down in the gully was dry but the grass on the lawn.

Carol, 53, was full of love, talent, energy, and caring for her kangaroos.

"Here's your bedroom mate. You have your own room. Aalina has her own room next door and you two share the bathroom. It's just the two of you now. Because the only water we have is what we collect in the tank in the winter, please take very short showers. We'll all eat dinner together but you have to make your own breakfast and lunch. If there's any special food you want from the store, you can drive to town. Let's go see what you'll be doing here." We immediately set off to meet the two baby joeys that were napping in her bedroom.

"Here are Kiah and Leila, the girls," she said, pointing to two quilted pouches hanging from her closet doorknobs. Inside the quilt was a pillowcase and a napping joey. "They are too young to be out with the mob yet and this is where they take their naps."

"What a very clever solution to mimic the comfort of the mother kangaroos pouch!" I exclaimed.

Carol smiled. "I'll show you how to make their bottles after they wake up. Over here is where Tina, Turner, and Tyke sleep, the three young wallabies. All of the young need bottles three times a day and your job is to mix the milk and feed them. I am so glad you have come with experience. I am working hard now to get a documentary completed about the roos here, and if you can do all of the feeding, that will really free me up."

With memories of lion cubs dancing in my head, I told her, "Yes. I am quite sure that I can do all of the feedings that you need me to."

Carol trained me by first explaining personality differences between my five charges and then showed me the formula, the bottles, and the process. What a great change from the Wildlife Hospital in Lesvos and way more need here for help than weeding in Melbourne. Each project had its own feel depending on the person whose heart was running it. Carol's love for her wildlife warmed my heart, and I looked forward to a cuddle with these roos during their feeding time.

With the roos and wallabies napping, we walked outside to meet the other creatures that Carol had saved.

"Here's our kookaburra."

"I have been singing the kookaburra song since I was a little girl and here we are, face to beak. Carol, does he really laugh?"

Smiling, she said, "Just you wait. He has a rather different interpretation of the song but he'll sing for you. A rather wacky kind of laughing song. He has only one wing. Watch this."

And she threw him a dead baby chicken for his morning feeding. He caught it in his beak and then whacked it a few times against the tree limb to kill it even though it was already dead. Once he was convinced it was dead, he swallowed it whole. I could see the bulge in his throat.

"If you can catch mice for him, he'll like that plenty."

"Okay, just show me the traps. I've got lots of experience."

"Now meet Mel, another small bird of prey, who has lived here a long time." Mel looked like a small owl.

"He has a damaged eye and one bad wing. Dangle a piece of raw meat in front of him like this thunking it against his beak to get him to feed, but make sure your fingers are clear. His beak is sharp."

I tried it and eventually he grabbed it and then swallowed it whole.

"Over here we have Betty."

Expecting some lovely creature to match the name, I was shocked when a hopping rat jumped to our feet from the tall grass inside her hut. My first reaction when I saw her was to scream RAT, but she was actually another type of marsupial, a rat kangaroo, and she flipped on her belly for a good scratch from Carol.

"You feed Betty only at night." she said as we walked to another area. Then she changed the subject. "I am looking for a life mate for this injured male parrot. Parrots are able to live to over 60 years and mate for life! And then over here we have a walk-in cage full of injured magpies that need tending as well. What do you think, mate? Are you with me so far? The other volunteer here has slacked off. Seems she likes to sleep late and go to bed early. I really need your help if you are ready."

"I am so glad to be here, Carol. Just tell me if there is more that you want me to do or to do things differently. I'm here to help."

"Let's walk down to the gully and I'll introduce you to the mob of kangaroos that have come to live here over the years. There are 30 in all of various ages and sizes that wander the property by day and then come up to the house for water, grain, nuts, and attention in the evening."

Telling me each one's story, she patted them and scratched them, talking to them and to me. Lying down in the gully, resting in the shade, I realized I had never really looked at a kangaroo close up before.

Kangaroos are one of those creatures that make me wonder about who was in charge of design. A sweet face and warm eyes like a deer with long big ears but their front legs are short and rather delicate like human arms. Move down to their legs and its pure power with strong, big muscles and huge feet, the only large animal that moves by hopping except for the Easter bunny. With three toes on a foot, roos can hop up to 40 mph and leap up to 12 feet, and their tail is so big and heavy that they can't go in reverse. I find the amazing pouch that holds the joey safe, a really clever design feature that every mother could appreciate. How easy for the mom! "Hop in, time for a nap now." Roos seemed like gentle creatures from a cartoon to make children smile with hopping and pouches and even boxing.

When European explorers first saw these animals, they asked a native Australian, the aborigine, what they were called. The Aborigine replied, "gangurru," which easily changed to kangaroo. In the wild, they are generally in a mob of 10 roos, with an "old man" or a "'boomer" who is dominant. At birth, they are the size of a jelly bean and immediately after birth, they make an upward trek crawling along a line that their mother has dampened with her tongue leading them to her pouch and hidden nipples. Like a fetus, they stay in the pouch continuing to mature until they are ready for adventures out of the pouch though always returning for safety and naps. They don't become totally independent for 7 to 10 months.

Back at the house, Carol showed me how to hold Kiah to feed her and what was different about feeding Leila. While they had their bottles, they liked a cuddle inside their pillowcases like babies and their blankets. Once the girls were fed, we moved on to the wallabies, who were chunkier and built lower to the ground. Their fur had patterned markings.

Aalina came back home from an afternoon swim and we had a chance to visit. From Germany, she was only 19 and this was her first trip away from the continent. I enjoyed talking to her but understood Carol's frustration because she didn't wake up for morning chores and never offered to do much more than bottle feed the girls.

To keep the peace, the roos had the entire acreage in the back of the house and the four wallabies the front. The wallabies didn't need cuddles and drank from the bottles with their feet on the ground. All the young had the run of the house including the huge living room with tiled floor and comfy couches. At different times throughout the day and evenings, we had lots of hopping going on from the living room to the kitchen and into Carol's bedroom, the nursery, a source of constant amusement for me.

Working long hours to finish the documentary, Carol stayed back in the office putting together the materials for Peter, the producer of the film. As she had done most of the filming herself or with her husband when he was there, I was in awe of Carol, who had never put together a documentary before. She amazed me with her hard work and drive and her creativity. She had even written the music for the documentary!

My work here at the sanctuary at this time of year was not too strenuous and often in the heat of the day I fell asleep on the couch holding one of the girls. It reminded me of cuddling with Joe and Dan when they were babies. Besides helping feed the wildlife, Carol gave me some detail work on the computer to help her with the documentary. Aalina and I both worked on this project. We all worked well together, but I noticed that Carol rarely took time to fix herself anything proper to eat. I took on the task of fixing our lunches and dinners to keep her healthy and strong as she would always rather keep working than stop to eat.

As we worked and ate together, her story unfolded. "We came from England to start a bed and breakfast. We bought this property for that but then we found a baby kangaroo in his dead mother's pouch. She had been hit by a car. Caring for that baby was the beginning of this sanctuary. We found our love of kangaroos much stronger than the drive to start a bed and breakfast. Over the years, we learned more about the roos and rescued more injured ones. We decided that rather than having a bed and breakfast, we wanted to have a kangaroo sanctuary. Everything we did, we did together to build this place for the kangaroos using volunteers to help us with everything from construction to wildlife care. Our website told about the sanctuary and our need for volunteers and was popular on the continent, which is where most of our volunteers come from. Occasionally Americans come. And then a young Dutch girl came, volunteered, and got it into her head to go after my husband."

"Oh, shit, Carol, I'm going to hate this story."

"My husband of 33 years abandoned me, our marriage, and the sanctuary and they ran off together. Now he expects to divorce me, kick me off this property, and return with his volunteer just like that."

"The bastard. He'll never get this place. Never!"

"He thinks he can wear me down. That I won't be able to function on my own. But he's wrong. Once this documentary sells, I will find a way to continue my work."

"Carol, you are so strong. I find your story so disheartening. It's hard not to just hate them both and be discouraged. But a man who would turn away from you, your marriage, and the roos, well, he is not worthy to be with you. Truly. I don't know him. I don't know anything about your relationship but you are loving. I see that everyone who comes here to help you, to join your cause comes because of who you are. I don't know but I can sense that happiness is going to be yours. Once you get through what seems like a whole bunch of junk that you really didn't need, you'll be a new woman-- freer, stronger, and happier. I can see that. How can I help? Tell me what you need."

"I like having you here, Joyce. I haven't had a woman to talk this stuff out with, mate. For now, keep helping with the feeding, the tracking on the computer, and we'll see. He's not going to get this place. Not after that."

So here was a marriage of 33 years, a bucket of love that Carol thought was full. What once was a healthy love working together building this sanctuary was now ruined. How did it change? Is the love shared between two people over time not enough? Couples sometimes run out of love, the water draining from a bucket from some small unseen hole. The leak goes unnoticed till the bucket is dry. And what happened to make it spring a leak? Is there no love pump to refill it? Can't a patch fix the hole? Or is it just two people on empty heading for disaster as soon as one finds a new mate? Better to be a parrot guaranteed to mate for life.

Every day we talked about hearts and hearts broken with things we shared in common, always finding something of sadness and something of joy to talk about. Carol felt like a lifelong friend to me with her openness and vulnerability about her feelings. Aalina just listened. That kitchen table became our place to talk, to laugh, and to become friends. Everyone from town who came to the house to help with the sanctuary had the same closeness to Carol and respect for her spirit.

So even in far away Australia, men and women confused their relationships and hurt each other with the lack of a lifetime commitment, Mozart's infidelity a worldwide issue. Apparently either the man or the woman could turn their head and decide that what they saw all shiny and new on their left was way better than their life partner who had been walking by their side for years and years. One person all whoopdedoo in love with their new, bright shiny toy leaves the other person in the dust, sad and hurt trying to figure out how they missed it, didn't see it coming. The shock of betrayal. And then the chaos of a hurricane blowing through everything they thought was rock solid. To heal from the hurt. To reorganize their lives into an entirely new life not of their choosing. Is it ever possible to trust a person who has made a commitment to stay?

And with betrayal came heartbreak and sadness, pain and anger. I was sad to know that Carol was going to have to suffer through a divorce, sort through all of the emotions, divide up the cash, and now fight to keep the sanctuary with the very person who had helped her build it. It seemed like a lot of crap from where I was sitting, but I knew she'd fight back and be the better for it. Her spirit was much stronger than one man's goofy ego. Her directness was refreshing. Our long talks helped us both, and I hoped she and I would be friends forever.

Evenings were lovely at the sanctuary. After Aalina left for home, Carol and I would sit in the backyard drinking a beer and watching the roos eat the grain that she put out for them each evening. One night two of the males faced off with each other, each one straightening their spines to be the tallest like they had an extension in their backs. Once they reached their tallest height, one back foot went out in a karate kick. The other roo leaned slowly way back balancing on his tail to avoid the hit, and when he came back up, he sent out a kick. Carol said that this boxing match was for fun, not for a female. They continued in slow motion, kicking, backing onto their tails, never hitting each other and it really was amazing to see them rock back and then kick out. They looked like the blow-up toys that go backwards and then right themselves. It was slow and graceful and funny to watch, like a cartoon.

For the Australia Day Breakfast, Carol and I went to the central park in town to eat sausage and eggs with the entire town gathered together in celebration. It was a perfect opportunity for a taste of Australian culture and I wasn't let me down. Straight shooting conversations and lots of jokes about America that I found hysterical. Carol had found many friends here and each person who greeted her wanted to know how she was holding up under all of the stress. There was a warm feeling of concern.

I met a woman in town who told me that after 24 years, her husband came in one day and said "It's not working."

She said, "What, the car?"

He said, "No, the marriage."

And that was it. He divorced her and starting living with another woman. She told me the story like it was a joke!

"I'm remarried and happier than I was," she said, smiling at me.

Ah, the other way to deal with betrayal. Just blow it off and get on with life. Some people had an easier time trusting again, but I was not one of those people. I survived betrayal and the slide downhill, but I hesitated to jump full on into love again for many years. Trusting, believing, and loving were scary words for me though at times I felt certain that I would love a man again and be loved in return.

But these seven months were the first seven months of true freedom in my entire life. I wanted to treasure the freedom and see what it would create. I had not worried about earning money, saving money, building a business, taking care of my car, taking care of my house, or making sure I had enough money for my sons to go to college. Gone was the pressure of earning money and the responsibility of being somewhere every damn day. I was on vacation from responsibility and celebrating my life. Celebrating that if I had my choice of people to talk to and spend time with, it would be Dan and Joe at the top of the list.

A long, long time ago when they were quite small and I was a single mom, I was incredibly scared that as a divorced mom, a single mom, I was not going to be able to earn enough money without working a full-time job, which would force me to send them to daycare. I wanted to be the mom. I wanted to be the person who loved them, raised them, held them when they were sick or hurt, read them stories. By some miracle, selling Discovery Toys eked out enough money to keep them out of daycare and us warm and safe with food and comfort. When our expenses increased, along came real estate to bring more prosperity and still with the freedom to take summer days off if I wanted to take them to the lake or to volunteer in their classroom.

Those years were a struggle with lots of pressure. I felt like a juggler with too many balls in the air, but I got through it and so did they. Celebration time! Like a tethered balloon whose string had popped, I was floating in the air now, sailing freely around the world.

As my stay went on, the kangaroos, the joeys, and the wallabies got used to me as I fit into the routine. Leila and Kiah, the girls, graduated to spending more and more time outside adjusting to the mob. Usually they stayed in the backyard, but they were starting to follow the mob down to the gully, and Carol encouraged their independence. After a couple of hours with the mob, I walked down to get them holding two empty oversized pillow cases. When I found them, I opened the sacks and they hopped over to me somersaulting into their "pouch" ready to go to the house to take a nap! I carried both pouches over my shoulder and walked up the hill to the house. At night, I cuddled with the girls on the couch, feeding them seeds and wild leaves.

One morning a couple of people arrived at the sanctuary with a very young wallaroo that they had found inside the pouch of a run-over roo. Unable to take care of him themselves, they came to Carol. Nicky was a wallaroo, a first for Carol. He was so tiny as Carol held him in her hands. He was built like a miniature with delicate facial features, sweet big bug eyes, long ears, and long back jumping legs. Carol set him up on a feeding schedule and situated him in a new pouch. Nicky, the mighty Nick, the sweetest little wallaroo and small enough to hold in your hands, stormed into all of our hearts. He hopped mightily around the lounge, fists clenched, hopping with determination, reaching me and then giving my hand a hug. He jumped around the room zooming quickly back to my feet to make sure all was well. He leaned way back on his tail, scratched his belly, and then off he went again till he hurried back to his pillow pouch exhausted from his journey. Hopping amidst the mighty baby wallabies, he jumped into them scaring himself by his own friendliness. With an abundance of personality and attitude, he always made us all laugh.

"Hiss," the wallaby Tyke said. "Get out of here you little runt. You are not a wallaby."

"But I am the mighty Nicky and everyone loves me."

" Ha, not me mate, you look like a scrawny little runt to me not a handsome wallaby. Get lost."

"Are you sure you don't want to cuddle me?"

"Hrmmpphhh no," said Tina. "You are not a wallaby. You are bugging me. Go away now."

And so Nicky jumped to the nearest ankles certain that someone would bend down and cuddle him, tell him he was wonderful, love him. At feeding when I held him in my arms, Nicky lay down on his back, put his long thin legs straight out and his arms above his head, and opened his fists to enjoy his bottle. When finished, he loved a tummy rub.

Sometimes during those night feedings when the sanctuary was quiet, I thought about my life in the United States. Images of people back home passed through my mind. I never saw them clearly; they were always blurred like fast cars zooming by on the freeway. My American life. Multi-tasking my way through the day. Too busy heading to the next place to stop to be in the time of now. A blur of a life.

But I wanted to be here, not thinking about somewhere else. I wanted my physical presence to be connected to my thoughts. I wanted to be in this moment. Smiling the Able smile. To feel the sunset, not just glance at it as I drove over the I-520 bridge on the way to somewhere else. I wanted to hear birds sing, wings flapping when they flew. One life. One ticket for Planet Earth. Right now on this beautiful planet, one life.

One afternoon I could not find the girls. Heading down to the gully to bring them up for their nap, I walked to all of their favorite spots but I could not find them. Really worried I headed up to the house to get Carol.

"Carol, I've looked everywhere and I can't find them! I'm so worried."

We walked together through the area where normally the roos and girls were resting but nothing. Suddenly, off in the distance on the far side of the property, we saw the entire gang hopping at full speed in what looked like panic. Were they running from a fire or gunshots?

"They're definitely scared jumping along the outside perimeter of the compound like they're trying to get out. Something has set them off." She spotted the girls running with the mob and screamed. "The girls can really get hurt. They could be trampled or just outrun their little hearts. We've got to get them. "

"What? What are you saying? How can we help?"

"Let's go catch them."

We went flying through the tall grass hoping to cut off the gang and grab the girls. I wasn't worrying about all those poisonous snakes and spiders living in the tall grass. I just wanted to help Carol get the girls. I couldn't believe the speed of the mob as we ran to intersect them. They were flying but Carol timed it perfectly grabbing Leia out of the mob that kept flying by. But we still needed to find Kiah. Where was she?

Roos sweat on their front feet and legs to keep themselves cool when they are in an emergency. Poor little Leia was covered in a foamy sweat and her heart was racing. While Carol cradled her, we found Kiah lying down. She was exhausted from overexerting herself.

"These girls are in bad shape but they'll make it."

We held them in our arms and brought them up to the house. After making sure that they were okay, they gladly went into their pouches for a nap. I was a wreck from worry.

"I can't figure what happened to the gang? I didn't hear anything unless they were over by that tree when a big limb broke off. If they were nearby, the loud thump would have spooked them."

As Carol said this, we noticed that the gang had finally slowed down nearby. All of them were lathered up on their front legs in a protective, cooling sweat. We never did figure out what it was that had spooked them.

During my last night I closed my eyes listening to the crunch of corn from the mob as they ate outside my window. At Roo Gully Sanctuary in small town Boyup Brook, I awoke to wild green parrots chirping on the lawn in the morning and saw the stars at night. I listened to the laughing song of the kookaburra and smelled the eucalyptus leaves growing wild. I cuddled a joey, a sweet wallaby, and a handsome wallaroo. The tranquility of a sanctuary. All of these things filled my senses as I breathed in the air of Australia, a peacefulness in spirit.

If I could sign up to be a native in a friendly tribe, I would do it. Feeling love, connection, and admiration. All of these were here at this sanctuary. Connections. We are always looking for connections, it seems. People are happy when they love and are loved. They walk around sad and angry when they are not in love, with their spirit suffering from a constant low-grade fever.

My year-long celebration felt perfect here and I loved talking to Carol. We had talked about men, visited with her friends, worked hard when needed, which, for Carol, was all of the time. She was completely devoted and her talent meant that the roos had someone to help them.

Carol wanted me to stay longer and I wished that I could, but I was scheduled to fly to the North Island of New Zealand to volunteer for five weeks at the Tararu Valley Sanctuary where I would learn about sustainability by living it. I had a very hard time saying goodbye to Carol and all of the wildlife. I admired her in so many ways. I hoped I would come back someday to work together with Carol.

CHAPTER 14

The Tararu Valley Sanctuary in New Zealand

ARRIVING IN NEW ZEALAND after a marathon trip from Boyup Brook that involved a bus, a train, a midnight plane to Sydney, and then a 7am flight to catch a bus from Auckland to the small town of Thames on the North Island, I was flat-out exhausted, grungy, and wrinkly but I wasn't upset and I wasn't crying! I chuckled to myself at these little signs that I was adjusting to international travel after only 7 months. The little town of Thames looked like it was deserted as I stood on the sidewalk looking for my ride.

Dagmar, an attractive German redhead in her 30s and bursting with energy, met me at the bus stop and we hopped into a beat-up old 60s VW bus that reminded me of Tony and the Restoration Project in Italy. We drove about 20 minutes out of town turning onto a winding narrow gravel road up a steep hill. There was a beautiful river flowing below in the valley. I hoped we wouldn't meet another vehicle coming down though because the road was only wide enough for one car and the edge of the road was an abrupt drop off right down to the river. The land around me looked like a combination of forest greens of the Northwest, rainforests of Australia, and cattle ranches from the Midwestern American States. Most of the trees though had been cleared for sheep herding, which supported the population here for many years.

Arriving at the Tararu Valley Sanctuary's original house, I was really back in the 1960s. There was a ramshackle hippy dark-green wood house, big vegetable gardens, sheds, a large barn-like structure, and something that looked like an earth house.

"This is where we all used to live when the sanctuary started. The family that lived at the top of the hill let their sheep loose continually, and they ate our vegetables and ruined our land, creating a constant source of frustration for us. Finally we purchased their property through the Tararu Sanctuary Trust, and now we work on this entire side of the hill. The Tararu Sanctuary has a goal to replant all of this pasture to return it to its natural state. You'll learn all about our projects from John."

Dagmar drove us up an even steeper gravel road to the top of the hill to a big rambler that housed the volunteers, a smaller separate house for John and Dagmar, the managers of the project, plus an office building and a barn. Surrounded by the 140,000 acres of the Coromandel State Forest, I looked out at the sparkling bay below and the clear blue sky and fluffy white clouds above and felt at home. When Dagmar showed me my room, it surprised me to learn that I had my own room with a view of the bay. Though I knew I wouldn't be spending any daylight hours here--no siestas in New Zealand--it was lovely to have privacy.

My fellow volunteers were all under 27 and, for the first time, surprisingly all American except for one British woman. John Traylen, our leader was a tall, handsome, lean and muscular New Zealander, who started this sanctuary while following his passion to help the planet by living and teaching others to live sustainably. Intense times three, intelligent, a bundle of energy in constant movement, John understood the need for sustainability at a very young age, before the word had a following. The driving force at Tararu, he epitomized what one man could create by following his dream. Dagmar, who was a biologist and John's girlfriend, was a light touch at the sanctuary, softly smiling at all of us and giving it her best at all times as she patiently worked with everyone including John. Yin and yang.

But my first dinner with the group felt strange. The team on dinner prepared our vegetarian food and then we all sat down at a long table to eat. Remembering the fun at the Monkey Sanctuary, I looked forward to lots of chatter and laughter but John talked while everyone else was quiet, strangely quiet. Were they tired? Shy? Was dinner traditionally a lecture format? Whatever was going on, I noticed a discomfort here but put it off to my adjustment to a new project.

John explained sustainability, a topic that I knew very little about.

"Sustainable living is a lifestyle that harmonizes both human and environmental ecologies, meeting the needs of the present without compromising the ability of future generations to meet their own needs. Sustainable living is an ethic of stewardship for the environment. We need to think about living with a smaller ecological footprint.

"We have extremely huge footprints today. If every person lived as the average wealthy American does today, we'd need almost ten planets worth of resources to sustain ourselves. When we throw out our old television, we don't think about the toxic chemicals and heavy metals that will seep into the landfill and then flow into the groundwater. When we install a new hardwood floor rather than bamboo, we don't see the forests disappearing in a cloud of chainsaw smoke.

"But we ought to see these things. Every day I want you to think about your footprint here and when you go home to continue making it smaller. Don't go to the store and buy something small in a plastic carton in a cardboard box with cellophane around it put in a plastic bag to take home. Live your life using resources that are sustainable. While you are here, I will teach you how to live sustainably."

This first lesson in sustainability struck a chord with me. Instead of just admiring the beauty of the planet and wanting to protect it, I could learn to live with a smaller footprint, to make conscious decisions and help to make change. I was excited to learn more.

John went on with the lesson. "My goal here is to grow most of our own food supplemented with beans and grains. With three wind turbines on the hill near the house, we produce our own electricity but it is turned off at 10pm to conserve power. Flashlights and candles are fine and for reading at night in bed, wear your headlamp. To conserve water, our showers are set to 10 minutes maximum with warm water heated by solar power. We cook with either propane in the gas stove or with wood in the cast iron stove. Because refrigerators are huge electricity consumers, we have a small half refrigerator that holds only yogurt and a bit of milk. Fresh veggies are growing in our organic vegetable patch that we fertilize with worm tea, fish tea, and a plant mixture to keep the bugs away. We recycle and compost in an attempt to keep our ecological footprint small. We do not buy processed foods and avoid unnecessary packaging.

"You must become aware of waste reduction, which means using less of the earth's resources to live our lives. Sustainable living means taking no more than 'your fair share' and giving back as much as you can to the Earth and its people."

I listened intently and then at a pause, I spoke up. "All of this is an entirely new concept for me, John, but one that I feel very close to. What you say makes sense to me but I live more with my eyes shut than open. I'm ready to change that."

He smiled at me. "My perspective on the need for environmental action is a bit like this: Humanity can be thought to be riding a big bus. Call the bus 'modern civilization. In terms of the global environment, virtually every intelligent mind on earth agrees we are driving this bus of ours towards a cliff—planetary ecological disaster. But we're in a thick fog, we don't know where the cliff is, nor how far away our bus is from the cliff. We certainly don't know what the minimal braking distance is. Even with the brakes on full, the bus may still find the unseen cliff. So rather than slow down our bus, we argue over the details, and meanwhile we're accelerating, as more and more humans join us on the planet, and the footprint of each person grows heavier. Our bus is in fact speeding up! Since we've never tried to slow down, and we don't know if we can, it might be wise to test the brakes."

I thought about how much I had to learn here in order to help the earth, not just use her but protect her. This sanctuary would be a great way to begin a new way of living but I still wondered why it was so quiet at the table.

"We have several projects that are ongoing here every day. The trap lines need to be walked each day to collect any dead possums and reset the traps. (What I thought was that about? dead possums?) We have the organic garden, building the nursery building, and planting the tiny trees in the outdoor nursery. All of us take turns with the trap lines and Josh can take you up and show you what to do."

On my first full day, all eight volunteers drove off in the VW bus for a 6-hour training hike in preparation for a tough 5-day hike coming up. Besides working on sustainability, the sanctuary offered hikes, rock climbing, and kayaking as part of the project. Arriving at a beautiful rainforest, the hike up the mountain followed an old pack mule track and after the first hour I felt like an old pack mule that desperately needed to be turned out to pasture. With no strenuous activity in Australia for the last month, I was out of shape and unable to stay with the young volunteers up this really steep trail. Had they never heard of switchbacks in New Zealand? If I saw one more step, I was gonna collapse. Jet lag? Old age? Or just out of shape?

"You guys go on up without me. I am clean out of energy and will just slow you down," I said panting.

"No, come on, we can do it together." Dawn said. Dawn was a pretty young woman with long brown hair, sweet and spiritual. She worked with young children at home. We would get to know each other working on the garden and on a kayaking trip. Her compassion was heart-warming.

"No," I said, "I'm so sorry. I must be channeling a stubborn mule on this path I think and without a good kick I'm staying put. Total body refusal! My knees hurt and my feet say no more. I might be able to crawl but that's it. Sorry, I am totally out of shape."

Reluctantly they hiked up the mountain leaving me to breath in the gorgeous green, moist rainforest, the fresh smell of the damp earth while listening to the song of nearby birds. I sat down on the path step completely disappointed in myself for not being able to keep up. I felt old and decrepit for the first time in a long time as I rubbed my old knees encouraging them. I grumbled, not used to calling uncle when I wanted to hike. As I hiked down the too steep steps, I made a plan to get in shape here. Stopping by the river listening to the water flow over the rocks, I took a quick nap until the rest of the volunteers returned.

On the return trip home, Steve slowly navigated up the narrow road being extra cautious in the dark because he was new to driving on the right side of the car on the right side of the road. But by staying too far from the scary edge that went straight down to the river, he landed us in a ditch on the hill side of the road. We all bailed out of the van to have a look. We were high-ended in the ditch in a beat-up old VW bus but the guys heard the call of the macho and wanted to push it out of the ditch.

"Shouldn't we send someone up the hill to get John?" I asked.

Everyone groaned in unison. "You don't know John yet."

"What do you mean? We need his help."

And that was when it began, my education about the tension at the sanctuary. A combination of not wanting to disappoint John, not wanting to ask for his help, not wanting to suffer from his temper, kept the young men trying to sort it out while we females gathered outside the bus, looked at the stars, and talked about the atmosphere at the sanctuary.

I really liked all of the volunteers here and I was about to learn that it was the tension between them and John that was distracting. They felt totally unappreciated and John was continually unhappy with the quality of their work.

Steve revved up the engine and we all got behind the bus to push it but the wheels were spinning. I was convinced we were going to either ruin the bus or hurt someone. As the resident mom, I finally put my foot down and told them to call John. How mean could this man be? This was like being with teenagers when they didn't want to get in trouble with their parents.

Finally someone called John for help and in a short time he had us back up the hill in the other car with a plan to rescue the van the following day. John was not yelling though the tension in the air was palpable.

Morning came and the van was easily pulled out of the ditch without any harm, but there was definitely the feeling of anger in the air. I explained the circumstances to John to clear the air, but the tension lingered. John seemed, in many ways, like an ogre to me. His gruffness set a tone here that I didn't like at all. Thinking of my primate friends, I saw that John was the dominant male gathering the troop around him and ordering us all about. If sustainability was the theme here, I thought that first we'd better work on sustainable attitudes and learn to create harmony as we worked together.

Lunch time brought another of the strange mealtime routines with John doing all of the talking. Somehow this particular group of volunteers and John were not grooving on each other. The volunteers thought he was unhappy with the lack of intensity of their work and that he was just plain grumpy. He treated the group without respect and they responded to him like children. Everyone turned their faces down and ate while John lectured.

"I want to explain the purpose of heritage seeds and their importance in sustainability. If you compare a seed catalog from the early 1900s and look at beans, peas, lettuce, broccoli, and carrots, you'll find over 70 different types of broccoli, as well as many kinds of the other vegetables. If you look at a catalog today, maybe three types of each vegetable are sold. What does this mean? When a farmer plants his fields, the more different varieties of a crop he plants, the better he can withstand a disease that may only wipe out one variety. Using heritage seeds encourages diversity, keeping seeds around that would otherwise be in danger of permanently disappearing. Heritage seeds help insure plant diversity and it is this diversity that works to promote food security. We'll be visiting an organic farm today where they are also producing heritage seeds to sell."

"I had no idea about heritage seeds." I said.

"Nor did I," Dawn chimed in.

"Yes, there are many things that people are unaware of," John said. "Humans are no longer as healthy as they were in earlier times."

"What do you mean?" I asked. "We live longer than we did before. How can you say we are not as healthy?" I was probably just looking for a point of conflict to see where it would go, testing the waters.

"Because of antibiotics, which create a false health," John said, looking squarely at me.

"But penicillin means someone doesn't have to die from an infection. Now that is not a false health," I replied.

Feeling a wave of stubbornness, I asked, "What is your definition of healthy, John?"

"What is yours?" he asked me, probably sensing the tug of war.

"I asked you first." I said, smiling at him.

He gave me a definition that I couldn't understand, but I didn't back down. I was in a mood for some verbal ping pong, and the others were all watching intently.

I told him mine. "For me healthy is having an awareness of what my body is doing and what it needs and finding a balance."

"Only a yogi could do that," he said with that "I'm right, you're wrong" tone that always gets my goat.

Sighing, I said, "Well, that's true but it is possible to begin having an awareness to guide yourself towards health and it is still my definition of health. I wonder what the dictionary says."

I also wondered how to change the energy here. This man really needed control and he was making me a little crazy. I loved his cause and his passion. I loved his knowledge. He knew so much about things that I wanted to learn about but jez, someone had to give him some people skills. When I thought about different atmospheres at the volunteer projects, it was the leader who set the tone, bringing energy to the group. That just wasn't happening here.

John pushed his chair back to end the conversation. "Here are some heritage seeds that have been germinating in a plastic bag and are now ready to be planted," he said.

So we left our tug of war for the excitement of learning to help the planet.

After lunch we drove to the little town of Thames to an organic farm run by a couple in their 50s who grew heritage seeds and organic vegetable starts to sell in town. There was a little farmhouse straight out of rural Illinois surrounded by large gardens, an enormous greenhouse, and cows out in the pasture. John took most everyone out to the field to cut some wood, but Dawn and I stayed to help Paul and learn about organic gardening to increase the crops in our own gardens.

Paul was a tall, burly man around 60 with a straightforward attitude. "You know I had no idea this little potting thing would take off. I was headed in an entirely different direction and my wife started selling these starts. Before we knew it, my plan wasn't really working and her plan was flying. Well, the people came from everywhere to buy her starts and get her advice. Now this is what we do entirely. Smart woman, she is," he said smiling. "So do you know how to transfer these starts to larger pots?"

"Yes, we do." Dawn and I nodded at Paul.

"Okay, well, I'll just leave you to it and if you have any questions, I'll be in the greenhouse. Thanks for your help."

"Dawn, we are on our own," I said. I loved the work and getting to know gentle Dawn.

When he returned, Paul told us, "John wants you two to head down to the field and help load the wood onto the truck."

When we arrived on the scene, John was giving orders. "Start using the saws to cut the smaller pieces and then help load them onto the truck."

Walking over to the logs, we crossed a wet area of land and I got my foot stuck in the muck, which stunk something awful. "What is this stuff, John? The smell is horrible."

"Oh, nothing to worry about," he replied.

Everyone else was exhausted from the work and rather than complain, I worked in the wet, smelly muck, sawing and loading wood. John ignored the apparent exhaustion on everyone's faces. He's the type of man who could easily do an Ironman, I thought, boundless energy and figuring that everyone else could keep up. After felling one last tree that landed onto the neighbor's fence, he finally decided we could stop. We loaded ourselves onto the van smelly, wet, tired, and hungry but I had to admit it did feel great to have worked hard.

On the way home we stopped to talk to Paul, who commented on our smell. "What in the world is that nasty odor coming from the van?"

We told him where we were working.

"Oh dear," he said. "That's not water, that's where all of the cow waste collects. John, didn't you know that? Now you kids get home and wash well."

As wet cow crap seeped into my shoes and pants and skin, everyone was grossed out and grumpy with John, who obviously knew but didn't warn us.

WE HAD A WEEKLY chore schedule just like at the Monkey Sanctuary. The morning began with a complete house cleanup. Josh and I were on kitchen duty, a room in dire need of a thorough scrubbing. At 19, Josh, a tall, lanky young man on his way to college, who probably drank and smoked too much weed, had an easy-going nature, and we laughed together while we cleaned. Josh told me that he liked being around my energy and believed it was a healing energy. Over our weeks together, Josh and I would become great bread-making friends. I prepared the dough and he used his enormous strong hands to knead. We built a fire in the stove and everyone celebrated when the warm bread was ready to eat.

On our first afternoon off, everyone walked down the road to Thames with our laundry bags over our shoulders smelling of cow crap stinky pants.

When we reached the main road I told Josh and Dawn, "I'm gonna hitchhike to town. Care to join me?"

Dawn and Josh laughed. They didn't quite believe me but they agreed to join me if anyone stopped. Sure enough a man stopped and we piled into his car. He was just a bit younger than me, medium build, grey hair, and average looks. He was from Thames.

"My name is Joe," he said. "So what kind of a group are you three?"

"We're working at the Tararu Valley Sanctuary up the road," I said. "Please pardon the smell. We were working in a cow poo field. Sorry."

He laughed, "Well, I don't know what you are doing up there. Never heard of the place but maybe I'll see you later in town."

"Thanks for the ride."

While our laundry washed, I checked emails and was happy to have one from Leonard, whom I'd met in the London train station. His literary poetic writings to me were appealing in a new way. He was so honest about his feelings with no need to hide his emotions, and we communicated on a much different level than usual for me. We wrote each other ever since meeting in England four months earlier, and we both wanted to see each other again when I went to Ireland. Having an email romance was sweet though after never hearing from Robert, I had little faith in long-distance romances going anywhere. I resigned myself to 'holidating.'

After the laundry was done, we all wanted a beer and some red meat, so we walked to a local pub where we spent a great night meeting the locals and eating a juicy burger. Joe showed up and we had a chance to talk.

"So how did you come to be working at a place in Thames?"

I explained my yearlong trip.

We talked some more and he issued an invitation. "Would you like to go fishing with me and my friends on the ocean tomorrow?"

Hmm, I thought, how great to be out on a boat. "Sure. Sounds great but we only have one phone and it's not in our house. I might not be around to answer."

"Well, here's my phone. Call me and we'll go."

"Okay. I'm a definite maybe. Being on the water in a kayak is great but I usually get seasick and throw up when I'm fishing. You might be better off without me!"

With drinks and laughter, we felt great. I liked Joe's easy-going nature but I wasn't sure about spending the day with strangers on a boat getting seasick. Besides I'd have to see what I felt like in the morning. I doubted I'd call him.

JOHN ORGANIZED A camping trip with a 2-day training hike but he decided the weather was too crappy for us to go. After my first hiking experience, I was relieved because I still felt out of shape. Instead, he sent some of us out to work on the trap lines while others worked on carpentry projects.

Josh and I took the trail called Tararu. There were about 5 different trap lines and thank goodness Josh had brought trekking poles and didn't need them because the steep trail of slippery mud wasn't an easy path to hike. Stopping at each trap to check them, we found a dead possum, a dead ferret, and a dead rat. Poor Josh had to be the one to grab them and put them into plastic bags. Then we stored them into the old yucky backpack that I was wearing. He taught me how to reset the traps. Neither one of us liked this job at all, nor did it feel right walking with dead animals in my pack at a vegetarian sanctuary.

This New Zealand possum was nothing like our ugly North American possum; it had a cute little face and was about the size of a cat with a fat tail. But like the prickly pear of Australia, they were not indigenous to New Zealand and they had no natural enemies.

"I hate doing this trapping even though I know the possums ruin the forest." Josh said.

"Yea, me too, but how else can we protect the tree buds? It's strange that an animal that is considered cute in Australia is public enemy number one here. What do we do with them when we get back down?"

"There's a disgusting pit that we bury them in. Really gross."

Josh did everything slowly and our walk was at a lovely slow pace. But even using the poles, my damn knees were achy from the constant pressure down a slippery, steep mud path.

"I'll have to ask Dagmar how she rationalizes being a vegetarian and trapping possums. Tough choice between killing something and letting it kill instead."

Arriving home just in time for lunch, we sat down hungry.

"Dagmar, can you explain the possum problem here?

John answered, "Possums were introduced here around 1837 from Australia to start a fur trade. In Australia the trees have natural defenses like spines, prickles, and poisonous leaves, and the possum is actually protected there. But the ecosystem here has trees like pohutukawa, rata, totara, kowhai, and kohekohe with no defenses. The number one enemy of the pohutukawa and rata trees is the possum! They eat new growth and will go back every night eating the same tree till it is almost dead. Not only do they kill the tree destroying bird food and habitat, but they also eat bird eggs. They are a perfect example of how the introduction of a non-indigenous species takes an ecosystem out of balance."

"They ravage the native bush and are nearly single-handedly responsible for putting Kiwis on the endangered list. The New Zealand government has all sorts of incentives to create industries and crafts using possum, the most successful of which has been high-end woolen knits of possum fur spun with merino wool, marketed as 'merino mink.' Without trapping, the 70 million possum here in New Zealand will eat 20,000 tons of vegetation every night! We'll lose our ecosystem." Dagmar explained. As a biologist, she was committed to protecting the environment and I decided to follow her lead.

Then John made another of his announcements. "We'll be taking a hike at three today."

"How steep is the hike, John?" I asked.

He answered by telling me it would be fine. Obviously, he doesn't have achy knees.

I persisted. "John, can you tell me how the hike compares to the trail I just walked up the trapline? What level of steepness is it?"

"I can't really say."

"I'm worried about my knees that are really achy after that trap line. Can you give me a clue? Just hold your hand at the angle that the hike may be."

But no answer again. I didn't think that an answer to my question was too much to ask for. The man had been ordering teenagers and 20-somethings around for so long he had no idea how to treat a woman. I really didn't know how to turn this around.

I decided to just speak up for myself. "I am going to go to the Buddhist Shrine down the hill instead, John. I'm nervous about going somewhere too steep."

"Well, the hike to the shrine will be steeper than what we are doing."

Again a tug of war. My stubbornness took charge faced with a male who thought he could get control of me. Issues. Always issues even in New Zealand. I said, "Well, I want to meditate today."

Completely frustrated with John and our inability to communicate, I put on my shoes and walked down the driveway chastising myself for getting into a control battle with him. Why did it always feel like he was telling me things instead of talking to me? How could I keep from getting frustrated? I wanted to learn but not be ordered about. Issues.

Passing me in the car with the other volunteers, he said nicely, "Don't you want to go to the beach with us and hike?"

"No, John. I don't." shaking my head and continuing to walk obviously frustrated.

He drove on but stopped ahead to once again ask me if I would like to join them. But I was all caught up in my own issues, having an old knee jerk reaction to difficult men. Even if I wanted to go with them, I was way too stubborn by then to allow John to "win." We were definitely bringing up old stuff with each other, and this walk on my own was necessary to blow off steam and get a grip.

Here at Tararu the stress from a tense working environment uncovered questions about my path and my growth. John provided the perfect opportunity for me to either get ticked or get over it. We could communicate or play tug of war. Stubbornness was not a solution.

Wandering down the road and up to the Buddhist shrine, I had no idea if the road was steep because I was too filled with frustration to pay attention to it. Could I adjust to this energy for another four weeks as it was? There was some male energy that was just too macho, too out of touch, and too damn bossy for me to be around. Was that the case here? Out of balance. No laughter and no light. The world doesn't need macho fire. And I didn't need to go stubborn.

I still didn't know what to do when a feeling like a giant wave washed over me. On this journey of my soul, I was uncertain where to go to find my peace. If I stayed here, I needed to relieve the stress. I wanted to find a way to make it work.

Arriving at the Buddhist shrine, I sat down and meditated looking for a breath of fresh air to clear out my unhappy mood. This place of peace, meditation, and silence faced our hill. Here people were encouraged to walk with grace, to live in peace, and over there people were living with dissatisfaction, unrest, grumpiness, and a constant tug of war between personalities. Two hills facing. Two different energies.

The walk back to the house was a strenuous uphill trek. John was probably right about the steepness but the meditation had been a good idea.

When the crew returned, they were all smiles.

"Hey Joyce, you would have loved it. It was pretty flat and nice." Dawn said.

"Yea, we had a great time." Josh told me.

"Great, glad it worked out."

"How was the Buddhist shrine?"

"It was very quiet. I didn't see anyone at the houses there but I had a chance to meditate and clear out some cobwebs. I feel better but John was right. It was really steep."

OUR ORGANIC GARDEN grew strong using only completely natural products to control insects and to fertilize. Bunnies were our only problem. Never having done any organic gardening, the process of making our "teas" from worms working in a box, from different leaves we gathered for pest control, and from fish bones for fertilizer fascinated me. Jo, Dawn, and I worked well together on the garden talking about guys, love, sex and the atmosphere here. Sometimes I felt like the struggle here was too much for me but at other times, I felt it was up to me to use my wisdom to change things.

I was here again with youth. I wondered why this journey had me consistently in the presence of kids, volunteering, listening and laughing with people my sons' ages. I listened to them as they wondered about the world, wondered what they would do next. I too wondered about my life.

Generally youth thinks age and maturity are from a different planet. Youth judges maturity as lacking in energy and life-force. I kept hearing that from talks with younger volunteers. Why was that? How was it that maturity was not respected for its wisdom? Why would my vitality, my silliness, and my openness surprise these kids?

I was not an extraordinary human by any measure. I believe in questioning my life hoping to learn and to prevent habits from boxing me in. I nourished my sense of wonder. I knew that I was getting stronger by being away, getting stronger by living with people in many different settings.

Each country gave me something new to stretch my viewpoint and something new to reflect on about myself. Now New Zealand asked me to find harmony and a way to communicate with a controlling man. To bring one side of the mountain to the other side, one hell of a challenge for me! Here at Tararu Valley Sanctuary, there was agreement as well as conflict. I understood John; I disagreed with John.

At a breakfast meeting to talk about our work, John was being rather curt with everyone about chores that needed to be done. I was sick of listening to his bad attitude. Everyone here was a volunteer, not a slave, and John gave orders like it was an army.

I decided to speak up. "John, I disagree with how you are handling this situation."

"Well, that's not really your place, Joyce," he replied, frowning.

"Well, I think it is. I am here as a volunteer. I would like to feel some respect from you for the time and energy I'm putting in."

We stared at each other. Everyone watched the showdown at the OK Corral.

"I would like to talk to you after the meeting, Joyce."

"Sounds great to me," I answered, nodding.

We met outside the house, like two gunfighters, our hands on our guns ready to draw.

"John, I don't like the way you are treating me."

"Well, I don't like the way you are treating me."

"Well, I believe that I said it first and it deserves a discussion to clear the air."

"I think you need to be more respectful to me, Joyce."

Were we two children sticking out our tongues at each other?

One more time I tried to communicate. "I have asked you to be polite to me, John. That issue needs to be dealt with first. Now if you have nothing to say to that, I'm out of here."

He said nothing and I walked away to work in the garden. I really liked John, all of his devotion and fire to work for the planet was passion that I respected. Somehow I wasn't communicating this respect to him, and he in turn needed to understand my earnest desire to really help here and to learn from him. All but one of the volunteers was unhappy here because of his gruffness.

In the middle of my talking to Dawn and pulling weeds in the garden, Dagmar came over, "Joyce, how about if you, John, and I have a conversation?"

"Yea," I said, "that is fine with me but I am not talking to him unless you are there."

Dagmar was the sweetness here at the sanctuary, always kind and working well with all of the volunteers.

We talked in the old hippie house near the garden. Tension was the biggest player and poor Dagmar attempted to keep a lid on the anger in the room, making us each stop and listen to each other. For two hours we hammered it out. Two hours.

John shared his frustration with the group of volunteers not working hard enough, his stress about meeting the demands that the property was making financially, and his attitude towards me. He felt that I was undermining his authority by criticizing him. I discussed the atmosphere here and how difficult it was to volunteer in this unappreciative, tense environment. I told him how his attitude made me feel. I cried when I spoke from the stress of the confrontation.

We barked at each other till there was no bark left. A battle of titans. Dagmar kept us from chewing each other up and somehow when all the anger was gone, we both took a deep breath. The tone changed.

We spoke then from the heart about our feelings under the anger. We spoke about our shared passion for helping the earth. I told John how much I respected his work and sincerely wanted to help. He listened and heard me. With Dagmar's gentle prodding, we found common ground and started on a path towards solutions. It was like watching the sun come out after a miserable storm.

What did the volunteers need here? We needed a free day; we needed things to cheer up, to feel respected. I wanted the volunteers to be happier here. John wanted more work out of everyone here. No slackers. He was under a lot of pressure. We talked long and hard.

I wanted John's dream to work. He loved the earth. He carried frustrations from the world's lack of caring for the land, the air, the trees, and nature as he focused on sustainability. He passionately believed that we were heading for a disaster unless we learned to live within our resources respecting the earth. He wanted the volunteers to share his vision and commitment to this project. Commitment to a cause that his entire being was passionate about.

I looked at it with different eyes, explaining the atmosphere at other places where I had volunteered. I explained that the emotional energy of a place was as important as getting the work done. John knew about sustainability. I knew about group dynamics. He listened. We were finally on the same page. I too wanted the earth protected. I also wanted people to learn to work together with respect and understanding. We listened to each other and gained understanding. A lovely transformation, truly amazing.

John and I hugged with a new respect for each other. Life at the sanctuary changed for all of us.

Through conflict I learned about myself. Through conflict, I spoke my truth about what I felt. A conflict with a strong man was resolved through honest, open communication. It was celebration time for that one.

Balance. Balance was the goal. Surrounding myself with differences to allow myself to see who I was and learn to communicate through conflict. Surrounding myself with kindred spirits to feel the comfort of understanding. I needed both as I carved out the path of my life. Age. Wisdom. Spirit. Courage.

The atmosphere at the sanctuary improved almost immediately. I heard more laughter. Dinner was no longer a lecture but conversations. We got a full free day and afterwards everyone worked harder. I walked around feeling very satisfied. Tararu had really needed our conversation. Both John and I needed to blow off steam. I could have left this place in disgust but instead I stayed and with Dagmar's patience and guidance, we talked.

Why did I feel the need to bother? Why not just leave? Because I wanted to improve my ability to communicate through tough situations. Because I wanted success here in atmosphere as well as in education. I was very proud of our outcome.

John planned a weekend kayaking trip to Tiritiri Matangi Island, a 550-acre bird sanctuary. One hundred and fifty years ago the island had been cleared for cultivation and livestock grazing but all of that changed when it became a sanctuary. Millions of hours of volunteer time were spent replanting and removing all mammals - rats, possums, feral cats, and mice. The sanctuary was now home to rare birds: stitch birds, North Island saddlebacks, takahe, brown teal, and the little spotted kiwi, among others. Now only 20 years later, the birds flourished a true conservation success story.

John knew that I had kayaked before and he gave me a light, fast kayak that flew across the waters of the calm Hauraki Gulf 15 miles from Auckland, New Zealand's largest city. Thrilled to be kayaking on the open sea with the sound of water and little penguins swimming near us, the 3-hour paddle was pure heaven. My kayak was fast!

Arriving at this island sanctuary, we took our supplies to the bunk house where we'd be staying. John warned us to stay away from the takahe bird because they had been known to poke at people with their sharp beaks. I headed to the beach to read and sleep before our nature walk and paddle around the island, but there was a surprise in store for me.

The takahe, found only in New Zealand, is built like a turkey, a flightless bird that apparently looks like it did about 80 million years ago with black, bright blue and green feathers, a reddish-orange beak, and big three-toed feet. Tiri is known for its takahes with a colony of 20, who hang out at the beach greeting tourists, posing for cameras, and generally stalking humans through the many paths of the island.

I fell asleep in the sun on the beach, not thinking about birds at all. Suddenly I heard shouts.

"Get up!"

"Wake up! Old Blue is on your towel!"

I opened my eyes to a big bright reddish-orange beak and strange toes moving dangerously close to my eyes! Flying off my towel, my heart racing and thankful that my top was tied, I watched him peck through my stuff. His feet were really amazing and his feathers shone in the sunshine like a peacock, the hues of blues and greens blending together. But with prehistoric-looking birds invading my beach time, it was definitely time to leave for a paddle around the island.

ALTHOUGH I WAS in New Zealand working on a conservation project, it had certainly been a people project in the beginning. Emotions, tension, stresses and miscommunication had all distracted me from the main goal. People learning to cope with each other, to talk to each other, to appreciate each other. A team getting built amidst different goals, different needs, different abilities, and different energy levels with management stressed from too much responsibility. No wonder it took me four weeks to see the conservation work!

After a month, I finally had a feel for what I was doing here. Conservation work was not sexy. There was no tree that came running up to me or looked at me with big brown eyes. I didn't get a hug. If I repotted a plant or fed it, I couldn't see the smile of appreciation. But I began to wake up anxious to get started.

A combination of events opened my eyes to the wonder of this project. First, I walked up a trap line with Ninja, the dog, to reset the traps. I discovered that my knees were getting stronger. The tree ferns had my heart with fronds up to a meter long sprouting into an umbrella on top of their black trunk, which could grow 15 feet tall. As I walked through this wet green, I breathed in pure nature surrounded by the singing of birds and the buzzing of insects. Conservation work would keep this beauty alive on our planet.

I come from a place where forests are lush and beautiful, and a drive from the city takes me to a mountain with an evergreen forest full of pine, cedar, and oak. At Tararu hiking up the steep path, I was under the cover of tree ferns providing an umbrella for me of gorgeous green leaves, under the closed canopy of a rainforest, a moist shaded world of immense beauty. Freshness in the air from the damp moss on the earth. So healing to breathe in this air.

An enormous fallen tree blocked my path that day, and I lay down on it to take in the ceiling of green in all directions. I listened to the sounds of the forest, felt the freshness of the air, and understood my connection with nature. I am the quiet found only in a forest. The overgrown forest leaves reached out to touch me, touch my face, little drops of moisture falling to my cheek, the incomparable smell of an undisturbed rainforest. I had been here with my eyes on the people, but now I saw the beautiful ferns and trees, the forests that John and Dagmar were working hard to protect. Magic in the middle of a forest. Nature brought me peace. All things easy not to notice, easy to take for granted. The magic of trees. The beauty of the forest. The connection. I am the quiet found only in a forest.

After I finished resetting the trap line, my next job was to make more seed balls, a fun project that was like making snowballs out of wet dirt with seeds inside and then throwing them over the hill where they would germinate on their own. Finishing with seed balls, I moved to the tall grass to weed and mulch the 1-year-old trees.

John planned to reforest the cleared hills and over the years volunteers had planted young trees all over this hill. They need to be mulched to keep them growing strong. Each tree was weeded, mulched with scraps of old clothes, and then mulched on top with compost. I thought back to caring for baby lions and joeys and now caring for young trees.

One day this ridge would be filled with trees, a forest like the nearby Coromandel Forest. Someone would hike through this ridge full of beautiful trees because of the passions and dreams of one man and his group of volunteers. Things changed because the land had a hero; the land had someone who cared. Today I finally understood what I was doing here. Though I could not cuddle a tree, I could still smile when it was planted. John taught us all to look at the earth as he did.

I tumbled onto my back resting in the tall grass gazing up at the sky and thought about how many of us ignored the earth and used her resources, cut her trees, polluted the air with our cars, and took her for granted. Time to think about doing things in a different way. But it was not sexy, this conservation work. Weeding, mulching, planting, building nurseries, this was not glamorous work.

"Yea, baby, I planted 20 trees today."

What was exciting about this?

"I ate today entirely from the garden. I baked bread on a stove that used wood. I recycled everything I used and composted all of the waste."

It was just not sexy, not cool, not exciting. And yet, it was. Healing our atmosphere was important. Healing our earth.

The lesson for the sanctuary? Volunteers needed to feel that their contributions were a part of something bigger in order to recognize the importance of the task at hand. We as a tribe needed to have a connection first; then we could recognize our work.

And maybe that was why we destroyed the earth, not bothering to protect it. We didn't feel a part of the tribe, the family of man. We saw individual people all living in individual houses taking care of individual problems buying individual food, clothing, and housing. The problems of the earth were someone else's problem.

We missed the connection we had with each other. We missed the connection we had with the earth. Both were present. Both were necessary to really be alive. Each tree we helped to grow in turn helped us. Why was it easy to be part of the disconnect? Easy to feel unappreciated, misunderstood, and alone both from each other and from the earth that houses us. Easy to be distracted by jobs, stress, and money. A lack of love, a lack of inspiration, and the inability to see how to close the gap. The gap between what our soul seeks and what we are doing.

My lesson here was profound. I had always felt a connection to the planet, to the wonder of trees, but now I felt the connection between it all...the people, the trees, the wildlife, Planet Earth. Sustainability was the solution.

Tribes understood the earth. It was a part of their life. The American Indians, the Aborigines, the Maoris, the Mayans, and more. Earth was always a part of each of their rituals but a big old group of white folk called these cultures primitive. We "advanced" beyond the "primitive" beliefs to honor the Earth and we cut ourselves off from ourselves. A huge part of life spent floating along the top of the water, getting what we needed but ignoring what was around us.

Earlier that day I had been asked, "What have you learned, Joyce, learned here?"

I had replied, "I am still putting it together."

Now lying on my back taking in nature, I had my answer. I was waking up new parts of my heart and seeing how to put them to work. I was allowing rarely used parts of my heart to flourish, backing away from making money and opening up to help the planet. This journey volunteering was teaching me, healing me, and allowing me to see myself in new ways. I was so easily distracted by humans, that I almost lost the trees. Here at Tararu, I learned about my connection to the planet and became committed to living sustainably in the future. John had passed me his passion and drive to reduce my footprint.

My last day at the sanctuary I walked my favorite trap line. It was easy to understand John's passion about trees here. To cut trees down, to use the land for herding sheep, the trees for lumber, the planet could not survive. With no forests, no old growth forests left, our entire ecosystem would be out of balance teetering on the edge of disaster. Surely we as intelligent planet dwellers could stop our unrelenting buying, using, getting, and throwing away in enormous quantities wasting the earth's resources.

I hiked the trap line that last day without sore knees. I had finally adjusted to New Zealand hills, though Josh's poles had saved me. I finished resetting all of the traps and luckily didn't find any possum. Back at the house, I was sad to be leaving. There was so much to do at Tararu Valley Sanctuary. I walked to the ridge to mulch more trees but couldn't resist taking time to lie down and look up.

How different from the rain forest! No smells, no fronds, no forest sounds. I felt John's dream. One man had a vision and made the earth his priority.

The volunteers asked Josh and me to bake bread one more time before I left, bread and chocolate chip cookies. At dinner we talked about bananas.

"Why don't we ever buy bananas, John?" one of the volunteers asked.

"Bananas themselves are tough on the land using up all the nutrients and making it hard to grown anything afterwards," he replied. "The plantations eat up the land and worse than that, the bug sprays are poisonous to the plantation workers."

So now how was I ever going to eat bananas?

My last night was sentimental with hugs and tears and laughter with all of the volunteers. John and I had a long talk, a friendship formed since we had hammered out our differences. When John and Dagmar drove me to Thames to catch the bus to Auckland, we all cried when we hugged goodbye but quite certain that we would meet again.

I thanked them each for all that they had given me. A very important piece of my puzzle had been found here.

It was time to move on to Thailand to work at the Elephant Nature Park in Chiang Mai. Back to wildlife for me, but sustainability was a part of my lifestyle now. John was with me in my heart, his tenacious fight for the Earth inspiring me.

CHAPTER 15

The Elephant Nature Park in Thailand

ON THE FLIGHT FROM Auckland to Bangkok, we stopped in Brisbane and picked up two Aussies, who sat next to me. Eric, who sat in the seat next to mine, was a tall, handsome Viking of a man with blonde hair and blue eyes, chiseled cheekbones, muscular build, and a fast smile. They tipped more than a few beers back and kept me laughing.

"You're beautiful" Eric said. "Are you with someone then? Some lucky man?"

"No, no, I am flying solo." Flattered by his attention, I had not had a good flirt for some time.

"What would it take to hook you up? I am sure there are hundreds of men out there who would love to be with you. What's the problem?"

"I'm not sure. What do you think?"

"I think you must be turning them away, love." And the talk moved on.

"I own a daycare in Brisbane with my wife." Paul said. "Do you know that more and more young Aussie kids are speaking with American accents?"

"No, how can that be?"

"Because they're watching so much American TV, including your commercials."

"And how do you feel about that?" I asked.

"Well, it's frustrating for us. We're getting to be more like you though, less direct."

"That's not good. I love the clear communication here, unaffected and down to earth."

"Yea, we are about 20 years behind America but adopting your ways."

As we finished dinner, we giggled and laughed, their Aussie humor cracking me up. They were going to Thailand for a golf holiday. When the lights dimmed in the plane, Eric put his arm around me.

"Curl up on my shoulder, babe. It's time to go to sleep. Don't worry I won't try anything" he said with a wicked giggle.

I decided that a big warm chest and an arm around me would be a perfect way to sleep, so sitting in the bulkhead, we stretched our legs out, put a blanket over us, and slept. I had not slept with a man's arms around me since Robert and it felt great.

Where was Robert anyway? Someday I would talk to him again. I was certain of that. For now this cuddle was just what I needed, listening to Eric breathe, the movement of his chest, his arm secure around me gave us both solid sleep, but we woke up a bit surprised to still be in a cuddle.

Looking out the window, I could see Bangkok below us as the plane went into its decent. I was so excited. I knew that here I would no longer be comforted by the Western culture of soft Aussie and kiwi travel, speaking in my own language. Filled with anticipation, only one more short plane ride separated me from my next destination, Chiang Mai and the Elephant Nature Park.

Chiang Mai seemed exotic like I was really traveling. When the plane landed, this was evident immediately from the strange cooked things hanging in the airport restaurants and the surrounding chaos that was reminiscent of Rio. My four-star hotel with its king-sized bed and breakfast buffet was a bargain at 32 dollars a night and right in the heart of the city!

The famous night bazaar was just outside my door. Always watchful of evening safety issues in a foreign city, rather timidly I ventured outside joining the evening tourist parade past hundreds of vendors lining the streets and inside the enormous bazaar. If I had been a shopper, this would have been heaven with beautiful items awaiting barter. Even with so much sensory stimulation, I instantly took in the great smiles of the Thai people, gentleness in the air.

But I was starving as I walked past McDonald's and Starbucks, amazed to have these two icons following me everywhere on this trip. I passed them right by and stepped into a small local restaurant, where I ordered Phad Thai, a favorite at home. Oh, my, this was the most delicious Thai food I had ever eaten and the flavors were much different than the restaurants at home. And this meal would be only the beginning as little did I know that the Elephant Nature Park would be a delicious culinary adventure.

Sitting at my table outside on the patio, I noticed in particular a lot of one type of couple: overweight, middle-aged white men, who were generally unattractive, walking around with pretty, young petite Thai women. Were they getting paid to walk with these blokes? On the surface they seemed to be oddly matched couples in large quantities.

Morning came early with jet lag fuzzing my brain. Hungry, I walked to the hotel buffet breakfast. It was loaded with American dishes like eggs, pancakes, and toast and then there were more interesting Thai dishes: soups, stir fries, fried rice, and lots of unknown things to taste. I loved the spicy *kho tom koong*, a breakfast rice soup, and I ate three helpings of *kuatiao radna*, a sweet noodle dish with vegetables. I tried to sample almost everything else leaving with a very full belly.

Walking around the city with a big smile on my face, I was surprised and sad to see smog everywhere as I looked at the distant hills. No wonder. The streets were packed with scooters, bikes, taxis, buses, and cars all zooming around never staying in a lane. There were little taxis called *putputs* that looked like converted golf carts with a covered passenger bench and bicycle taxis.

Temples with gold ornate detail abounded here as frequently as coffee shops at home. This was my first time in a Buddhist country, and I had many questions. Was Buddhism responsible for the agreeable energy I felt as soon as I landed here? I saw it in the smiles, a different version of the Able smile. I wanted to know how the religion viewed wildlife. Why was there a need for a sanctuary for abused elephants here in Thailand? What was the problem? What was happening to the Asian elephant population with only 30,000 left on the planet?

The next day a group of new volunteers met at the sanctuary's office in Chiang Mai and Lek, the mighty force who had started the park, welcomed us all with a flurry of energy and fast talking. She was maybe 4'10" tall, very petite, and very beautiful with a kindness surrounding her.

"First we go to vegetable and fruit stall buy food for elephant. Elephant need much food. You ready? We go now."

At the market, which was a madhouse of activity, we bought pineapple, watermelon, corn, cucumbers, and other fruits for the elephants, who eat up to 200 kilograms a day each! We loaded up the trucks and the van, and an excited, nervous bunch of volunteers drove to The Elephant Nature Park 60 km outside of Chiang Mai.

As we drove through the gates down the dirt road and arrived at the camp, I was overwhelmed. It was spectacular! The hills surrounding the park were dry this time of year with a haze blanketing them glowing in a beautiful light that brought a feeling of tranquility. A river ran through the park and bamboo huts built on stilts were sprinkled around the park. Most amazing were the elephants roaming around, big enormous dusty elephants. They were grand! I had only seen elephants at the circus and to see them ambling along freely was intimidating and awe-inspiring!

Our vans stopped at a large platform, probably 30' x 40' and raised 7' off the ground. It was open on all sides and had a bamboo roof. There we unloaded all of the food.

Currently there were 19 elephants, 32 dogs, and 9 cats in residence here plus one young boy, whom Lek had rescued from the streets because his mother was dead and his father was in jail. Each elephant had a mahout, a full-time caretaker, who also lived at the park with his family.

Lek thought nothing of her expanding circle of love that lived at the park. When she was asked by a volunteer how she did all this, she replied, "You not run out of love. Heart has plenty enough love. No limit to love. Always more love."

I listened to this wisdom and the simple truth hit a bull's eye on my heart. I was now beginning to sense the melody of my journey as I traveled the globe, and Lek's wisdom had given me the words to carry with me, to clarify my quest. My journey was a journey into love and all of its facets. This sanctuary operated with an abundance of love for elephants, volunteers, dogs, cats, mahouts, and one little boy.

Soung Yo, a lovely man who worked at the park, showed me to my lodgings. Walking up the stairs to the platform, I settled into my bamboo hut built around a beautiful tree overlooking the grounds. My first tree house was built on bamboo stilts and had a bamboo floor, bamboo walls, and a lovely thatched roof. There was one window and a sleeping mat on the floor surrounded by mosquito netting. Simple living. One other hut shared the space under the shade of the tree plus a bathroom.

Our shower consisted of a trickle of river water and a pot in a garbage can full of river water for rinsing. Well, I guess if the river water was good for the elephants, it was good for me! The cold water was always shocking but quite refreshing except when it came to rinsing my hair. Our sit-down toilet was cause for celebration rather than a hole in the ground and it got flushed using a pot of river water.

That first day, all of the volunteers gathered at the large platform for lunch, which was the beginning of a series of incredible meals: six different Thai dishes! I'd had no idea that amazing food was going to be part of this volunteer project. We sat on benches all getting to know each other and reveling in the delicious flavors. The atmosphere seemed very relaxed.

After we ate, the experienced volunteers taught the new volunteers our first daily chore, washing the fruit and veggies for the elephants to remove pesticides. The mahouts, who didn't speak any English, helped us cut the pineapple into fourths, elephant-sized chunks with bananas and cucumbers all put in large garbage containers around the large platform.

Knowing it was lunchtime, the elephants gathered around three sides of the platform, resting their trunks on the wide ledge. For a moment I stood in awe. I was on a platform with 17 elephants ready for lunch, their heads lined up anxious to be fed. Timid at first, I put a chunk of pineapple near an elephant's trunk and was shocked when he wrapped his trunk quickly around the pineapple and put it in his mouth. Amazing! Not exactly comfortable with this job yet, I was just fascinated to watch them.

They lined up as family units that were formed as new elephants arrived. It made sense to me to eat lunch with your family! I soon got brave enough to put chunks of food right into their trunks, quickly moving my fingers to avoid getting them curled up inside with the food. I felt the rough skin, the prickly hairs, the strength of their trunks and the quickness with which they tightened around the food. Their trunks squeezed hard! We kept feeding them until all of the food was gone.

Once they were fed, we walked down to the river for our next daily chore: washing elephants in the river! The mahouts each walked their elephants down to the river while the volunteers followed. The mahouts stayed with their elephants all day taking them for walks, keeping them out of trouble until they were tied up in the evening to their individual home base. Ideally, the same mahout would be with them for their lifetime. However, since these were rescued elephants recovering from different forms of abuse, their mahouts had only been with them as long as they had been here at the park. The entire group of elephants, including two very frisky 5-year-old babies, was now in the water, lying down, rolling around, getting scrubbed with brushes by their mahouts and volunteers to rid their skins of any pests. I must say the vision of elephants playing in the water, rolling around on their sides, stunned me.

In my wildest dreams, I never expected this to be a part of my life. The babies especially were wonderful to watch as they played with the adults. A crazy scene, a river full of playful elephants. Still very tentative, I took a bucket and threw water on the elephants, too uncertain yet to grab a brush and scrub.

And then Greg introduced himself to me. A returning volunteer from California, he was a tall pony-tailed fellow in his forties with a very kind, gentle way.

"Hi. I'm Greg," he said. "I've been coming here for three years. I love these elephants. Come over here and scrub Lilly's side with me. I'll make sure you're safe."

Lilly looked enormous to me, like a beached whale lying on her side in the water. I grabbed a brush, waded past my knees, and started to scrub her back well aware that I was standing in an elephant bath tub.

"Always have an escape path in case one of the elephants is having a bad day," Greg said.

I tried to imagine an elephant on a bad day stomping around, throwing his trunk in the air.

"One of the elephants here is not allowed to come down to the river. She killed two mahouts at her previous gig after being beaten badly. You can tell this elephant by the hole in one ear. She is kept separate from the rest of us but still keep an eye out for her just in case her mahout loses control."

"An elephant that's having a bad day? An elephant with a hole in her ear who kills mahouts?" I said. I scanned elephant ears. "Hmm, this all makes me nervous, Greg."

"I'll stay with you and make sure you are safe."

"Great!" Meanwhile, I kept looking at all the elephant ears just in case.

After the bath, some of the volunteers rode the elephants but I just watched still timid. Next stop was their mud pit to reapply the dirt we just removed because they need to protect their skin. What a hoot watching them play in the mud! Elephants definitely smile. These were happy elephants sliding and wrestling with each other in the mud throwing a glop of mud on top of their backs. Each one seemed to have a different personality, a different shape and color to their eye.

With no chores now, I went back to my hut for a relaxing afternoon of reading and watching the elephants wander through the park with their mahouts until it was time for dinner. The mahouts tied the elephants to their separate spots for the evening for their own safety. If they were left to wander, they would head straight to a farmer's field to graze, ending with injury to the elephants or enormous costs to Lek to pay for the damage. In the past one of the babies had wandered into a farmer's field and eaten his crop. In revenge the farmer had poisoned the young elephant, who later died, breaking Lek's heart. Killing a baby elephant for revenge was completely outside of my understanding. I was shocked and confused. Obviously, there were many things here that I did not understand.

Our dinner platform near the kitchen was smaller and more intimate with benches lining the three sides and a long table filled with 10 different dishes, each one more delicious than the next. The flavors, the variety, everything was delicious and not like anything I ate at home.

"The food here is amazing!" I said.

"Every lunch you'll get 6 different dishes and 10 at dinner." Kelly told me, another returning volunteer. "You'll never get tired of anything because it keeps changing. I am working on a cookbook of the recipes used here to sell as a fundraiser for the sanctuary. They don't have written recipes though so I sit in the kitchen and try to write down what they put in the pots. I return here every year for my vacation."

"I had no idea that Thai food could be this delicious or that the food here would be this good. Everywhere but Italy, we have done communal cooking. This dinner is a taste treat! I want one of those cook books when they are ready."

On this evening, we ate spiced rice with pork, *koa mu ap gapi mor din;* vegetarian mushroom noodle pot soup, *ga por je;* green curry, *khaeng khieo wan.* There was a steaming whole fish poached in ginger, onions, and soy sauce, *pla jian,* and a mild chicken fried with vegetables and cashew nuts, *kai phat met ma muang;* a spicy papaya salad with a myriad of herbaceous ingredients, *somtam;* spicy sausage, *sai ua;* curry noodles, *khao soy;* pork curry casserole with ginger and peanuts, *kaeng hang lae;* and banana palm curry, *kaen yuak.* And those with a sweet tooth loved Lek's specialty: the coconut-sweetened sticky rice and mangoes with coconut milk. Each evening the menu changed!

With volunteers from all over the world, our conversations were filled with many accents as we talked about the day, the elephants, and life. As I looked around, I felt grateful for this year and for my real estate business that had always provided for my sons and me. I was grateful that someone like Lek had the drive and the strength of character to protect elephants, to fight for their safety, and to make the elephant sanctuary thrive.

The following morning when I asked Lek where to find a list of my chores, she smiled at me, "You be with elephant. You love elephant. This your chore. Go now and walk with elephant to watch them. Very beautiful. Very beautiful."

"What's your favorite part of an elephant, Lek?" I asked.

"The bottom. I think elephant have cutest bottom and I love watch them walk. You go walk with elephants." Lek smiled when she said this, admiring a passing elephant. She walked up to the elephant to tell it a secret, I think, and tiptoed up her hands stroking the trunk. Over my weeks here, I would watch tiny Lek talk to all of these enormous elephants. What an amazing woman!

Greg walked by and said, "Come on, Joyce. Let's go watch the elephants. They graze with their mahouts most of the morning and we can talk more."

"Always happy to go with you, Greg."

We walked behind the elephants following the river until we crossed through to the other side. The mahouts kept the elephants out of the farmers' nearby fields, no easy task with lots of sweet corn growing there. I found it amazing that a big old elephant took orders from a tiny mahout. The elephants slowly grazed through the grass by the riverside, and then Greg and I followed them back. Returning back to the sanctuary for lunch, we again washed their food and fed them. After lunch we walked down to the river again for elephant washing!

After they were clean, Johnny, one of the mahouts, told me to get on Lilly, who was lying on her stomach in the water.

"What? Me climb on this huge elephant? You must be joking."

No, he wasn't joking. So I reached up thinking that I could pull myself up but I wasn't strong enough to climb this round, rough mountain with nothing to grasp. However, a team of mahouts came to the rescue. Built small like our jockeys, they put their hands on my bottom and hoisted me up, totally cracking me up. It must have looked pretty damn funny. From way up on top of Lilly, I was scared and she hadn't even gotten up yet! Pum, the woman who helped run the camp, told me to move forward so that my knees were right behind her ears leaning forward with my hands on her head! As I nervously scooted forward, her skin felt tough, stubs of hair prickly through my shorts and on my legs, but damn, I was on an elephant!

Her mahout commanded her to get up and suddenly I was on a rising elephant that felt very wobbly and a long way up! We started our walk back from the river following the other elephants. This was not as stable of a ride as you might think. Every step of her legs was a movement I felt under my bum. With my hands resting on her forehead, I had nothing but her ears to hold on to as she picked up speed. But her mahout was there and I almost felt safe. When we got to the trees, he commanded her to drop down. And down we went. She was a big elephant as I turned to slide down her rough skin.

"Thank you, Lilly." I stroked her head as she looked me in the eyes. Now curious about Lilly, I asked Greg why she was here at the park.

"Lilly was born in Burma but sold in Thailand as a logging elephant when she was only 8 years old. Her life was one of pulling logs and was maybe manageable until she gave birth to a baby. That baby was taken from her after a year and a half because she could not or would not pull logs with her baby nearby. Elephant moms are very devoted mothers and this cruel custom is beyond my comprehension."

"I don't understand. Why is this cruelty necessary?"

Moira, who had spent her life working with wildlife in Africa, was standing nearby. She was here working as a mahout for Mae Tong Bai, an 80+-year-old elephant.

"In Africa elephants are trained only with patience and love and it works perfectly. Lek is trying to change the custom here. To show the locals that love can work better than pain and fear," she explained. Moira was my age and at every opportunity, I spent time talking with her or Greg.

Greg continued, "When the logging industry was banned in 1989, the domestic elephants were out of work. Lilly's Karen tribe could not support her and sold her to a logging company doing illegal logging. Lilly was beaten severely there, and when she could no longer work hard even with her beatings, she was sold to two families doing logging work. They drugged her with amphetamines to make her work all day and all night. The more she worked the more they gave her amphetamines until that was the only way she could work needing more and more drugs just to stand up. Within two years, she could no longer stand; her legs were shaking all of the time, her eyes rolled. She became stubborn, unable to work, and her owner beat her even more.

"When Lek and her Jumbo Express, a mission that goes out in the field with volunteers to help care for sick elephants, found Lilly, she was tied to a tree. She was covered with fresh cuts and wounds, and she was dying. The group of volunteers and Lek encouraged Lilly to walk to the river to find the will to live. It is a miracle that she survived her ordeal."

"Lek told the owners that she would take her to the sanctuary and nurse her back to health. Using homeopathic cures, Lek weaned her body away from the drugs and cleared her brain. After three months Lilly's body recovered and then the owners were ready to take her back from Lek. But Lek had decided never to make Lilly go back to being a drugged slave. Gathering her savings with financial help from volunteers, she bought Lilly. Now Lilly is happy here. As the adoptive mother for one of the young ones, she and the other aunties look out for him."

"Greg, to watch these elephants and listen to their stories of abuse at the hands of humans, I feel so sad. It breaks my heart to listen to this and each elephant here has a story of abuse. How can humans abuse these magnificent animals and maim them? I am unable to understand cruelty."

"There is a *National Geographic* video of the plight of elephants in Thailand that uses Lek as the source of information. Lek wants all of the volunteers to watch it as part of our education. You'll have a chance to understand."

When Lek gathered us together to watch the video, I found the documentary so cruel and heart-wrenching as they covered the young elephants' training process that I could not watch it. Young elephants were beaten into submission as their training began. I walked out sobbing and returned to my hut filled with sadness. I didn't get it. What was wrong with mankind that we were unable to understand the preciousness of wildlife? We must take care of wildlife as we care for our own families. We are all our family. Throughout this trip, I was being forced to ponder mankind's cruelty, shortsightedness, and greed. Yet Lek answered it here with love, always with more love. So much to think about and so much to be aware of.

Rather than walk with the elephants one morning, I asked Greg if there was a chore that I could do.

"Sure. Let's shovel elephant pancakes. It's bad for their feet to stand in it. We can start at the big platform and then move to their sleeping areas."

With pitch forks and a wheel barrow, we worked together talking and enjoying the physical labor.

"What do you do at home, Greg?"

"I work as a therapist at an asylum. It's a pretty crazy place most days," he said smiling.

"Ah, that explains your calm nature. I bet you are great there."

"Well, the plan is to retire early and come here to live. My retirement money will go far here and I want to be near the elephants. Lek said I could build a hut here and she's going to help me find a good Thai woman who speaks English."

"Hmm, you don't want to marry an American woman who speaks English?" I said, smiling at him.

"Well, I like this culture a lot."

"Less feisty than ours?"

"It is a gentle, warm culture."

I was really enjoying the dung cleanup but as the sun warmed up, I had to take a break. Tomorrow there would be more dung. After the cleanup, Jeff, a mahout from Australia, told us to come with him as elephant love was in the air. They had one of the females chained up and I wasn't sure how I felt about that. One of the males who would be coming into musth was ready to mount her.

"He make good effort but need more bananas," Lek said.

"Are bananas like Viagra?" I asked.

"Yes, yes. Banana help."

Musth was the males' gradual hormonal surge that came when it was time for mating. It created a super-stud of an elephant when the hormones reached their maximum levels. In the wild in this super-charged state, they tore through the forest mounting females, defying the strongest dominant male to challenge them. The dominant males sensed that a battle with a male in musth would be a loss and generally avoided the fight. Apparently, this was nature's way of giving the gene pool variety.

However, in the limited space of this sanctuary, the hyped-up male in musth was dangerous, and once the hormone started oozing from their glands down their faces into their mouths, the elephant needed to be tied up. If they mated before musth was in full bloom, the storm of hormones was not nearly as intense, which explained tying up a female. During musth at the sanctuary, no one goes near the male elephant, even their mahout, because they are maniacs. During the time that they are tied up, they lose lots of weight and get very rundown.

I went to my room most days in the mid-afternoon to read a bit during the heat of the day. Contrary to the New Zealand project where we were expected to work all day, no one here really seemed to care how hard we worked as long as we loved the elephants. Each project where I volunteered reflected the culture—and the organization—in their demands on volunteers. Here, the Thai culture welcomed us to enjoy the food, a rest, and the elephants, and to do as much work as we wanted to do.

After my rest, I gathered tamarind seed pods, which were long brown dried pods and walked over to talk to Moira.

"I know these pods have many medicinal purposes. Do elephants like them?"

"Yes, Max really needs them for the arthritis in his legs. I'll come with you and help collect seeds."

So off we went under the tree while she told me the story of her life.

"My husband of 39 years lost his will to keep fighting for life in Africa. Our only son was murdered and after that my husband refused to work. We had spent our lives in Africa making documentaries together about all the wildlife there. He is an amazing photographer but he lost his will, and I just couldn't cope with him anymore without his spirit.

He lives in a small flat in London now. I still love him but I left him 10 years ago."

Moira was obviously still deeply in love with her husband. There were tears in her eyes when she told me this story. "I live in Botswana now and try to make a living as a guide. I sold everything but my house to afford this trip here. I love watching over Mae Tong Bai. She is over 80 years old now and I want to spoil her. When Lek found her, she was standing with her trunk down ready to die after a miserable life of working hard and being beaten. Lek bought her and asked me to come take care of her. I love her so much."

"I'm 56 years old and still scrapping together money to survive now. Seems we were never very clever at making money living in the jungle most of the time. Your lifestyle was a better plan, Joyce."

"Moira, don't be sure about that. It's just different, Moira. You have lived working with your passion for your entire life. What happened to your son is an unimaginable tragedy. How could it not have left you and your husband reeling? It's a tragedy beyond compare, I think. I'm so sorry. Can I give you a hug? Maybe with more time somehow he will heal. Maybe love will find a way. For now, Mae Tong Bai certainly loves you. You two are sweet together."

As we gathered seeds, Max walked over with his mahout, Carl. He is known as the tallest elephant in Thailand. Max had been a begging elephant in Bangkok. In this custom, tourists pay the owner money to feed an elephant a piece of fruit. However with the insane traffic in Bangkok, this way of making a living is very dangerous for the elephant and is supposedly illegal. Poor Max got hit by a truck. He crumpled in a heap with both of his legs broken. But after his accident, no one took care of him to make sure his legs healed properly. They healed into stiff poles that are unable to bend at the joint, and arthritis made standing painful. As an injured male, he could not really deal with the other male elephants in the park though the females adored him. Most of the time he stayed in Carl's yard for safety or went for walks when the other elephants were back at the sanctuary. Carl only brought him over to the center of the sanctuary when the other elephants were gone to keep him safe.

However, somehow Boon Khum, the enormous dominant male, had been left wandering without his mahout and upon seeing Max charged him ferociously, pushing him from the back. It was horrible to see Boon Khum crash into Max. Moira and I were very frightened. Carl was only able to throw stones at Boon Khum and yell at him as he had no authority to control the dominant male. Boon Khum took running starts pushing Max into the barbed wire fence cutting his legs. It seemed only a matter of time before Max would lose his balance and collapse. Boon Khum kept backing up and crashing into poor Max, who knew he couldn't turn to fight with his bad front legs. I screamed my hardest from the safety of the platform, horrified at seeing Max attacked when he was always so afraid to leave the safety of his yard.

Finally, Baut, Boon Khum's mahout, came running down the road yelling at his elephant. In one instant this enormous, angry, charging elephant stopped his attack on Max and turned to his mahout. I was floored by this show of discipline. Baut jumped up, bit his ear, and hung there for a minute, punishing the elephant.

"Now that is an amazing show of authority." Moira said. "None of the other mahouts will work with Boon Khum because he is too powerful. Baut is a perfect mahout for this strong male. He has such good control."

Poor Max was injured, frightened, and unable to defend himself. He returned with Carl to the safety of his yard.

"I won't get him out for a walk now for a long time after this!" Carl said.

"I'll collect seeds for him every afternoon Carl. Maybe that will help his pain." I said with tears in my eyes.

Later in the afternoon, I sat with Carl by the river as the light changed with the sunset from a white haze to a beautiful rosy glow settling over the hills. One of his other elephant charges was playing in the water.

"My wife and I came here the first time as volunteers from Australia and fell in love with the place. Lek told us she would build us a house if we would come back and live here and take care of Max. We sold everything and have been here ever since. I love the life here with Max and the elephants."

"Do you ever miss home?"

"Yes, but what we are doing here feels better to us than our life in Australia."

AFTER ANOTHER good dinner and more interesting conversation, I walked back to my cozy room but Greg caught up with me.

"Come with me to sit by Mae Tong Bai as she eats her grass."

"Okay," I replied.

With only the light of the moon, we sat down and listened to Mae Tong Bai make noises of contentment as she ate her evening meal of cut grass. The crescent moon high in the sky, the hills with just a bit of light upon them, and this lovely elephant's silhouette outlined against the light from the main platform. We listened to her crunching the grass while we talked.

Greg was easy to talk to and such a gentle man. I felt the peace of this beautiful setting with stars in the sky, sounds of all the nearby elephants, and Greg telling me stories about the park. I listened and watched the beautiful elephant. Finally Mae Tong Bai had found contentment. Me, too, Mae Tong Bai. Me too. I felt contentment here.

On the walk back to my hut, Greg and I hugged and that hug turned into a long kiss. We stared at each other, wondering the same thing, where from here? With more kisses, neither one of us was certain if we wanted more, neither one of us ready to push it further. I decided to wait a bit and to see if things would heat up before rushing in. I wasn't quite ready for another hot romance.

When Greg and I weren't shoveling dung, we walked with Moira, Mae Tong Bai, the stately queen and Ben, an 18-year-old high-school dropout from Australia, joined us as now he too was acting as a part-time mahout for Mae Tong Bai. Ben was brilliant around wildlife and he was traveling the world following his love of animals. He had worked at the zoo in Australia and then an orangutan sanctuary in Borneo before coming to the park to learn about elephants. Ben was a glowing light full of ancient wisdom, beautiful knowing, and monkey business, and

Greg was a great example of a wonderful American man. The elephant was in her glory as she learned that finally she was safe. In her 80 years she had never known a single moment of freedom and now she had a new lease on life.

But Moira was sad. She knew that Mae Tong Bai had fallen in love with this young whippersnapper and was now completely attached to Ben. Having left her life in Botswana to care for Mae, she felt betrayed by Lek as her place with the elephant she loved was being replaced by Ben. Moira and I talked about life, about planning, about her future.

IN FACT, THOSE mornings, we all talked. We sat watching Mae Tong Bai graze on grass and wander freely. Why did being in the presence of an elephant bring us all peaceful and soul-satisfying conversations? Was it the contentment of our elephant? I would always remember these conversations and lovely mornings with three of my favorite people by the river's edge.

Ah, what wonderful days I was having here at the sanctuary for elephants. I hoped that in the future I would be lucky enough to fine a way to bring joy and peace to others and to connect the dots of the planet. Here feelings of sorrow, anger, and unhappiness about abused elephants lived alongside feelings of joy, love and caring when they were rescued. On this planet we have people killing, stealing, and raping, and we have the gentleness of a doctor caring for a sick child, a woman holding a baby kangaroo until it is strong enough to be on its own, a man devoting his life to protect a species of trees to heal the air.

I wanted all the good, all the caring, and all the love to radiate out. I wanted money to find the places where it could do the most good, to help where it was needed. I wanted people to feel love and to believe in it. I wanted children to have faith in us again, to have hope. Somehow I would find a way to brighten the planet to help those working so hard for good to keep up their strength. To cover the world with love and smother the sorrow, smother the evil.

After washing the elephants at the river one afternoon, I stayed with Greg to watch Hope and Jungle Boy, the two baby male elephants, and Phu Pa, the 20-year-old elephant, play in the water with their aunties standing guard to make sure the play didn't get too rough! Phu Pa was lying down in the water while the babies climbed on him. The two young males put their heads down in the water submerged like little boys in a pond. Climbing on each other, the three were full of mischief and it was beautiful to watch their antics. These young babies would never be trained by the harsh painful methods used here. Lek used love. They would never be used for tourist trekking with a sharp iron hook poked into the soft places on their head or have the weight of riders on their backs day in and day out or be tied to pillars in a cement garage all night so hard on their feet or be taken from their babies. Here they would live lives of joy, safe and protected at the sanctuary because one woman had the energy to create this center.

After watching the swim, it was time to head back to my lovely tree house that I never wanted to leave. I rested with the first rain of the year making lovely sounds on my rooftop. My two favorite dogs were standing guard at my door. There are no demands on me here, only peacefulness and time to think, create, and love. Perhaps this sanctuary was for humans, too?

WE WERE ALL getting excited for the weekly trip to Heaven with the elephants, a special place that the elephants go each week to have the freedom to graze all day and night. Heaven was about 5 miles from the sanctuary! The volunteers could ride elephants all the way to Heaven, but Greg and I decided to walk instead of making them work carrying us. The rest of the volunteers rode elephants, and it was quite a sight to watch an entire group of elephants walk down a road and then cross a river. Greg and I forged the river that came to the tops of my legs and then up into the green hills passing farms, giant rocks, and big trees.

I loved getting up into the hills to see some green and to watch the elephants maneuver their way up the path moving slowly and deliberately. Elephants have a spongy, air pad above their soles that absorbs the shock of their weight. Did Nike Air copy elephant technology?

Even Jokia, the blind elephant, could sense where to put her feet on the narrow part feeling first with her trunk. We walked behind Boon

Khum, who was giving his mahout a patience test as he kept going off the path eating tall green grass though Baut was yelling at him. I was nervous about passing him on the narrow path after watching him with Max plus he was going into musth. He was here because thieves had stolen his tusks. When he was tied to his sleeping tree one evening, bandits drugged him and then used a chain saw to remove his tusks way high up into his nostrils. Infection was killing him when Lek found him and brought him to the sanctuary. The vet saved his life. Now each day Baut takes his hand and a rag and puts medicine up his tusk holes. It was gross to watch and yet fascinating to see the trust between Boom Khum and Baut.

Arriving at our overnight camping spot, I saw a large elevated platform with a cooking area, a fire pit, and a sleeping area with a thatched roof. Our campsite. Pum set about getting our food ready with the help of the mahouts. I sat in the middle of the cooking watching Pum, while Boon Khum did the same on the forest side of the platform with Pum talking to him the entire time! The mahouts set up our mosquito nets and mats, and each of us put down our sleeping bags. Dinner cooked by Pum was delicious and spicier than usual though not nearly as hot as the food the mahouts ate, which I tasted one night.

After dinner the mahouts built a fire and we all relaxed around the fire pit in the moonlight while the elephants enjoyed an evening of grazing. No wonder they called this Heaven.

But some of the volunteers heard another fire and we asked Pum, "What is that fire, Pum? It sounds very close."

"Just same as Elephant Park. Villagers burn forest floor for mushrooms and easy farming."

"But it sounds so close Pum. Are you sure we are safe?"

"No worry. Villager do all time. No problem."

But as we looked up the hill, we could actually see the light from the fire on the other side of the hill with the sound of burning growing in intensity!

"Pum, it's getting closer."

"No problem. No problem. Time for sleep now."

I didn't know how it could be no problem when we were in a bamboo hut with dried leaves for a roof, dried vegetation all around us. It was definitely pretty damn tough to believe her seeing the light from the fire but like good little children we went to bed with "no problem" the last words we heard.

In the middle of the night, I awoke to the sound, not a distant sound, but the loud sound of a fire! I lifted my head to see what looked like a forest fire to me at the top of the hill and working its way down. All of the volunteers were awake and scared.

"Okay, now what do we do?"

We were all pretty damn scared and Pum heard us talking.

"No problem. You be fine. Go to sleep!"

"But our roof is dried leaves, we are surrounded by leaves. Even one spark can set this platform on fire. Can't you see the headlines? Volunteers burn in forest fire. Investigators have no idea why they didn't leave when they saw the fire coming!"

"But what shall we do? We can't find out way out of here alone?"

"Well, I don't know about you but I am putting on my shoes and my clothes and when my face feels hot, I'm out of here!" I said.

I sat at the edge of the platform for a while watching the fire head slowly down the hill. The mahouts were sound asleep as was Greg. Just another forest fire to them. Was this part of cultural adjusting? Finally too tired to stay awake, I lay down with my shoes on and fell asleep to the sound and smell of burning leaves.

When we all woke up, everyone ran to the edge of the platform. I would NEVER understand what I saw. The fire went down the hill and then took a turn away from our platform rather than towards our platform! Pum just shook her head saying, "No problem."

Every time volunteers come up to Heaven, they are armed with red scarves that have been blessed by monks. We tied the scarves around some of the trees and because the scarves were blessed, the villagers would not cut these trees down. What a lovely way to save the forest!

OUR NEXT EXCURSION was an outreach program to give polio vaccine to the children of a nearby village. We brought balloons for the children and other medicine for the adults. As we drove into this little village, everyone gathered to greet us. Old women, old men, young children all lined up to welcome us. The vaccine was oral and we volunteers gave a dose of the vaccine to each child, another great project that Lek had organized.

Each evening after dinner, Greg and I had been sitting with Mae Tung Bai to watch her eat her grass. Afterwards we walked to my hut and gave each other a long goodnight hug. It always felt good to have a hug. I looked up at him wondering what next.

"Are you flirting with me? he asked.

"Probably," I said, "though I thought you were kind of with Kelly." She was one of the other returning volunteers.

"No, we're just friends. It's just not my style to hook up just for hooking up. How about you?"

"No. One-night stands are not my forte."

"Hmm, wonder what we should do from here then? I can just come in and we can cuddle through the night. It would feel wonderful. I would take good care of you."

"If you come in, it is not to cuddle through the night, Greg. That never works."

With neither Greg nor I aggressively moving forward, we left it at a hug but I had an impossible time falling to sleep that night wondering if I had made the right decision.

ANOTHER PEACEFUL DAY at the sanctuary but with new chores in the morning. We were using machetes to cut bamboo into small angled pieces to plant them in the field. The Thai workers cut and sharpened each piece easily and quickly while all of the volunteers suffered from a lack of machete skills.

After too many missed cuts, I decided to plant the bamboo in the field instead. A man working in the field taught me to put two stalks of the bamboo into the side of the row so that when water came down the valley the bamboo would draw it up inside. This bamboo would rest until the rainy season came and then it would take only 20 days to mature enough to become elephant food. Squatting down working row by row, I planted two long rows until my legs could no longer maintain the classic crouch. Thank goodness it was time for lunch!

One of the males was coming into musth and Lilly was backing into him ready to have sex. One of the other females, Mekeo, kept getting in between them trying to stop it from happening. The male kept pushing her out of the way to try to get to Lilly, but then Lilly decided she didn't want anything to do with him. All three elephants were frustrated.

Lek was watching and said, "This elephant Mekeo wants so much a baby she turn her back toward every male. They no like. They think she too easy and walk away. She like slut. How she ever get pregnant I don't know."

Besides my little flirt with Greg, I had fallen in love with the 20-year-old elephant, Phu Pa, who slept right near my hut. He was playful, always hitting the tire swing with his back feet or wrestling with the two baby males.

"I brought him here to maybe make baby but the females no like him. Think he too silly. Too immature."

"Well, Lek, I'm crazy about him."

At night I always stopped and talked to him to check on how he was doing. One of his favorite things was to have his tongue patted with a hand. If I stood up on my tiptoes, I could reach his tongue. Pretty damn weird to put my hand in an elephant's mouth but I was in love with this young rascal. When I walked to my hut, he made a sound that must have meant good night. As I lay in my hut looking for sleep, I heard his steady breathing through the night. Lions roaring, kangaroos crunching and elephants breathing.

I was waking up my ability to love more than just my corner of the world. Seeing what it was like to step away from the cramped corner of thinking that love needed to be one man when it could be a cause, a passion, a world.

"When I marry, I tell husband, 'mother number one, elephant number two, and you number three.'" Lek told me. "When mother die, my husband say, 'Now am I number two?' I say, 'No, mother number one, elephant number two, and you still number three.'"

LEK HAD RESCUED another elephant, called the Purple Elephant because when she found him, he was covered with purple antibiotic to heal his many wounds. He had been recovering in the hospital too sick to come here. (I wondered what an elephant hospital looked like. Did they have little elephant beds?)

About four of the volunteers were meeting the truck at the foot of the dirt road and we would help walk him up the hill to the sanctuary with Pum and a couple of mahouts. When he was unloaded from the truck, we fed him fruit to welcome him and then we all walked up the hill, each of us holding a piece of fruit to encourage the elephant as he made the trek up the hill.

When it was my turn, I gave him his fruit just like I had when we started the walk. However, something snapped in Purple Elephant. Suddenly he became afraid and thought that I was going to take the fruit away. With lightning speed, he turned his head and thumped me on my chest bone with his head and trunk lifting me completely off the ground and sending me flying to land 10 feet away on my butt. I was in shock and gasping for air. It had all happened so fast.

The volunteers came running to see if I was okay. Though the wind was knocked out of me and I was shaking from fear, my breast bone and my body was fine. It seemed like a miracle that I wasn't injured but now I was scared of the elephants.

When we got back and I told Moira what had happened, she was furious.

"They should never let the volunteers with an elephant who hasn't even adapted to the park. You could have been killed. That is so stupid. I'm so glad you are okay. You did nothing wrong. This park needs to start paying attention. They would be shut down in a minute if you were injured."

I walked away thanking the angels who take care of me. "Nice job you guys. Thank you. Nice job."

One night lying in bed listening to Phu Pa, I realized something was very wrong. He was gasping for air. I grabbed my flashlight and flew out the door. He was laying flat on his side, a very dangerous sign in an elephant. I ran to Lek's hut screaming for help, afraid that Phu Pa might die. She ran out with me and felt his tongue and talked to him and called the vet, who came immediately and gave him an elephant-sized shot. He had an intestinal disease.

"Thank you, Joyce. You help Phu Pa. He be okay now."

After they all left, I stayed and talked to him for a while. I had been so scared. Finally too tired to keep my eyes open, I said goodnight. The next day he was standing but I could tell he still was not feeling great. The dickens in his eyes was missing. But the doc came again to give him another injection and then he was fine.

THE CURRENT MUD PIT was just a wee little spot like an inflatable pool for a bunch of NFL players. Somehow we all decided that it would be really great to dig a giant Olympic-sized mud pit but little did we know what a hard job that would be moving the stinky, wet mud. Looking for muscle, we enlisted the help of some of the mahouts and dug and dug and dug. Covered in mud, full of laughter and happiness at our work, we were very proud of the new huge mud pit.

When the elephants inaugurated it after their river bath, we were ecstatic with their response. There was room for entire families in this pit. Jungle Boy and Hope went crazy wrestling with Phu Pa and getting stuck in the mud. We couldn't stop laughing at their antics. Big elephant butts up in the air while they slipped playing in the mud. The aunties keeping a steady eye on the play making sure it didn't get out of control. Of all that we had done here, I was sure that the mud pit was our best effort.

After the hard work and a long shower in the river water, I collapsed exhausted after all of that digging and in need of a long nap. That was it for me for my last day here! I had a delicious farewell dinner, a great talk with Moira, and Ben, a tearful goodbye with Phu Pa, and a long hug from Greg. Then it was time to leave. But I wanted to stay. After recovering from my scare with the purple elephant, I was now getting comfortable with the elephants again and I was sad to be leaving.

When the van came for me, I was standing on my tiptoes patting Phu Pa's tongue sad to be leaving him but convinced I'd be back again. My time with the gracious Mae Tong Bai, my friendship with Greg, Moira, and Ben, my respect for Lek and what she was accomplishing at this park were memories to cherish.

I found myself wishing there was a way for me to keep traveling to let the world know how much love there is in it and how much more needs to be done. Could I get a job with a travel company researching volunteer trips that they could take? Or teach a class on how to take a trip like this or write a book telling the story of my travels? How could I create a life that would support me? Wondering still what I wanted my life to look like. Maybe what it looked like now.

The music that I heard now had nothing to do with pretty things that cost money. The music that I heard now was gentleness and caring. I was more open now and felt more loved than when I left. I felt more connected with myself but I had a serious case of Mom longing to see her sons. If I really took off and kept traveling, could I find a place to call home? Would this quest ever end? I still had three months to find my way.

It was time to head to Beijing and then to Yantai, China, to spend a month teaching English at a high school. These magnificent elephants and the people at the sanctuary would forever be in my heart. Like the elephants, I would remember forever.

CHAPTER 16

Teaching English in China

ON THE FLIGHT TO China, I found myself thinking about Len in England. I wondered what it was about him that made me look forward to seeing him so much. Perhaps it was his Scottish accent and his English professor demeanor. And his intelligence and dry humor were fascinating to me. Well, soon enough we'd have another meeting in Scotland.

BEIJING AIRPORT WAS mad and a bit like being on a merry-go-round too long. I was dizzy from the commotion, overwhelmed by all of the people, the sounds of a new language, the constant motion. But there was Margot, a friend of my good friend Bev, to pick me up and guide me through the maze. An expat, she and her daughter had moved here from Australia and she taught at an English school.

We drove to their lovely condo in a security complex as we got acquainted. Their condo project reminded me of living in the Seattle suburbs as it had tidy streets, lovely landscaping, a health club and dining facility, and kids playing on swing sets. A tall, brick wall separated them from the hordes of people and lack of order on the other side. The juxtaposition of their pretty condo beautifully furnished in a safe, landscaped complex sequestered from the dirt yards, littered streets, lack of color, and obvious poverty boggled my brain.

During my first days in China, I toured Tiananmen Square and the Forbidden City, finally standing in front of that enormous painting of Chairman Mao that I had seen on every TV broadcast about China. I looked up at him thinking about the contrast between how I felt about him and how his people felt. Here was a man who had encouraged his people to have as many children as they could in preparation for WWIII figuring that sheer numbers of human beings would beat weapons and ammunition. The plan obviously worked. Hordes of people in numbers I never imagined walked past me wearing Chairman Mao coats. Bike lanes as wide as a car lane were filled to capacity. Buses and cars dangerously changed lanes playing dodge ball with pedestrians. No one used their brakes. In a fast growing culture, braking wasn't an option. I crossed the street to my tour group, safely tucked behind a group of locals who seemed to know what they were doing.

Maylin, our guide, was a young educated woman who spoke perfect English. "Mao Tse Tung was the founder of the People's Republic of China in 1949 and one of the founders of the Chinese Communist party in 1921. He is honored and loved by the people here."

My information had portrayed him as a man who in the late 1950s started the Great Leap Forward, which ended in famine. Mao was a man who had absolute power over the lives of one-quarter of the world's population and was responsible for over 70 million deaths during peacetime. I was perplexed by the conflict of information. What was I missing?

Someone in our group asked, "Is the one-child policy still in effect?"

According to my version, after Mao's population explosion and the problems associated with too many people and too little food, China's leaders went in the opposite direction to correct the problem of overpopulation by initiating China's controversial One-Child Policy. However, because elderly parents live out their years in their son's home, the cultural preference has always been to keep male infants, thus not allowing many female infants to live.

Maylin explained, "In reality, only the cities have the one-child policy, but in the countryside, it's been two kids. We call it the one-and-a-half-child policy."

Walking with us in Tiananmen Square, our guide was surprised to hear that all of us knew about the massacre in 1989. Outside news was still censored here. My version: almost 5000 civilian protestors, mostly students, were shot dead by the Chinese army during a bloody military operation to crush a democratic uprising in Tiananmen Square with tanks rumbling through the capital's streets firing on unarmed protesters.

She listened patiently to what everyone said, then quickly changed the subject describing the amazing architecture, the concubine houses, and ancient lifestyles.

My second day tour found me alone with Maylin on our way to the Great Wall, a place I never dreamed I would visit. We had time and privacy for her to be more open about Tiananmen Square, about Chinese government propaganda, and about the one-child policy though everything still had a positive spin. She was very curious about the outside world and asked me many questions.

"I think the one-child policy has meant that the one child is very spoiled as I am. Luckily my family kept me even though this means in their old age they will have no one to take care of them."

"What does that mean, Maylin?"

"Well, parents in their old age can only move in with their son and his wife. With a daughter, my parents will have no one to care for them as they age. Our culture does not allow parents to live with their daughter only the son's parents live there. My parents will grow old taking care of each other but with no help from me."

We talked about the pollution problem caused from the impurities in the coal-burning used for fuel. Everywhere I looked the air was thick with pollution, the worst I had ever seen.

"I think," said Maylin, "that we are similar to your country 100 years ago in burning low-grade coal that causes pollution. There isn't any stopping for environmental issues. Neither China nor the United States wanted to sign the Kyoto Provision to reduce pollution. We want to move ahead quickly to catch up with the world. You can see that everywhere you look and we are succeeding. We are moving ahead. Everything even in my short lifetime is changing rapidly. There has been a huge increase in building in the last 20 years. Buildings are put up in a month so quickly I wonder if they can continue standing."

"So these tall buildings are completed in a month?"

"Yes. Everyone is very excited about the Olympics and there are many new buildings."

Our visit to The Great Wall was pure tourist glitz including a ride up a track in a carnival car. The ancient wall clashed with the tourist mania, but once on the wall I walked freely up and down the path looking out, touching bricks and imagining ancient times, ancient workers, and ancient soldiers standing guard over desolation 2000 years ago. The Wall was much higher and wider than I had expected. The barren, desolate, dark and hilly terrain could never be captured in photographs, the vastness needed to be felt. It was a bit like I imagine the landscape of the moon except with a long wall winding out as far as my eye could see, a wall separating a country from invading barbarians charging on Arabian horses.

My VOLUNTEER WORK here would return me to my first profession, and I was excited to be teaching English to high school students, my first volunteer project helping people. When I arrived in Yantai, located in Shandong Province on the Yellow Sea, Jack from the volunteer office met me and introduced me to Frank, a volunteer from Canada, who would become a great friend and traveling buddy. Frank was a handsome man in his 50s who was a high school teacher in Canada and an experienced world traveler. About my height, he had a kind smile. He seemed very relaxed to be here.

Jack was also in his 50s and had an entrepreneurial spirit. He wanted our month-long stay in Yantai to go well. He took us on a tour of the city from the old to the new, to the shopping center past McDonalds and KFC, by the waterfront with its fishing, beaches, and ferries. Jack drove Chinese-style, aggressively and with impulsive turns without caution or blinkers. I found myself gripping the car seat and scrunching my eyes even while his calming Chinese music played. Were we trying to lose a tail?

Right off the bat, the air pollution and litter shocked me. No one ever threw anything in a garbage can apparently. Litter was definitely something to adjust to, not at all like my life in clean, conscientious Seattle.

Jack filled us in on the local culture. "Twenty years ago there were no cars here. Only bicycles and no high buildings. Everything is changing rapidly. There are 6.3 million people here now and 3000 students in your school."

"This many cars in 20 years? Unimaginable!" I replied. The streets were jammed with vehicles, and I wondered if the Sears driving school could put order into this chaos.

"Yes, things are changing rapidly here. These are boom times."

We arrived at a school campus with four large brick buildings and a big dirt playing field.

"We'll go find your rooms," said Jack.

In the dormitory where about one-fourth of the students lived, Frank and I had rooms next to each other with the other volunteers down the hall. It was a pretty typical dorm room with brick walls and a very high ceiling—some things are universal! I had a TV, a water jug with hot or cold water, and a small refrigerator. My bed had a one-inch hard mattress and I was glad that I had brought my Thermaflex air mattress around the world for extra padding. I had a big desk and my own phone! My private bathroom had a hole in the floor for my toilet and a shower nozzle on the wall that drained into my toilet! There was no shower curtain and if I didn't pay attention while taking my shower, I could step into my toilet! But after the cold, river water of Thailand, a hot-water shower was a miracle.

But I was freezing. Absolutely freezing. Because it was April, the school had turned the heat off. I had on long pants, a shirt and another shirt on top of that with a fleece. There were just two choices either wear more clothes or stay under the covers! I jumped around, unpacked, and went to visit Frank, who was not at all cold, his Canadian blood much better here than my now below-the-equator body thermometer.

We were not there long before the head English teacher came by to introduce herself.

"Welcome. My name is Madame Xin. We are pleased to have you here. Let me take you to the dining room."

We walked to an enormous lunchroom where we would eat all of our meals for free with the students or in a smaller room with the teachers if we preferred. Both Frank and I wanted to talk to the students as did the other volunteers.

Looking at the food, I recognized only rice and broth but everything looked interesting.

"I want to try it all, Frank," I said.

"Me, too. Okay, let's jump in."

"I'm going for this deep-fried piece of bread and the potato and carrot stir fry. Did you know there was so much deep fried food here?"

"No," he said, "all of this is new to me."

A man was making noodles pulling and twisting the dough magically, turning it into long noodles for soup, a process that amazed me. They had many different versions of bean curd that were deep fried in big vats of oil and then served with a spicy red sauce. Fried fish on a stick, green beans, new veggies, and a chicken stir fry each served in small bowls. The students put their dishes together to share from each other's bowls.

With chop sticks that were washed and reused, I ate some of mine, some of Frank's, lots of rice, and steamed bread. It was either all good or I was really hungry. Most of the teachers did not speak English but we had a nice conversation with Madame Xin, who seemed very gracious and welcoming, and we met Mr. Pong, one of the other English teachers.

After lunch we walked back to our rooms but I was still freezing.

"Hey, Frank, want to go for a walk. I'm freezing!"

Walking through our neighborhood, Frank told me about his adventures, running marathons in Athens and other countries, trekking for a month in Nepal and yearly trips to Croatia--so many different things. He had a passion for travel. His wife of 20-some years didn't like to travel, but I liked his smile when he talked about her.

Passing through the huge food market near the school, some stands looked like the Pike Place Market at home but others were full of squiggly stuff from the sea or things that I didn't recognize. One man had big strands of kelp laid out on the ground to sell. People brought plastic bags to fill with beer from the beer man! Everywhere I looked there were raw vegetables and cooked food, spices I'd never smelled and fish I'd never imagined, some right out of Dr Seuss. I was surprised to find so many different types of bread, and I bought some yummy fried bread. I loved that we were totally safe here with no worries about robbery or pick-pockets.

But as we walked around, all eyes were on us. I felt like I must be either naked or an alien. A path of turned heads and long stares opened as we walked along. Not frightening stares but deeply curious.

"Frank, do you think we look strange? Everyone is staring at us." I said, my eyes looking to the left and the right at all of the faces turned in our direction. "Do we look famous?"

"It's you they are looking at, Joyce."

"Yea, right, Frank. Very funny. Why are we creating such a stir here?"

Frank smiled too polite to go into detail.

I wondered if it was my height, my nose, my dark tan, or my breasts, all more extreme than their Chinese equivalents!

Back at school, we introduced ourselves to the six Chinese English teachers, who were all very gracious and polite.

"We do not yet have your assignments, either times, classes, or books. When you come on Monday at 7:30 am, we will tell you what you are teaching." Madame Xin explained smiling at us both.

Frank and I spent time together as if we had known each other for years. After dinner, we walked through our neighborhood. Stopping at an Internet café that had 100 computers! After checking email, we went to the grocery store where each of us bought a bit of home: instant coffee and bread for the morning, juice, yogurt, and wine. As we shopped, the long stares continued, and I always smiled back, sorry that I couldn't have a conversation. Obviously staring at foreigners was not considered rude!

"Want to come over for a glass of wine before turning in?" Frank asked.

"Sounds great."

That first evening began a tradition of talking in the evening with a glass of wine to wind us down. Instantly comfortable, over time I told

Frank about Robert, about Len and Harley, and about my trip. He filled me in on his adventures, too.

One night we decided to eat at a local restaurant for dinner, but when we sat down and looked at the menu, we both looked up smiling at each other. Of course, it was in Chinese with no photos.

"Well, do you have any ideas?" I asked looking around at the other diners.

When the petite woman came to take our order, I pantomimed that I didn't understand the menu. Understanding me perfectly, she grabbed me by the arm pulling me up and dragging me through the kitchen doors! Once in the kitchen, she wanted me to point to everything that I wanted. I looked around at the grills while the cooks looked at me. I still didn't recognize most of the food and chuckled at being in the kitchen. I pointed my finger at lots of different foods, which she wrote down on her pad.

Returning to the table I said, "Frank, I don't know what I ordered or how much it will cost but we are getting lots of food!"

"What happened?" he said, obviously enjoying this.

I told him what had transpired in the kitchen, and he cracked up. In a short time, the woman arrived with a large lazy Susan covered with dishes filled with all of my choices plus some French fries. She was smiling proudly and we thanked her profusely, an adventure in eating for us both.

OUR STUDENTS WORKED a grueling schedule by American standards with classes six days a week from 8-5 with a dinner break and then classes from 6-9. For the 25% of the students who lived too far to go home during the week, their wakeup call was 6:30 am, even on Saturdays. Students staying in our dorm were allowed to make noise and yell in the halls for exactly 30 minutes when they got back at 9 pm and then it was study time until bedtime. The competition to succeed and rise above the masses kept them working hard. Motivation did not seem to be an issue, but I wondered how they survived the stress.

Students were classified into 12 sections according to their abilities from smartest to slowest. Within these sections, they were seated in their classrooms according to their grades with the brightest students at the front winding to the back of the room and the slowest students. I remembered my dad telling me that when he went to school in Chicago, they used the same system. But my democratic nature was appalled. How did a student in section 12 in the back row feel about himself? Could you ever break out of your classification?

The school program was very regimented, and the classrooms were rigid and strict. At midmorning break, the entire school exercised out on the playground: all 3000 kids in straight lines following the instructor in a tai chi exercise, an amazing sight. The halls were jam-packed between classes, but no one ever pushed. I never saw a fight or even anger, only smiles.

When we met Monday with the teaching staff, they gave us only three classes each, apparently not wanting us to think that they were slackers passing off their students and workload to us. But neither Frank nor I felt that this was enough work. We politely asked them for more classes to teach explaining that we loved teaching and wanted to spend more time with their students. If we were here to improve conversational and listening skills, then we wanted more exposure to the students. The teachers relented and gave us 12 classes each enough to fill our week and see the progress of our students.

But now what? There was no set curriculum. Here in restricted, regimented China, the school system gave us free range in whatever we wanted to teach, an anomaly that surprised me. There were no forbidden topics and no books to use. I needed to come up with some lesson plans that would be of interest to them. I had four weeks to improve their English skills. I wanted my classes to be dynamic, interesting, and fun! To talk to them about the world and about life for students in the United States, and to give them practice speaking.

"Just talk. Tell them about your country. We want the students to listen to a native speaker," Madame Xin told us.

I was nervous when I approached my classes that first day. Each class had about 70 students and I worried about discipline. I introduced myself, speaking slowly and stopping often to see if they understood.

But each classroom was perfectly quiet for the entire 50-minute session. There were no discipline issues in China!

I was the first American to teach in their school and I felt pressure to excel, to make a good and lasting impression. Sadly, I had found many bad impressions of Americans as I traveled the world, usually beginning with our President and then moving to our movies, the ambassadors of our culture. I wanted to give them a more positive feeling about my country and a more realistic view of a typical American lifestyle.

As I told the story of how I came to China and my trip around the world, it was lovely to see such intensity on each face. I found an enormous range of comprehension between the high sections and the low sections, but the biggest problem overall was shyness. No one raised a hand to ask a question. No one raised a hand to answer one. Actually in all of my classes, no one was willing to talk to me! How could I have them practice conversation if they wouldn't speak?

And then I laughed my big boisterous laugh. A laugh that comes on fast and loud with nothing held back. In the middle of telling them a story, I said something that amused me. The laugh came out. They sat looking at me stunned. I was quite sure that the teachers here were very serious in the classroom, neither smiling nor laughing. Looking at their surprised faces made me laugh more. Some of the girls covered their faces embarrassed to be laughing.

And so I explained my laugh, "Now don't think that all Americans have this big boisterous laugh. It's just something that I have. And it is okay if my laughter makes you laugh, too. We can enjoy ourselves while you learn."

The ice was broken. Although everyone was still too shy to answer questions, they didn't seem afraid of me now. I decided to work with them in rows. I wrote sentences on the board and had each row repeat what I had written seeing if I could develop a sense of pride by rows to speak clearly and with authority. I started by writing a poem by Mother Teresa on the board. I wanted to know if the vocabulary was in the correct range and if they comprehended the meaning. They recited the stanzas out loud in rows and I loved hearing them recite it. They were all attentive, really listening to me. It was unlike any school I had ever taught at in America. Dream-school China.

After class Meeko, who spoke fluent English, told me he thought the poem was too easy. Intrigued because he sat at the back of the room, I told him, "I see that you sit at the back of the room and yet your English is beautiful. Why is that?"

"I just am not motivated by the way they teach. Everything has to be the same. No one is allowed to be an individual. Maybe I am fighting the system."

"But how will you do if you buck the system?"

"Maybe not well but I hate it."

We tried to talk a bit every day. He would have loved American schools and I understood his frustrations, but there was no solution. He had to follow the rigid path to find success. What had happened here to uniqueness? I had just started teaching and I was already sad that I would only be here for a short time.

With my lessons learned in New Zealand, conservation was our next topic. We discussed recycling and pollution. Of the top 20 most polluted cities in the world, 16 of them are in China. My students were shocked to learn this and probably didn't believe me. Like all countries, the spin on how great they were was different than how another country judged it. I found an enormous amount of Chinese pride but criticism was not part of their psyche.

I was beginning to really love my built-in American ability to both love my country and also be critical of certain things. Freedom was glorious. The spirit of freedom that filled my soul was a sharp contrast to life here in China. The feeling that I could do whatever I saw in my mind's eye was part of growing up as an American. Make a wish and strive for it to come true. Voice my opinion. Be self-employed. Be a woman, independent and strong. America's many gifts to me allowed me to grow up in a safe environment that honored individuals and promoted creativity.

However, with everything we understood at home, I wished that the United States could be a leader in the fight against pollution. In my world, the United States as a world leader would show that a strong economy could grow without destroying the air we breathe. Perhaps China, working so hard to copy us, would see that the environment was not for polluting but rather for protecting. But I did not want to be critical here in China. My country had no flags to wave when it came to conservation.

I wanted to introduce new concepts. Only 22% of waste water was treated here. The rest was released untreated causing problems in lakes, rivers, the ocean, and the ground water here. I talked to the class about the long-term effects.

Thinking about John in New Zealand, I discussed reforestation and everything that I had learned about sustainability and living with a smaller footprint. I told them about my commitment to change my lifestyle to become more aware. Captive audience as they were, I watched their eyes to see if they understood or caught some inspiration. I explained my love of the earth…slowly and with a lot of emotion.

"Are you willing to take on the responsibility of the future? To live with a smaller footprint, to plant a tree, to recycle everything you can? Do you think that each of you in the next five years could plant one tree for each member of your family? Have any of you planted a tree before? Me neither till I went to New Zealand! What do you think would be the effect on air pollution if each of you did plant a tree?"

Moving on to recycling paper and litter control, I wished that I had brought more photos of Seattle to show them streets without litter. They had never seen streets without litter, and I wondered if they had ever seen a true blue sky. I explained that my city of Seattle recycled glass, aluminum, plastic, and paper and even composted veggie and fruit waste. I told them about our policy on litter and how clean our streets were. We were having some great discussions even if I was the only one talking!

"Can you each make a commitment never to litter again?"

Did they understand my words? I believed from the lights in their eyes that they did understand me. After class, I got hugs from some of the girls.

Whenever I woke up in China, I was so happy to be warm that I fought to stay in of bed. Grabbing a hot cup of coffee, some yummy Chinese bread, and a yogurt, I burrowed back under the covers to watch TV! The English-speaking channel covered ancient culture to modern China to the news but with censorship. China courted many different countries for economic growth. Currently they were working out agreements with the Arab nations for more trade and were busy making friends with Indonesia and Tonga, building them a school for 1000 students. They were also helping Pakistan and India. Like a game of diplomacy, they were branching outside of their country for allies. The news explained that they were upset that the US would limit their textile exporting and upset with Japan for textbooks that downplayed the Japanese destruction of China, but there was no coverage of the current riots in Beijing over Japanese issues. How intriguing to leave out chunks of news!

On another adventure through our neighborhood, Frank and I swiftly and agilely crossed the insanity of the wide main street dodging bikes, buses, and cars to walk to a larger market area. I was not used to standing out in a crowd. Everywhere I had gone except Thailand, I looked kind of native with my olive-colored skin, but here wherever we walked, all eyes were on us, looking, staring, and smiling.

I wanted to taste the food cooking in rows upon rows of food stands filled with things I had never seen, smells I didn't recognize. I bought warm gloves for only one yuan, socks for five yuan, and a beautiful long radish. We walked for blocks and I truly had never had so many eyes on me. I felt like a celebrity. Were we that strange-looking? Did no other tourists ever come here?

A group of women had been watching us as we walked along the market. One woman from the group approached me looking at my purse. Was she playing truth or dare with her friends? Was she going to say something I wondered? What was she staring at? I had no idea what she was doing, but I stood there looking down at her. Then suddenly she looked me in the eye, reached up her hand and quickly tweaked my nose between her fingers! I was shocked and drew my head back, a surprised look on my face. Her group of friends burst into laughter and she smiled grandly at her prank! Laughing as well but not wanted to be outdone, I figured that I too could be playful; I smiled coyly at her and then quickly tweaked her nose back! The group almost fell over laughing hysterically! My tweak was the last thing she was expecting from the Western giant. After our big laugh, we waved goodbye still smiling, both pleased with our interaction. Oh, how I wish I could have spoken to her. Frank was chuckling, too.

Our teachers had graciously invited us to Gwa Wat, dinner at a chafing dish restaurant. We were led to a private room where our round table had a hole in the center filled with an enormous chafing dish full of steaming hot stock. Inside the large chafing dish was another smaller dish with a hot spicy stock. They were called "mother and son" because the mother kept the son warm. The teachers ordered lots of beef, cut paper thin with more fat than meat, vegetables, and noodles, and guided us by putting the beef and vegetables into the two different stocks to cook while showing us how to mix the sauce ingredients of cilantro, onions, and bean curd into our little bowls to dip the beef and lamb into. There was also lotus root, crown daisy, potatoes, dumplings, broccoli, a bean salad, and delicious pickled cabbage. Mr. Pong poured lots of beer for Frank, himself, and me while the other teachers drank wine. It was a lovely evening with lots of laughter and enjoyment. Frank and I knew how expensive this meal was compared to their meager salaries. They made only $400/month, but they absolutely refused to let us help them with the bill, waving us off when we offered to contribute.

BACK IN THE CLASSROOM, I discovered that poems were too difficult for most of my classes. I realized that the vocabulary and stories from music would give better practice, so I started using Beatles' songs on the board for our oral recitation: "Hard Day's Night," "I Want to Hold your Hand," and "She Loves You." They had never heard of the group! I loved listening to them repeat the words to songs that I loved and their pronunciations improved steadily. What a shame that I had no way to play music during class.

Each evening on the Internet, I looked up the words to different songs. Besides looking up songs and catching up with friends, Len and I were still writing each other and I loved getting his emails. His writing was beautiful and I was looking forward to spending time with him again. We had picked a time to visit in Scotland at his mom's house after I completed my ride on the Trans-Siberian Express. I was excited to see him but curious about our meeting location. He said his mom loved animals and would love to see my photos.

We went for another day of shopping, with Frank, the forever gentleman, carrying my packages. Being around good natured Frank every day was making me think that a thoughtful man with patience would be lovely to travel through life with. When he spoke about his wife, it was always with a smile. Rather than feel the tension that I sometimes felt when people talked about their relationships, I felt happy listening to Frank. Our conversations flowed easily. We talked about our classes, travel, marriage, and relationships and how we felt about the Chinese culture.

Heading off to the big shopping area, I said, "Let's find some food!"

Following our noses, we found a street filled with vendors, steam from cooking filling the air, odors unknown, lots of food and people. A crowd gathered around some cooks pouring batter on a griddle forming round, thin bread like a small pizza fried in oil. One of the cooks cracked an egg under the bread and fried them together. Judging from the waiting line, Frank and I decided to eat one and they were delicious! Eating the meat or chicken here was always a worry since they hung in the open air markets like fly paper but the breads were amazing.

"I'm freezing, Frank," I said, wondering if he would get tired of my whining.

Wandering through the open markets in the freezing rain, finally I found some heavy long johns that fit and snapped them up. On through the winding corridors, shoe stores lined both sides of the hallway all exactly the same, maybe 25 stores in a row. Waving at us to come in, the owners then looked down at my shoe size, their eyes stunned. When they looked back at my face, I saw the look of astonishment. A giant in their midst.

I wondered how so many stores with exactly the same product stayed in business. Imagine seeing a block of stores exactly the same. I was amazed by this philosophy of identical stores with the exact same products displayed in exactly the same way. This style of marketing was difficult for me to understand. Individualism was as foreign of a concept here and as difficult for them to understand as blanket conformity was for me. I wondered what thoughts were like inside a woman's mind in a culture that had such strong group thought. Did anyone ever see things in a different way? What kept the conformity going?

I tried to understand group thought. Obviously the goal here was to strive to be like your neighbor, not to stand out. How different from home where individualism flourished, the home of the free. Curious, very curious. Wrapping my head around conformity as a goal that stifled the individual was like learning Portuguese for me. It boggled my brain. I had no way to understand their lifestyle. How could people live like this? Maybe it was like our housing projects that had only small differences between the houses? I never understood that either. A maverick thinker would go mad here. There just wasn't an opportunity to see things from a new angle. Group thought versus individual power. Control versus freedom.

IN A YARN SHOP, I bought inexpensive purple mohair yarn and a pair of wooden knitting needles. I planned to knit a scarf on the Trans-Siberian Express, which was next on my travel agenda. And for the rain outside, a delicate, beautifully flowered red umbrella. The umbrella woman, a very good sales clerk, pantomimed with me, negotiating a good price for herself and then decided to sell me more. What else do you need? Socks? No. Gloves? No. A bra? I laughed looking down at my chest. And then she looked at me and at my chest. Once she realized the joke, she laughed and laughed because all of the bras were exactly the same size, A cups. (So even breasts conformed here!) But laughter always came easily even without knowing the language.

Frank was great at organizing weekend trips, which I wouldn't have done without him. He asked Jack to drive us to the bus station for a daytrip to Penglai on the coast. Arriving at Penglai into sunshine and mild weather, we walked to the beach to see an enormous granite full-body sculpture of the Eight Immortals, who were thought to have gained their immortality here in Penglai. It was said that the eight immortals got drunk at Penglai Pavilion and crossed the sea without boats by using their different tricks. They now inhabited this supernatural mountain.

But before walking up to see the world-famous Penglai Pavilion, which was built a thousand years ago, I stopped at a shop starving for an apple to tide me over. I pantomimed eating an apple and the woman showed me packaged dried fish. Hmm, better work on my pantomime, I thought, but a man walked over who understood me and he reached behind his desk handing me his apple! I pantomimed that no, no, no, I couldn't take his apple but he insisted. Because everyone in China peels their apples to be safe from pesticides, I pantomimed a knife. By now the other store owners gathered around us curious to watch Caucasians as we were still quite a novelty. With the crowd watching, he peeled my apple but he wouldn't allow me to pay! The people here had a consistent sweetness. Frank was amused as always and took photographs, smiling.

Leaving my generous apple donor, we walked toward the pavilion but I saw a man selling baked sweet potatoes out of a portable oven.

"Frank, I have to have one. They look great, blackened on the outside. I bet they're unbelievably sweet."

"Are you ready now?" Frank asked patiently after I finished snarfing down the potato.

"Well, I should make it for a couple of hours now," smiling at my kindly travel buddy. Somewhere along the way, my metabolism had changed. Every few hours I needed to eat or I felt the agony of hunger turning my mood to madness. I must have been rather a giant pain for Frank to travel with though he was always patient.

Walking up the cliff to the pavilions, the palaces, and the temples used by emperors as a place of relaxation, we wandered through looking at the architecture, ancient artifacts, calligraphy, and stone inscriptions.

Exquisite details and beauty everywhere I looked. I wondered about life here with the emperors 1000 years ago.

Walking back to the city, we stopped to visit my apple friend and I bought a big bag of dried squid that was absolutely delicious! Hungry again, we walked up the street where all of the restaurants served fresh fish, kept alive with an aerator in separate plastic bins on the floor. Each restaurant looked exactly the same except that each had different furniture. A woman stood in front of each restaurant inviting us inside. Again, I noticed the lack of individuality. Conformity was treasured here, a mindset that created spritz cookies in restaurant design, food and clothing stalls. Did everyone think the same thoughts here, too?

WHEN WE WERE NOT in class, Frank and I hung out in the teacher's room helping grade papers. Finally the teachers understood that we wanted to help and did not consider them lazy. With 70 students in each class, they had an enormous amount of paperwork. All of the English teachers loved to practice their English with us asking us questions and laughing and joking with each other. I loved the atmosphere here.

But one day Meeko, my favorite student, misbehaved in one of his classes. The teacher he had offended brought him into the teacher's room for a very public yelling session. She screamed at him for a solid five minutes. He hung his head in humiliation. I wondered if she would pinch his ear or smack his bottom. When she was finally finished, he humbly left the room. How many high school students in the States would have taken that kind of verbal shakedown?

The teachers asked me to stay the year, a compliment that went straight to my heart. For so many reasons, I would have loved to teach there for a year. I smiled thinking that Beatle songs were acceptable curriculum! But I knew that I would miss Frank if I stayed a year! His patience, love of the students, and easy-going nature were a big part of my enjoyment there.

Because most of the students at the school were boys, the NBA was extremely popular there especially Yao Ming. Basketball games were intense at lunchtime. One of my students asked if we could learn about the NBA and smiling I said yes. However, that meant that every night I had to go to the Internet café to learn about the teams!

Introducing geography lessons by placing the teams in their respective states on a map, I talked about those states and what they were known for. Even explaining the team names and mascots was fun. The boys were very anxious to learn about each team and we even started posting scores on the board and team standings. "The NBA goes to China" was a very successful lesson.

As frosting on the NBA cake, Claude Berghorn, an old high school buddy, sent me a Houston Rocket T-shirt, 2 wrist bands, and a headband to use as rewards. With the class that had worked the hardest, I told them, "Four students will be given one of these items for a prize."

They gasped with delight at the prospect.

I asked, "How should we decide who gets a gift?"

And for the first time, I had individuals raising their hands with opinions!

"I think the person who speaks the best English should win the prizes," said the smartest girl in the class.

"I think you should just pick," said another.

"I think you can draw a number from our student numbers and that will be the student who wins."

I was so excited to have a conversation! "How are we going to decide what to do?"

"You can just decide," said one of the boys used to teacher rules.

"No, let's do it like we would in a classroom in America. I will write each idea on the board and then your raise your hands for the idea you support."

And democracy twinkled for a moment in China as they voted in my class on what to do! When all four items were distributed, everyone congratulated the winners. There were no sour grapes. I was impressed.

FRANK PLANNED A train trip to Mount Taishan, a sacred mountain, to walk up the 6566 steps to the top and then spend the night so we could watch the sunrise. Taking this walk in ancient China meant you would live to be 100 years old and the sunrise would give you and your family a blessing of health, wealth, and happiness. The original treadmill test had existed for 3000 years as 72 emperors had successfully made the climb, including Confucius and Chairman Mao.

But Frank ran marathons, and I hoped I could keep up. We rode for 10 hours in a sleeper train in a berth with six bunks. Between noise, lights, and the rock hard mattress, I was without sleep.

Arriving in town, we walked to a park full of apple blossoms, beautiful sculptures, and a temple and then past kites for sale, the only souvenir I was dying to buy. Without bargaining, which shocked the vendor, I bought an enormous kite with an ancient design in bright colors for 100 Yuan. Frank, of course, carried it for me all the way up the mountain. Great guy, this Frank!

As we walked away, the man sent along his 10-year-old daughter, who spoke no English but was all smiles and excited to join us.

"Frank, did I buy the daughter?" I asked.

"No, but since you didn't negotiate, I think he figures that you are rich and will give his daughter money for helping us up the mountain."

"But the kite only cost $12! How could I negotiate that? We are staying overnight. What can we do?"

I pantomimed to the little girl that after we walked up the mountain, we would spend the night. She understood me and said goodbye!

It was a glorious sunny day. We got the usual number of stares from people wondering why we were following an ancient Chinese tradition and after two hours on the Ancient Chinese Stairmaster, I started wondering, too.

Thousands of people were climbing up and down with us. Bounding down the stairs finished with their trek, groups of young people laughed playfully with each other full of energy. I glanced over at a pair of lovers sitting on a rock taking a rest, a contented look on her face as she rested her head on his shoulder. Families climbed together with grandparents using their canes and slowly working their way up the stairs. How did they manage to climb these steep stairs hour after hour?

Mount Taishan symbolizes the Chinese spirit, the physical challenge signifying the ability to overcome difficulty. This trek gave me insight into that spirit. Along the path, cypress trees with limbs twisted as if by some ancient god took my mind off the never-ending steps. There were tall rock towers built from small rocks along the way as if each passerby had added one small rock to the tower.

Lost in the meditation of the constant steps, I imagined the procession 3000 years ago. What clothes did they wear? The ornate silk clothes that I saw in the museums and the small ballet slipper shoes? How many people climbed in the grand ceremony to thank heaven for peace and prosperity?

Back from my daydream, I noticed a man with a long pole stretched across his shoulders with two enormous bags on either end. Without the strength or possibly time to remove his load, his head bent and his shoulders curved as he rested the weight of his load on the nearby wall. Much of what was needed at the top of Taishan was still taken up by porters in this manner, rain or shine. He was a slight man, and I was amazed at his strength, balance, and endurance.

We continued upwards finding a group of three Chinese women walking at the same, steady pace as Frank and I were. We smiled as we climbed the stairs together encouraging each other, our bond the challenge of the climb. Frank easily kept up his steady pace patiently walking with us. Along the path to the top of Taishan, people stopped to offer prayers and burn tall joss sticks of incense in beautiful temples as they had done for thousands of years. Our climbing companions stopped to make an offering. Frank and I happily stopped enjoying a moment of rest on a small bench.

A beggar, who had watched me climb up the last group of stairs, moved to sit near me. Very curious he stared at me, probably amazed by the number of sweat drops falling off my face. Never one to hold back on drama, I acted out my walk for him showing my exhaustion and rubbing my tired feet. Obviously amused, he laughed and then pointed me in the direction of the temple signaling me to make a prayer. Not certain if asking for more energy was a proper prayer, I took his advice hoping it would work and made a stop at the temple. We waved at each other as our group continued up the mountain.

My second wind kicked in after my stop or perhaps an ancient Taoist god graciously helped me. We climbed the final hour, 1000 steps, in good time and good spirits, and when we rounded a bend, I saw the tram. Proud of myself for making it this far as we passed through the Mid-heaven Gate, there were still 2000 steps left on The Road to Heaven and from a distance it looked straight up.

Arriving in the tram at the top of the mountain, the stark beauty of the 72 peaks that made up Mount Taishan overwhelmed me. There were ancient cypress and pine trees, beautiful rock formations, pagodas on distant misty hills, and ancient writings with enormous letters in red ink carved into the rocks. We walked up more stairs to the top of the mountain, where the small village catered to tourists with little shops where one could buy souvenirs and pieces of rock, restaurants, and a couple of hotels. But most of these people would not stay overnight in hotels. They rented green Mao winter army coats with fur collars and huddled together outside through the night! Already cold and gusty, nightfall had to be freezing even with a big army coat. I couldn't even imagine a night in the blustering cold.

Out our hotel door at 5:30 am, wearing our hotel's long down green coats with hoods, we were blown around by big, cold gusts of wind and our faces reddened from the cold. The darkness of night just before dawn made climbing the path difficult but seeing the silhouettes of hundreds of Chinese people wearing green army coats and walking silently towards the eastern peaks inspired me as we joined their march happy to be a part of this ancient Chinese pilgrimage. Everywhere on the top of the mountain thousands of people huddled together, dark hair flying in the wind and happy faces contrasting sharply with the stark, rock clusters.

Frank and I found a place to sit protected from the cold wind gusts as we all anxiously waited for the big show. Finally, as the time for sunrise approached, anticipation and excitement filled the air and a hush came over the crowd as slowly dark turned to light.

Sadly, that morning there were too many clouds in the sky and though we saw the light changing, we could not see the sun. A simultaneous sound of disappointment wafted up from the crowd. I pointed my camera in the eastern direction and took a photo anyway. As everyone got up to walk back, I looked at their faces and saw happiness in their smiles even without the sun. Blessings of happiness, health, and wealth were in the air.

Later in my room, I was amazed, flabbergasted, and totally stymied when I looked at the photo in my digital camera.

"Frank, come here and look at this. What do you see?"

"It's the sun, Joyce," he said as calmly as he said everything.

"But how? How can it be the sun? There was no sun this morning."

"I don't know," he replied. "It looks like a miracle, a true ancient magical mystery." He was smiling at me.

Later when I returned to school and told my classes the story of my trip there, I showed them the photo and explained what had happened. I asked each group, "How did the sun appear on this photo if no one saw it?"

They all replied, "Mount Taishan gave you a miracle." They too were in awe.

Frank and I bought food for the 10-hour daytime train ride back to Yantai from Taishan but with a packed train, our first "seats" were on the floor between the cars with some pretty scruffy looking characters. Glad that Frank was with me, I was also happy to be there with common people, who were equally thrilled to be there with us.

Luckily after an hour or so, we moved to seats for the long ride home but what an education that trip proved to be. The countryside along the train was a trail of cardboard, plastic bags, and paper waste left there as the train chugged past. In a total disregard for the beauty of the land, any scraps of paper or food were either thrown on the floor or out the window. With amazement, I watched a man peel an apple letting the skin fall to the floor. Another person finished his big bowl of noodles and threw the container out the window. Every couple of hours, the conductor came by sweeping the floor of the train, which was covered with litter.

I had waited to use the bathroom till I knew there was no choice. Dreading the filth, it was far grosser than I had feared. It was a tiny room with a hole in the floor that went straight to the tracks. Urine was everywhere. A gross smell hung in the air. I wanted a mask to cover my nose. Better than that, I wanted to be a man. I crouched down hoping to hit the hole without slipping into it while somehow keeping from peeing into my own shoes. Nothing like a deep crouch with nothing to hold onto in a rocking train with my face in a twisted grimace from the nastiness around me! Absolutely the worst toilet in my entire life.

Returning to my seat, I took out my pretty purple mohair and wooden needles and began to knit the scarf. Every woman in the vicinity froze staring at me as I knit including the young woman next to me. What now? I wondered. Women walked by and stopped in the aisles hiding their laughter behind their hands. An entire commotion stirred up about my knitting. A man asked to take my photo! I shrugged at Frank, smiled at everyone else, and kept knitting.

Finally the young woman sitting next to me could bear it no longer. In a very bold move, she grabbed the needles right out of my hands and started knitting as if to take me out of my misery.

Smiling, she seemed to be saying, "Here, let me show you the right way! And by the way, these needles are much too thick."

Chuckling at her grab, I watched her nimble fingers show me the correct way to knit. My free, loose knitting done without throwing the wool was unacceptable (even though my mom had taught me that way). She knit a tight, exact stitch. She knit for an hour happy to be busy on the long train ride. I watched her and was hesitant to take it from her. When she finally gave it back, her portion of my scarf was perfect, each stitch an exact duplicate of the last one. Even knitting was controlled here. We smiled at each other and I thanked her, but then continued on with my wild freestyle knitting! Frank smiled at us both and took photos.

As my last week of teaching approached, in my higher-level classes, I was able to have some question-and-answer sessions. At first tentative, the students became more bold as they saw how happy I was to answer their questions. They wanted to know about my family. Obviously having two sons and no husband was out of their paradigm, especially because I was neither embarrassed about that fact nor weak and dependent.

Divorce in China had been quite a stigma and until the end of 2003, a separating couple needed their work unit's permission to separate. The welfare of the state was always more important than individual happiness. Now with the rule change, unhappy couples could go to the town center and pay about one dollar and in 10 minutes, they would be divorced. Still I had the sense that being a single mom raising two sons was a difficult concept for my students to understand. When I talked about my divorce and raising my sons, Meeko said that he felt sad for me that I had been alone. There was a lovely look of compassion in his eyes.

They had many questions about my trip as a single woman around the world for a year—a totally impossible concept for them to understand. How could I explain my sense of individuality? It would be like describing green to someone who was colorblind. Questions surfaced about money, safety, leaving my family, and what had motivated me to travel. Questions about courage and independence, too. As I ruminated over their conformity, they questioned my individuality. Any questions that they were brave enough to ask, I answered openly. The topics changed from questions about my life in America to more political ones. I was ecstatic to have them speaking after three weeks of shyness and frustrated that I would be leaving so soon.

"What do you think about the war in Iraq?"

"Why does your country bomb and kill people?"

"Do you support your President?"

Remembering that I was the first American to teach here, I wanted to impart both my love for my country and the precious freedom that I feel to voice my opinion openly, to be critical. What were the words to use that conveyed the joy I had from growing up free and the despair I felt from a war that I didn't understand?

After this very intense class, I wracked my brain thinking of peace songs that I could use to explain my heart. I loved John Lennon's song, "Imagine" and decided to let his words speak for me and my heart's deep desire for peace. I wrote the words on the board and then as always they recited them back to me in rows. Their English had improved tremendously in a short time both in understanding and pronunciation.

An individual hand went up, "Can you sing this song for us?"

"Oh, dear, this is a beautiful song and I do not have a beautiful voice. I'd better say no."

Another hand went up. "We think your voice will be fine."

I was happy that they were comfortable with me now but sing? How embarrassing!

But 70 students looked at me waiting. I sang the first performance of my life in China shyly but with a tear falling from the wave of feeling for the world to be one.

When I finished, they clapped full of smiles but I was completely embarrassed, and I changed the focus.

"Now is there anyone who will sing it for me?"

Thinking for certain no one would be bold enough, I was surprised when all of the students pointed to a boy towards the back of the room.

"Do you want to sing this?"

Everyone answered "yes" for him and he nodded yes. He rose from his seat and though he only had heard it once, he sang in a clear, beautiful voice in what will always be the sweetest version of "Imagine." I was speechless. Tears fell down my cheeks.

Full of emotion, I said, "I want to thank you for that beautiful song. My tears are in gratitude for being able to spend this time with all of you. My tears are for my dream of peace. I want you to remember me when you see things about that war. Many people desperately want peace in America. Just like you, I am against the war."

Class ended with me on the bright side of many hugs. Lucky me. The young man's song in his beautiful voice would be with me for a long, long time.

I COULDN'T BELIEVE that I would be leaving soon on the Trans-Siberian Express through China, Mongolia, and Russia, and I prayed that it would be a cleaner train than the Taishan had been.

With more time in the classroom and more familiarity, my students talked to me now over lunch or outside during recess. We had conversations about their future, their dreams, and the careers they hoped to have.

"I have a dream to be a world-famous journalist. I will travel everywhere," one of our lunchtime companions told us.

"I don't know what I want to do yet. Here in China I must decide or my family will not be proud of me," said another.

"I will be a top engineer. That is my dream."

Meeko saw it differently. "Maybe someday I will find a way not to be like everyone else and have it be acceptable. Maybe after the Olympics come, my dream will come true."

I wanted to stay. I wanted to hear more dreams. Things were finally comfortable in all of my classes, and it was way too soon to leave. On the last day I told my students goodbye, thanking them for an amazing month, and saying that I had loved teaching them. They clapped and gave me little notes of thanks and love saying how much they would miss me. I bid a sad farewell to the English teachers too, who had been so much fun. And to Frank, the best travel companion possible, a hug and a promise to stay in touch as we both traveled the planet.

Would I return someday? I hoped so.

Now it was time to fly to Beijing to get ready for the Trans-Siberian Express, my longest train ride ever.

CHAPTER 17

The Trans-Siberian Express

BEIJING WAS INSANE with noise. Buses, cars, bicycles, and people all just a split second from colliding. People spitting and hacking and blowing their noses on the sidewalk. Pollution that hung on my eyelashes.

Across the street from the train station, I arrived at a $15/night hostel where I got a clean private room, a clean shared bathroom down the hall, free laundry and Internet, and an in-house bar. Before I could leave on the next leg of my trip, I had chores to complete: a huge package to mail home and a visa to get for Belarus.

The embassy neighborhood was beautiful, like a walk into another world with trees and grass, quiet streets, and wrought iron fences around stately embassy buildings. The nearby restaurants catered to wealthy clientele, and I hopped into a French bakery playing quiet French music for a lovely croissant and cup of coffee, an oasis. I dropped off my passport with $100 at the Belarus embassy and walked away nervous as usual that I wouldn't get my passport back for two days.

Walking by the Silk Warehouse, I ventured inside but it was crazy intense with hawkers standing in front of their booths shouting, screaming "Come here. Good price." "You like our stuff. Best price." If they could have used a hook to grab me, they would have. Unable to take the pressure, the closeness, the shouting, or the crowds, I found my way back outside to a small booth.

A young Chinese woman, excited to talk to an American, introduced herself.

"My name is Yong. I am an English teacher, 27 years old.

"How nice to meet you, Yong." We exchanged more small talk.

Anxious to continue talking, Yong said, "Would you like to go to a park and talk? I love to practice my English if you have time."

"Sure. Let's go." Sitting down, I explained about my trip, which fascinated her.

"I don't want to teach English anymore," she said. "I want to travel like you are doing."

"Great. I hope you can do that someday."

"No, it may never happen." She shook her head. "I had a chance to leave China and work in Canada but my country would not allow me to leave."

"They wouldn't allow you to leave?" I asked incredulously.

"Yes, I cannot get permission."

"Hmm, why don't you apply at Microsoft here in China? Maybe sometime you would be able to transfer out of the country. Why don't you find out about applying there?"

"Can I ask you about American men?"

"Well, yes."

"There is a black man here from America and we were together. Now I think we are not. Have I made a mistake?"

How was it possible for two women from any country to easily talk about men?

"Okay, if you are in a relationship with an American man and you are unhappy, then you need to either walk away and forget him or talk to him to see if you can get him to understand your problem. He might be thinking he can get away with more here than at home. Stick up for yourself."

"Do I believe him when he says he love me?"

"Ah, for this you have to see how he behaves and how he treats you. Talk is cheap. Trust your instincts. His idea of love and yours may be totally different. You want marriage. He may only want to play."

We talked for two more hours about my trip, her life, and relationships, not my specialty at all.

"I am very old by standards here for marriage."

"Oh, not in America. You have plenty of time."

It felt like I had met an old friend as we talked so comfortably, and when it was time for her to leave, we exchanged emails.

"The government censors emails here. We may not be able to stay in touch but I will try to write you," she said. She looked wistful as we parted.

When I returned to pick up my Belarus visa, the obviously bored diplomat asked me, "What is your reason for needing this visa?"

"I am taking the Trains-Siberian Express to Moscow and then through to Brussels though I'll only spend a couple of nights in Moscow. My father and a large part of my family were born near Kiev."

Ah, now he was interested. "You must go again, stay longer then, and find your lost family. You will be able to find them if you look. For now you will only be traveling through my country. Best wishes for a good journey."

I left figuring that this was a positive sign that another trip was in the hopper to find my family. But now I had everything that I needed for the trip that my MonkeyShrine travel agent had told me: some snacks, some US dollar bills, some yuans, and the same $1000 in travelers checks that I had been carrying around the world in my money belt for 10 months!

I was beyond excited to board the longest continuous rail line on earth completed in 1905. The route I'd be taking around Lake Baikal was completed in 1916, the year before my dad was born. On this epic journey of almost 6,000 miles, 7 time zones, across two continents and one-third of the globe, I'd pass through China and the Great Wall, Mongolia and the Gobi desert, and finally across Siberia onto Moscow. Then onward across Belarus, Poland, and Germany before getting off the train in Brussels and flying to Scotland! Train girl would be getting her fill!

Walking into my second class compartment, I found a million boxes on the floor and on the beds and cramped between the boxes were three Mongolians, who, of course, only spoke Mongolian. A friendly round-faced, short woman; her husband, who with his open pimples, red marks all over his face, and nasty glare, gave me the creeps, and their tall, dark, handsome friend. They cleared off my bunk and I lifted the lid to store my backpack. I wasn't sure how I'd change clothes if at all since our entire car shared a bathroom. What had I gotten myself into now? No first class for me.

I wanted to travel with the real people. Real people meant the creepy man who was currently staring at me. Something just felt wrong here but I had signed on for adventure and from an adjustment standpoint that was what I would have to do. Apparently from the words on their boxes, these three were returning from a computer buying expedition in Beijing. I offered them some peanuts and the woman helped me roll my purple mohair yarn into a large ball. The windows neither opened in this room nor in the corridor and it felt warm and stuffy and too close. Adjust. Adjust. Adjust.

Our two car attendants were Chinese and spoke no English. Water boiled in a coal-fired samovar at one end of the car to make tea and instant noodle dishes. There were no showers in second class, but the toilet at the end of the car had a sink and warm water. Each country had its own dining car that would be attached at border crossings.

I moved to the corridor lining up with my Chinese train mates, all men, gazing out the window. As the train pulled away, our excitement even without a common language was in our faces.

"Woo hoo! We're on our way! Moscow, here I come!" I said. My Chinese travel companions smiled and said something to each other. We were all hypnotized with the changing sites of the jumble of Beijing with skyscrapers, vast construction projects, and cars flying over expressways. People on bikes or walking along the tracks and women hanging their laundry in crowded old residential compounds changed as we headed toward rural northern China to people driving horse and carts, people working in the fields, and a look of dire poverty.

And then the Great Wall appeared. "Oh, my gosh, there it is. Going on for miles!"

My Chinese train mates smiled at my excitement. Gazing out the window, I suddenly felt something along my butt like a hand but I thought it must have been an accidental passing. As I turned to look, the creepy husband was looking back at me with that evil glare on his nasty face. The bastard! I was not putting up with his crap.

I stomped to the dining car steaming. What the fuck was that? At the dining car, I told an English-speaking conductor what had happened, and asked him to transfer me to another car no matter what the cost.

"Sorry, the first class section is full. The entire train is full. Give me a minute."

Shit. I plopped myself down and ordered a Chinese beer. I was in a foul mood. The Chinese dining car was American 50s diner-style with a plain décor. The lace curtains were the only detail, but the beer was cold and I was safe.

The scenery was amazing until we started into the Gobi desert towards Mongolia. As I gazed out the window, I heard no song from the earth. It was desolate, not even close to pretty. A landscape of bleakness. The color of depression. An earth barren and burnt, rolling sorrow. Joy was lost here. Sky, the color of earth. Perhaps I rode a train over the moon. No cowboys. No cows. Trees too sad to bloom. Patiently I watched this totally depressing environment fly by festering about Mr. Mongolia. I wondered where to hide from a man so gross. I wondered how to survive. Was this going to be the train ride from hell spent hiding in a dining car?

A happy couple from Sweden joined me, and I told them my tale of woe. They told me about life in Sweden, their dreams, and their lovely first-class car. They brightened up my day with laughter.

But when the conductor returned, he had bad news. "Sorry but there is no where I can move you. However, those three people will only be with you tonight. Then you will ride alone."

"Thank you, but now what? How long does the dining car stay open?"

"It closes at around 8 PM."

We ate really bad Chinese food and another cold beer and talked till they went to their compartment.

When the Swedes left, I moved to sit by an Irish guy and a British woman, who were also traveling first class. The Canadian woman, who worked at a zoo, was volunteering at animal sanctuaries! We were instant friends. She was going to work with snow leopards in Mongolia. Paul, the Irish chap, was doing a lecture as part of his year away from work. We talked about being a tourist, places they had seen, and the benefits of taking time off. With stories to exchange and laughter, I almost forgot that I was going to have to sleep in the room with the bastard. We stayed until the dining car closed.

The walk of dread back to my berth left me with only a plan to sleep lightly. Just one night I told myself. As I entered the berth, the men were gone and I started knitting the Trans-Siberian Scarf while the wife and I pantomimed about this purple mohair scarf that I planned to work on every day until I reached Brussels.

I loved the sound and rhythm of this train on the tracks, like a meditation with no effort. This train was really the king of trains unlike any other I had ridden. Was it something in the wheels, the pull of the engine, the speed, or the gentle rocking? I always found peacefulness on trains. But this time, nightfall was approaching and I wasn't sure what to do about Genghis Khan.

The immediate solution came at the Chinese-Mongolian border. At each border crossing, there was a huge production changing the wheels to fit the next country's tracks. Each car was jacked up to change the wheels. But first Chinese customs dressed in tidy uniforms with very solemn faces checked each room to make sure nothing illegal was stashed aboard or anyone illegal leaving the country. Should I tell them we had a bastard on board?

After customs gave us back our passports, the wife signaled me to hop off the train with her. Walking out into the cold, eerie night with dim spotlights lighting the old train station, I found fog whirled at my feet. It was a classic scary movie scene. Passengers bought crates of fruit on the platform, and the Mongolian wife bought four huge crates of fruit to somehow fit into our room.

She and I waited in the small train station as it filled with cigarette smoke. The wife was very protective of me, even teaching me to roll up my pant legs before entering the filthy bathroom. Genghis and his friend thankfully were off somewhere else.

Finally we got back on the train, but we immediately stopped at the border in Mongolia where a new set of nicely uniformed customs officers checked the boxes and the passports of everyone aboard. This entire process took till well past midnight, probably four hours or more. I was exhausted but I walked the length of the train on the off chance that the new Mongolian dining car would be open. It was locked. I walked slowly back to my car.

When I opened the door, everyone was in bed. The bastard was sleeping on the low berth across from me with his wife on the upper berth and the friend above me. Damn! But the floor between us was filled with fruit boxes and the table separated our heads. Not feeling safe at all, I backed myself up against the wall promising myself to sleep lightly.

Suddenly I jerked awake. Terror shook my body when, gasping with fear, I felt hands on either side of my head, a leg pinning me down, and that evil, pimply face closing in on me.

Full on awake, I screamed, "Jesus, what the fuck are you doing?" and I shoved him backwards, my arms tense with the strength and fury of 20 women.

The bastard had climbed over all the fruit and the computers boxes in the aisle to climb on top of me. My warrior's shove pushed him right over the fruit boxes while I kept screaming. The room was pitch-black.

"Aaaah…aah…aaah…" I screamed. I was pissed, frightened, angry, ready to cry and ready to kill. Somewhere a logical woman plotted what to do next but Screaming Woman was in charge at the moment.

"Jesus Christ, you asshole, what the fuck do you think you are doing? How dare you! How dare you! Fucking asshole"….and on and on I ranted, furious, almost beyond anger and ready to throw the asshole from the train. Now! At the same time, I was frightened to death wondering why no one was helping me.

My tirade was definitely loud. But the wife stayed in her bed. The friend stayed in his bed. The conductors in the next room ignored my screams as did the whole car. I continued to swear at the bastard loudly for the next five minutes interspersed with screams. While I screamed, I tried to think of what to do. What the hell was I supposed to do now?

Obviously, the conductors were staying out of this. Shit. The bastard. Who did he think he was messing with? What if I pounded on the conductor's door...what then? No one understood English. I was a woman in a foreign country screaming about attempted rape. Why weren't they coming?

I decided I needed some kind of protection in case he tried it again and unfortunately my knife was tucked in my backpack under my seat. Damn! I grabbed my knitting needle in my fist knowing that for certain I would puncture him if he came near me. Make my day. I was ferocious. Fucking son of a bitch! A curse on him!

I held the wooden knitting needle like a weapon up in my hand shaking it in the dark screaming, "You come near me and you're dead, bastard." Somewhere inside a totally frightened woman wondered if I'd be hung in Mongolia for stabbing the bastard. I stayed there griping a knitting needle ready to put it through his chest. But he left me alone. My shaking stopped but I was really scared, too scared to even think clearly. There would be no crying tonight. I gripped my knitting needle in terror till dawn.

In the morning he and his wife sat on his bunk smiling and trying to talk to me. I bolted up, knitting needle gripped tightly.

"Look, asshole, and you, stupid wife, shut the fuck up! You both go to hell!" I stormed off in disgust taking giant steps down the corridor to the dining car. I was shaking. Mad. What the hell had just happened? Did I handle it okay? Could I have turned him in? Storming through eight cars cooled me off. I was safe now and they were leaving.

Arriving in the Mongolian dining car, I was a mess of emotions and after no sleep, one wreck of a warrior. But I looked around at my surroundings and calmed down. Gorgeous ornate wood carvings lined the walls, silver tea sets were placed on each table, and old Mongolian carvings hung on the wall. The sun was shining. I was far way from my berth.

I sat near Ireland and Canada telling them about my trauma. They hugged me and told me they would stay with me till we reached Ulan Bator.

"Do you think I should have told my conductor or come to get yours?"

"No, yours obviously heard you and ignored you," Canada said. "Ours would not have gotten involved."

We discussed wildlife and the environment. The chattering kept my mind off things. Lunch was delicious—mutton stew with more beer, Mongolian beer now.

Gazing out the window at the desolate stretches of sand with mountains and hills in the distance. The sand blew constantly, creating a blur across my vision. In the distance three enormous vultures were sitting patiently waiting perhaps for someone to fall off the train. Vultures as big as Great Danes with giant wings and skinny heads on big bodies. They looked evil in their patient stance, waiting and watching for Death. Standing on a sand dune watching the train like a gang of thugs waiting for someone, something to die. I thought about a Mongolian I would love to feed them. What were the chances of me pushing him off this train as a dinner offering to the vulture gang?

The endless expanse of the Gobi desert was gorgeous beyond description, with a glowing blue sky. I imagined Mongols racing across the desert on Arabian horses with sword in hand, and camel riders flying across the desert carrying goods from village to village. The train zoomed past and the desert changed to small villages of wooden houses surrounded by intricate fences and the *gers* (the word for "dwelling") that nomads lived in. Sheep, buffalo, horses, and goats grazed in the endless pastures with very little grass like the South West in the United States. Men on horseback herded cattle.

But I was an emotional mess not yet recovered from the attack. In my day-old, night-old outfit, I felt forlorn, scared, angry, and grubby. I needed clean clothes and a clean bathroom, too. Maybe I could use the first-class bathroom.

Thankfully, the Mongolian bastard left the train at Ulan Bator! I shivered when I entered my room wishing I had sage to burn. I said a prayer to clear away the bad energy. It still felt nasty in my room. Filling a bowl with hot water from our samovar, I treated myself to a "bath," using lovely smelling soap and a small green rag that turned the water green. With the bath and fresh clothes, I felt better though I still refused to look at the other berths. Terror lingered.

The Gobi Desert changed to grassy steppe. Mongolia. The earth screamed at me here to protect it. Her trees had been heavily logged, leaving barren mountains. Horses ran wild. Looking out the window, watching the front of the train snake around a corner, I saw cattle with long thick coats to keep them warm as they came out of winter. Snow on the river banks and an evergreen standing tall were messengers from home.

What was Mongolian life like? Simple farming with sheep, horses, cows. Camels and gers. Now safe and alone in my compartment, I began to experience profound happiness on this train, watching everything fly by. At the same time, I was totally exhausted from a lack of sleep.

I longed for a friend to talk to, to help me recover from last night's attack. I kept playing it over and over again in my mind, which only scared and angered me more. I was having a bout of the lonelies and yet I was full of joy. I needed a hug. Animal people knew how to love. I needed sleep.

Arriving at the Mongolian border crossing and heading into Russia, the train stopped for customs and a new set of wheels.

A woman customs officer in a down army coat, short sexy skirt, fur hat, and tall boots stood outside my room and asked with a Mongolian accent, "You passport?"

No smile. I handed it to her and start humming, "From Russia with Love."

Taking my passport, opening to the photo, she looked at me. I smiled.

"Vat is your name?"

"My name is Joyce...Joyce Bond. I mean, Joyce Major." Now the theme from *Mission Impossible* clouded my mind.

"Vhere are you from?"

"America" I said wondering if I would ever get over loving accents.

A handsome man in the same coat, hat, and uniform—but not the skirt—entered and searched my room while I hummed, "The Spy Who Loved Me." Imagination gone wild. They both took my passport and left. I sat wondering what my mission was.

I decided to stay on the train this time and watch as my car was jacked up in the air and the wheels were changed. Unbelievable all of these wheel changes to match each country's different gauge rail tracks. We crossed the border into Russia, and Russian passport control questioned me.

"Your passport." (darlink?)

After six hours of wheels and passports, we left Mongolia. The purple mohair scarf was definitely getting longer.

I was excited to travel through the land that my family came from. A land that was off limits for so long, enemy number 1, but now I was here. As night fell in Dr Zhivago land, forests of silver birches and tiny villages rushed by. Homes made of squared-off logs with steep gable roofs to shed the snow flew by as well. Some had cheery pastel paint.

I awoke and thought I was dreaming. Out the window was a beautiful snow-covered lake that looked like the ocean. It was completely frozen. Snow-covered trees and a lake frozen in waves. Where was I? The train was so cold in the morning that I didn't want to get out of bed. Were we out of coal? I pulled out the map of the train journey. Finally, I was looking at Lake Baikal, the deepest fresh water lake in the world at over a mile and the world's oldest lake at 30 million years. It contains 20% of the world's freshwater. I took a bath in my room looking out at Lake Baikal wondering how cold it was outside to make this lake freeze into a solid chunk.

My stomach craved something fresh and I needed a shower. My body was wound up, ready to move with only two 30-minute breaks each day. I wished that I could find just one breath of fresh air. Our car always smelled like Chinese noodles. Whenever the train stopped, I would burst through the doors. I jogged around while my Chinese friends smoked cigarettes smiling at me. At the stops, babushka women sold fruit, water, crawdads, fish, bread, and schnitzel, but I only had those damn $1 US bills and they wouldn't take them. I did manage some bananas and a loaf of bread.

The train pulled us through Russia as the sun set like a fire through the skinny trees. Chinese music played in the corridor of my car, and Chinese conversation blended into the rhythm of the train as I knit the Purple Trans-Siberian Scarf. The rhythm of the train matching with my joy had me thinking about love, Harley, more tears, and a dream.

My dad was born in Russia. I spent his last days in the hospital with him being close, helping. The rhythm and constant repetition of the train worked as a therapy session of meditation bringing up emotions, helping me feel everything. The sounds of the train matched my heartbeat while the rhythm of my thoughts matched the sound of metal on metal, clicking and clanking. The power from the engine pulling us along. Homeland, Pops, I'm in your birth country. I wish I knew where your family was now but I'll come back someday. I was feeling love for my dad and remembering sorrow when he died as the train rocked me gently. Days on a train with my heart and head my sole companions. Remembering received and accepted love. Eyes of elephants, kangaroos in my arms, young volunteers, lion cubs, and a man. On the Trans Siberian Express as my mind flitted about. I wanted to slow it down, slow it down to focus.

My MIND AND HEART needed to get to know each other and work together. Heart the dreamer, the feeler. Mind made the plans, brought ideas to earth. Time, how did time figure in? It interrupts flow. Gotta be, gotta go. Be back. Maybe tomorrow. Time the reason why mind wins over heart. Time drives results to give a sense of accomplishment yet little heart satisfaction. People live in so many ways. Interpreting time. Listening to heart or just surviving?

Seeking is different from doing. What are you doing? What are you seeking? Where does your joy come from? Heart, Mind, Time, now Money.

Money hops on and insists on driving the car with three passengers aboard: Heart, Mind, and Time. With different destinations and no conversation, Money keeps driving. Respect, fame, appreciation, wisdom. What does it all mean?

The definition of success, please, from the three passengers and the driver, too. Let's talk and get things out in the open.

Money has it easiest and begins the discussion. Success is getting more money, more than the other guy, more than I need, more and then more and then more. Me, I am Money, what everyone needs and I become, in that process, what most live their life seeking, more of, more Money. Yet around the world, not everyone holds money as the most important measure of a life well spent.

All right, Time, it's your turn. What is success for you? So, Time says, getting things done in the agreed-upon time, respecting time, allowing the clock to be in control of the project. That's #1 as to how your life is run. Time is money. I am King. Success is getting things done in the allotted time. How many things can you get done in a day? Race with time. Pencils down; your time is up. You see, I control everything you do. You are always thinking of me. I would like to do that but I don't have time. Oh, I can't do that today, not enough time. Me, I am Time, I control all actions. I should be driving so we get there on time.

Mind, it's your turn. Ah, more complicated here. I have the vast ability to create, to think, to imagine, to communicate, and to get things done. I keep things rational, grounded, real. I both create the idea and put the idea into reality. Without me driving, there is no map, no streets, and no car. I can control Heart, Time, and Money. I am the absolute ruler. Success can only come from a strong mind in charge. Success is getting things done, creating wealth, using my full abilities, rising to the challenge, overcoming difficulties, solving problems, gaining respect from others. I am the natural leader of all. Mind over matter. What's on your mind today? My thinking is my reality. Whatever I think is how I feel. I can solve all of your problems through thought. Success then is a well-thought-out plan, executed to attain a goal. I can get you to your goals. I am the natural driver.

Heart, Heart, are you there? Heart is gentle, swinging back and forth on a swing with the sun on her face and the breeze in her hair feeling the moment. The pure joy of the moment. I am too gentle to drive until all of you have taken a turn. You must all take control, you must all drive, you must all feel the emptiness. I am the moment. I am the smell of warm cookies filling the air. I am the sun's sweet colors painted on a sky. The stirring you feel looking into the eyes of someone or something you love. I am contentment. I am sorrow. I am breathing in the forest after the rain. A baby giggles. I am what you feel when you give. You feel me, you notice me, but you will allow me to speak only when the emptiness gets too strong and the pain is all you feel. Heart driving? Ah, still your Mind. Put away your clock. Allow worries of money to take a rest. Gently now. Listen. Heart will not be heard rushing in traffic, cell phones ringing. Heart will not speak. Make a space for me. You who never leave 10 minutes unscheduled. If you truly want to hear Heart, put everything down. Listen. Give up control. Listen. But Fear steps in. Fear of change. Fear of stepping off the tracks and making a mistake.

Heart is gentle. Bring the world to people with my loving eyes. Bring the love of earth out. Bring the love of earth, animals, trees, and people. Give a voice to my love of earth, animals, and people. Earth wants to be noticed. She speaks to me at sunrise and again at dusk. Honor me. Protect me. It is in your heart.

Heart as driver means love is first. Feelings are full and rich and take priority. Heart as driver means dreams of life direct the path. A pause. Then a dream. Heart says it is happy to make dreams of highest purpose for all. Heart recognizes who you are. Let me dream, give me the freedom to dream, and I will give you a piece of yourself or a peace for yourself. The wondering, the nagging questions, allow me to speak. First, you must be quiet and listen. Success? When your soul is alive and you are full of life, purpose and questions, you are in a state of love. This is success. When you hear my dreams, give it to mind to orchestrate. Always let my music play in your soul. Always.

Heart takes the wheel now. Mind sits in the front. Time and Money are in the back having difficulty adjusting to all this change. Are you sure Heart can drive? Heart is gushy, full of feelings, Heart in control? Yes, yes, yes, says Mind. Each of us has had a turn but all we do is get stuff done. We do not know how to make the soul sing. We must let heart drive for the joy, the pure joy. For the song of the earth is understood by Heart. Animals talking are understood by Heart. Nature? Only Heart knows her music. A gentleness and peace will come. The beauty of Heart helping us all. And with that Heart begins to sing and the dreams she longs to create are set free. Mind sees the road ahead clearly. Time and Money finally understand. The soul feeling the changes sighs and welcomes the day and all of its beauty.

As the wheels methodically sent me into a trance of clickety clack, clickety clack, the train gave me time to think. What a great idea traveling the world turned out to be! My lightness shined brighter, reinforced as I traveled. Always being heart-warmed, shown kindness, without language. I felt more understood without language than with it. Heart always showed through as I traveled.

HUNGER DROVE ME to the dining car where the beer was cold. The music in the dining car was what, Russian rock? I ordered borscht and beef stroganoff. The borscht was almost as good as mine with intense flavors though no beets, just potatoes, fresh dill, sour cream, onion, and lots of fat in the beet broth. The food on the Russian train was good!

The couple from Sweden was great fun to talk to teasing me about all of the nice things they had in first class as we chugged along together to Moscow. "We love to travel together." the husband said smiling at his wife. "We just sold our houseboat for a big profit so that we can buy a boat to sail around the world. I was a commercial diver but my hearing is fading and so I have retired."

I was jealous of their relationship. We ate and talked some more.

On the way back to my car, I noticed a handsome, tall Chinese conductor who was definitely flirting with me but just with his eyes. He watched me walk. Subtle flirting each time I walked by. Each country with its different style of communication between the sexes.

And it wasn't just flirting that was different here. The Chinese men in my car thought that a toilet seat was as weird as a hole in the ground was to me. They had no idea how to use it. How did I know this?

Shoeprints were all over the seat! For showering, they must have been throwing water from a bucket because there was always water all over the floor. Well, if you can't beat 'em, join 'em. I hopped on the toilet seat, too perched like a bird laughing at myself. Ah, the differences.

I stood in the corridor looking out the window with some of my train mates. Chinese music played in our car as always. Suddenly I heard a beautiful voice, high, crystal clear, and full of emotion singing along. I turned and saw one of my buddies looking out the window singing. I watched him and listened, fascinated by the differences. A man singing. The music continued and more men along the corridor of our car joined in the song. I was serenaded now on my left and on my right with a beautiful Chinese song. A spontaneous chorus. I was in love. In love with a culture that lets men sing when they look out a window and will let us be friends even without a language. There is more that people have in common than they have in differences and somehow that needs to be remembered. Laughter, joy sadness, all the emotions need no language at all. Feeling the happiness, I started to sing along at the chorus mimicking their Chinese words. Smiles. Our car was full of smiles while we all sang together.

Whenever we stopped, we all piled out so happy to touch the earth and breathe the fresh air. The train only stopped at major cities—Kirov, Perm, and Yekaterinburg—long enough for us to stretch our legs. Not having exercise or fresh air most of the day was like being in jail for me. Usually I jogged outside the train as soon as I hit the pavement. Occasionally I could get one of my Chinese buddies to put down their cigarette to jog with me. The babushkas selling food at each stop were bundled up in big coats and big fur hats to fight the cold but they always had solemn faces and never any smiles.

"May I take your photo?"

"отсутствие фотоего" The look reprimanded me and I heard "nyet" that I remembered from my dad…No!

They sold delicious treats and I was desperate to sample them but I had been given the wrong information. US dollars were worthless in Russia. No one wanted them. I went from vendor to vendor begging them to take my money. Just one orange, one loaf of bread. My hands together for a bit of drama asking for food but getting a refusal each time. Finally able to buy a loaf of bread, I jumped around because of my success. But little did I know that my Chinese buddies were watching me at each stop interpreting my begging as actual hunger. They had decided that I was broke because I only had $1 bills and hungry because I was pleading for food. Because they always ate noodles from home in their rooms, they had no idea that I was eating large in the dining car.

When I returned to my room, one man came in through my open door leaving a box of noodles on my table.

"Ah, thank you." I said wondering what was up. Then another came in with dried meats, another one with drinks, and another with fruit. Soon everyone on my car had donated food to me! They even offered me money. Their sweetness was overwhelming. I thanked them for all the food.

I was really stunned. My table piled high with their generosity and caring. They had watched me at each stop trying to buy food and thought that I was starving. I was sorry that I could not explain that my begging was just me being expressive, dramatic, silly. How could I describe the feeling of being cared for by my train mates, people I did not know and could not understand?

I was thinking about life and what choices to make now. I was thinking about freedom. The obvious lack of freedom in China versus the subtle lack of freedom created by staying in the same environment doing the same thing because, because... Why? Why? A self-created prison built by expectations and unclear dreams would still hold me if I didn't change.

Generally, I was a success in life because I followed the path that everyone decided was successful. But when I died and looked at the movie of my life, I would not for the life of me be able to figure out how I came to make my life so small, so restricted, and so lifeless. Staying the same was not an option. Change was imperative.

But the ability of humans to be sheep, to follow, was stronger than their ability to follow their own music. What to do with my life now when I wanted something different? I wanted freedom for my soul, to be living in the moment, to be absolutely in touch with who I am.

Everywhere I had traveled, I had been caressed and warmed by loving people and loving animals. I knew the language of the earth, the one that had no words. The Soul of the World had touched me with her love and joy. I had spent my time laughing and enjoying people with no common language, only smiles. The universal language of joy and acceptance.

Out my window, I saw the dunes changed by the wind but the desert stayed the same. I wanted change.

I LOOKED OUT MY window and saw a bright red engine pulling with incredible power. Nothing can describe lying in my bed with the gentle rocking of this iron train. Sound repeats sound, rhythm patterns moving hard, iron hard molded by fire, wheels gliding on tracks, pistons pumping. I lay here, a slave to the train as it rocked me, swayed me, and moved me. I lay here under warm blankets, the sounds of wheels I loved to hear.

I saw a teardrop on my pillow as I rode the magnificent train. I realized that I was afraid of love. I had been giving love around the world, loving people, loving animals, loving the earth, and in return I had been loved. My love accepted, understood, returned, and I was safe. And in that love, I had grown and been nourished and seen myself as I am. Now I wanted this love to continue to grow, to trust love again.

The trip around the world had been a chance for me to fall in love, to give my heart, and to be loved by the earth. I didn't think I had quite understood my heart's problem until now—all that love bottled inside needed some place to express itself.

Flying by my window were quaint towns with window shutters painted royal blue on brown wooden houses. And poverty was everywhere. We crossed another river and the town was flooded. Every house stood surrounded by water with just a few chimneys with smoke. The economy drowning.

But the train was getting closer to Moscow, and my Chinese friends and I were really excited. All packed, we stared out the window together in anticipation. As we pulled into the train station, we all had the same thought. "I am in Moscow!"

It had been a grand adventure with enough time left to my own thoughts to feel like I had been wise to take this journey across two continents and seven time zones. Leaving the train I found my driver. Tomorrow I would tour Moscow and then on to see Leonard!

CHAPTER 18

Trainman in Scotland

AFTER A TOUR OF a more cheerful Moscow than I had ever imagined and a pledge to return someday, I boarded the train to Brussels. First I noticed that I was the only passenger in my car and second that there was no dining car! Thank goodness my Chinese friends had given me so many noodles.

The train sped along through the countryside but I was ready to get off. Without my charming Chinese train mates, I felt lonely and this was definitely not the Trans-Siberian Express. I watched the countryside turn green through Belarus and then rolling into Poland, where a SWAT team in black uniforms with white letters searched every empty compartment. It looked like a drug bust and they seemed like a rough bunch.

Poland flowed into Germany with lovely villages on green rolling hills, horses in fields, brick and stone buildings, all postcard-perfect! Finally we were in Belgium with more rolling green hills. It had been a fast ride, an uneventful ride, ending in Brussels where I ate a delicious Belgium waffle and some Belgium chocolate and then retreated to my bed and breakfast for a luxurious, long hot bubble bath, my first in five months! I spent the evening submerged amidst bubbles thinking about Leonard, whom I would spend 3 days with in Scotland. I had met him back in September on the train to London when I left the Monkey Sanctuary and we had been emailing ever since.

I had some Cinderella fantasies that still played whenever I met an intriguing man. Soaking in my bubble bath, I imagined my future life in England with Professor Leonard creating poetry while we listened to Beethoven in a room lined with books, two large leather chairs facing a fireplace, rain hitting the windows of our room.

We had both been surprised by our attraction to each other. Leonard had a history of young, thin women and I liked brawny men, smart and athletic with silliness. But after seven months of continual emails, I was ready to test the waters. Meeting him for the weekend in Scotland would definitely be an adventure in romance. Was there the possibility of love here? Nervous about seeing him, I remembered that he was very clever, deliciously handsome, extremely nervous, and uncertain.

Leaving Brussels the following morning, I flew to Scotland and looked around for Len, who I remembered as tall, handsome like Liam Neeson with blue eyes.

"Hello. Welcome to Scotland," he said nervously, looking down at me with a shy smile.

"Hello," I said feeling nervous, too. I hugged him for comfort.

"We'll take the train to my mother's house in Troon," he said. "She is looking forward to meeting you. I told her that you are an animal psychiatrist!" He laughed. "She's anxious to see your photos and she wants you to help her with her neurotic cat. Can you do that?"

"You're too funny. An animal psychiatrist? Sure I'll put the cat on the couch and sort out his problems." I jabbered away wondering when we would both calm down!

When we arrived at his mom's house, she was sitting in a chair in her living room. She had white hair and a warm smile, and I felt instantly comfortable around her.

"I have been looking forward to meeting the woman who caught Leonard's eye on the train. I can see why he was attracted to you! He calls you 'Traingirl.' I want to hear all about your travels."

"It was very romantic when we met," I said to her. "Your son, 'Trainman,' is very charismatic. I'm looking forward to telling you about my trip."

But we only stayed with his mother for a short time as Len was anxious to leave.

"Let's go for a walk, okay?" Len said obviously still uncomfortable with my visit.

Heading to a local pub, I saw that Len was much more nervous than I remembered him. He was having a difficult time adjusting to my presence. We were after all strangers having only spent four hours together eight months earlier with only emails since then. Our rhythm together was definitely not established. I was still chugging along on a train contemplating my entire life and not yet fully present with Leonard. But I felt it important to communicate.

"It is going to take us a little time to adjust to our own spontaneity at wanting to see each other, isn't it? I know that I wanted to see you again but I'm a bit uncomfortable right now. I loved your emails, Leonard. Your words are delicious. They are like music to me."

Leonard looked at me without saying anything and in that split second I thought about connections that people have when there is some place within both that magically connects. I felt peaceful in that moment. Emotional intensity, our common ground. I could absolutely feel Leonard's energy...like it was tangible. No small talk for us. I felt Leonard in my solar plexus but I was anxious to get him to relax. I wanted all of those beautiful words to come pouring out as they did when he was calm. I was a connoisseur of words and listening to Leonard was like attending the symphony. But that moment of noticing our connection passed in the blink of an eye as the waitress came to take our order interrupting my thoughts.

After a beer or two, we walked back for dinner. Getting to know each other at his mother's house was quite a humorous undertaking. Len and his mom were quite close, and he cared for her deeply and worried about her health. She wanted the best for him and she encouraged me to choose him for my number-one boyfriend! It was very sweet to see their interaction including their frustrations with each other.

When night came in her two-bedroom home, Len asked me, "Would you mind if I slept in the room with you? If you are uncomfortable, I can sleep out on the couch?"

Ah, decisions, decisions. The white room was pretty typical with two twin beds pushed together a flowered bedspread on each one, a dresser and a desk. How funny to spend our first night together at his mother's house. I was chuckling to myself about this situation. I didn't feel that it would be a wild crazy night of passion but I wanted us to connect. I wanted to know more about the place inside of me that felt at home with Leonard. What exactly was my connection with a poet's soul?

"Leonard, will you tell me a story or read me poems? I would love to have you read to me."

"Yes, I will." he said, looking into my eyes again, searching for some answers. No doubt he was probably wondering how this woman had come into his life. An American woman was in his mother's house sleeping in the extra bedroom after a brief encounter on a train to London. No wonder he was searching my eyes.

But I was thinking of something different as I decided to snuggle with Len. On my list of things I love were babies' giggles, the smell of rain in the forest, music and hot bubble baths, and something else really high on my list: talking in bed, telling secrets, sharing thoughts in the dark of night. So there I was, lapping it up, enjoying the moment and connecting to a new part of myself. His voice, his words, the gentleness of this man and his willingness to be vulnerable felt like eating an ice cream sundae with thick hot chocolate sauce sliding down as it melted the ice cream.

Feeling like I was having a sleepover with my new best friend, I smiled mischievously as Len got into his bed. I hungered for a long, hot night of words with a sensitive, intelligent man and I wasn't disappointed. We talked late into the night as we both relaxed. I was entranced with his ability to transport me and I wondered how I could keep him talking. His words soothed me, tickling my brain.

"Leonard, can you read me a poem? I know little of poetry and I want to hear you read."

He left the bed to find a book of poetry and returned to read to me. Cuddling near the poet as he read was a brand new experience. Ah, life is good. I soaked in every word and like a contented little girl being read a story, I listened until I fell asleep.

When morning came, Leonard was already up. He was not one to stay in one place too long. He opened the door and smiled at me.

"Good morning, Joyce. How did you sleep? Can I bring you a cup of coffee?" he said gently.

"I would love a cup of coffee and I'd feel like a princess drinking it in bed." Such a simple thing but I had no memory of the last time a man did that for me so cheerfully. By our second cup, we were talking easily.

"Would you like to go to Ayr for the day? It's a bigger town along the train line and I have a friend that I would like to meet up with for a beer."

"Sure. I'd love to see the countryside and walk along with you. Talking to you tickles me in a new way."

With that, we said goodbye to his mother and left on the train. But right from the start, there was an incompatibility: Our eating patterns were exactly the opposite. We arrived at Ayr and as in China I was starving. My metabolism had somehow switched to fast and furious on this trip and hunger attacked often.

"Len, I'm starving." I said, feeling like I'd fall over if I didn't eat immediately.

Len's stare was one of total amazement. "But you just ate breakfast. How can you be hungry again?"

"Well, in my stomach apparently they are now ready to celebrate lunch. It's a very busy stomach and gets cranky if it doesn't get fed often. Aren't you hungry?"

"No, I only eat once a day in the evening."

"Okay, well, get ready to watch a woman eat often then. It's three times a day for me with snacks. Just pretend you are walking with a wild beast that needs to be fed or she'll roar in protest."

After lunch, we walked through the village, which was filled with people. I was paying more attention to Leonard than my surroundings and he seemed unsettled. I wondered what was wrong. It was almost like he had lost his bearings in the unfamiliar town with all of the tourist energy rattling his calm. His temperament changed.

"Are you okay, Leonard? You seem unsettled."

And indeed he was. I guess it was like a giant case of what I get when I enter Costco: over-stimulation from too many sources. I always feel assaulted in that store and looking at Leonard, I could tell that something like that was going on for him. He seemed to be having trouble processing.

"Hey, let's go grab a beer and find your friend." I said, hoping a familiar face would be comforting.

We found his friend and the two men covered a lot of ground over beers. For a bit I watched the intellectuals banter, and then bored, I went out to shop around town and get a snack. Browsing around thinking more about Len than actually looking at the town, I knew that he was working with delicate emotions. He was straightforward about his inner workings, which I really appreciated.

Like a plane correcting its course, my dating went one way and then the opposite direction to correct its course. I had sworn off macho men who could not express themselves and now I was with a man who expressed himself beautifully, the full gamut of emotions. Was there a middle course perhaps?

As we left town to head back to his mother's, he lost his cool with a tourist and I was at a loss what to do. Even Leonard seemed at a loss. A gentle man with ghosts haunting him. Magical Len with the beautiful words was fighting ghosts.

"I don't understand all that you are going through, Len," I said, as we rode the train back.

"I do not understand it either. I apologize. I just am not myself lately. The days of lecturing and being on top of the world seem a long way away."

But there was still a connection. There was something in his emotions, his honesty that I liked. When Len was comfortable and having fun with words, he was brilliant, stimulating, and a great listener. I told him things that I was feeling that were deeply hidden secrets and he completely understood and comforted me. The depth of my emotions didn't frighten him at all.

"Let's get takeout tonight and bring it home for dinner with my mom."

But I had to chuckle during dinner as I watched the dynamic between him and his mom. She was losing patience with him in that mom way and Len was reacting by losing patience with her. I was happy to be there with them both.

"How about if I show you both photographs of lions, elephants, kangaroos, baboons, and monkeys until you scream 'Stop'?" I suggested, thinking that a change was in order.

I sat on the couch between the two of them, the animal psychiatrist discussing her wildlife. I hadn't shown my photos to anyone and their ooohs and ahs continued for a good long time. Even I was amazed at all that I had done. After we looked at my photos, his mom showed me her wedding photos and baby photos of her son. I had a chance to ooh and ah over sweet baby Len. It was absolutely a classic evening for all of us, with his mom letting me know how much she'd like it if we were together, the wildlife psychiatrist and the poet.

Off to bed and another good cuddle. He read me a poem and then told me an amazing story full of beautiful images and his lovely imagination. There was a part of me that was totally enamored of this man, his voice and his words. I could imagine evenings of being together listening to music and poetry but then there was also the outside world that I love. Len seemed to like staying inside with his poems now rather than traveling to foreign places. I fell asleep listening to his stories.

Morning came with an offer of fresh coffee from Leonard, who was also still in bed. "It is 10 am and I can't remember when I have slept till 10," he said. "Would you like toast?"

"Yes. Wonderful!" I said, smiling at this man who wanted to take care of me in the morning.

"Would you like a rasher of bacon?"

"Sure, thank you."

He brought food back into the bedroom and we both ate our fill. We had a chat with his mom and then we were off for a long walk through Troon.

"I want to show you my childhood house and fill your ears with tales of my youth," he told me.

After walking and talking our way through most of the day, we decided to head home to cook dinner for his mom. But his mom got testy with him again and they did their dinnertime love bickering. What a funny way to get to know a man!

Our last night together was filled with more poetry, stories, and cuddles. Being with someone who was very emotional was new for me. I was usually the one in the relationship who was getting led around by emotions, but Len was way more sensitive than I was. As I saw it, our friendship was good for both of us. My understanding of love was more encompassing now.

On the train to the airport I told him how I felt. "Leonard, thank you for bringing me into your life here in Troon. You and your mom are sweet to watch together. I appreciate the love between you and the bickering as well. All of our time together has been real, nothing hidden and I feel like I know the real you. Your vulnerability and willingness to be honest with me are not typical when getting to know a man. You allowed me to feel safe, to be open about my feelings. I hope that you feel the same way about me – that you know who I am in my soul. Listening to your poetry and your stories was magical for me. I really want to see you again and please, please take good care of yourself. "

"Yes, we can see each other again. I don't know about me going to Ireland but maybe we can meet here again. I'm going to miss you, Joyce. Your compassion and kindness have helped me."

We hugged and kissed each other at the airport with promises for more visits. It was time for me to head to Ireland to start volunteering as a newspaper reporter for the last two months of my journey.

CHAPTER 19

The Imokilly People in Ireland

As I flew to Cork, I had a vision of myself at a restaurant.

She sat down at the table and looked at the menu. "I would like to order," she said, as the waiter approached her.

"What will you have, Madam?"

"I would like to order a new life. What is good here?"

"Well, most of our customers come in and order the same thing they always have."

"But I would like to try something new."

"Well, we will give you whatever you want but you do have to figure that out."

"Oh, dear, that is so much pressure and so much freedom all at the same time. All right, I want to be loved. I want to feel good, purposeful about what I am doing with my life like being in China, like holding lions on my lap, like making friends with other volunteers. The closeness, I want the closeness. I like living together in a group, eating together. And then of course, a man who I can count on, to trust."

"Might I suggest you start with the one most important thing and order that? The cooks get confused when you order too much."

Around the world in 304 days through 17 countries and thousands of miles, my grand finale landed me in Ireland. Here I would volunteer as a reporter at a weekly newspaper in Midleton, County Cork! I had zero experience as a writer. I had only written real estate ads over the last 16 years, which hardly qualified me to become a reporter. But when I had searched for projects, I had only found this one and though I was fueled by a long time desire to see Ireland, I lacked the confidence to even apply. Me a reporter? Hardly!

Enter Susan, the astrologer. I had never gone to an astrologer before but as the reality of my trip settled in, uncertainty over my decision increased and I decided to check in with the stars. Timidly I met Susan, who had been recommended by a friend. I was wary of the entire chart-reading process. What was I doing here? But as we talked, I relaxed and started enjoying myself. According to what she saw, it seemed that the trip was all over my chart!

And she repeated what she saw. "This trip is excellent now, Joyce! But there is writing in your chart. Are you planning a book?"

"No, I wasn't thinking of that but there is a volunteer project as a reporter in Ireland that I thought about but I have no experience."

"Oh, that doesn't matter. It's very clear here," she said, pointing to my chart (maybe somewhere between Mars and Jupiter, my moon sign was lining up with my birth sign?). "Sign up to be a reporter! And yes, this trip is an excellent idea but I really think there is a book somewhere. Think about that, okay?"

Off I went to write an application to be a newspaper reporter, an application that included several "sample articles" for the editor to read. Amazingly, Mr. O'Brien, the editor of *The Imokilly People,* accepted me as a volunteer reporter for two months. My final project was a perfect way to end my kaleidoscope year of amazing experiences with even a bit of reentry into the Western culture thrown in because I would be working in an office with computers and living in a house with no wild animals in the backyard.

When I arrived in Cork, my volunteer coordinator picked me up for the short ride to Midleton, a quiet, quaint small town.

"Midleton dates back to the 12th century and is the home of Irish whisky," she told me. "It boasts the largest still in the world! We'll drive to your house to meet Margaret and Noel and their little boy. They are a very nice family. I'm sure you'll enjoy living there. Tomorrow you can go to the newspaper office and meet Patrick, your editor. He'll give you your assignments for the next two months. If you need anything, call me."

We drove into town through streets lined with old grey stone houses built side by side. The grey was cheered up by their brightly painted doors, each one a different color. Leaving the older section of town, we entered a development and stopped at a new house that could have been anywhere in Surburbia, USA. The similarity confused me for a moment. Was I in Ireland or Seattle? The resemblance was eerie.

Inside I met my home-stay family. Noel, the dad, a tall, strong man in his 40s with a welcoming smile, was a prison officer and charming to talk to with a twinkle in his eyes. Margaret, the mother, a short woman with dark hair, fair skin, and a no-nonsense manner, was all business. Mathew, their 5-year-old son, shyly said hello with equal parts curiosity and trepidation. Garfield, the cat, and the two dogs helped me ease back into Western culture. Whitney, a smart, young woman in her 20s from Oregon, had already been living in the house for a few weeks volunteering at the paper. I felt very much at home almost immediately.

But the adjustment wasn't going to be easy. TVism slapped me in the face instantly. After a year of only minimal watching, I wasn't ready for the constant barrage. They had one TV in the kitchen on during all meals (why did we need that constant noise!), another one in the family room, one in the living room, and one in Noel and Margaret's bedroom. Why were we spending our lives watching someone else's make-believe life on TV? Always jabbering away interrupting everyone, the TV seemed to be a member of the family talking in every room except my bedroom.

My bedroom was pure luxury with a comfy bed, pillow, and blanket, a dresser and closet! It looked out onto a swing set in the back yard and the neighbors' houses. Wow, neighbors! I felt like a foreigner adjusting to Western ways. I shared a big bathroom with Noel, Margaret and Mathew; Whitney's room was next door with her own private bath. Everything felt familiar and yet shockingly strange. I couldn't quite grasp all of the luxury around me.

Whitney and I each cooked our own separate meals but because we all ate dinner together, we had lots of time to talk and get to know each other. Noel loved telling us stories to make us laugh and was always sweet to Mathew. Margaret scoffed lovingly at Noel's stories and reprimanded Mathew constantly yelling his name loudly: "Mathew!" She had a much more serious view of life. But with Noel's lightness and Mathew's sweetness, our dinners were really enjoyable.

Each morning Whitney and I talked our way to work walking a mile to our office through our neighborhood, past the old church and the quaint part of town until we reached the six or seven blocks of the downtown area where the newspaper office was located. Downtown Midleton had lots of little shops, bakeries, and pubs, and I laughed when I found out that the luscious smell that filled my nostrils every morning wasn't the yummy Irish bread baking that I was visualizing but rather whiskey brewing at our local distillery.

Arriving at the newspaper office, I was sent upstairs to work at the internet café. Apparently my editor, whom I had not yet met, had nothing for Lois Lane to do and I was chomping at the bit. Though I knew nothing about reporting, I was like a race horse kicking at the gate. I read every back issue of the newspaper, which had a big section devoted to color photographs of local students and general news from around the area. I spoke to the other volunteers about my lack of work. They told me to be patient. Right!

I emailed my volunteer contact. "I have been here three days. I am ready to report, even obituaries will be great. Can you help me?"

Finally, Patrick, my editor called me to give me my first assignment.

"Joyce, go to Cork and cover the annual convention of the Green Party."

"Sure thing. Thank you," I said confidently, glad that he couldn't see the puzzled, nervous look on my face. Now what? I took the bus to Cork and scouted out my surroundings. No doubt about it, I knew nothing about reporting and I was a nervous wreck. Truth be told, I wasn't even a good notetaker in college. But I listened intently to the speakers taking careful notes wishing that I had a tape recorder for better accuracy. I focused on their speeches keeping myself from drifting off into a daydream that lately seemed very easy to do.

But when the speakers were finished, I was too shy to approach the candidates individually figuring they would detect that I was only masquerading as a reporter.

"Hey, you're not a reporter. What do you think you're doing here?" they'd say, showing me to the door.

I practiced my introduction, "Hello, my name is Lois Lane. I am here with *The Imokilly People* in Midleton." Finally, I mustered up my courage to interview a candidate, approached him and then afraid of screwing up and embarrassing myself, I did a sharp 180-degree turn and walked away. I was failing the challenge.

I decided to warm up by talking to some of the people attending the convention to get their views on the issues, but I was still too afraid to tell them that I was a reporter. Shyness and uncertainty are not good qualities in a reporter. I gave myself pep talks but I was failing miserably. I had notes for this story but no quotes. But I could not get myself to approach anyone. Fear of failure had me in her talons and wasn't letting go. With no interviews, I left the hotel for the bus, my tail between my legs, chastising myself for my miserable performance. What kind of reporter was I going to be? Completely worthless?

Returning home, I researched the current issues facing the Green Party to get more depth. I took hours and hours to write the story and one thing was clear. I loved the process. It challenged me in an exciting new way. Every part of my intellect was involved here. How to write with facts and yet because this was a "friendly" weekly paper, the article also needed to be interesting and easy to read. Thinking, analyzing, researching, and playing with words, I was having fun! When the story was completed, I nervously turned it in with my fingers crossed. I expected a well-deserved reprimand from my editor for the lack of interviews.

But when the paper was published, my story was in print and I reread it several times feeling both proud and critical. Lois Lane had her first article published. My name was in print! I mailed a copy to my mom, my biggest fan. Even though this was a wee little paper in a small town with more advertising and photographs than hard news, I still loved seeing my writing in print. I was proud of myself for applying here, proud of myself for writing an article when I knew nothing about journalism, and proud of myself for jumping into something completely foreign. But I had a long chat with myself about my lack of confidence. There could be no more shy reporter behavior. I might make mistakes but I was not going to whimper in the corner without confidence. Lois Lane was bold!

Patrick next sent me to Dungarvan, a coastal town, to report on the launch of a retirement home, very soft news. The opening of the launch began with a short concert from the visiting Polish symphony followed by lovely hors d'oeuvres and wine. Always hungry, I sampled everything pretending I was a food critic. Given 16 years of meeting strangers in real estate and getting to know them, it was uncharacteristic for me to be this awkward and reserved. I was still afraid of making a mistake. I scouted whom to talk to but I stayed on the outskirts. A dark-haired man in his 30s with a camera around his neck introduced himself to me.

"Hi, I'm Ian, the paper's photographer. Let's get some photos of you interviewing people if you can put down your plate of food, that is." He smiled at me in that teasing manner that I would encounter often in Ireland.

"Okay, but I am a failure so far, too shy to talk to anyone and I don't know who to interview," I confessed, rolling my eyes.

Ian took pity on me and coached me on how to conduct an interview, encouraging me to ask questions. "These people are advertisers. You'll want to be complimentary."

Everyone was very pleased when I introduced myself as a reporter covering this story. But where was the story? Finally I stumbled onto the man who actually owned the building and we had a bit of a chat. My ear was not yet tuned to Irish accents though and I missed some of what he said. However, I asked questions and the conversation had good flow.

Someone offered me a glass of champagne and then another and suddenly my reporting skills improved tremendously. I relaxed and met all kinds of people who were anxious to talk to a reporter. What a grand way to get to know a culture!

Returning home, I went to work writing the article. This launch was not breaking news but obviously I got it right because when the story "broke," the retirement home owner liked it so much that they called Patrick to thank him! Patrick in turn called me to praise his newest cub reporter. I smiled.

Culturally, I had a lot to learn here in Ireland and my interviews brought me into a wide range of activities. But there was more to learn. One day having left my reading glasses at home, I got a lift from Shane, who worked at the paper. When I got back to the Internet cafe, Whitney asked me if I had had to walk home.

I said, "No, Shane gave me a ride."

When she asked, "Did you have to walk back?"

"No, Shane gave me a ride again. Shane is the man!"

Strangely the entire café burst out laughing. I looked puzzled. I didn't have a clue what was funny.

Whitney, who was obviously enjoying the joke, explained, "In Ireland, 'a ride' means having sex. Think about what you just said!"

LIFE AT THE HOUSE was steady, like living in a suburban household with a typical family. Margaret and Noel watched TV each evening while Mathew played with his toys. Margaret cooked different versions of meat and potatoes and watched me cook fish.

"Joyce, are you going to cook fish and vegetables every night? Is that how you stay in shape? Garfield is getting used to having a taste of fish every day, and I will have to cook him some when you leave, I suppose!" she said to me one night.

Garfield, the cat, who loved my cooking, was my new best friend and he started hanging out in my room in the evenings. Home was relaxing and uneventful except for the hourly screams from Margaret: "Mathew!"

Though work was on the rise, my social life was below negative. I had always found Irish men attractive, ever since my first love, Ed, in high school. Probably on some level I was hoping to go to the land where they grew Irish men for some romance. However, that plan wasn't close to happening because divorce had only recently become legal in Ireland and only 4% of the population was divorced. Though the men in pubs were happy to chat me up, they were definitely just full of the blarney. As for dating and flirting, my pickings were slim to none, but that made it easy to focus on being a reporter and giving total concentration to developing my new skills.

Len and I continued to email each other after my visit but I think we both knew we were friends for life, not lovers, though I always smiled whenever I thought about him. In my spare time, I occasionally googled Robert but still I could only find his athletic records and nothing personal. We had completely lost touch but I still held a thin thread of hope that we would talk again.

Back at the paper, my next assignment tested me in a novel way. From the Green Party to a retirement home, I was now to interview a famous hunk of a soap opera star from *Coronation Street*!

I prepared a list of questions to ask him but I got so flustered when I saw him, I was speechless. The man was gorgeous, buff with great muscular arms and a sexy smile. Women were standing in line to get his autograph and I was supposed to walk up to him for an interview? My goodness, Elsa Mae, I needed way more makeup to properly bat my eyes at this handsome man...phew! Ian, my photographer, fanned me to cool me off, laughing at my reaction to the hunk. Working hard to conceal the low growl that was coming from somewhere deep inside, I approached him. (Grrrrrowl...Hey, baby, how ya doing? Wanna go somewhere quiet for this interview, grr...)

But no, I held it together and because he was both open and humble, the interview went smooth as honey.

Looking into his dreamy, steamy eyes, I asked him, "How long will you stay with the show?" And he gave me hot scoop!

"This will be my last season."

"Why would you leave something successful?" I asked.

He told me, "One of my children has special needs. I feel it's more important to spend time with my family now. I've also started a charity for other special needs children."

We discussed how he'd spend his time off from the show. His vulnerability and heartfulness kept our conversation comfortable and interesting. I was having a grand time learning about his life and his passions. He gave me a hug when the interview was finished, undoubtedly making me the envy of the still long line of women waiting for an autograph.

After I had completed three articles, the newspaper rewarded me with a cell phone, a tape recorder, 200 euros to cover my bus fares, and a reporter's notebook. All I needed was a visor that said, "REPORTER" and a pencil behind my ear! The challenge of learning to interview and write had 100% of my attention.

But there were questions beginning to surface both about this project and my future. Though I loved the challenge of reporting, it was only intellectual. Why was I gathering writing skills if my heart was in love with the earth? How could I put it all together? How would my future evolve? My stories, though personally fascinating as a glimpse into Irish culture, were hardly supporting the planet, humanity, or wildlife, aspects of my life that I had come to cherish.

After all of my soul-enriching experiences over the last year, what was my heart doing here in Ireland? How could I take everything that I had learned and settle for writing small-town articles? With my return to Seattle less than 6 weeks away now, I wondered where heart and soul would lead me. Somehow the pieces of the puzzle of my future would all fit together but I still couldn't visualize what that future would be.

When I listened to my inner voice, I heard only one reply, "Continue to write. Continue focusing on your newspaper work."

My next assignment was the Cork Art Festival launch, a private function in Cork, which was a gorgeous colorful seaport with graceful bridges crossing the river. Held in a pub with more free champagne and lots of people, I sat with another reporter, who graciously gave me some basic reporting skills when I told her my situation. I thanked her for all of her tips and, after the ceremony per her advice, I mingled with the crowd boldly looking for interviews as my mentor had taught me.

I met Johnny, a feisty artist who was more than happy to fill me in on the art scene in Cork, the Art Festival, and life as an artist in Ireland. My pencil was flying across the pages of my notepad as he described being on the dole to create art and the politics involved in getting a showing at the Art Festival.

"Can I take you for a drive and show you the area?" Johnny asked, pushing his curly dark hair out of his eyes.

"That would be great if I can interview you for my paper on the drive." I wasn't sure if my editor would use the story but I wanted the practice and Johnny was interesting to talk to, all fired up! Patrick gave me the go-ahead and before we met, I looked up Johnny's website to view his art. His work was beautiful.

Johnny was in his 40s, my height, with a medium build and curly black hair that bounced when he walked and fell over his eyes while he talked. But it was the intensity in his eyes that grabbed me demanding 100% of my attention. Though when he wanted to tease me or tell a funny story, a twinkle of mischief and a charming smile disarmed me easily. He drove us to his favorite dreaming spot and we sat on a brick wall looking out to the sea and breathing in fresh air in the sunlight. Settling into my best imitation of Barbara Walters, I asked piercing questions about his life as an artist. He was open and honest and didn't sugarcoat the struggles. I was enthralled with his view of creativity and art, the first artist I had talked to at length.

"I have been in a slump. I could do what I have been doing, which is commercially successful, but I don't feel that is using my creativity. I want to develop new ways, new styles, but that means no money right away. I need time to develop something new without worrying about income. That is why most beginning artists here are on the dole. There is no other choice for us. But I am committed to change. Can you understand that, Joyce? A friend is letting me stay at her house at the ocean for two weeks to work on this new style, to give it a chance to develop."

I took notes but I knew the tape recorder was backing me up. I asked soul-searching questions and he answered them. A rambunctious man full of outspoken opinions, who saw things in his own strong-willed way, Johnny was not afraid to alienate anyone in the Cork art scene. Early on he had been instrumental in creating more art venues in Cork, but his radical approaches had alienated the art festival personnel. I loved his iconoclastic philosophies.

I followed the art line and then asked about his personal life. Barbara W. would have been proud.

"I am lonely. I have been searching for a good woman to love. I need to have that inspiration of a love and a family," He said, looking me square in the eyes.

Seems we were all wondering where our best friend was hiding and when we would meet them. Asking questions and listening intently to his answers, getting to his soul, interviewing Johnny was making me smile deep inside. I loved this process. What a great excuse to really get to know someone and allow my own curiosity to surface without worrying about infringing on his privacy.

After we had covered his art, his love life, and the financial struggle of being an artist, we went to an old pub along the road with friendly patrons and large glasses of Guinness, my new favorite drink. (How had I never drunk one before?)

"Do you want to come to the radio station that I work at? You might find my interviews interesting," he asked.

"Sure, it sounds great." I answered. He was a charming rascal. An outspoken man. I liked his style.

When I got home, I turned on the recorder anxious to begin the article but my interview had a problem. Stupid me had put the recorder on pause, not play. Not one word had been recorded. Barbara Walters had screwed up! Argh! Now how was I going to write an article that reflected Johnny's spirit and his art? I pounded my head on the wall until Garfield came in wondering what was wrong. Once I calmed down and looked at my notes and in my memory, there was plenty of information to write a good article and my editor wanted to run it with a photo of Johnny taken by Whitney, who was doing more photography for the paper.

Heading into Cork with Whitney to take Johnny's photo, Whitney too thought he was a charmer as he joked with us both while posing for the camera.

"Joyce, can I have your email address. Maybe someday I'll come to America and visit you? Would that be okay?" Johnny asked.

"Of course, you charming rascal. Maybe I can find someplace to show your work!"

"Then I'll say 'see you soon' and give you a hug."

PATRICK WAS SENDING me to a wide variety of events and my next assignment was in the small town of Milford (*Áth an Mhuilinn*), for a book launch of *The History of the Old Creamery*. Gathered in an old schoolhouse with people who had lived in the parish for generations, we listened to the author talk about the history of butter with everyone clapping and listening intently! Everyone but me. The old parish was an Irish-speaking town. The book launch was entirely in Gaelic! I had no notes! But afterwards, I interviewed the author, who gave me a copy of his book to read.

Everyone in the town came up to meet me. "Are you from the parish?"

"No," I replied smiling, "I am working in Midleton at *The Imokilly People*. I will be here for two months. I'm from America."

"Well, why don't you stay longer? Welcome to our parish."

Patrick, whom I still had never met, called to give me my next assignment. I was given my first feature story, a full-page interview of a local woman who had become a very successful TV reporter. The interview was to be conducted on the phone, yet another new experience. Before the interview, I researched her background. I wanted to be professional.

But when she answered the phone, I realized that her deep Cork accent and the speed of her conversation were going to make this one of my toughest assignments. I didn't think that I could keep saying, "Pardon me."

However, upon hearing my own accent, she said, "I'll try to speak slower but please just stop me if you can't understand. I completely understand how hard it is."

We had a great interview. She was delightful with the same straightforward honesty that Johnny had. Was this then a characteristic of the Irish? No sugarcoating; everything didn't have to be great. She explained her low points. She was real and vulnerable. I was learning a lot! But I strained to understand her answers and wrote notes furiously my pen flying across the page to keep up with her witty conversation.

Writing this article was a walk in a new land for me even; figuring out how to start it was challenging. I realized that my creativity in real estate had been asleep and never needed. Here at the paper, I combined my people skills and a love of research that I hadn't even known about with my creativity. After the article was published, the TV reporter called my editor to let him know that she thought it was very well written! I was on a high.

The Swedish Ambassador was having a reception for a Swedish Navy vessel anchored in Cork and I was sent to interview him. Me? Interview an ambassador? Looking at my three interchangeable Lois Lane outfits, I picked the most conservative one and took the bus to Cork. My nerves were way over the top. Wasn't he going to catch on that I was a cub reporter or wonder about my American accent? Ambassador sounded important and stuffy to me. How would it go?

I boarded the ship for a tour and then filled my plate with delicious Swedish delicacies and white wine mingling with the guests, mostly men. An aide approached me and I was taken to the ambassador. This wasn't a press conference but rather a one-on-one interview with the ambassador and I was completely intimidated. The ambassador, a tall perfectly groomed formal man, sat facing me, his back as straight as a board, his face solemn, intelligent. Forget warm, Irish characters full of jokes and friendliness. This was Sweden, reserved and proper. His aides nodded, giving me the go-ahead to begin my interview. Forget Barbara Walters. Now I was channeling Tom Brokaw. I asked questions about the economic connections between Ireland and Sweden.

"How do you think the partnership between the two countries is progressing? What would you like to see improved? Are there projects that the two countries are working on together? How are these cultures similar?" I finished, feeling exhausted from the stress of asking questions, taking notes, and attempting to look professional with one month of reporter experience backing me up.

After the interview and the subsequent story, Patrick, my mystery editor, actually asked me to join him for lunch. I felt like one of the angels meeting Charley, curious about this man who had given me so many great stories to cover! I braced myself for a lesson in what a real reporter would ask an ambassador. Patrick had not given me any advice the entire first month but had published all of my stories.

Patrick looked like an editor. With brown hair, glasses, and curved shoulders from bending over a computer all day, he was definitely more brains than another pretty face. But the twinkle in his eyes was a welcome sight as we sat down.

"Joyce, you are doing a great job." he said. "You have risen to every challenge I have given you! I purposely have not given you any advice to see how you would fare. You've done an excellent job! I am going to send you many more assignments now. You go through them and choose the ones you want to cover. Is there anything in particular you would like to cover?"

Floored by his praise, I responded, "I've loved the wide variety but if there is any music to review, that would be my first wish. I love music."

I returned home flabbergasted by his compliment. The challenge of this work stimulated both my intellect and my curiosity, but Patrick's approval meant the world to me. Even though *The Imokilly People* was just a small weekly newspaper with soft news, I was tickled by his praise and ready to take on the world. Patrick, true to his word, gave me almost more assignments than I could handle but with no social life in Midleton, I loved being busy and each interview gave me a small piece of Ireland.

In response to my desire to cover music events, I was sent to review a viola concert celebrating a concert held in 1831 at the Theatre Royal, which was now the Cork Post Office building. The organizer of the concert was a postman known as "Irish Jack," so christened by his years with the rock group The Who. He delivered mail to Constantin Zanidache, a well-known Romanian-born viola master. When Irish Jack told Zanidache about the Paganini concert and his proposed celebration, Zanidache offered to play.

With Irish Jack and Zanidache dressed in period clothes and with dim lighting to change the mood of the post office waiting area, we were all drawn back to the original concert. Zanidache played the Paganini piece beautifully and the concert was a huge success. After the concert, all of the audience enjoyed champagne while I worked on my interviews. I interviewed Irish Jack, Zanidache, and people in the small audience including a lovely Cork couple who took me under their wing, inviting me to their home for dinner the following evening. My reporting was on a roll!

Patrick next sent Whitney and me to the Maritime Song Festival on the coast of County Cork in Cobh, a beautiful seaport city famous as the departing port for *The Titanic*. There was Irish folk music by Liam Clancy of the Clancy brothers, and other famous Irish folk musicians and storytellers. Whitney took photos while I gathered storylines.

My favorite concert was held outside in the promenade where *Banana Boat,* a Polish male vocal sextet, stole the show with classical sea shanties featuring close harmonies. When I asked for an interview, we all sat outside of a pub, each of us with a Guinness in hand. The group was made up of a doctor, a lawyer, a whiskey salesman, a professor, a banker, and a dentist, and they had been friends for a long time.

"With your professions, I find it interesting that you take the time to practice the exacting harmonies of these sea shanties. What motivates you?" I asked.

"We use our group as a chance to get together and a chance to see the world because none of us makes enough money in Poland to travel. Even with our education, the economy in Poland does not afford us any luxuries. But our singing provides us with the adventure of travel," Pawel answered in perfect English.

We sat drinking our beers and discussing life in Poland, the history of sea shanties, and the popular Sea Shanty Contest in Poland.

"Each year we compete in the Krakow Shanty Festival in Poland. This is the biggest shanty festival in the world celebrating our heritage on the sea," Tomasz explained.

"Singing together keeps our friendship alive and we all love to travel," Maciej told me smiling.

I asked them the same questions I had been asking people all around the world, questions about time, about love, and about the position of women in Poland. I couldn't imagine sitting down in America with a doctor, a lawyer, a whiskey salesman, a professor, a banker, and a dentist and having so much fun. All of my curiosity was satisfied delving into people's lives. I loved asking questions. We laughed the afternoon away and they gave me a complimentary CD!

"You must come to our Shanty Festival and see how Poland celebrates! You can contact us and we will find housing for you both," Maciej told Whitney and me.

I WAS NOW WRITING up to five stories a week for the paper, but most of the articles were light features. Given my growing confidence as a reporter, I wanted to do more serious articles to test my skills.

I called Patrick. "Can I do an article on hormone replacement therapy for menopause? Most women in Ireland are on HRT therapy during menopause and I want to present alternatives."

"If you want to do the research, go ahead." he answered.

I scheduled an interview with an herbalist, a doctor, and a kinesthesiologist, who were all anxious to give their views. I researched data. As I put the story together, I talked a lot with Margaret, my home-stay mom. She was very supportive of the article. "If that paper is going to charge people 2 euros, they need stories like this, Joyce. I want to read it! It's a good thing that Patrick O'Brien has approved the story but I will be surprised if he will print it. Indeed I will be surprised."

When I finished the article, I was pleased with the results. But as Margaret had foretold, Patrick told me he was going to hold it for a couple of weeks. He never published it. I was extremely disappointed.

Margaret explained, "Ah, Patrick must have thought it would be too controversial for the paper. He was wrong. Of that I am certain."

Not one to be easily discouraged, I read about a conference, Fueling the Future, in Kinsale on the seaside that would be held during my last weekend in Ireland. Now here was something I could put my teeth into, an environmental issue discussing peak oil and definitely in need of a reporter. It seemed like the perfect culminating story after a year of volunteer work around the world that had developed my strong passion for saving the planet.

"Patrick, can I do a story on this conference?"

"Yes. Sounds good. I'll pay for your lodging," he said, really surprising me.

I was excited though still nervous but I felt almost prepared to cover this event after two months of reporting. Arriving at the conference, I was given a press badge, my first. Memories of Lois Lane who just 8 weeks earlier had been too timid to interview anyone at the Green Party Convention, made me smile. How things had changed! I asked for an appointment to interview each of the speakers and attended the lectures to learn about *peak oil,* a term that I knew nothing about.

I sat with Dr. Colin Campbell, a retired oil geologist. He had joined the oil industry as an exploration geologist in 1957 and traveled around the world. He was now a Trustee of the Oil Depletion Analysis Centre, a charitable organization in London dedicated to researching the date and impact of the peak and raising awareness of the serious consequences. A very witty man, he was full of stories about peak oil and his humor lightened the serious topic of our interview.

"Understanding depletion is simple. Think of an Irish pub. The glass starts full and ends empty. There are only so many more drinks to closing time. It's the same with oil. We have to find the bar before we can drink what's in it."

"In truth, every year for the past two decades the industry has pumped more oil than it has discovered, and production will soon be unable to keep up with rising demand.

The U.S. has to somehow find a way to cut its demand by at least 5% a year. It won't be easy, but as the octogenarian said of old age, 'The alternative is even worse.'"

"But why don't I know about any of this?" I asked shocked to think the world would run out of oil.

"The inexplicable part is our great reluctance to look reality in the face and at least make some plans for what promises to be one of the greatest economic and political discontinuities of all time. Time is of the essence. It is later than you think.

"The second half of the Age of Oil will be characterized by a decline in the supply of oil, and all that depends upon it....That speaks of a second Great Depression and the End of Economics as presently understood," he concluded.

"All of this is shocking to me," I said. "Have I been living with my head in the sand? Now I feel like the world will be coming to an end." My head was reeling.

"That is probably why they call me Dr. Doom." he said, smiling. "I am not surprised that you knew nothing about the term *peak oil*. That is consistent with what I hear. The governments, the newspapers play it down like it doesn't exist or isn't a pending disaster."

"Your government desperately wants me to come tell them how to solve their problem. They've sent numerous people including Dick Haines from the Office of US Naval Intelligence over here to persuade me to go to Washington DC, but I've got quite enough to do here."

Richard Douthwaite, a contemporary economist and co-founder of the Foundation for the Economics of Sustainability, an Irish economic think tank studying the effects of the oil depletion on Ireland, was less pessimistic in his speech, a sharp contrast from Dr. Campbell.

"What do you do when a vital commodity becomes scarce? The rich cannot be allowed to take it all. The only option may be for a world rationing system for oil. Handled correctly, the lower output of oil may be environmentally and socially good."

"How can less oil possible be good for us when we are totally dependent on it?" I asked.

"It gives us a chance to change a lot of things that are clearly going wrong now, he explained. "The climate crisis and the energy crisis are coming together."

Richard Heinberg, author of *The Party's Over: Oil, War and the Fate of Industrial Societies,* was very pessimistic about the world's future. He felt that global oil production as a whole was about to peak and warned that there were fewer nations in the category of oil exporters and more nations in the category of oil importers. "As we move into an era of oil depletion and energy constraint, everything from transportation to medicine to food to climate change response strategies will be affected. Almost everything we do is dependent on oil."

He grimly explained about the reality of oil deletion and its effects on modern society as we know it. He gave a gloom and doom description of how he saw the world unfolding if we didn't start changing our lifestyles. I wondered how the world could survive especially if this information was currently being kept a secret.

My interview with David Holmgren, from Australia, the co-originator of the permaculture concept and author of *Permaculture One,* was more encouraging as he felt there was still an opportunity for people around the world to change their lifestyles.

"Permaculture is a design system for sustainable living and land use. It's always going to be a fringe thing." he explained.

"Do you think that everyone will have a vegetable garden someday?" I asked.

"No, but the thinking behind permaculture is based on how to work with reduced energy supplies and that requires a complete overturning of a lot of our inherited culture. We have an opportunity to positively engage with the energy-descent and to learn and to change as we've done in the past. Most people can't get off the treadmill because of peer pressure and individual and collective addiction in society. Sometimes people recognize a problem, want to change, but they need a crisis, something that affects their peers, so they can all change together."

"Is that what you think it will take, a crisis?" I asked.

"I hope not. But I recommend that everyone begins with a total audit of their household's consumption of food, energy, and water usage. Permaculture can be in part a solution."

Interviewing these speakers and attending the conference jolted my sense of calm about the planet. I was shocked by what I was learning.

SMILING AT THE WORLD

Why was this the first time I heard the term *peak oil?* The speakers believed that the collective world governments were tucking it under their arms, away from the news. We watched a shocking film called *The End of Suburbia.* Was it a collective "See no evil, hear no evil, speak no evil" on this looming problem? If it was even only half as serious as these experts discussed, it was still an enormous problem.

After a year spent traveling the globe opening my eyes to world issues, attending a conference about peak oil in many ways seemed like a reward for me even if the information terrified me. As I had traveled, I had learned about problems facing different cultures, wildlife issues, conservation problems and sustainability solutions. My global awareness had started at zero with no commitment to live in a conscious manner. I had been blind to all global issues much more interested in the World of Joyce. But I had changed, changed drastically and this conference heightened my sense of responsibility as a global citizen.

Attending the conference and writing about it for the paper added fire to my environmentally conscious awakening heart. Here was an opportunity to communicate important information about the environment, both a challenge and a reward. My goal was to write this article in a way that would be easy to absorb for readers.

Patrick called me when I returned to Midleton with my story. "I am going to pay you 250 euros for the Peak Oil story! Can you stay for another month?"

"Oh, Patrick, I am grateful for this opportunity. You have opened up an entirely new world for me and the conference was frosting on the cake. But home is calling me. I've got two sons to see and a life to figure out. Again, I thank you for every article you have assigned me. Maybe I can come back some day and write more."

After I hung up the phone, I reviewed our conversation. How could that be? Paid for work I loved? I was beyond happy. Even as my time in Ireland was wrapping up, I was not thinking too much about heading home. I just wanted to keep writing articles for *The Imokilly People.*

I had absorbed this culture in a very different way from the other countries that I had volunteered in. Interviewing my way through many different aspects of Irish life, I learned about lifestyles and customs in

County Cork. I had never asked so many questions. I liked the honesty and directness here. People were not politically correct but rather spoke their truth. Families were tight. People lived in the same town for generations and a move 30 minutes away was a calamity! The humor and storytelling kept me enthralled during my interviews and I found smiles very close to the surface. And Guinness. Ah, Guinness! Never much of a beer drinker, I had found myself lapping up a Guinness here like a woman parched from a long walk across a desert.

BUT IT WAS TIME to leave Ireland and *The Imokilly People*. I bid farewell to Margaret and Noel and Garfield the cat. Whitney and I promised to stay in touch with each other and hopefully our paths would cross again.

My last weekend in Ireland would be spent in Dublin at a reunion of the gang of volunteers I had met in South Africa the year before! We all had kept in touch and planned a gala weekend. However, U2 was in town for a concert, which meant that I could find nowhere to stay.

But Patrick rescued me and told me that he would be happy to give me a ride, no make that a lift, to Dublin. He even arranged for a place for me to stay.

"I attended Priest's College when I thought I wanted to be a priest. You can stay there for a couple of nights. Now, Joyce, you must behave. You are not to be blasphemous!" he told me as we drove to Dublin.

"Of course, Patrick. How could it be otherwise?" I said, chuckling about spending my last weekend of a yearlong journey in a monastery with priests, the grand finale of my trip around the world.

"Could I be just a little bit naughty, Patrick?" I teased him with a smile.

AS I TRAVELED AROUND the world, I appreciated the gift of growing up in the United States as a free woman unafraid to voice my opinion. I loved America and the lifestyle that had made me independent and strong. I had grown up well loved, well fed, and well provided for in a small Midwestern town, a fine upbringing when compared to many places that I had seen.

But I was still an idealist. Traveling the world, I saw how strong America was for a young country. Our economy succeeded in bringing riches and success to many people. We were a society full of beautiful houses, cars, clothes, schools, fast food, TV, strip malls, computers, and gadgets. A society moving ahead faster and faster. In the contest between the countries of the world to become the frontrunner, in a very short amount of time we had developed into the most powerful country in the world.

But why did only 30% of Americans have passports? We didn't get out much. Why not? We didn't see firsthand what the rest of the world was doing or thinking or what their cultures were like. We read newspapers or watched TV. So, the world didn't know us and we didn't know the world. But we thought we knew the world based on the media. And the world thought they knew us from listening to George Bush and from our TV shows and movies. Nobody had it right.

I had more questions now than when I left. Why had my country, which produced 36% of the carbon emissions emitted into the atmosphere, refused to sign the Kyoto Protocol? Why did my country of the free allow the primate trade? How did my advanced country create more garbage than we had room to throw away, never looking back at the resources that were wasted to create the packaging? How did we rationalize cutting down more trees than we planted? Was everyone asleep or did no one care? And what about peak oil? Was everyone so busy on their personal treadmill that they could not think about the environment, the wildlife, and the trees?

I had no answers for these questions. In my heart, I wanted America to be the leader of the world lighting the way in how we cared for each other and the environment. I was actually tired of defending my country. Blue sky with clean air meant something to me. Protecting the earth was my job. I cared. I hoped that somehow we would turn around and look at what we had done and change. We needed to change. We could not go to the store for another earth or more air or fresh water.

And I needed to change. If I went home to live in my sweet houseboat and began my real estate career again, it would be like I had never taken this trip. It would be like a dream with memories fading over time of elephants, lions, and roos; of China, Greece, and Brazil. Before long I would be back in a lifestyle that was good but not alive.

I had jumped out of my old life and into the open arms of the world for a yearlong adventure. Volunteer projects had taught me about wildlife, conservation, different cultures, and myself. I knew that the beauty of the world was in all of her differences. I had a strong sense of my place here in the world. Taking the risk to seize my life had changed me forever. My soul had urged me forward and I had listened. Now, it was time to trust my feelings as I created my new life using my heart.

Imagining heading home after a full year of travel, I wondered what it would be like now. With visions of lovely lions, elephants, roos, monkeys, and the people that I had met dancing around in my head, I was sad to end my year of adventure. Did I want to go home now? Was I ready? How would I adjust to being back home? What would I do with my life now? My first trip around the world had been a giant success, an enormous education, a year of gradually unfolding new aspects of myself.

My clarity on Joyce was much better than when I left. The novocain that had blocked my heart feelings had finally worn off. In the journey of my heart – opening what I thought was open – I had found my center, my soul. Layers of unnecessary emotional stuff were peeled off now. How funny to travel as a volunteer for a year to get to know who I really am. I had been loved and accepted around the world finding pieces of myself scattered everywhere that I went. Like heading off on a scavenger hunt, I had picked up pieces of Joyce from each country that I volunteered in.

After a year of falling in love with the earth – for that is what happened – my heart was strong and open. I believed. I believed in the power of people to help each other, to help wildlife and to help the earth. I had been loved in so many different ways that I felt brand-new. I was in love with the world and I wanted to protect her. Now Seattle no longer felt like home, the earth did. When I stood with my feet on the earth, I felt a connection to the entire planet, a concept I would not have understood before this trip.

SMILING AT THE WORLD

I had Able's South African smile still in my heart and I wanted my smile to shine like today was the only day in my life. So, how would my life unfold returning home? Would I keep traveling and volunteering? Would I find work as a reporter? What was my one thing? My heart wants to be put to work every day. In the end my one thing was simpler than I had originally thought: To live each day with passion, love and a smile.

Gratitude
Jumping off the cliff
I was given wings to fly
In a choice of heart, my path would be clear
Trust the future